EDUGORILLA
PUBLICATION

UPSESSB PGT

Post Graduate Teacher - Geography

Latest Edition
Practice Kit

10 Tests
10 Mock Test

Based On Real Exam Pattern

✓ Thoroughly Revised and Updated

✓ Detailed Analysis of all MCQs

<table>
<tr><td>Title</td><td>: UPSESSB PGT Post Graduate Teacher - Geography</td></tr>
<tr><td>Author Name</td><td>: Mr. Rohit Manglik</td></tr>
<tr><td>Published By</td><td>: EduGorilla Community Pvt. Ltd.</td></tr>
<tr><td>Publishers Address</td><td>: 12/651, First Floor Opp. Arvindo Park, Near Jama Masjid,
Indira Nagar, Lucknow, Uttar Pradesh-226016, India</td></tr>
</table>

Copyright EduGorilla

Disclaimer EduGorilla

ROHIT MANGLIK
CEO, EduGorilla

Dear Applicants,

People say *"Success comes to those who work hard."* But I've seen people working hard for their exams day in and day out for marginal success. While others succeed in their examinations by putting in just half the work. So are they God Gifted? No! I believe that it's because they work *smart* and not just *hard*. Similarly, for your exams, you should strategize your preparation so as to increase the likelihood of success. Well with EduGorilla get ready to increase your *chances of selection* in your exam by *16x*.

EduGorilla helps you in not only working *hard* but also working in a *smart and strategic* manner. With EduGorilla's preparation package, you get a chance to make your exam preparation easy, and a fun learning path towards selection. Finding the right path to your preparations can be difficult if you don't know in which direction to head. Don't worry, we have you covered! EduGorilla will be your guide to success in your journey. With our Preparation Package, you can prepare strategically and beat the exam in just one attempt.

EduGorilla's Preparation Package includes-

- **Test Series**
- **Books**

Our preparation package is handcrafted as per the latest changes, expert opinions, and students' discretion. Thus, enabling you to get through each stage of the selection process for your exam.

Our Books are designed by the teachers and experts of the respective exam with a combined 150+ years of experience; to provide you with easy, efficient, and effective learning. Our books are smart, in the sense that not only do they give you the answers to the questions but also provide similar questions for practice.

EduGorilla's competent Test Series gives you real-time experience and confidence through which you can clear your offline or online exam in just one attempt. We currently host 83,000+ mock tests for 1,440+ competitive and academic exams.

Thus, EduGorilla misses no chance to assist you in your preparation and covers all stages of the exam, so that you don't have to look anywhere else.

We provide complete preparation packages for defense, banking, teaching, and other National & State-Level exams. Hence, it doesn't matter which exam you aspire to because you will reach your success.

ALL THE BEST !
Let EduGorilla be your Guide to Success.

Rohit Manglik,
Founder and CEO, EduGorilla

INTRODUCTION

EduGorilla focuses on guiding students to succeed in their examinations. With that in mind, our book, titled "UPSESSB PGT : Post Graduate Teacher - Geography", has been drafted through the collective efforts of our distinguished experts with 150+ years of combined experience. This book consists of questions that are created following the latest changes in the syllabus and exam pattern. We compiled the book on the basis of questions that are most likely to appear in the UPSESSB PGT Geography. Through EduGorilla's "UPSESSB PGT : Post Graduate Teacher - Geography" your chances of success will increase 16x.

EduGorilla does this through our Complete Preparation Package. This package consists of well-conceptualized and structured content in the form of questions that are tailor-made according to your needs and will help you practice for exams in a smart way by pinpointing all the necessary information. It also provides hints and solutions, along with a smart answer sheet for your self-evaluation. You can assess your shortcomings and work accordingly on areas that may require more of your attention.

EduGorilla promises to help you succeed in your examination and accomplish your dream goals. We believe in our aspirants and see them at the top of the merit list. And the first step towards the top is to start preparing with us. EduGorilla's "UPSESSB PGT : Post Graduate Teacher - Geography" includes the following attributes.

➤ Well-Researched Content

➤ Top-Notch Quality

➤ Detailed Answers and Analysis

➤ Smart Answer Sheet

➤ Exam Relevant Questions

Therefore, EduGorilla fortifies your preparation and makes it durable enough to help you stand tall and beat the examination.

UPSESSB PGT Geography
Scan QR code for Eligibility, Exam Pattern, Syllabus and more.

Book ID: 0752

TABLE OF CONTENTS

Mock Test 01

Q.1 Which one of the following is the best description of the term "Biome"?

A. Community of plants and animals that share the same environmental conditions.

B. That part of the Earth which is inhabited by living organisms.

C. A community of organisms interacting with one another.

D. Transitional area between two geographical areas with diverse environmental conditions.

Q.2 Which of the following is associated with biological nitrogen fixation?

A. Red algae

B. Brown algae

C. Green algae

D. Blue-green algae

Q.3 Which of the following does not contribute to the formation of Photochemical fog?

A. NO

B. O_3

C. SO_2

D. Voltatile Organic Compound

Q.4 Which of the following is a Persistent Organic Pollutant (POP)?

A. SO_2 **B.** CO_2 **C.** DDT   **D.** NO_2

Q.5 Which one of the following is not a protected area?

A. National park

B. Sanctuary

C. Zoo

D. Biosphere reserves

Q.6 _______species are not in the IUCN classification of threatened species.

A. Harmful

B. Extinct

C. Vulnerable

D. Endangered

Q.7 Which declaration was signed at UNCED 1992 at Rio De Janeiro, Brazil?

A. Agenda 39

B. Agenda 19

C. Agenda 22

D. Agenda 21

Q.8 Which of the following was the first conference/convention on the depletion of the ozone layer?

A. United Nations Framework Convention on Climate Change (UNFCCC)

B. Saving the Ozone Layer conference

C. Convention on Biological Diversity

D. Vienna Conference

Q.9 Red data book contains data of which of the following?

A. All plant species

B. All animal species

C. All endangered species

D. All extinct species

Q.10 _______________ is the largest tiger reserve in India.

A. Jim Corbett Tiger Reserve

B. Nagarjuna Sagar-Srisailam Tiger Reserve

C. Satpura Tiger Reserve

D. Sunderbans Tiger Reserve

Q.11 Which crops does not come under kharif crops?

A. Rice   **B.** Wheat   **C.** Makai   **D.** Bajra

Q.12 A set of non - conventional sources of energy out of the following is:

[Haryana Primary Teacher (PRT), 2020]

A. Mineral oil, natural gas, coal

B. Coal, wind energy, bio gas

C. Solar energy, atomic energy, wind energy

D. Geo - thermal energy, natural gas, petroleum

Q.13 What are the three pillars of production?

A. Land, Market, Labour

B. Land, Labour, Capital

C. Market, Capital, Labour

D. Capital, Land, Market

Q.14 Which irrigation practice leads to maximum water conservation?

A. Water wheel

B. Tube-well

C. Drip irrigation

D. Sprinkle

Q.15 Limonite ore is the ore of which metal?

A. Iron

B. Aluminium

C. Zinc

D. Cobalt

Q.16 The plateau richest in minerals in India is:

A. Chhota Nagpur Plateau

B. Mysore Plateau

C. Deccan Plateau

D. Malwa Plateau

Q.17 Match List-I with List-II and select the correct answer using the code given below the Lists:

List - I (Manufacturing site)	List - II (Industry
A. Ludhiana	1. Auto part
B. Kanpur	2. Woolen garments
C. Varanasi	3. Leather
D. Vijayawada	4. Handloom

A. A-1, B- 4, C- 3, D- 2

B. A-2, B- 3, C- 4, D- 1

C. A-2, B- 4, C- 3, D- 1

D. A-1, B- 3, C- 4, D- 2

Q.18 Which five years plan is also known as the liberalization of the economy?

A. 7th   **B.** 8th   **C.** 9th   **D.** 10th

Q.19 Consider the following statements about the location of the jute industry in India in the Hooghly basin and select the correct answer using the code given below:

1. West Bengal is one of the leading producers of jute.
2. Cheap and skilled labor is available.
3. Low cost of transport
4. Adequate water supply is available

A. 1, 2 and 3
B. 1, 3 and 4
C. 1, 2 and 4
D. 1, 2, 3 and 4

Q.20 The resources of water on the earth are:

A. Sea/Ocean
B. Snow on mountain and near poles
C. Monsoon rain
D. Ocean, snow, rain and underground water

Q.21 Which of the following indicators is not used to calculate Human Development Index (HDI)?

A. Life Expectancy
B. Education
C. Per Capital Income
D. Social Inequality

Q.22 What is Gini coefficient used for?

A. To measure income equality
B. To measure income inequality
C. To measure distribution of income
D. To measure profit and loss

Q.23 What is meant by the term Dollarization in economy?

A. Use of the currency of another country along with its own currency
B. Use of dollar as currency by country
C. Process of converting rupee to dollar
D. Adopting Dollar as national currency by a country

Q.24 The custom duty on which of the following are to be rationalized under union budget 2021 - 22?

A. Gold and Silver
B. Tin and Silver
C. Copper and Gold
D. Tin and Copper

Q.25 During which five-year plan, the Government of India adopted a regional approach to agricultural planning?

A. Fifth Five Year Plan
B. Sixth Five Year Plan
C. Eighth Five Year Plan
D. Tenth Five Year Plan

Q.26 There are three types of ration cards in India. Which among the following ration cards is for the poorest of the poor people?

A. Suraksha Card
B. BPL Card
C. BBPL Card
D. Antyodaya Card

Q.27 "Absence of minimum income to get the minimum needs of life" is concerned with which of the following types of poverty?

[Maharashtra Public Service Commission, 2018]

A. Absolute poverty
B. Relative poverty
C. Both the above
D. None of the above

Q.28 What is the growth rate of Service Sector in India in 2019-20?

A. 8%
B. 7%
C. 2%
D. 5%

Q.29 Omkareshwar project is associated with which of the following rivers?

A. Narmada
B. Ganga
C. Brahmaputra
D. Tapi

Q.30 Which of the following rivers is associated with Mahatma Gandhi Hydroelectric Project?

A. Godavari
B. Sharavati
C. Subansiri
D. Krishna

Q.31 Which of the following layers of the Earth's atmosphere provide ideal flying conditions for Jet aircraft?

A. Mesosphere
B. Thermosphere
C. Stratosphere
D. Troposphere

Q.32 Doldrums are ________.

A. High latitudes with heavy snow
B. Equatorial zone with low pressure
C. High pressure areas on mountains
D. Sub-polar zone with high pressure

Q.33 Which of the following places are favourably influenced by the Trade winds?

I. West Indies
II. Brazil
III. Mexico
IV. Madagascar

A. I and II
B. I, II, III and IV
C. III and IV
D. II and IV

Q.34 In the northern hemisphere, the wind blowing from the Horse latitudes to the Doldrums is called ________.

A. Westerly wind
B. Trade wind
C. Polar Easterly
D. Jet Stream

Q.35 The dense mass of small water drops on smoke particles in the lower layers of the atmosphere is ________.

A. Smog
B. Frost
C. Fog
D. Dew

Q.36 The chemically inactive gas present in the atmosphere is ________.

A. Nitrogen
B. Argon
C. Water vapour
D. Oxygen

Q.37 In which layer, temperature increases dramatically?

A. Ionosphere
B. Exosphere
C. Stratosphere
D. Troposphere

Q.38 Which one of the following pairs is NOT correctly matched?

[Madhya Pradesh Public Service Commission (MPPSC), 2017]

A. Lipulekh - Uttarakhand
B. Nathu La - Arunachal Pradesh
C. Rohtang - Himachal Pradesh
D. Palghat - Kerala

Q.39 Temperature generally decreases towards the poles because ______.

A. Air movement is generally towards the. equator

B. Cold polar air masses prevent surface heating of the land

C. Cold surfaces do not absorb solar energy as readily as warm surfaces

D. Progressively lesser solar energy per unit area falls on the earth's surface as we move to polar regions

Q.40 Excess carbon dioxide in the atmosphere due to pollution will cause:

A. Earth's temperature to rise

B. Earth's temperature to fall

C. No change in earth's temperature

D. Increase in ultra-violet radiation reaching the earth

Q.41 Atmospheric pressure exerted on earth is due to ______.

A. Gravitational pull of the earth

B. Rotation of earth

C. Revolution of earth

D. Uneven heating of earth

Q.42 Is the following statement correct?

Hurricanes ______.

A. Form at the equator

B. Are not as large as tornadoes

C. Develop over warm ocean areas

D. Tend to intensify when they move over land surfaces

Q.43 Rain shadow effect is associated with:

A. Cyclonic rainfall

B. Orographic rainfall

C. Convectional rainfall

D. Frontal rainfall

Q.44 Which one of the following layers of the atmosphere is responsible for the deflection of radio waves?

A. Troposphere   **B.** Stratosphere

C. Mesosphere   **D.** Ionosphere

Q.45 The monsoon has well-developed cycle in ______.

A. South and South East Asia

B. North Australia

C. East United States

D. Africa

Q.46 Consider the following statements with respect to Taiga forests:

1. It is a forest of the temperate and tropical region.

2. Coniferous trees, such as spruce, pine, and fir, are common in these forests.

3. Taiga ecosystems are threatened by direct human activity and climate change.

Which of the statements given above are correct?

A. 1 and 2 only   **B.** 2 and 3 only

C. 1 and 3 only   **D.** 1, 2 and 3

Q.47 Consider the following statements with respect to Ring of Fire:

1. It is located along the Atlantic ocean.

2. It is characterized by active volcanoes and frequent earthquakes.

Which of the statements given above is/are not correct?

A. 1 only   **B.** 2 only

C. Both 1 and 2   **D.** Neither 1 nor 2

Q.48 Which of the following statements is correct with respect to Extra Tropical Cyclone?

A. It develops in the tropical region.

B. It originates only over the seas.

C. The wind velocity is higher compared to tropical cyclones.

D. It moves from west to east.

Q.49 The Gulf of Aden connects which of the following?

A. Red Sea and the Arabian Sea

B. Mediterranean sea and the Red sea

C. Arabian Peninsula and Indian ocean

D. Indian ocean and south China sea

Q.50 Consider the following statements with respect to Savanna Climate:

1. It can be found in tropical regions.

2. It is characterized by Shortgrass and tall trees.

3. It has a distinct wet and dry season.

Which of the statements given above is/are correct?

A. 1 and 2 only   **B.** 2 and 3 only

C. 1 and 3 only   **D.** 1, 2 and 3

Q.51 Which of the following countries are Landlocked countries?

1. Mongolia

2. Bolivia

3. Sudan

4. Rwanda

Select the correct answer from the code given below.

A. 1 and 3 only   **B.** 1, 2 and 4 only

C. 2, 3 and 4 only   **D.** 1, 2, 3 and 4

Q.52 Consider the following statements with respect to the Appalachian Mountains:

1. They are among the youngest mountains on Earth.

2. They are located in South America.

Which of the statement given above is/are correct?

A. 1 only   **B.** 2 only

C. Both 1 and 2   **D.** Neither 1 nor 2

Q.53 Which of the following best describes 'Birth rate'?

A. It is the difference between total births and total deaths in a given time period.

B. It is the number of live births per thousand persons in a year.

C. It is the change of population in particular area between two points of time.

D. It is the number of live births per million persons in a year.

Q.54 Which of the following is the tallest plateau in the world?

A. Deccan Plateau   **B.** Tibetan Plateau

C. Columbia Plateau   **D.** Katanga Plateau

Q.55 Vanadium reserves have been found in which state of India?

A. Karnataka   **B.** Arunachal Pradesh

C. Odisha   **D.** Jharkhand

Q.56 Consider the following statements with respect to Estuary:

1. It is an area where a freshwater river or stream meets the sea or an ocean

2. Estuary is a biologically low productive zone.

Which of the statements given above is/are correct?

A. 1 only   **B.** 2 only

C. Both 1 and 2   **D.** Neither 1 nor 2

Q.57 Consider the following pairs:

Type of tide	Characteristic
1. Semi-diurnal tide	Two high tides and two low tides each day
2. Spring tides	Occur when the sun, the moon and the earth are in a straight line
3. Neap tides	Occur when the sun and moon are at right angles to each other

Which of the pairs given above are correctly matched?

A. 1 and 2 only   **B.** 2 and 3 only

C. 1 and 3 only   **D.** 1, 2 and 3

Q.58 The method of soil conservation in which rocks are piled up to slow down the flow of water which prevents gullies and further soil loss is called?

A. Mulching   **B.** Contour barriers

C. Rock dam   **D.** Terrace farming

Q.59 Which of the following countries does not Border the east China sea?

1. Taiwan

2. North Korea

3. Japan

4. The Philippines

5. Indonesia

Select the correct answer from the code given below.

A. 2, 3 and 4 only   **B.** 1, 2 and 3 only

C. 2, 4 and 5 only   **D.** 1, 3 and 5 only

Q.60 Consider the following statements with respect to Inter-Tropical Convergence Zone (ITCZ):

1. It is a belt of low pressure that circles the Earth generally near the equator.

2. Trade winds of the Northern and Southern Hemispheres converge here.

3. The position of the ITCZ is the same throughout the year.

Which of the statements given above are correct?

A. 1 and 2 only   **B.** 2 and 3 only

C. 1 and 3 only   **D.** 1, 2 and 3

Q.61 Which of the following statement is incorrect regarding air front?

A. The boundary zone between air masses is called a front.

B. The process of formation of the fronts is known as frontogenesis.

C. There are only two types of fronts.

D. When the cold air moves towards the warm air mass, its contact zone is called the cold front.

Q.62 Consider the following statements with respect to Tropical Monsoon climate:

1. It is characterized by the distinct wet and dry seasons.

2. It can be found in the Indian subcontinent only.

3. It is associated with the seasonal reversal of winds.

Which of the statements given above are correct?

A. 1 and 2 only   **B.** 2 only

C. 1 and 3 only   **D.** 2 and 3 only

Q.63 Consider the following statements with respect to convectional rainfall :

1. It is common in the regions that are intensely heated.

2. It is mostly found in the temperate regions of the earth.

Which of the statements given above is/are correct?

A. 1 only   **B.** 2 only

C. Both 1 and 2   **D.** Neither 1 nor 2

Q.64 Consider the following statements with respect to the atmosphere of the earth:

1. More than 90 percent of the total mass of the atmosphere is confined to the height of 32 km from the earth's surface.

2. Carbon dioxide and water vapour are found only up to 90 km from the surface of the earth.

3. Ozone is found between 10 and 50 km above the earth's surface.

Which of the statements given above are correct?

A. 1 and 2 only   **B.** 2 and 3 only

C. 1 and 3 only   **D.** 1, 2 and 3

Q.65 Consider the following pairs:

Discontinuity	Layer of the earth
1. Mohorovicic Discontinuity	Between crust and mantle
2. Conrad Discontinuity	Between upper and lower mantle
3. Lehman Discontinuity	Between Outer core and Inner core

Which of the pairs given above are correctly matched?

A. 1 and 2 only   **B.** 2 and 3 only

C. 1 and 3 only   **D.** 1, 2 and 3

Q.66 Which of the following industry and its related city are mismatch?

A. Software Technology Park - Indore

B. Industrial leather complex - Dewas

C. BHEL Plant - Jabalpur

D. Sarees - Chanderi

Q.67 Which of the following is the busiest airport in Madhya Pradesh?

A. Raja Bhoj International Airport

B. Khajuraho International Airport

C. Devi Ahilyabai Holkar Airport

D. Gwalior International Airport

Q.68 India shares its land boundaries with which countries in the east?
A. China, Nepal and Bhutan
B. Bhutan and Afghanistan
C. Myanmar and Bangladesh
D. Pakistan and Afghanistan

Q.69 River Narmada flows through a rift valley in which mountain range?
A. Aravalli
B. Vindhya
C. Satpura
D. Both (B) and (C)

Q.70 Which district of Madhya Pradesh has the highest urban population?
A. Bhopal
B. Dindori
C. Morena
D. Indore

Q.71 According to the Census 2011, which district has the highest literacy rate in Madhya Pradesh?
A. Indore
B. Bhopal
C. Jabalpur
D. Balaghat

Q.72 The Koyna, Tungabhadra and Bhima rivers are the major tributaries of the river:
A. Tapti
B. Ganga
C. Godavari
D. Krishna

Q.73 The districts in which the Tropic of Cancer does not pass through are:
A. Shahpur and Rajgarh
B. Indore and Balaghat
C. Bhopal and Jabalpur
D. Ratlam and Ujain

Q.74 Which of the following passes are NOT correctly matched with their location?
A. Nathu - la pass - Sikkim
B. Shipki-la pass - Arunachal Pradesh
C. Zojila pass - Jammu and Kashmir
D. Mana pass - Uttarakhand

Q.75 Backwaters or Kayals are commonly found in which state?
A. Tamil Nadu
B. Kerala
C. Andhra Pradesh
D. Telengana

Q.76 Which district of Madhya Pradesh has the maximum child sex ratio?
A. Alirajpur
B. Morena
C. Indore
D. Bhopal

Q.77 Which one of the following is the leading producer of Copper?
A. Bihar
B. Jharkhand
C. Orissa
D. Madhya Pradesh

Q.78 Which one of the following is the highest peak of the Aravalli mountain?
A. Achalgarh
B. Jarga
C. Guru Shikhar
D. Ser

Q.79 The river island Majuli which became "India's first and only island district" is located in ________.

A. Karnatak
B. Jammu and Kashmir
C. Himachal Pradesh
D. Assam

Q.80 Tsangpo river flowing through Tibet is known in India as:
[Intelligence Bureau Security Assistant, 2019]
A. Brahmaputra
B. Gangas
C. Sutlej
D. Beas

Q.81 Which of the following areas is the original habitat of the 'Toda tribe'?
[Madhya Pradesh Public Service Commission (MPPSC), 2017]
A. Jaunsar Hills
B. Garo Hills
C. Nilgiri Hills
D. Jaintia Hills

Q.82 Which of the following can not be drawn from the Population Pyramid of a country?
A. Dependancy ratio
B. Population Growth Rate
C. Gender distribution within population
D. Total population size

Q.83 From which State does Monpha tribe belong to?
A. Arunachal Pradesh
B. Assam
C. Sikkim
D. Mizoram

Q.84 In India, the steel production industry requires the import of:
A. Saltpetre
B. Rock phosphate
C. Coking coal
D. All of the above

Q.85 The Panama Canal opened in 1914, links:
[UPSC NDA, 2020]
A. Red Sea and Mediterranean Sea
B. Atlantic Ocean and Pacific Ocean
C. Indian Ocean and Pacific Ocean
D. Adriatic Sea and Black Sea

Q.86 Which of the following modes of transport is very flexible?
A. Water
B. Pipeline
C. Air
D. Railways

Q.87 Which of the following is the major copper producing country?
A. Indonesia
B. Sri Lanka
C. Russia
D. Chile

Q.88 Carajas mine is the largest iron ore mine in the world. In which country is it located?
A. Brazil
B. USA
C. China
D. Australia

Q.89 Which type of coal is the first stage of coal formation from vegetation?
A. Anthracite
B. Bituminous
C. Lignite
D. Peat

Q.90 Which of the following industries manufactures telephones, computers, etc?

[MPTET Paper I - Varg 3, 2012]

A. Steel
B. Electronic
C. Aluminum
D. Information Technology

Q.91 A person living in Gandhidham (Gujarat) wants to visit first Bhopal (Madhya Pradesh) and then Hyderabad (Andhra Pradesh). The directions of his journey will be-
A. First towards East and then towards South
B. First towards West and then towards South
C. First towards South and then towards west
D. First towards South and then towards East

Q.92 Asteroids are found in between the orbits of:
A. Saturn and Jupiter
B. Mars and Jupiter
C. Earth and Mars
D. Saturn and Uranus

Q.93 Delhi is the capital of India and it is located on the River?
A. Godavari
B. Yamuna
C. Krishna
D. Tapti

Q.94 Which country is also known as the Playground of Europe?
A. Osaka
B. Switzerland
C. Philadelphia
D. Cuba

Q.95 Gwadar port is located in:
[UPSC Central Armed Police Forces AC, 2019]
A. Pakistan
B. Iran
C. India
D. Sri Lanka

Q.96 Which among the following Rivers act as boundary between North and South India?
A. River Periyar
B. River Mandovi
C. River Narmada
D. River Penner

Q.97 Name the Tri - Equilibrium factors of human geography?
A. Biotic
B. Abiotic
C. Cultural factors
D. All of the Above

Q.98 Which of the following river is flowing through Jammu & Kashmir?
A. Chenab
B. Mahi
C. Godavari
D. Krishna

Q.99 As per Census 2011 data, which is the most populated metro city in India?
A. Delhi
B. Mumbai
C. Chennai
D. Kolkata

Q.100 In which state is the Nokrek National Park located?
A. Tripura
B. Manipur
C. Assam
D. Meghalaya

Q.101 Ayodhya is situated on the banks of which river?
A. River Sarayu
B. River Periyar
C. River Narmada
D. River Mandovi

Q.102 Which of the following is the origin of Godavari river?
A. Nasik hill
B. Amarkantak

C. Cardomom hills
D. Vindhyas

Q.103 This is the longest irrigation canal in India-
A. Indira Gandhi canal
B. Buckingham canal
C. Agra canal
D. Conolly canal

Q.104 Teak wood trees grow in the following type of forests:
A. Temperature forests
B. Tropical Deciduous forests
C. Dry deciduous forests
D. Beach forests

Q.105 Which of the following dams has been built on the river Krishna?
A. Narmada Sagar
B. Hirakund
C. Bhakra Nangal
D. Nagarjuna Sagar

Q.106 Which of the following rocks formed from the existing rocks by undergoing the process of recrystallization?
A. Igneous rocks
B. Metamorphic rocks
C. Sedimentary rocks
D. None of the above

Q.107 About 90% of the world's earthquakes and 80% of the world's largest earthquakes occur along the Ring of Fire. In which sea this Ring of Fire lies?
A. Himalayan Area
B. Atlantic Ocean
C. Pacific Ocean
D. Mediterranean Area

Q.108 Hydraulic Brakes work on which principle?
A. Pascal's Principle
B. Archimedes Principle
C. Newton's Laws
D. Casini's Laws

Q.109 Northern Europe is characterized by?
A. Tundra
B. Taiga
C. Temperate coniferous forests
D. Alpine

Q.110 Santa Ana, Brickfielder, Sirocco & Khamsin are examples of _____?
A. Currents
B. Volcanoes
C. Winds
D. Deserts

Q.111 Which of the following rivers does NOT flow through Punjab?
A. Sutlej
B. Yamuna
C. Ravi
D. Jhelum

Q.112 Which among the following is the largest freshwater lake in India?
[Nagaland PSC (NPSC), 2018]
A. Dal Lake
B. Pulicat lake
C. Wular Lake
D. Chilka Lake

Q.113 Which of the following rivers does not originate in India?
A. Beas
B. Chenab
C. Ravi
D. Sutlej

Q.114 Which is the longest river in India?
A. Godavari
B. Yamuna
C. Ganga
D. Brahmaputra

Q.115 Which among the following is the highest waterfall in the world?

A. Mutarazi   **B.** Monge   **C.** Tugela   **D.** Angel

Q.116 Which of the following is the tallest of the dams in India?

A. Bhakra   **B.** Koyena   **C.** Pong   **D.** Tehri

Q.117 The largest brackish water lake in Asia is:

A. Chilika Lake   **B.** Vembanad Lake
C. Wular Lake   **D.** None of the above

Q.118 Which of the following River is also known as 'Twin of Narmada'?

A. Sabarmati   **B.** Tapti
C. Godavari   **D.** Mahi

Q.119 The river Godavari originates in the state of:

A. Madhya Pradesh   **B.** Chhatisgarh
C. Maharashtra   **D.** Odisha

Q.120 In which state is the Sharavati Power Project situated?

A. Maharashtra   **B.** Karnataka
C. Kerala   **D.** Tamil Nadu

Q.121 The Betwa river flows through the states of -

A. Only Madhya Pradesh
B. Madhya Pradesh and Uttar Pradesh
C. Madhya Pradesh and Chhattisgarh
D. Madhya Pradesh and Rajasthan

Q.122 In which state is Jog Falls located?

[Territorial Army Officer, 2019]

A. Uttarakhand   **B.** Karnataka
C. Jharkhand   **D.** Sikkim

Q.123 On which river is the Bhakra Nangal Dam situated?

A. Sutlej   **B.** Ghaggar   **C.** Ravi   **D.** Chenab

Q.124 Which of the following states is the Nizam Sagar Dam situated?

A. Karnataka   **B.** Telangana
C. West Bengal   **D.** Andhra Pradesh

Q.125 On the banks of which river is the city of Vijayawada located?

A. Krishna   **B.** Godavari
C. Tungabadhra   **D.** Manjeera

// Smart Answer Sheet //

Correct — Indicates percentage of students who answered questions correctly.

Skipped — Indicates percentage of students who skipped questions.

Q.	Ans.	Correct	Skipped
1	A	53.02 %	7.92 %
2	D	51.7 %	20.38 %
3	C	20.38 %	17.54 %
4	C	33.4 %	22.64 %
5	C	42.64 %	20.94 %
6	A	55.66 %	19.43 %
7	D	54.72 %	21.88 %
8	D	30.38 %	21.7 %
9	C	48.3 %	21.7 %
10	B	28.68 %	20.75 %
11	B	60.94 %	18.49 %
12	C	52.64 %	21.7 %
13	B	51.89 %	14.34 %
14	C	51.13 %	21.7 %
15	A	42.64 %	17.74 %
16	A	68.68 %	17.74 %
17	B	59.25 %	21.88 %
18	B	27.74 %	21.69 %
19	D	70.19 %	8.11 %
20	D	75.85 %	16.23 %
21	D	60.0 %	14.72 %
22	B	41.51 %	21.7 %
23	A	26.23 %	8.3 %
24	A	46.23 %	22.07 %
25	B	25.85 %	21.7 %
26	D	43.02 %	21.89 %
27	A	44.91 %	13.39 %
28	B	38.11 %	22.46 %
29	A	55.28 %	15.47 %
30	B	41.32 %	19.81 %
31	C	67.55 %	19.24 %
32	B	62.08 %	17.54 %
33	B	45.09 %	11.7 %
34	B	55.85 %	21.7 %
35	A	36.98 %	18.11 %
36	B	58.49 %	18.87 %
37	A	22.08 %	22.83 %
38	B	53.21 %	21.32 %
39	D	61.13 %	21.89 %
40	A	59.43 %	22.27 %
41	A	62.83 %	14.34 %
42	C	27.55 %	21.7 %
43	B	36.04 %	17.73 %
44	D	54.91 %	21.88 %
45	A	73.21 %	15.28 %
46	B	41.51 %	21.51 %
47	A	17.74 %	18.11 %
48	D	24.34 %	22.26 %
49	A	33.4 %	22.83 %
50	C	26.04 %	20.56 %
51	B	25.47 %	16.79 %
52	D	29.81 %	16.42 %
53	B	55.28 %	22.27 %
54	B	66.79 %	20.0 %
55	B	22.26 %	18.31 %
56	A	32.26 %	21.7 %
57	D	40.38 %	21.88 %
58	C	22.08 %	20.18 %
59	C	40.75 %	17.93 %
60	A	48.11 %	16.98 %
61	C	30.94 %	21.51 %
62	C	44.72 %	21.32 %
63	A	43.02 %	18.11 %
64	D	34.72 %	22.07 %
65	C	39.62 %	21.13 %
66	C	20.57 %	20.56 %
67	C	27.74 %	21.51 %
68	C	56.04 %	21.88 %
69	D	60.75 %	21.89 %
70	D	39.06 %	22.26 %
71	C	15.47 %	10.38 %
72	D	51.13 %	16.98 %
73	B	18.87 %	23.02 %
74	B	51.13 %	21.7 %
75	B	50.75 %	21.33 %
76	A	21.13 %	18.87 %
77	D	23.77 %	22.46 %
78	C	70.75 %	21.7 %
79	D	68.49 %	11.7 %
80	A	72.83 %	18.49 %

Q.	Ans.	Correct / Skipped
81	C	65.09 % / 13.78 %
82	D	19.62 % / 20.57 %
83	A	31.13 % / 21.51 %
84	C	17.74 % / 19.43 %
85	B	53.96 % / 22.46 %
86	A	42.08 % / 21.69 %
87	D	51.51 % / 22.07 %
88	A	27.92 % / 22.27 %
89	D	43.77 % / 21.89 %

Q.	Ans.	Correct / Skipped
90	B	42.45 % / 21.7 %
91	A	56.23 % / 22.07 %
92	B	56.79 % / 21.32 %
93	B	80.57 % / 13.96 %
94	B	53.77 % / 22.46 %
95	A	43.02 % / 18.68 %
96	C	62.64 % / 19.62 %
97	D	67.55 % / 22.64 %
98	A	70.19 % / 21.89 %

Q.	Ans.	Correct / Skipped
99	B	46.42 % / 17.92 %
100	D	38.87 % / 18.3 %
101	A	72.08 % / 21.88 %
102	A	47.55 % / 21.88 %
103	A	72.08 % / 22.64 %
104	B	60.94 % / 19.44 %
105	D	63.4 % / 22.07 %
106	B	50.0 % / 22.08 %
107	C	68.87 % / 18.11 %

Q.	Ans.	Correct / Skipped
108	A	40.75 % / 22.46 %
109	B	29.25 % / 14.9 %
110	C	63.96 % / 21.7 %
111	B	58.49 % / 12.08 %
112	C	62.08 % / 22.07 %
113	D	63.4 % / 13.2 %
114	C	69.62 % / 22.08 %
115	D	69.43 % / 18.87 %
116	D	37.17 % / 21.7 %

Q.	Ans.	Correct / Skipped
117	A	60.57 % / 12.83 %
118	B	64.15 % / 21.7 %
119	C	61.89 % / 13.02 %
120	B	58.11 % / 16.42 %
121	B	55.28 % / 15.85 %
122	B	57.74 % / 22.45 %
123	A	72.64 % / 17.55 %
124	B	34.15 % / 22.27 %
125	A	36.6 % / 22.27 %

Performance Analysis

Avg. Score (%)	47.29%
Toppers Score (%)	100.0%
Your Score	

//Hints and Solutions//

1. A biome is an area of the planet that can be classified according to the plants and animals that live in it. Temperature, soil, and the amount of light and water help determine what life exists in a biome. Biomes are distinct biological communities that have formed in response to a shared physical climate. A biome is a broader term than habitat. A biome is different from an ecosystem. An ecosystem is the interaction of living and nonliving things in an environment. A biome is a specific geographic area notable for the species living there. A biome can be made up of many ecosystems.
Hence, the correct option is (A).

2. Blue-green algae(BGA) are actually types of bacteria known as Cyanobacteria. They normally look green and sometimes may turn bluish when scums are dying. BGA is widely distributed all over the earth. While fixing carbon from CO_2, certain BGA can fix dinitrogen from the atmosphere and are called nitrogen-fixing BGA, including free-living and symbiotic forms.
Hence, the correct option is (D).

3. The photochemical reaction is caused by the absorption of energy in the form of light. The word smog is formed of smoke and fog. Photochemical smog is the major contributor to air pollution and is composed of primary and secondary pollutants. Primary being the nitrogen oxides and volatile organic compounds. Unsaturated hydrocarbons are those that have double or triple covalent bonds between adjacent carbon atoms. e.g., Ethylene, Gasoline and natural gas are the major sources of unsaturated hydrocarbon.
Hence, the correct option is (C).

4. Persistent organic pollutants (POPs) are persistent, mainly lipid-soluble chemicals which bioaccumulate in fatty tissues and are biomagnified up the food web, and pose a risk to human health and the environment. Dichlorodiphenyltrichloroethane, commonly known as DDT, is a colorless, tasteless, and almost odorless crystalline chemical compound, an organochlorine. Originally developed as an insecticide, it became infamous for its environmental impacts.

Hence, the correct option is (C).

5. A national park, Sanctuary, and Biosphere is a park in use for conservation purposes, created and protected by national governments. Often it is a reserve of natural, semi-natural, or developed land that a sovereign state declares or owns but a Zoo is a facility in which animals are housed within enclosures, cared for, displayed to the public, and in some cases bred. The term "zoological garden" refers to zoology, the study of animals.
Hence, the correct option is (C).

6. Harmful species are not in the IUCN classification of threatened species. IUCN Red List of Threatened Species, also called IUCN Red List, one of the most well-known objective assessment systems for classifying the status of plants, animals, and other organisms threatened with extinction. IUCN red list was founded in 1964. It uses a set of criteria to evaluate the extinction risk of a thousand of species and subspecies.
Hence, the correct option is (A).

7. Agenda 21 was the declaration signed at UNCED 1992 in Rio De Janeiro, Brazil. Agenda 21 is a comprehensive plan of action recommended by the UN summit to be taken globally, nationally, and locally by organizations of the United Nations System, Governments, and Major Groups in every area in which human impacts environment. Agenda 21 signed with an aim to achieve global sustainable development. It was adopted by more than 178 governments at the United Nations Conference on Environment and Development in 1992. Agenda 21 is divided into 40 chapters that have been grouped into 4 sections and 351-page.
Hence, the correct option is (D).

8. The Vienna conference was the first global conference on the depletion of the ozone layer, held in Vienna, Austria in 1985. It was held after a hole as large as the size of the US was discovered in the ozone layer. At this conference, the Vienna Convention for the protection of the Ozone layer was agreed upon.
Hence, the correct option is (D).

9. Red Data Book is a public document that contains the data of endangered and rare species including animals, plants, fungi as well as some local subspecies present in the country. It was published by the International Union for Conservation of Nature. This book is responsible for the evaluation of the total number of wild animals present, identification of all animals and birds and their extinct species.
Hence, the correct option is (C).

10. Nagarjunasagar - Srisailam Tiger Reserve is the largest tiger reserve in India. It is present in Andhra Pradesh. The core area of this reserve is 1200 km^2.
Hence, the correct option is (B).

11. Rabi Crops: These are agricultural crops sown in winter and harvested in the spring in South Asia. Rabi crop season is form (October - March). Ex- Wheat, Barley, Oats (Cereals), Linseed, Mustard, Peals, etc.

Kharif crops: Kharif crops as monsoon crops are domesticated plants that are cultivated and harvested during the rainy season. (Kharif crop season is from April to October). Ex- Rice, Maize, Pearliament, Bajara, Pulses(Arhar), Cotton, Makai, etc.
Hence, the correct option is (B).

12. Sunlight (Solar energy) - Non-Conventional.

Wind - Non-Conventional.

Atomic energy - Non-Conventional.
Hence, the correct option is (C).

13. The factors of production are land, labour, capital, and entrepreneurship. 'Land' is quite a broad category as a factor of production in that it refers to all natural resources. 'Labor', as a factor of production, involves any human input. The quality of

labour depends on the workforce's skills, education, and motivation. 'Capital' refers to manufactured resources such as factories and machines. 'Entrepreneurship' - An entrepreneur is someone who takes on the economic risk involved in bringing the other three factors of production together.
Hence, the correct option is (B).

14. Drip irrigation practice leads to maximum water conservation. It delivers water and nutrients directly to the plant's roots zone.

Drip irrigation: Each dripper emits drops containing water and fertilizers, resulting in the uniform application of water and nutrients directly to each plant's root zone, across an entire field. Water and nutrients are delivered across the field in pipes called 'dripper lines'.
Hence, the correct option is (C).

15. Limonite ore is one of the principal iron ore. Limonite ore is also called lemon rock or yellow iron ore. Limonite is used as a pigment. Important ores of Iron are: Limonite, Hematite, and Magnetite.
Hence, the correct option is (A).

16. Chotanagpur plateau represents the north-eastern projection of the Indian Peninsula. It covers Jharkhand, the northern part of Chhatisgarh, and the Purulia district of West Bengal. This plateau is composed mainly of Gondwana rocks. The Damodar valley has vast coal reserves, and the Hazaribagh region is one of the main sources of mica in the world. Other minerals are copper, limestone, bauxite, iron ore, asbestos, and apatite (useful in the manufacture of phosphate fertilizers).
Hence, the correct option is (A).

17.

List - I (Manufacturing site)	List - II (Industry)
A. Ludhiana	2. Woolen garments
B. Kanpur	3. Leather
C. Varanasi	4. Handloom
D. Vijayawada	1. Auto parts

Hence, the correct option is (B).

18. 8th Plan of 1992 to 1997 is also known as the liberalization of the economy. It was also considered as the beginning of liberalization, privatization, and globalization (LPG) in India.
Hence, the correct option is (B).

19. The factors for the growth of the jute industry in Hooghly region are- The nearness of the jute producing areas. Low-cost water transport, supported by a good network of railways, roadways and waterways to help the movement of raw material to the mills. Abundant water for processing raw jute. Cheap labour from West Bengal and adjoining states of Bihar, Orissa and Uttar Pradesh. Kolkata as an urban centre provides banking, insurance and port facilities for the export of jute goods. 90% of Jute is cultivated in the Kolkata hinterland. Jute is the only crop that can withstand flooding of this region. West Bengal alone accounts for over 50 percent raw jute production.
Hence, the correct option is (D).

20. Water resources available on earth are:

Freshwater: Glaciers, ice caps, and snow

Groundwater: Oceans, seas, streams, rivers, lakes, ponds

Wetlands: Lagoons, swamps, and marshes

Precipitation: Rain, snow, and dew

Therefore, from the above points, we can clearly infer that the resources of water on the earth are the ocean, snow, rain and underground water.
Hence, the correct option is (D).

21. The Human Development Index (HDI) is a statistical tool that is used to measure a country's overall achievement in social and economic dimensions. The social and economic dimensions of a country depending on the health of people, their level of educational attainment, and their standard of living. A country scores a higher HDI if the lifespan is higher, the education level is higher, and the GDP per capital is higher.
Hence, the correct option is (D).

22. Gini Coefficient represent the Distribution of Income. It measures the degree of income inequality in the country's population. The value of the Gini Coefficient varies from 0 to 1. 0 means perfect equality where everyone has the same income, and 1 means perfect inequality where all the income is received by a single individual. Graphical Representation of the Gini Index (Lorenz curve).

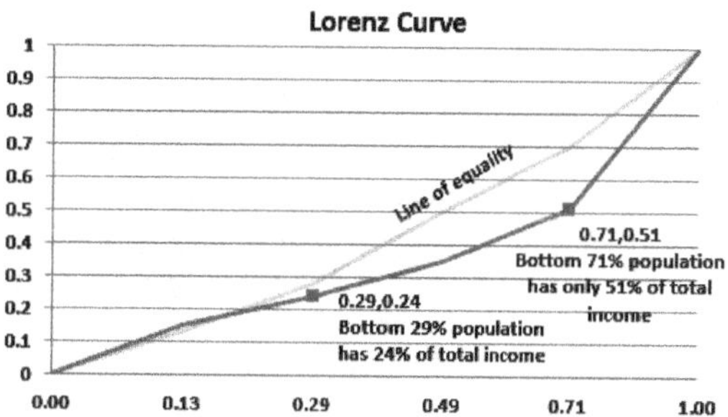

Hence, the correct option is (B).

23. When a country uses the currency of another country along with its own currency or by official substitution, it is called Dollarization. Example Nepal and Bhutan hold Indian rupee along with their own official currencies' Nepalese rupee and Bhutanese Ngultrum respectively. It is done for financial security and for trade across the border.
Hence, the correct option is (A).

24. The custom duty on gold and silver is rationalized under the union budget 2021-22. This will reduce the prices of gold and silver. At present, Gold and silver attract a basic customs duty of 12.5%. The customs duty on gold and silver will be reduced from the existing 12.5% to 7.5%. The gold dore bars will attract customs duty of 6.9%(the existing rate is 11.85 %) The silver dore bars will now attract a customs duty of 6.1% (the existing rate is 11%). Customs duty on gold and silver findings will be halved to 10% from the current 20%.
Hence, the correct option is (A).

25. The Sixth Five-Year Plan marked the beginning of economic liberalization. Price controls were eliminated and ration shops were closed. This led to an increase in food prices and an increase in the cost of living. The National Bank for Agriculture and Rural

Development was established for the development of rural areas on 12 July 1982 by recommendation of the Shivaraman Committee. Family planning was also expanded. NCR planning board in 1985 and Integrated Development of Small and Medium Towns (IDMST) The Sixth Five-Year Plan was a great success for the Indian economy. The target growth rate was 5.2% and the actual growth rate was 5.7%.
Hence, the correct option is (B).

26. There are three types of ration cards in India:

Antyodaya cards for the poorest of the poor

BPL cards for those below the poverty line

APL cards for all others

The rationing system was revived in the wake of an acute food shortage during the 1960s, prior to the Green Revolution. The food procured by the FCI is distributed through government-regulated ration shops among the poorer section of the society. This is called the Public Distribution System.
Hence, the correct option is (D).

27. Absolute poverty can be defined as the state in which a subject lacks the means to meet his or her basic needs. Such basic needs are often listed in international poverty reduction programs, and usually include food, water, shelter, basic education, and basic medical care. Extreme poverty is typically defined as a state in which a person lacks access to all, or several, of the goods needed for meeting these basic needs.
Hence, the correct option is (A).

28. The service sectors in India had an estimated growth rate of nearly seven percent in the financial year 2020, marking a decrease of 0.7 percent in growth compared to the previous year. These services included trade, hospitality, transport and communication services, finance, real estate, and public administration.
Hence, the correct option is (B).

29. Maheshwar Project: The Maheshwar Hydel Project 400 MW located about 40 km downstream of Omkareshwar multi-purpose project on main Narmada river near Mandleshwar town in Khargone district of Madhya Pradesh.
Hence, the correct option is (A).

30. The Mahatma Gandhi Hydroelectric Power Station and the Sharavati Valley Project, a short distance downstream (east) of the cataract, generate much of the electricity for Karnataka state.
Hence, the correct option is (B).

31. The stratosphere is said to be ideal for flying jet aircraft. This is because this layer is rich in ozone which reduces fuel consumption, the temperature is constant and ideal for aircraft engine efficiency, this layer is out of the firing range of anti-aircraft guns and of the absence of clouds and other weather phenomena.
Hence, the correct option is (C).

32. Doldrums are Equatorial zone with low pressure. As this region lies along the equator, it receives highest amount of insolation. Due to intense heating, the air gets warmed up and rises over the equatorial region (convection). Whenever there is vertically upward movement of air, the region at the surface will be at low pressure. Thus the belt along the equator is called equatorial low pressure belt.
Hence, the correct option is (B).

33. The following places that are favourably influenced by the Trade winds are West Indies, Brazil, Mexico and Madagascar.

Trade winds: When you're outside, you might notice that one day the wind blows one direction and the next day, the wind is blowing a different direction. That's a pretty common occurrence. However, many winds on Earth are quite predictable. For example, high in the atmosphere, the jet streams typically blow across Earth from west to east. The trade winds are air currents closer to Earth's surface that blow from east to west near the equator.
Hence, the correct option is (B).

34. In the northern hemisphere, the wind blowing from the Horse latitudes to the Doldrums is called Trade wind. Trade wind blow out from the Subtropical High Pressure belts. In the northern hemisphere, they blow towards the equatorial low and called North East Trade Winds. In the Southern hemisphere they blow towards the equatorial low and become the South East Trade winds.
Hence, the correct option is (B).

35. The dense mass of small water drops on smoke particles in the lower layers of the atmosphere is Smog. Smog is a kind of air pollution, originally named for the mixture of smoke and fog in the air. Classic smog results from large amounts of coal burning in an area and is caused by a mixture of smoke and sulfur dioxide.
Hence, the correct option is (A).

36. Argon is the chemically inactive gas present in the atmosphere. Argon is a chemical element. The symbol for argon is Ar, and its atomic number (or proton number) is 18. It is a noble gas and no electrons or protons can be lost or gained from this atom.
Hence, the correct option is (B).

37. As Ionosphere is one of the upper most layers, the solar and cosmic radiations heat it up rapidly, the gaseous material available here is in ionic state. Hence temperature increases rapidly.
Hence, the correct option is (A).

38. Nathu La - Arunachal Pradesh is not correctly matched.

- The Nathu La Pass connects the Indian state of Sikkim.
- Its height is about 14450 feet.
- The capital of Sikkim is Gangtok.
- There is also Jelep La Pass in Sikkim.

Hence, the correct option is (B).

39. Temperature generally decreases towards the poles because progressively lesser solar energy per unit area falls on the earth's surface as we move to polar regions. Longer the path of the sun's rays, greater is the amount of reflection and absorption of heat by the atmosphere. As a result, the intensity of insolation is less.
Hence, the correct option is (D).

40. Excess carbon in the atmosphere warms the planet, when carbon dioxide concentrations rise, air temperatures go up, and more water vapor evaporates into the atmosphere which then amplifies greenhouse heating.
Hence, the correct option is (A).

41. Atmospheric pressure exerted on earth is due to gravitational pull of the earth. The air around you has weight, and it presses against everything it touches. That pressure is called atmospheric pressure, or air pressure.
Hence, the correct option is (A).

42. Only tropical cyclones that form over the Atlantic Ocean or eastern Pacific Ocean are called "hurricanes." Tropical cyclones are like giant engines that use warm, moist air as fuel. That is why they form only over warm ocean waters near the equator. The warm, moist air over the ocean rises upward from near the surface.
Hence, the correct option is (C).

43. Orographic precipitation or Rain produced when moist air is lifted as it moves over a mountain range. As the air rises and cools, orographic clouds form and serve as the source of the precipitation, most of which falls upwind of the mountain ridge. Some also falls a short distance downwind of the ridge and is sometimes called spillover. On the lee side of the mountain range, rainfall is usually low, and the area is said to be in a Rain Shadow.
Hence, the correct option is (B).

44. Ionosphere is the top layer of the atmosphere. Radio waves are deflected in the ionosphere of the atmosphere. It ranges from about 60 km to 1000 km. It's ionized by solar radiation.
Hence, the correct option is (D).

45. The monsoon has well-developed cycle in South and South East Asia. The monsoon through axis experiences considerable day to day variation in its position, which has a vital bearing on the monsoon rainfall distribution in the region.
Hence, the correct option is (A).

46. The taiga is a forest of the cold, sub-arctic region. The subarctic is an area of the Northern Hemisphere that lies just south of the Arctic Circle. The taiga lies between the tundra to the north and temperate forests to the south.

Taigas are thick forests. Coniferous trees, such as spruce, pine, and fir, are common. Coniferous trees have needles instead of broad leaves, and their seeds grow inside protective, woody cones. While deciduous trees of temperate forests lose their leaves in winter, conifers never lose their needles.
Hence, the correct option is (B).

47. The Ring of Fire is also referred to as the Circum-Pacific Belt. It is a path along the Pacific Ocean. Hence, statement 1 is incorrect. It is characterized by active volcanoes and frequent earthquakes. Its length is approximately 40,000 kilometers (24,900 miles). It traces boundaries between several tectonic plates-including the Pacific, Juan de Fuca, Cocos, Indian-Australian, Nazca, North American, and Philippine Plates.
Hence, the correct option is (A).

48. The passage of the front causes abrupt changes in the weather conditions over the area in the middle and high latitudes. Extratropical cyclones form along the polar front. Initially, the front is stationary. In the northern hemisphere, warm air blows from the south and cold air from the north of the front. When the pressure drops along the front, the warm air moves northwards, and the cold air move towards, south setting in motion an anticlockwise cyclonic circulation. The cyclonic circulation leads to a well-developed extratropical cyclone, with a warm front and a cold front.
Hence, the correct option is (D).

49. It is a deepwater basin that forms a natural sea link between the Red Sea and the Arabian Sea. Hence, statement 1 is correct. Named for the seaport of Aden, in southern Yemen, the gulf is situated between the coasts of Arabia and the Horn of Africa. To the west, it narrows into the Gulf of Tadjoura; its eastern geographic limits are defined by the meridian of Cape Guardafui (5116 E). In oceanographic and geologic terms, however, it extends to the eastern limits of the continental shelf beyond the Kuria Muria Islands to the north and the island of Socotra to the south, covering an area of some 205,000 square miles (530,000 square km).
Hence, the correct option is (A).

50. It is a transitional type of climate found between the equatorial forests and the trade winds and the hot desert. It is confined within the tropical region. It is best developed in Sudan. It is also called Sudan climate. It is characterized by an alternate hot, rainy season and cool, dry season. The monthly temperature hovers between 70 degrees F to 90 degrees F. The annual temperature range is 20 degrees F but it increases when moving away from the equator.
Hence, the correct option is (C).

51. These are countries lacking any direct territorial access to the seas. Because of this geographical barrier, they are almost entirely dependent on neighboring transit countries for their external trade. They usually suffer from high transaction costs, especially due to huge transportation expenses, inadequate infrastructure, and bottlenecks associated with importation and exportation requirements, as well as inefficient customs and transit procedures.
Hence, the correct option is (B).

52. They are also called the Appalachians, a great highland system of North America, the eastern counterpart of the Rocky Mountains. Extending for almost 2,000 miles (3,200 km) from the Canadian province of Newfoundland and Labrador to central Alabama in the United States, the Appalachian Mountains form a natural barrier between the eastern Coastal Plain and the vast Interior Lowlands of North America. As a result, they have played a vital role in the settlement and development of the entire continent. They combine a heritage of natural beauty and a distinctive regional culture with contemporary problems of economic deprivation and environmental deterioration. The system may be divided into three large physiographic regions: northern, central, and southern Appalachia. The highest elevations in the Appalachians are in the northern division.
Hence, the correct option is (D).

53. Birth rate - It is the number of live births per thousand persons in a year. It is a major component of growth because, in India, birth rates have always been higher than death rates.

Death rate - It is the number of deaths per thousand persons in a year. The main cause of the rate of growth of the Indian population has been the rapid decline in death rates. The natural increase in population is the difference between birth rates and death rates.
Hence, the correct option is (B).

54. Tibetan Plateau is the tallest plateau in the world. Tibetan Plateau is also known as the "Roof of the world". The region lies between the Kunlun Mountains and its associated ranges to the north and the Himalayas and Karakoram Range to the south and southwest.

Hence, the correct option is (B).

55. Geological Survey of India (GSI) has found reserves of Vanadium in Depo and Tamang regions of Papum Pare district of Arunachal Pradesh. GSI is an attached office to the Ministry of Mines.
Hence, the correct option is (B).

56. An estuary is an area where a freshwater river or stream meets the ocean. In estuaries, the salty ocean mixes with a freshwater river, resulting in brackish water. An estuary may also be called a bay, lagoon, sound, or slough.
Hence, the correct option is (A).

57. The periodical rise and fall of the sea level, once or twice a day, mainly due to the attraction of the sun and the moon, is called a tide. The movement of water caused by meteorological effects (winds and atmospheric pressure changes) are called surges. Surges are not regular like tides. The study of tides is very complex, spatially and temporally, as it has great variations in frequency, magnitude, and height. The moon's gravitational pull to a great extent and to a lesser extent the sun's gravitational pull, are the major causes for the occurrence of tides.
Hence, the correct option is (D).

58. The method of soil conservation in which rocks are piled up to slow down the flow of water which prevents gullies and further soil loss is called Rock dam.

As we know that much of soil erosion is caused due to the high flow of water i.e floods, so to decrease the flow the water, small rock dam made of stone gravel and some other durable material are constructed in the path of flow , which hence helps in checking the soil erosion.

Hence, the correct option is (C).

59. It is an arm of the Pacific Ocean bordering the East Asian mainland and extending northeastward from the South China Sea, to which it is connected by the shallow Taiwan Strait between Taiwan and mainland China. The East China Sea and the South China Sea together form the China Sea. It is bordered by Japan also.
Hence, the correct option is (C).

60. The Intertropical Convergence Zone, or ITCZ, is the region that circles the Earth, near the equator, where the trade winds of the Northern and Southern Hemispheres come together.
Hence, the correct option is (A).

61. When two different air masses meet, the boundary zone between them is called a front. The process of formation of the fronts is known as frontogenesis. When the cold air moves towards the warm air mass, its contact zone is called the cold front. There are four types of fronts: cold fronts, warm fronts, stationary fronts, and occluded fronts.
Hence, the correct option is (C).

62. Monsoons are the sea and land breezes on a larger scale. It is the seasonal reversal of wind with the change in the heating of the earth's surface. Monsoon climate is characterized by distinct wet and dry seasons.
Hence, the correct option is (C).

63. This type of rainfall is most common in regions that are intensely heated. It is mostly found in tropical regions. In temperate regions, it can be observed during summers. When the earth's surface is heated by the sun's heat, it creates rising pockets of warm air, known as convection currents. Warm air rises rapidly, where it starts to cool and condenses to form clouds. These clouds cause rainfall and thunderstorms.
Hence, the correct option is (A).

64. The atmosphere is a mixture of different gases and it envelopes the earth all around. It contains life-giving gases like oxygen for humans and animals and carbon dioxide for plants. The air is an integral part of the earth's mass and 99 percent of the total mass of the atmosphere is confined to the height of 32 km from the earth's surface. Ozone is found between 10 and 50 Km above the earth's surface.
Hence, the correct option is (D).

65. Mohorovicic Discontinuity: Transition zone between the Crust and Mantle.

Conrad Discontinuity: Transition zone between upper and lower crust

Lehman Discontinuity: Transition zone between Outer core and Inner core.
Hence, the correct option is (C).

66. BHEL plant is located in Bhopal from the collaboration of Britain. Gun Carriage Factory is located in Jabalpur. Agro Complex is located in Chhindwara. Stainless Steel Complex is located in Sagar. Orient Paper Mill is located in Amlai. The factory for making biscuits from soybean is located in Bhopal. The headquarters of Madhya Pradesh Finance Corporation is located in Indore.
Hence, the correct option is (C).

67. The airport is located in Indore. The airport was the brainchild of the Holkar State Administration. The land was selected in 1935 after consulting Nevill Vintcent of Messrs Tata and Sons (Aviation Department). The airport is named after Maharani Ahilya Bai Holkar of Holkar dynasty of the Maratha Empire. In July 1948 air services from Indore to Gwalior, Delhi and Mumbai began. The Indian government took control over the operations in 1950.
Hence, the correct option is (C).

68. India shares a 1,643-km-long border with Myanmar which touches the states of Arunachal Pradesh, Nagaland, Manipur and Mizoram. India shares a 4,096-km-long border with Bangladesh which touches Assam, Tripura, Mizoram, Meghalaya and West Bengal.
Hence, the correct option is (C).

69. The Narmada river originates in eastern Madhya Pradesh and flows west across the state, through a narrow valley between the Vindhya Range and spurs of the Satpura Range. It flows into the Gulf of Khambhat. The Vindhya Range separates northern India from the southern mainland.
Hence, the correct option is (D).

70. The Indore district of Madhya Pradesh has the highest urban population. The most populated urban agglomeration in Madhya Pradesh is Indore where 21,67,447 persons reside followed by Bhopal (U.A.) with 18,83,381 persons and Jabalpur (U.A.) which has reported 12,67,564 persons is seen in third place. Madhya Pradesh's population growth rate (2001-2011) was 20.35%. The rural population growth was 18.42% and the urban growth was 25.69%. Madhya Pradesh's child sex ratio (2011) is 918. Madhya Pradesh's Child sex ratio in 2001 was 932.
Hence, the correct option is (D).

71. Jabalpur district of Madhya Pradesh has the highest literacy rate (81.07%) among all the districts of the state as per the Census 2011. The top five districts with the highest literacy rate in MP are - Jabalpur (81.07%), Indore (80.87%), Bhopal (80.37%), Balaghat (77.09%), Gwalior (76.65%). The overall literacy rate of the state of Madhya Pradesh as per the Census 2011 was 69.32% The male literacy rate was 78.73% whereas the female literacy rate was 54.49%. The total number of literates in the state stood at 42,851,169. The districts with the lowest literacy rates in Madhya Pradesh are - Alirajpur (36.1%), Jhabua (43.3%).
Hence, the correct option is (C).

72. The major tributaries of the Krishna river are Koyna, Dudhganga, Panchganga, Malprabha, Ghatprabha, Bhima, Tungabhadra, Musi, etc. The rivers Venna, Koyna, Vasna, Panchganga, Dudhganga, Ghataprabha, Malaprabha and Tungabhadra join Krishna from the right bank; while the Yerla River, Musi River, Maneru and Bhima rivers join the Krishna from the left bank.
Hence, the correct option is (D).

73. The Tropic of Cancer, also known as Kark Rekha passes through 14 districts of Madhya Pradesh. These districts are Ratlam, Ujjain, Shajapur, Rajgarh, Sehore, Bhopal, Vidisha, Raisen, Sagar, Damoh, Katni, Jabalpur, Umariya, and Shahdol, but not from the Indore and Balghat.
Hence, the correct option is (B).

74. Shipki-la-Pass is located among the Zaskar ranges in Himachal Pradesh. The road from Shimla to Tibet goes through this pass. The Satluj River flows through this pass. The Nathula Pass is located in the Dogekya range in Sikkim. It connects the Indian state of Sikkim with China's Tibet autonomous region. Zojila Pass is a high mountain pass in Jammu and Kashmir. It is the second-highest pass after Fotu La on the Srinagar-Leh National Highway. Mana Pass is located in Uttarakhand.
Hence, the correct option is (B).

75. Backwaters are the shallow inlet of the sea in rivers lying parallel to the coastline. Backwater is water turned back in its course by an obstruction or the force of tides. In Kerala, these backwaters are locally known as Kayals. One of the very famous backwaters in the state is Vembanad. These Kayals are formed by wave action and shore currents which creates low barrier islands. The Kayals are a zone where freshwater is meeting with seawater

and thus it has diverse flora and fauna.
Hence, the correct option is (B).

76. Alirajpur district of Madhya Pradesh has the maximum child sex ratio. Alirajpur district of Madhya Pradesh has a 978 child sex ratio. Morena district of Madhya Pradesh has the minimum child sex ratio which is 829. Madhya Pradesh's child sex ratio (2011) is 918. Madhya Pradesh's Child sex ratio in 2001 was 932.
Hence, the correct option is (A).

77. Madhya Pradesh is the largest producer of copper in India. 2nd largest producer of copper in India is Rajasthan. India is a net importer of copper.
Hence, the correct option is (D).

78. Guru Shikhar is the highest peak of the Aravalli mountain. Guru Shikhar is located in the Arbuda Mountains of Rajasthan. The highest peak of the Aravalli Range at Guru Shikhar is at the elevation of 1,722 meters (5,650 ft). Aravalli hills one of the oldest ranges of the world borders the Peninsular plateau on the north-west side. Aravalli range starts near Delhi and crosses Haryana and Rajasthan, then ends at Gujarat.
Hence, the correct option is (C).

79. Majuli is the largest inhabited riverine island in the world located in the Brahmaputra River in Assam. It is India's first Island district consisting of nearly 144 villages with a population of approximately 1.6 Lakh. It is a centre of Neo Vaishnavite culture initiated by Saint reformer Srimanta Sankardev in the 15th century. It has nearly 65 Sattras which is the religious and cultural institution. It is surrounded by the Subhasini river in the north, Brahmaputra river on the south, and Kherkutia islands in the northeast.
Hence, the correct option is (D).

80. In India, the Tsangpo river is known as the Brahmaputra river. It is known by the name of the Yarlung Tsangpo in the Tibet region. It originates in the Chemayungdung glacier in the Himalayas and drains into the Bay of Bengal. It is about 2,900 km In length. After flowing through Tibet it enters India through Arunachal Pradesh and flows through Assam and Bangladesh before it joins the Bay of Bengal. The river crosses Assam and enters Bangladesh where the river is known as Jamuna and joins Ganga and then finally drains into the Bay of Bengal.
Hence, the correct option is (A).

81. Nilgiri Hills is the native area of the Toda tribe. Nilgiri hills are located in South India. Part of western ghats, spread in Karnataka, Kerela, and Tamil Nadu. The highest peak of the Nilgiri hills is being Doddabetta.
Hence, the correct option is (C).

82. It is a graphical illustration that shows the distribution of various age groups in a population (typically that of a country or region of the world), which forms the shape of a pyramid when the population is growing. It is also used in ecology to determine the overall age distribution of a population; an indication of the reproductive capabilities and likelihood of the continuation of a species. It mentions percentage-wise distribution within major age groups.
Hence, the correct option is (D).

83. Monpha Tribe is found in the state of Arunachal Pradesh. They are found in the West Kameng District and Tawang District

of Arunachal Pradesh. They perform Mopha dance to celebrate Losar Festival (Tribe's New Year).
Hence, the correct option is (A).

84. Saltpetre (Potassium nitrate) is not used in the production of Steel. It is used in the production of fertilizers, tree stump removal, rocket propellants and fireworks. It is one of the major constituents of gunpowder (black powder) and has been used since the Middle Ages as a food preservative. Rock phosphate is used in the production of fertilizer and not for the production of Steel.
Hence, the correct option is (C).

85. The Panama Canal opened in 1914 linked the Atlantic Ocean and the Pacific Ocean. It connects the Atlantic and Pacific oceans through the narrow Isthmus of Panama. It is an artificial 82 km waterway in Panama.
Hence, the correct option is (B).

86. Water transport in India is one of the cheapest modes of transportation. 6 national waterways were set-up by Inland waterways Authority of India in 1986. 13 major ports and 187 minor ports.
Hence, the correct option is (A).

87. Chile, the world's leading copper producer by far, produced an estimated 5.6 million metric tons of copper in 2019. In second place is Peru, with an estimated copper mine production of 2.4 million metric tons in the same year. The world's third-largest copper producer from mines is China. In 2019, China produced an estimated 1.6 million metric tons of copper from mines, which is over three times less than Chile's production.
Hence, the correct option is (D).

88. The Carajas mine is the largest iron ore mine in the world. It is located in the state of Para in the Carajas Mountains of northern Brazil. The mine is operated as an open-pit mine, and is estimated to contain roughly 7.2 billion tons of iron ore, plus gold, manganese, bauxite, copper, and nickel. The mine is located in the mining concession area of the Carajas National Forest, which contains known reserves of the order of 18 billion tons with an average grade of 65.4% of Fe(iron). The mine is largely powered by hydroelectric power from the Tucurui Dam.
Hence, the correct option is (A).

89. It is the first stage of coal formation from vegetation and has minimum carbon content of about 40%. Light brown in color with high humidity content, it is the most inferior type of coal.
Hence, the correct option is (D).

90. Industries of Electronic equipment manufactures Computers, Cell-phones, Telephones, Laptops and various other products where electronic components. Steel Industry is the backbone of the country, it manufactures building materials cars, bridges and many more steel products. Aluminium industry is widely used in various components like Transmission wires, Utensils, Aeroplanes etc.
Hence, the correct option is (B).

91. Gujarat is the westernmost state of India and Madhya Pradesh lies in the East of Gujarat. Andhra Pradesh is located to the south of Madhya Pradesh. Therefore while going from Gandhidham to Bhopal he will travel towards the East direction and then will move in the Southern direction towards Hyderabad.

Gandhidham is a city in the Kutch region of Gujarat and should not be confused with Gandhinagar- the capital of Gujarat. Bhopal is the capital of Madhya Pradesh and Hyderabad is the capital of Andhra Pradesh and Telangana. Hyderabad is now a part of Telangana (after the partition of Andhra Pradesh).
Hence, the correct option is (A).

92. There is a large gap in between the orbits of Mars and Jupiter. This gap is occupied by a large number of small objects that revolve around the Sun. These are called asteroids. Out of the eight planets, Mercury, Venus, Earth and Mars are called as the inner planets as they lie between the sun. The belt of asteroids and the other four planets are called the outer planets.
Hence, the correct option is (B).

93. Delhi is the capital of India and it is located on the river Yamuna. Delhi is the National Capital Territory (NCT). and Union Territory of India Yamuna River is the longest tributary of the Ganga River which flows in Northern India. Yamuna River arises from Yamunotri glacier and merges with the Ganga River at Triveni Sangam Allahabad.
Hence, the correct option is (B).

94. Switzerland is also known as the Playground of Europe. Writer Stephan Leslie called it so in his book also the country offers various adventurous activities. Osaka is known as the Manchester of Japan. Philadelphia is known as the Quaker City. Cuba is called the Sugarbowl of the World.
Hence, the correct option is (B).

95. For USD $ 3 million Pakistan purchased the Gwadar enclave from the Sultanate of Muscat and Oman on 7 September 1958 after four years of negotiations. After 174 years of Omani rule, on 8 December 1958 Gwadar formally became part of Pakistan and it is built and managed by China. The port holds great strategic and economic significance for Pakistan because it is located at the cross-junction of international sea shipping and oil trade routes.
Hence, the correct option is (A).

96. Narmada is the largest west flowing river. It acts as the boundary between North and South India. It originates in the Amarkantak plateau, where the Vindhya and Satpura mountain ranges meet. It flows through the states of Madhya Pradesh, Maharashtra, and Gujarat before emptying into the Arabian sea.
Hence, the correct option is (C).

97. The tri-equilibrium factors of human geography are: Biotic, abiotic and cultural factors. Abiotic factors refer to non-living physical and chemical elements in the ecosystem. Abiotic resources are usually obtained from the lithosphere, atmosphere, and hydrosphere. Examples of abiotic factors are water, air, soil, sunlight, and minerals. Biotic factors are living or once-living organisms in the ecosystem. Cultural factors are culture related.
Hence, the correct option is (D).

98. The Chenab River is a major river flowing through India and Pakistan and is one of the Punjab region's 5 main rivers. It begins in the upper Himalayas in the Himachal Pradesh state's Lahaul and Spiti district and passes across the Jammu valley of Jammu and Kashmir into the Punjab plains, Pakistan until it passes into the Indus River near Uch Sharif. The river is formed by two rivers, Chandra and Bhaga, which converge.
Hence, the correct option is (A).

99. Mumbai is the most populated metro city as per the 2011 Census data. It has a population of 18,394,392. It is followed by Delhi, Kolkata and Chennai.
Hence, the correct option is (B).

100. Nokrek National Park is a part of Nokrek Biosphere reserve located in the West Garo district (Tura range) of Meghalaya. In 1986 , the Government of India declared it as a National Park. This Biosphere reserve has been included in the list of UNESCO Biosphere reserves (designated in 2009). Ganol, Dareng and Simsang rivers flow through this biosphere reserve.
Hence, the correct option is (D).

101. The Sarayu originates from Lake Mansarovar in the Himalayas. It is also known as the Ghaghra and the Manas Nandini. It merges with the Ganga in Bihar. Ayodhya, city in Uttar Pradesh is situated on the banks of the River Sarayu.
Hence, the correct option is (A).

102. Nasik hill is the origin of the Godavari river. The Godavari is India's second-longest river after the Ganga (flowing only in India). Godavari river flows through the states of Maharashtra, Telangana, Andhra Pradesh, Chhattisgarh, Odisha.
Hence, the correct option is (A).

103. Indira Gandhi canal is the longest irrigation canal in India. It starts from the Harike Barrage at Harike. Indira Gandhi canal was formally known as Rajasthan Canal. Indira Gandhi Canal is 649 km long. Indira Gandhi Canal consists of the Rajasthan feeder canal and Rajasthan main canal. Indira Gandhi Canal runs through 167 km in Punjab and Haryana and the remaining 492 km in Rajasthan.
Hence, the correct option is (A).

104. Teak wood trees grow in tropical deciduous forests. Teak wood is moderately hard, and teak is durable and fire-resistant. It can be easily seasoned and worked. It takes up a good polish and is not attacked by white ants. It is among the most valuable timber trees in the world. Tropical deciduous forests are the most widespread forests of India. They are also called the monsoon forests. Tropical deciduous forests receive rainfall between 200 cm and 70 m.
Hence, the correct option is (B).

105. Nagarjuna Sagar dam has been built on the river Krishna. Nagarjunasagar Project is the largest and highest masonry dam in the world. It is built between Nalgonda district of Telangana and Guntur district of Andhra Pradesh. The Project was inaugurated on 10th December 1955 by Late Pandit Jawaharlal Nehru, the then Prime Minister of India. The dam has a storage capacity of nearly 11,472 million cubic meters with an irrigation capacity for 10 acres of land. The dam measures 150 m tall and 16 km in length.
Hence, the correct option is (D).

106. The type of rocks that are formed from existing rocks through recrystallization are known as metamorphic rocks. The word metamorphic means 'change of form'. Igneous rocks are formed by the solidification of hot molten material called magma or lava. The word igneous is derived from the Latin word 'ignis' meaning fire.

Sedimentary rocks are formed by the deposition of sediments of rocks by exogenous forces. The word 'sedimentary' is derived from the Latin word sedimentum, which means settling.
Hence, the correct option is (B).

107. Ring of Fire is a 40,000 km horseshoe shape in the Pacific Ocean basin associated with a nearly continuous series of oceanic trenches, volcanic arcs, and volcanic belts and/or plate movements.
Hence, the correct option is (C).

108. In 1647 the French scientist Blaise Pascal (1623–1662) discovered that water exerts the same pressure in all directions. This statement is known as Pascal's Principle.

Pascal's law states that increase in pressure at a point in the enclosed liquid in equilibrium is transmitted equally in all directions in liquid and to the Walls of the container. The working of hydraulic lift, hydraulic press and hydraulic brakes are based on Pascal's law.
Hence, the correct option is (A).

109. Taiga is generally referred to in North America as boreal forest or snow forest. It is a biome characterized by coniferous forests consisting mostly of pines, spruces, and larches. The taiga or boreal forest is the world's largest land biome.It is mostly in northern Europe.
Hence, the correct option is (B).

110. Santa Ana, Brickfielder, Sirocco & Khamsin are examples of hot Winds. Hot Local winds are occur because of the downslope compressional heating also known as adiabatic heating. Examples of the Hot Local Winds include Chinook, Harmattan, Foehn, Sirocco, Norwester, Brickfielder, Khamsin, Santa Ana, Loo, etc.
Hence, the correct option is (C).

111. Punjab is also known as the "Land of five rivers". The five rivers are Beas, Chenab, Jhelum, Ravi and Sutlej. Only Sutlej, Ravi and Beas rivers flow in today's Punjab. The other two rivers are now in the state of Punjab, situated in Pakistan.
Hence, the correct option is (B).

112. It lies in the Kashmir Valley. It is located in the Bandipora district in Jammu and Kashmir. It is also known as "Mahapadma Saras". It is the second-largest freshwater lake in Asia. Jhelum River is the main source of water for Wular Lake. It is formed as a result of tectonic activity. It also has a small island in its centre called the 'Zaina Lank'.
Hence, the correct option is (C).

113. Sutlej rises from the Manasarovar-Rakas Lakes in western Tibet. Before entering the Punjab plain, it cuts a gorge in Naina Devi Dhar, where the famous Bhakra dam has been constructed. It is the longest of the five tributaries of the Indus River. It eventually drains into the Indus in Pakistan.
Hence, the correct option is (D).

114. The Ganga is a great river of the plains of the northern Indian subcontinent. It flows through the Indian states of Uttrakhand, Uttar Pradesh, Bihar, Jharkhand, West Bengal. Ganga river length is 1,560 miles is short compared with the other great rivers of Asia or of the world. Ganga river is rising in the Himalayas Gangotri and emptying into the Bay of Bengal. It drains 1/4th of the territory of India, and its basin supports hundreds of millions of people.
Hence, the correct option is (C).

115. Angel height is about 3212 feet (979 m) is the highest waterfall in the world. it is followed by Tugela falls in South Africa whose height is 3110 feet (948 m) This waterfall falls at the edge of Auyan-Tepui which is also called Devil's mountain. It is an elevated piece of land with a flat surface. It is located in Canaima National Park in the Bolivar State of Venezuela. The water of the Churun river is added to this waterfall.
Hence, the correct option is (D).

116. Tehri Dam: It has a height of 261 m, a length of 575 meters and is the Highest dam in India and ranks the 8th tallest dam in the world. It is built across the Bhagirathi River in Uttarakhand. It has the reservoir capacity of 3,200,000 acres. This Dam generates electricity for entire Uttarakhand and is the primary resources for fisheries for tourism sector.
Hence, the correct option is (D).

117. Lake Chilika is the largest brackish water lagoon in Asia and the second largest coastal lagoon in the world. It spread across the Puri, Khurda and Ganjam districts of the state of Odisha on the east coast of India, at the mouth of the River Daya, which flows into the Bay of Bengal, covering an area of more than 1,100 km. It is the largest coastal lagoon in India and the second-largest brackish lagoon in the world after the New Caledonian Barrier Reef.
Hence, the correct option is (A).

118. Tapti River is one of the major Rivers of Peninsular India and is also known as twin of Narmada. Tapti River rises in the Satpura Range in Betul district of Madhya Pradesh. The Tapti River lies in central India. The River flows between the Godavari and Narmada River. The river flows westwards and drains into the Arabian Sea.
Hence, the correct option is (B).

119. The Godavari River rises from Trimbakeshwar in the Nashik district of Maharashtra. It is the oldest River in India. It is also known as the Ganga of South India. It is the second-longest river in India. Dams on the Godavari river are - Polavaram Dam (Andhra Pradesh), Pochampad Dam (Telangana).
Hence, the correct option is (C).

120. Sharavati Power Project is situated in Karnataka. The project is located on the river Sharavati. It rises in the western ghats. Mahatma Gandhi Hydroelectric Power Station is also situated on the river. Jog falls which is one of the highest waterfalls in India is located on this river.
Hence, the correct option is (B).

121. The Betwa is a river in Northern India and a tributary of the Yamuna. It rises in the Vindhya Range (Raisen) just north of Hoshangabad in Madhya Pradesh and flows north-east through Madhya Pradesh and Orchha to Uttar Pradesh. Nearly half of its course, which is not navigable, runs over the Malwa Plateau. The confluence of the Betwa and the Yamuna rivers is Hamirpur district in Uttar Pradesh, in the vicinity of Orchha. The Indian navy named one of its frigates INS Betwa in honour of the river Betwa.
Hence, the correct option is (B).

122. Jog Falls, is a waterfall on the Sharavati river located in the Western Ghats Sagara taluk, Shimoga district in Karnataka. It is the second-highest plunge waterfall in India. It is a segmented waterfall that depends on rain and season becomes a plunge waterfall. The falls are major attractions for tourists and are

ranked 36th in the list of freefalling waterfalls, 490th in the world by a list of waterfalls by total height, 128th in the list of single-drop waterfalls in the World by the waterfall database.
Hence, the correct option is (B).

123. Bhakra Dam is a concrete gravity dam on the Satluj River in Bilaspur, Himachal Pradesh in northern India. The dam forms the Gobind Sagar reservoir. The father of Bhakra Nangal dam is Sir Chaudhari Chhotu Ram. He conceived the Bhakhra Dam way back in 1923, to rid the farmers of the so-called economic plague-spots of erstwhile Punjab state. He was also the originator of the concept of compensating the farmer for at least the expenses incurred by him on farming, the concept has now evolved into 'Minimum Support Price'.
Hence, the correct option is (A).

124. Nizam Sagar Dam: The dam is located in Telangana. It is situated on the Manjira River. It was built in 1923 by Mir Osman Ali Khan, the then ruler of Hyderabad. Manijra river is a tributary of the Godavari.
Hence, the correct option is (B).

125. The City of Vijayawada is located on the bank of River Krishna. It is the second-largest city in Andhra Pradesh state behind the city of Visakhapatnam. It is the district headquarters of Krishna District and part of the New state capital of Andhra Pradesh called Amaravati. It also contains the famous Prakasam Barrage across River Krishna.
Hence, the correct option is (A).

Q.1 Which layer of atmosphere is suitable for flying airplanes?

A. Troposphere   **B.** Thermosphere

C. Stratosphere   **D.** Ionosphere

Q.2 Which layer of the atmosphere is also called the ozonosphere?

A. Troposphere   **B.** Stratosphere

C. Ionosphere   **D.** Mesosphere

Q.3 The equatorial low-pressure belt is extended from

A. $10°N - 10°S$ **B.** $0° - 5°N$

C. $5°N - 5°S$ **D.** None of the above

Q.4 Which layer of atmosphere is used for telecommunication?

A. Troposphere   **B.** Thermosphere

C. Stratosphere   **D.** Ionosphere

Q.5 When does the distance between the sun and the earth become shortest?

A. June 21   **B.** September 22

C. December 22   **D.** January 4

Q.6 _________ is an equatorial belt of low atmospheric pressure where the trade winds converge.

A. Moraine   **B.** La Nina

C. El Nino   **D.** Doldrums

Q.7 The nitrogen in the ecosystem is circulated by:-

[Territorial Army Officer, 2019]

A. Earthworms   **B.** Bacteria

C. Fungi   **D.** Protozoa

Q.8 The clouds that occur at the highest level are:-

[Army Public School (PRT), 2019]

A. Cumulus   **B.** Stratus   **C.** Cirrus   **D.** Nimbus

Q.9 In the context of climate, what is the full form of ITCZ?

[SSC Constable (GD), 2019]

A. Indian Trough Conversation Zone

B. Inter-Tropical Convergence Zone

C. Intra Temperate Control Zone

D. Islandic Tropical Climate Zone

Q.10 Lithosphere consists of:

A. Upper and lower mantle

B. Crust and core.

C. Crust and uppermost solid mantle

D. Mantle and core

Q.11 A deep valley characterized by a steep step-like slope is known as:

A. U-shaped valley   **B.** Blind valley

C. Gorge   **D.** Canyon

Q.12 Stalactite, stalagmite and pillars are the depositional landforms of:

A. Running water   **B.** Wind

C. Glacier   **D.** Underground water

Q.13 The normal lapse rate of the temperature of Earth's atmosphere drops to $0°C$ at the:

A. Upper part of ionosphere

B. Upper-boundary of the tropopause.

C. Lower part of the mesosphere

D. Upper boundary of stratopause

Q.14 Which one of the following statements about the Suez Canal is not correct?

[UPSC NDA, 2019]

A. The Suez Canal was constructed in 1869.

B. It links the Mediterranean Sea and the Red Sea.

C. It has a six lock system and ships cross the different levels through these locks.

D. It has given Europe a new gateway to the Indian Ocean.

Q.15 According to Koppen's climatic classification, the letter code Cfa denotes-

A. Tropical wet climate

B. Humid subtropical climate

C. Tundra climate

D. Tropical wet and dry climate

Q.16 Which one of the following land territories of Indonesia is not touched by the Equator?

[UPSC NDA, 2019]

A. Sumatra   **B.** Sulawesi

C. Java   **D.** Kalimantan

Q.17 Which one of the following hypotheses/theory explains the origin of the universe?

A. Nebular hypothesis

B. Binary theory

C. Big Bang theory

D. Planetesimal hypothesis

Q.18 Which one of the following ocean currents is a cold current?

[UPSC NDA, 2019]

A. South Atlantic Drift

B. Mozambique Current

C. East Australian Current

D. Caribbean Current

Q.19 The rivers of North-West Europe are good examples of-

A. Parallel pattern of drainage

B. Radial pattern of drainage

C. Barbed pattern of drainage

D. Trellis pattern of drainage

Q.20 Which one of the following can be said to be essentially related to 'Polar Front Theory'?
A. Anticyclone
B. Tropical Cyclone
C. Temperate Cyclone
D. Inter-Tropical Convergence

Q.21 Which one of the following ocean currents is not a cold ocean current?
A. Canary current
B. California current
C. Kuroshio current
D. Oyashio current

Q.22 "Shamal" warm and dry wind is a "Local" wind found in:
A. East Asia
B. West Coast of Africa
C. Sahara of Africa
D. Mesopotamia

Q.23 "Viticulture" is a common feature of which one of the following Australian cities?
A. Adelaide
B. Darwin
C. Hobart
D. Brisbane

Q.24 Which one of the following is not true in reference to Air mass?

[UPSC NDA, 2019]

A. Air mass forms either in tropical or in polar region
B. Air mass develops on continents as well as over ocean
C. Air mass develops in a cyclonic condition
D. Air mass changes the weather conditions

Q.25 For an area to be excluded from the drought-prone category, what percentage of its gross cropped area should be under irrigation-

[UPSC NDA, 2020]

A. 10 percent or more
B. 20 percent or more
C. 25 percent or more
D. 30 percent or more

Q.26 The Vindhyan system of rocks is important for the production of:
A. Iron ore and Manganese
B. Precious stone and Building materials
C. Copper and Mica
D. Uranium and Aluminium

Q.27 Which state is the largest producer of bajra in India?
A. Kerala
B. Rajasthan
C. Madhya Pradesh
D. Himachal Pradesh

Q.28 Which state is the largest producer of rice in India?
A. West Bengal
B. Uttar Pradesh
C. Andhra Pradesh
D. Punjab

Q.29 In which of the following states the largest coal reserves of India are found?
A. Assam
B. Jharkhand
C. Madhya Pradesh
D. Orissa

Q.30 Which state is the largest producer of tea in India?
A. Assam
B. West Bengal
C. Tripura
D. Sikkim

Q.31 Which of the following state is well known for terrace cultivation?
A. Punjab
B. Haryana
C. Plains of Uttar Pradesh
D. Uttarakhand

Q.32 Which of the following minerals is formed by the decomposition of rocks, leaving a residual mass of weathered material?
A. Coal
B. Bauxite
C. Gold
D. Zinc

Q.33 Which of the following mineral made the Koderma, Jharkhand famous?
A. Bauxite
B. Mica
C. Iron ore
D. Copper

Q.34 Which of the following rocks are deposited and accumulated in the strata's?
A. Sedimentary rocks
B. Igneous rocks
C. Metamorphic rocks
D. None of these

Q.35 Which of the following agencies markets steel for the public sector plants?
A. HAIL
B. SAIL
C. TATA Steel
D. MNCC

Q.36 Which of the following industry uses bauxite as a raw material?
A. Aluminium
B. Cement
C. Jute
D. Steel

Q.37 Which mode of transportation reduces trans-shipment losses and delays?
A. Railways
B. Pipeline
C. Roadways
D. Waterways

Q.38 Which of the following ports is the deepest land-locked and well-protected port along the east coast?
A. Chennai
B. Tuticorin
C. Paradip
D. Vishakhapatnam

Q.39 The Cold Desert of India is located in:
A. Shimla
B. Srinagar
C. Ladakh
D. None of the above

Q.40 Which of the following statements is not true?
A. Presence of water vapour is highly variable in the lower atmosphere.
B. The zone of maximum temperature is located along the equator.
C. Frigid zones are located in both the hemispheres between the polar circles and the poles.
D. Jet streams are high altitude winds affecting the surface weather conditions.

Q.41 "Roaring forties" is the term used to describe which of the following winds?
A. East-to-west air winds in the southern hemisphere

B. West-to east air winds in the northern hemisphere
C. East-to-west air winds in the northern hemisphere
D. West-to-east air winds in the southern hemisphere

Q.42 Which of the following mentioned layers is not a homosphere?
A. Exosphere
B. Troposphere
C. Ionosphere
D. Mesosphere

Q.43 What is the atmospheric pressure at sea level?
A. 1013.25 Pa
B. 14.696 psi
C. 760 Torr
D. All of the above

Q.44 By international convention, which line marks the outermost boundary of the Earth's atmosphere?
A. Space line
B. Boundary line
C. Karman line
D. Astronaut line

Q.45 Which layer of the atmosphere is responsible for aurora formation?
A. Ozone layer
B. Stratosphere
C. Exosphere
D. Ionosphere

Q.46 'Saving energy and other resources for the future without sacrificing people's comfort at present' is the definition of which of the following concepts?
A. Economic depreciation
B. Economic development
C. Sustainable development
D. Human development

Q.47 Placing of the threatened animals and plants in a special care unit for protection is called ________.
A. Ex-situ conservation
B. In situ conservation
C. Wildlife sanctuary
D. National park

Q.48 Which of the following pairs is incorrectly matched?
A. Bhitarkanika: Olive ridley turtles
B. Dalma Hills: Wild elephants
C. Kaziranga: One-horned rhinos
D. Dachigam: Asiatic lions

Q.49 Which of the following organizations released the Living Planet Report 2020?
A. International Union for Conservation of Nature
B. World Wide Fund for Nature
C. Ministry of Environment, Forest and Climate Change
D. World Nature Organization

Q.50 What is the 'Green House Effect'?
A. Increase in global temperature
B. Decrease in global temperature
C. Increase in seawater temperature
D. Increase in temperature of rivers and lakes

Q.51 World's only habitat for Asiatic lion found in which of the following National Park?
A. Bandhavgarh National Park
B. Gir National Park
C. Mukurthi National Park
D. None of the above

Q.52 Select the food chain found in forest Ecosystem?
A. Phytoplanktons → Water fleas → Small fish → Tuna
B. Grass → Grasshopper → Frog → Snake → Hawk
C. Leaf litter → Algae → Crabs → Small carnivorous fish → Large carnivorus fish
D. Dead organic matter → Fungi → Bacteria

Q.53 Where in Madhya Pradesh is the Central Institute of Agricultural Engineering located?
A. Bhopal
B. Indore
C. Gwalior
D. Jabalpur

Q.54 The correct group of diseases caused by water pollution is:
A. Cholera, Diarrhoea, Hepatitis A, Typhoid
B. Cholera, Jaundice, Typhoid, Anaemia
C. Anaemia, Scurvy, Emphysema, Typhoid
D. Cholera, Jaundice, Typhoid, Scurvy

Q.55 At the Central Government level, which agency was assigned the role of overseeing the implementation of Sustainable Developmental Goals (SDGs) in India?
A. The Energy Resource Institute (TERI)
B. NITI Aayog
C. Center for Environmental and Sustainable Development India (CESDI)
D. The Comptroller and Auditor General of India (CAG)

Q.56 The substance that causes the maximum air pollution is?
A. Smoke
B. Carbon monoxide
C. Sulphur dioxide
D. Nitrogen dioxide

Q.57 The process of using microbes to treat areas of land or sea that have been contaminated by pesticides, oil or solvents is known as:
A. Eutrophication
B. Nitrification
C. Ammonification
D. Bioremediation

Q.58 Which of the following States of India is on the way to becoming the first carbon-free State?
A. Kerala
B. Himachal Pradesh
C. Uttarakhand
D. Arunachal Pradesh

Q.59 Which of the following pairs does not match correctly?
A. Bandipur National Park - Karnataka
B. Manas Wildlife Sanctuary-Assam
C. Periyar Wildlife Sanctuary - Kerala
D. Simlipal National Park-Madhya Pradesh

Q.60 United Nations Conference on climate change, COP 21 was held in-
A. Moscow
B. Paris
C. Berlin
D. Tokyo

Q.61 'Sagarmatha' is the Nepali name for:
A. Mount Everest
B. Makalu
C. Kanchenjungha
D. Lhotse

Q.62 Which of the following is the largest freshwater lake in India?

A. Dal Lake

B. Loktak

C. Chilika

D. Wular

Q.63 The largest part of the Gangetic plain is covered by which of the following soil?

A. Bangar soil

B. Khadar soil

C. Bhur soil

D. Desert soil

Q.64 Which is the highest hydropower plant in India?

A. Tehri Dam

B. Srisailam Dam

C. Sardar Sarovar Dam

D. Nathpa Jhaki Dam

Q.65 Over how many Indian states does the Deccan Plateau extend?

A. 5

B. 8

C. 6

D. 3

Q.66 Which of the following parallels of latitude lies in the Southern Hemisphere?

A. Arctic Circle

B. Arctic Pole

C. Tropic of Capricorn

D. Tropic of Cancer

Q.67 Hot and dry winds blowing during the summer months in the Northern Plains is called:

A. Loo

B. Blossom Shower

C. Mango Shower

D. Kalbaisakhi

Q.68 Which one of the following is the main cause of land degradation in Punjab?

A. Intensive cultivation

B. Deforestation

C. Over irrigation

D. Overgrazing

Q.69 The Bhakra Nangal dam is situated on the _______ river.

[SSC Selection Post Phase IX, 2019]

A. Sutlej

B. Chenab

C. Ravi

D. Beas

Q.70 Which cities are connected by Golden Quadrilateral?

A. Srinagar-Tamilnadu- Silchar-Porbandar

B. Delhi-Amritsar

C. Delhi-Mumbai-Chennai-Kolkata

D. Delhi- Assam-Bangalore-Gujarat

Q.71 Which of the following river drain in Arabian Sea?

A. Banganga River

B. Sabarmati River

C. Gambhiri River

D. Kothari River

Q.72 Which of the following river is known as Dakshina Ganga?

A. Godavari

B. Tapti

C. Krishna

D. Kaveri

Q.73 Which of the following places in our country is a 'cold desert'?

A. Jaisalmer

B. Ladakh

C. Meghalaya

D. Darjeeling

Q.74 The northern part of the west coast in India is known as:

A. Konkan Coast

B. Coromandel Coast

C. Malabar Coast

D. Godavari Coast

Q.75 Which among the following groups in Koeppen's climate classification is referred as the climate of Highland region?

A. A

B. B

C. E

D. H

Q.76 Consider the following statements about Himalayan trillium:

1. The Himalayan trillium, a common herb of the Himalayas was declared 'vulnerable' by the IUCN.

2. The herb has numerous uses for human beings thus inviting people to utilize it, paving way for overutilization.

Which of the above statements is/are correct?

A. 1 only

B. 2 only

C. Both 1 and 2

D. Neither 1 nor 2

Q.77 Consider the following statements regarding the Himalayan serow.

1. The Himalayan serow, or Capricornis sumatraensis thar, is a subspecies of the mainland serow.

2. Himalayan serow is now been categorized as 'vulnerable' in the IUCN Red List of Threatened Species.

Which of the statements given above is/are correct?

A. 1 only

B. 2 only

C. Both 1 and 2

D. Neither 1 nor 2

Q.78 Among the following hills/ranges of Eastern Ghat, which is the southernmost:

A. Javadi Hills

B. Palkonda Range

C. Nallamala Hills

D. Shevaroy Hills

Q.79 Which of the following statements with respect to Ken-Betwa river Interlink project, is/are correct?

1. This is the country's first river interlinking project.

2. The project aims to transfer surplus water from the Betwa in UP to Ken river in MP.

Select the correct answer using the codes given below.

A. 1 only

B. 2 only

C. Both 1 and 2

D. Neither 1 nor 2

Q.80 A saltwater lake separated from the sea by the sandbars and splits is called a-

A. Lagoon

B. Glacier

C. Lake

D. Estuary

Q.81 Which of the following passes cuts through Pir Panjal range and links Manali and Leh by road?

A. Banihal Pass

B. Baralachala Pass

C. Rohtang Pass

D. Nathula Pass

Q.82 Directions: The following five (5) items consist of two statements, Statement I and Statement II. Examine these two statements carefully and select the correct answer using the code given below.

Statement I: The interior part of Maharashtra does not receive adequate rain in the summer season.

Statement II: The interior part of Maharashtra lies in the rain shadow of the Western Ghats.

A. Both the statements are individually true and Statement II is the correct explanation of Statement I.

B. Both the statements are individually true but Statement II is not the correct explanation of Statement I.

C. Statement I is true but Statement II is false.

D. Statement I is false but Statement II is true.

Q.83 Which of the following contains the World's largest area of mangrove forests?

A. Namdapha National Park

B. Rann of Kutch

C. Balphakram National Park

D. Sundarbans

Q.84 Pokkalli, a unique variety of rice which can sustain in salinity is endemic to which state of India?

[SSC Constable (GD), 2019]

A. Goa **B.** Andhra Pradesh

C. Kerala **D.** Telangana

Q.85 Which of the following river does not originate in the Himalayas?

A. Ganga **B.** Brahmaputra

C. Narmada **D.** Chenab

Q.86 Which one of the following points should be kept in mind while selecting the site for a rain gauge station?

A. The site where a rain gauge is set up should be close to a meteorological observatory

B. The rain gauge should be on the top of a hill

C. A fence, if erected to protect the rain gauge from cattle etc. should be located within twice the height of the fence

D. The distance between the rain gauge and the nearest object should be at least twice the height of the object.

Q.87 Infiltration rate is always:

A. Less than the infiltration capacity

B. Equal to or less than the infiltration capacity

C. Equal to or more than the infiltration capacity

D. More than the infiltration capacity

Q.88 Probability of a 10 year flood to occur at least once in the next 4 years is:

A. .25 **B.** .35 **C.** .50 **D.** .65

Q.89 Consider the following statements regarding water logging:

1. Water logging is the rise of groundwater table leading to a possible increase in salinity resulting in a reduction in the yield of crops

2. Water logging cannot be eliminated in certain areas but can be controlled only if the quantity of water percolating into that soil is checked and reduced

Which of the above statements is/are correct?

A. 1 only **B.** 2 only

C. Both 1 and 2 **D.** Neither 1 nor 2

Q.90 The highest water saving method of irrigation is:

A. Sprinkler **B.** Drip

C. Sub-surface **D.** Basin

Q.91 If the depth of water is $8.64\ cm$ on a field over a base period of 10 days, then the duty is:

A. 10 hectares per cum/s

B. 100 hectares per cum/s

C. 864 hectares per cum/s

D. 1000 hectares per cum/s

Q.92 Laysimeter is used to measure:

A. Infiltration **B.** Evaporation

C. Vapour pressure **D.** Evapotranspiration

Q.93 Victoria Falls in Africa are located on-

A. River Niger **B.** River Congo

C. River Zambezi **D.** River Nile

Q.94 The unit hydrograph is based on the assumption of:

A. Nonlinear response and time invariance

B. Linear response and non - linear time variance

C. Time invariance and linear response

D. Non - linear response and non - linear time invariance

Q.95 Consider the following statements concerning precipitation:

1. The Isohyetal map method of determining the average precipitation is considering to be better than the Thiessen method.

2. There is no possibility of damaging the storms because of cloud seeding activity.

3. Water that percolates through the soil emerges as the dry whether flow in streams.

Which of the above statements are correct?

A. 1 and 2 only **B.** 1 and 3 only

C. 2 and 3 only **D.** 1, 2 and 3

Q.96 The rates of rainfall for successive 20 min period of 140 minutes are $2.5, 2.5, 10, 7.6, 1.25,$ and 1.25 and $5\ cm/h$. Taking the value of phi-index as $3.2\ cm/h$, the total runoff (in cm) is:

A. 6 **B.** 4.33 **C.** 10 **D.** 5

Q.97 Crest level is kept low with large gates in the following:

A. Sluice **B.** Escape

C. Regulator **D.** Barrage

Q.98 A tube well having a capacity of $4\ m^3/$ hour operates for 20 hours each day during the irrigation season. How much area can be commanded if the irrigation interval is 20 days and depth of irrigation is $7\ cm$?

A. $1.71 \times 10^4\ m^2$ **B.** $1.14 \times 10^4\ m^2$

C. $22.9 \times 10^4\ m^2$ **D.** $2.29 \times 10^4\ m^2$

Q.99 A process determining outflow pattern from reservoirs for any given pattern of inflow, storage and tail-water condition is known as:

A. Hydrograph **B.** Flood discharge

C. Runoff estimate **D.** Flood routing

Q.100 The fall which is used to minimise the disturbance and water impact at the fall is -

A. Inglis falls   B. Rapid falls
C. Sarda Type falls   D. Ogee falls

Q.101 River Brahmaputra doesn't flow into:
A. India   B. Bangladesh
C. China   D. Bhutan

Q.102 The McMahon Line is a border line between:
A. India & Pakistan   B. India & China
C. India & Nepal   D. India & Bhutan

Q.103 Which of following states/UTs of India share boundary with Pakistan?
A. Jammu and Kashmir, Punjab, Gujarat and Himachal Pradesh
B. Himachal Pradesh, Punjab, Gujarat
C. Jammu and Kashmir, Punjab, Gujarat and Haryana
D. Jammu and Kashmir, Punjab, Gujarat and Rajasthan

Q.104 Which is the deepest lake in the world?

[HSSC Canal Patwari, 2019]

A. Lake Tanganyika   B. Lake Vostok
C. Lake Baikal   D. Lake Superior

Q.105 Source of River Nile is:

[Territorial Army Officer, 2019]

A. Lake Nassir   B. Lake Chad
C. Lake Victoria   D. Lake Tanganyika

Q.106 Alps mountains are of which type?
A. Volcanic   B. Volcanic   C. Residual   D. Block

Q.107 Which of the following countries share the longest international border with India?
A. Bangladesh   B. China
C. Pakistan   D. Myanmar

Q.108 Which one of the following is not an international boundary line?
A. Dresden Line   B. Durand Line
C. Maginot Line   D. 38th Parallel

Q.109 Which is the largest river island in the world?
A. Srirangam Island   B. Majuli Island
C. Bhavani Island   D. Agatti Island

Q.110 Which Strait divides Europe from Africa?
A. Bosporus   B. Bering
C. Gibraltar   D. Dover

Q.111 Which major river flows between the Vindhya and the Satpura Mountain ranges?
A. Narmada   B. Ken   C. Tapti   D. Sons

Q.112 Palk strait separates which of the following countries?
A. India and Sri Lanka
B. India and Bhutan
C. India and Maldives
D. India and Bangladesh

Q.113 Duncan passage is situated between:

A. Minicoy and Amindiv
B. South Andaman and Little Andaman
C. Minicoy and Maldives
D. Little Andaman and car Nicobar

Q.114 Which of the following countries does not have a boundary with India?
A. Myanmar   B. Bhutan
C. Mauritius   D. Nepal

Q.115 On which river bank is the City of 'Ujjain' situated?
A. Shipra   B. Narmada   C. Chambal   D. Betwa

Q.116 Among which of the following is considered as the actual "final frontier" of Earth's gaseous envelope?
A. Ionosphere   B. Exosphere
C. Stratosphere   D. None of these

Q.117 The two main branches of geography are:
A. Economic and Social
B. Physical and Urban
C. Political and Historical
D. Physical and Human

Q.118 Which of these scholars defined Human Geography as 'the synthetic study of relationship between human societies and earth's surface'?
A. Paul Vidal de la Blache
B. Ellen C. Semple
C. Fredrick Ratzel
D. Karl Marx

Q.119 Name the school of thought of Human Geography that employed the Marxian theory?
A. Deterministic school of thought
B. Behavioural school of thought
C. Radical school of thought
D. Humanistic school of thought

Q.120 Which one of the following country has higher population density than India?
A. Bangladesh   B. Nepal
C. Korea   D. Canada

Q.121 What percentage of India's population resides in the most populated state of India, Uttar Pradesh?
A. 38.96 percent   B. 14.37 percent
C. 16.16 percent   D. 20.56 percent

Q.122 Which one of the following state has a population density below 100 persons per square kilometre?
A. Jammu and Kashmir
B. Uttarakhand
C. Nagaland
D. All of these

Q.123 Which one of the following state in India has a population density below 250 persons per square km?
A. Punjab   B. Haryana
C. Chhattisgarh   D. None of these

Q.124 A large proportion of children in a population is a result of:

A. High death rate

B. High married rate

C. High birth rate

D. None of these

Q.125 What is the main cause for the high growth of our population?

A. Rise in death rate

B. Decline of death rate

C. Decline of birth rate

D. None of these

// Smart Answer Sheet //

Correct — Indicates percentage of students who answered questions correctly.

Skipped — Indicates percentage of students who skipped questions.

Q.	Ans.	Correct / Skipped
1	C	41.33 % / 2.67 %
2	B	30.67 % / 58.66 %
3	C	26.67 % / 58.66 %
4	D	34.67 % / 58.66 %
5	D	30.67 % / 58.66 %
6	D	36.0 % / 58.67 %
7	B	20.0 % / 58.67 %
8	C	32.0 % / 58.67 %
9	B	40.0 % / 58.67 %
10	C	38.67 % / 58.66 %
11	D	16.0 % / 58.67 %
12	D	28.0 % / 58.67 %
13	B	21.33 % / 58.67 %
14	C	29.33 % / 58.67 %
15	B	21.33 % / 58.67 %
16	C	10.67 % / 58.66 %
17	C	34.67 % / 58.66 %
18	A	16.0 % / 58.67 %
19	C	12.0 % / 56.0 %
20	C	28.0 % / 58.67 %
21	C	29.33 % / 58.67 %
22	D	12.0 % / 58.67 %
23	A	8.0 % / 56.0 %
24	A	12.0 % / 58.67 %
25	D	9.33 % / 58.67 %
26	B	24.0 % / 58.67 %
27	B	29.33 % / 58.67 %
28	A	32.0 % / 58.67 %
29	B	36.0 % / 58.67 %
30	A	38.67 % / 58.66 %
31	D	37.33 % / 58.67 %
32	B	14.67 % / 58.66 %
33	B	22.67 % / 58.66 %
34	A	33.33 % / 58.67 %
35	B	33.33 % / 58.67 %
36	A	36.0 % / 58.67 %
37	B	24.0 % / 58.67 %
38	D	28.0 % / 58.67 %
39	C	26.67 % / 58.66 %
40	B	24.0 % / 58.67 %
41	D	21.33 % / 58.67 %
42	A	22.67 % / 58.66 %
43	D	24.0 % / 58.67 %
44	C	18.67 % / 58.66 %
45	D	32.0 % / 58.67 %
46	C	36.0 % / 58.67 %
47	A	17.33 % / 58.67 %
48	D	28.0 % / 58.67 %
49	B	14.67 % / 58.66 %
50	A	38.67 % / 58.66 %
51	B	38.67 % / 58.66 %
52	B	34.67 % / 58.66 %
53	A	13.33 % / 58.67 %
54	A	28.0 % / 58.67 %
55	B	28.0 % / 58.67 %
56	C	14.67 % / 58.66 %
57	D	26.67 % / 58.66 %
58	B	14.67 % / 58.66 %
59	D	34.67 % / 58.66 %
60	B	34.67 % / 58.66 %
61	A	38.67 % / 58.66 %
62	D	32.0 % / 58.67 %
63	A	22.67 % / 58.66 %
64	A	34.67 % / 58.66 %
65	B	17.33 % / 58.67 %
66	C	33.33 % / 58.67 %
67	A	40.0 % / 58.67 %
68	C	25.33 % / 58.67 %
69	A	40.0 % / 58.67 %
70	C	37.33 % / 58.67 %
71	B	37.33 % / 58.67 %
72	A	32.0 % / 58.67 %
73	B	40.0 % / 58.67 %
74	A	32.0 % / 58.67 %
75	D	13.33 % / 58.67 %
76	B	12.0 % / 58.67 %
77	C	29.33 % / 58.67 %
78	D	17.33 % / 58.67 %
79	A	6.67 % / 58.66 %
80	A	34.67 % / 58.66 %

Q.	Ans.	Correct / Skipped
81	C	22.67 % / 58.66 %
82	A	36.0 % / 58.67 %
83	D	40.0 % / 58.67 %
84	C	22.67 % / 58.66 %
85	C	32.0 % / 58.67 %
86	D	14.67 % / 58.66 %
87	B	20.0 % / 58.67 %
88	B	9.33 % / 58.67 %
89	C	25.33 % / 58.67 %
90	B	34.67 % / 58.66 %
91	D	8.0 % / 58.67 %
92	D	16.0 % / 58.67 %
93	C	25.33 % / 58.67 %
94	C	9.33 % / 58.67 %
95	B	18.67 % / 58.66 %
96	B	18.67 % / 58.66 %
97	D	20.0 % / 58.67 %
98	D	10.67 % / 58.66 %
99	D	9.33 % / 58.67 %
100	D	9.33 % / 58.67 %
101	D	37.33 % / 58.67 %
102	B	38.67 % / 58.66 %
103	D	34.67 % / 58.66 %
104	C	34.67 % / 58.66 %
105	C	32.0 % / 58.67 %
106	B	24.0 % / 58.67 %
107	A	40.0 % / 58.67 %
108	A	26.67 % / 58.66 %
109	B	38.67 % / 58.66 %
110	C	29.33 % / 58.67 %
111	A	38.67 % / 58.66 %
112	A	38.67 % / 58.66 %
113	B	24.0 % / 58.67 %
114	C	41.33 % / 58.67 %
115	A	29.33 % / 58.67 %
116	B	20.0 % / 58.67 %
117	D	37.33 % / 58.67 %
118	C	18.67 % / 58.66 %
119	C	18.67 % / 58.66 %
120	A	40.0 % / 58.67 %
121	C	22.67 % / 58.66 %
122	A	6.67 % / 58.66 %
123	C	18.67 % / 58.66 %
124	C	34.67 % / 58.66 %
125	B	36.0 % / 58.67 %

Performance Analysis

Avg. Score (%)	45.65%
Toppers Score (%)	100.0%
Your Score	

//Hints and Solutions//

1. The stratosphere is the layer that is suitable for flying airplanes.

Stratosphere- It is the second layer of the atmosphere. It extends up to 50 km. of height. This layer is very dry as it contains little water vapour. This layer provides advantages for flight because it is above stormy weather and has steady and horizontal winds. The ozone layer is found in this layer.

Troposphere- It is considered the lowest layer of the Earth's atmosphere. Atmospheric layer between the earth's surface and an altitude of 8 km. at the poles and 18 km. at the equator. Thickness is greater at the equator because the heated air rises to greater heights. The troposphere is influenced by seasons and jet streams.

Thermosphere- The temperature rises very rapidly with increasing height. It helps in radio transmission. A person would not feel warm because of the thermosphere's extremely low pressure. International Space Station and Satellites orbit lies in this layer.

Ionosphere- Located between 80 km. and 400 km. and is an electrically charged layer. This layer is characterized by the ionization of atoms.
Hence, the correct option is (C).

2. Stratosphere is also called ozonosphere.

Stratosphere- The atmosphere consists of different layers with varying densities and temperatures. The stratosphere is the second-lowest layer of the earth's atmosphere. The stratosphere is found above the tropopause and extends up to a height of 50 km. The stratosphere of the atmosphere is also called the ozonosphere. The ozone layer is found in the stratosphere. The stratosphere absorbs ultra-violet radiation and shields life on the earth from the intense, and harmful forms of energy. The jet airplanes fly through the stratosphere. The temperature increases with altitude in the stratosphere.

Troposphere- The troposphere is the lowest atmospheric layer. Weather change occurs in the troposphere. Most of the weather and clouds are found in the troposphere.

Ionosphere- The ionosphere is a part of the thermosphere. Radio waves are found in the ionosphere.

Mesosphere- The mesosphere lies above the stratosphere. It extends up to a height of 80 km. The temperature starts decreasing with the increase in altitude in this layer.
Hence, the correct option is (B).

3. Atmospheric pressure belts: The distribution of atmospheric pressure across the latitude is termed the global horizontal distribution of pressure. Its main feature is its zonal character known as pressure belts. On the earth's surface, there are seven pressure belts. They are the Equatorial Low, the two Subtropical highs, the two Subpolar lows, and the two Polar highs.

This belt happens to be the zone of convergence of trade winds from two hemispheres from subtropical high-pressure belts. This belt is also called the Doldrums, because of the extremely calm air movements. The position of the belt varies with the apparent movement of the Sun. As this region lies along the equator, it receives the highest amount of insolation. Due to intense heating, the air gets warmed up and rises over the equatorial region (convection). Whenever there is vertically upward movement of air, the region at the surface will be at low pressure. Thus the belt along the equator is called the equatorial low-pressure belt. The low-pressure belt extends from 0 to 5° North and South of Equator. Due to the vertical rays of the sun here, there is intense heating. The air, therefore, expands and rises as convection current causing low pressure to develop here. This low-pressure belt is also called a doldrums because it is a zone of total calm without any breeze. Therefore the correct answer is $5°N - 5°S$.

Hence, the correct option is (C).

4. The ionosphere is the upper layer of the Earth's atmosphere. The atmosphere is partly ionized by solar UV light, and such ionization can persist at high altitudes. The ionosphere starts at about 80 km altitude and reaches up to more than 1000 km. This area of the atmosphere consists of several conductive layers that reflect radio waves, a characteristic that is of interest to scientists and engineers, especially in the telecommunications industry. Hence, the correct option is (D).

5. The earth is closest to the sun on January 4. The point that is nearest to the sun is called perihelion. The point that is farthest to the sun is called aphelion. Approx. an elliptical orbit is occupied by all planets, asteroids, and comets in our solar system. The flatness of the orbit is measured by the orbital eccentricity. On January 4, the earth comes closest to the sun every year. In the northern hemisphere, it is winter, when the earth is closest to the sun. At that time it is summer in the southern hemisphere. Apehilion occurs on July 4.
Hence, the correct option is (D).

6. Doldrums is an equatorial belt of low atmospheric pressure where the trade winds converge.

Moraines: Moraines are distinct ridges or mounds of debris that are directly laid down by a moving glacier. This material is usually soil and rock. Moraines only show up in places that have, or used to have glaciers. Glaciers are extremely large, moving rivers of ice. Glaciers shape the landscape in a process called glaciation. Glaciation can affect the land, rocks, and water in an area for thousands of years. That is why moraines are often very old.

La Nina: La Nina is a climate pattern that describes the cooling of surface ocean waters along the tropical west coast of South America. La Nina is the counterpart of El Nino. La Lina means Little Girl in Spanish. La Lina occurs at irregular intervals of about two to seven years. La Niña is caused by a build-up of cooler-than-normal waters in the tropical Pacific, the area of the Pacific Ocean between the Tropic of Cancer and the Tropic of Capricorn. Unusually strong, eastward-moving trade winds and ocean currents bring this cold water to the surface, a process known as upwelling.

El Nino: El Nino is a climate pattern that describes the unusual warming of surface waters in the eastern tropical Pacific Ocean. El Nino means Christ child or Littel Boy in Spanish During the time of El Nino, the trade winds weaken and warm water pushed back east towards the coast of Latin American countries. El Nino can affect our weather significantly and trade winds. El Nino has a

strong effect on marine life off the Pacific coast.
Hence, the correct option is (D).

7. The process of conversion of nitrogen (N_2) to ammonia is termed as nitrogen fixation. Bacteria play, a great role in nitrogen fixation. Nitrogen-fixing bacteria inhabit legume root nodules. Nitrogenase is the enzyme in nitrogen-fixing bacteria that catalyzes the conversion of atmospheric nitrogen into ammonia. Hence, the correct option is (B).

8. Cloud is a mass of minute water droplets or tiny crystals of ice formed by the condensation of the water vapour in free air at considerable elevations. As the clouds are formed at some height over the surface of the earth, they take various shapes. According to their height, expanse, density and transparency or opaqueness clouds are grouped under four types : (i) cirrus; (ii) cumulus; (iii) stratus; (iv) nimbus

Cirrus occur at the highest altitudes. Cirrus clouds are formed at high altitudes 8,000-12,000m. They are thin and detached clouds having a feathery appearance. They are always white in colour. Hence, the correct option is (C).

9. The Intertropical Convergence Zone, or ITCZ, is the region that circles the Earth, near the equator. Here the trade winds of the Northern and Southern hemispheres come together. The intense sun and warm water of the equator heat the air in the ITCZ, raising its humidity and making it buoyant. With the help of convergence of the trade winds, the buoyant air rises. As the air rises it expands and cools, releasing the accumulated moisture in an almost perpetual series of thunderstorms.
Hence, the correct option is (B).

10. Earth's lithosphere consists of Crust and the uppermost solid mantle. It extends to a depth of about $100 \; km$. The crust consists of a number of plates, and rigid blocks, as propounded by the Plate Tectonic Theory. The convection currents in the mantle generated by the interior heating, courtesy of radioactive material, is believed to be the cause of the movement of these plates. The mantle extends to a depth of $2,890 \; km$. It is the thickest layer of the Earth consisting of the upper mantle and lower mantle. While the inner core $(5,150 \; \text{to} \; 6,276 \; km)$ is solid, the outer core $(2,897 \; \text{to} \; 5,150 \; km)$ is liquid.
Hence, the correct option is (C).

11. The canyon is a deep, steep-walled, V-shaped valley. These valleys cut a river through rocks. These valleys occur in the upper courses of the rivers. The upper course is characterized by strong, swift currents digging its valleys. Example - Colorado in the United States.

A U-shaped valley is formed by strong lateral erosion of glaciers at high altitudes. The blind valley is a narrow, deep, and flat-bottomed valley that has an abrupt ending. Gorge is a narrow valley between steep mountains or hills.
Hence, the correct option is (D).

12. Stalactite, stalagmite and pillars are the depositional landforms of underground water. Therefore, these depositional landforms are formed by underground water running from the roofs in the cave. Stalactites are slender and sharp icicles having different diameters hanging from the roof of the caves. Stalagmites are formed by the dripping water from the cave

surface. Mergers of Stalactites and Stalagmites form pillars/columns.

Hence, the correct option is (D).

13. The normal Lapse rate is the rate of decrease in temperature with height at the upper boundary of the tropopause. It is $6.5°C$ per $1,000 \; m$ on an average. The temperature of the troposphere generally decreases as altitude increases. The temperature generally decreases with increasing height. Hence, the correct option is (B).

14. Suez Canal is a sea-level waterway that runs across the Egyptian Isthmus of Suez to connect the Red sea and Mediterranean sea. The Suez Canal was completely built by 1869. The Suez Canal is an open cut, without locks. The Canal is responsible for providing Europe with a new gateway to the Indian Ocean, as well as the Western Pacific Oceans. Hence, the correct option is (C).

15. Cfa denotes Humid Subtropical Climate according to Koppen's climatic classification. The Humid Subtropical Climate occurs on the eastern coasts of the continent, which is usually in the 20 s and 30 s degree latitude.

Tropical Wet Climate is denoted by Af and precipitation in this type of climate occurs all year-round. Tundra Climate is denoted by ET. Tropical Wet and Dry Climate or the Savanna type climate are denoted by Aw. It has an extended dry season during the winter.
Hence, the correct option is (B).

16. The Equator doesn't pass through Java, one of the land territories of Indonesia. Java lies between Sumatra and Bali. It is a volcano-dotted island. Located at the economic and geographic centre of Indonesia, it is the home to over half the people of Indonesia. Java is the largest modern city in Indonesia. Countries through which the Equator passes include - Ecuador, Colombia, Brazil, Sao Tome & Principe, Gabon, Republic of the Congo, the Democratic Republic of the Congo, Uganda, Kenya, Somalia, Maldives, Indonesia and Kiribati.
Hence, the correct option is (C).

17. Big Bang Theory is a hypothesis that explains how our universe originated from a small singularity. Nebular Hypothesis is about the origin of the Solar System, Sun, and Stars. Binary Theory states how all Chemical Compound are made up of two constituents of opposing characteristics. Planetesimal Hypothesis states that the planets are a result of the accumulation of small

bits of matter. Planetesimals planets revolve around the Sun. Hence, the correct option is (C).

18. South Atlantic Drift is also known as the Atlantic Drift or Westerlies Drift, and it is a cold current which is an eastward deflection of Brazil Current. Mozambique Current is a relatively warm surface current of the western Indian Ocean. East Australian Current is a warm ocean current in the South Western boundary of Australia. Caribbean Current is a warm ocean current that flows northwestward through the Caribbean from the east coast of South America, into the Gulf of Mexico. Hence, the correct option is (A).

19. The rivers of North-West Europe are good examples of barbed patterns of drainage. The great northwest European rivers include the drainage systems of the Elbe, Weser, Rhine, Meuse, Scheldt, Thames, Somme and Seine. This is because certain patterns in the North-Western Rivers emerge and indicate the presence of tectonically controlled variables. The barbed pattern is the drainage system where the stream suddenly bends back and flows in a reverse direction due to some tectonic activity.

Hence, the correct option is (C).

20. Temperate Cyclones are extra-tropical cyclones that emerge at mid and high latitudes. These low-pressure systems are associated with fronts - cold, warm, and occluded fronts. These cyclones are formed across the Polar front. Anticyclones are formed from air masses, are high-pressure cyclones affecting a larger area. Inter-Tropical Convergence is the area of convergence of trade winds between the North and South Hemisphere. Hence, the correct option is (C).

21. Kuroshio Current is a warm current, also called the Pacific/Japan current, a warm northeasterly coastal current off the coast of Japan. Canary Current is a cold current that is a part of the North Atlantic Gyre along the margin of West Africa, Portugal, Spain. California current is a Pacific Ocean cold current moving Southwards along the United States coast. Oyashio Current is a cold current that collides with the Kuroshio current off the Eastern shore of Japan and is an ideal location for fishing. Hence, the correct option is (C).

22. Shamal is a northwesterly wind that blows in the Mesopotamian region over Iraq, Persian Gulf, including Kuwait and Saudi Arabia. The winds are strong during the day but get weaker during the night. Results in sandstorms in the Iraq region, with sand, picked up from Jordan and Syria. Local Wind in East Asia is named Buran. Local Wind in the West Coast of Africa is Alize Maritime. Local Wind in Sahara is Kalima. Hence, the correct option is (D).

23. Adelaide, South Australia's capital city, is famous for Viticulture. The altitude and climate of Adelaide Hills are suitable for the cultivation of grapes and the production of wine. Viticulture is a branch of horticulture dealing with Grape cultivation and Wine Making. Suitable conditions for Viticulture - Light Sunshine, 65-70 cm of average rainfall throughout the year, frost-free season, Properly aerated soil. Hence, the correct option is (A).

24. Air mass can be formed in polar, as well as tropical regions. Air masses forming near the tropical regions or near the equator are warmer than those formed near the poles. Generally, there are four types of air masses - Continental, Tropical, Maritime, Polar. Maritime air masses have high humidity which takes moisture from the ocean and results in heavy rainfall. Continental air masses form over large landmasses and are dry. Hence, the correct option is (A).

25. For an area to be excluded from the drought-prone category, 30% or more of its gross cropped area should be under irrigation. The irrigation commission considers both rainfall and irrigation as factors in identifying a drought. It recommended that areas with more than 30% coverage of irrigation should be excluded from being listed as drought-prone areas. According to the vulnerability profile of NDMA, around 68 % of India's cultivable area is vulnerable to droughts. Areas that get up to 60 centimeters of rainfall annually are the most drought-prone. Hence, the correct option is (D).

26. The Vindhyan system of rocks is important for the production of precious stones and building materials. This system derives its name from the great Vindhyan mountains. The system comprises of ancient sedimentary rocks (4000 m thick) superimposed on the Archaean base. Mostly Unfossiliferous. The large area of this belt is covered by the Deccan trap. Hence, the correct option is (B).

27. Rajasthan has the highest area under Bajra with the highest production in the country. The stateoccupies nearly 4.43 million ha area with an average production of about 3.63 million tonnes and yieldof 818 kg/ha as in 2013-14.The semi-arid and arid parts of the western Rajasthan are important for bajra cultivation. Jodhpur,Barmer, Nagaur, Bikaner, Churu, Ganganagar, Sawai Madhopur, Alwar, Kota, Tonk, Jhunjhunu, Paliand Jaisalmer are important districts where the crop occupies 30-60% of the total cropped area.

Hence, the correct option is (B).

28. West Bengal is the largest producer of rice in India. Two crops of rice are raised in a year in this state. Rice is regarded as the master crop of coastal India and in few regions of eastern India. During the summer and monsoon season, both high temperature and heavy rainfall provide ideal conditions for rice cultivation. West Bengal state annual production in 2014-2015 was 14.68 %, which was the highest compared to any other state. Hence, the correct option is (A).

29. India has the fourth largest coal reserves in the world. As on 31 March 2019, India had 326.49 billion metric tons (359.89 billion short tons) of the resource. The known reserves of coal rose 2.34% over the previous year, with the discovery of an estimated 7.47 billion metric tons (8.23 billion short tons). The estimated total reserves of lignite coal as on 31 March 2019 was 45.76 billion metric tons (50.44 billion short tons), an increase of 0.22% from the previous year. Coal deposits are primarily found in eastern and south-central India. Jharkhand, Odisha, Chhattisgarh, West Bengal, Madhya Pradesh, Telangana and Maharashtra accounted for 98.09% of the total known coal reserves in India. As on 31 March 2019, Jharkhand and Odisha had the largest coal deposits of 25.88% and 24.76% respectively. Hence, the correct option is (B).

30. Assam produces the largest volume of tea in India, Assam Tea is known for its body, bright colour rich flavour and aroma. Tea estates of Assam are the world's largest tea-growing region, grown in the lowlands of Assam in the valley of the Brahmaputra river.
Hence, the correct option is (A).

31. Terrace farming is practised mainly in hilly areas. In India, it is practised in hilly areas mainly like Himachal Pradesh, Uttarakhand and some northeast states. It is also practised in the South area, like Andhra Pradesh. Uttaranchal (now Uttarakhand) is famous for terrace cultivation. In agriculture, a terrace is a levelled section of a hilly cultivated area, designed as a method of soil conservation to slow or prevent the rapid surface runoff. Terraced farming helps prevent the free flow of water.
Hence, the correct option is (D).

32. The mineral Bauxite is generated by the decomposition of rocks that leaves a residual mass of weathered material. Coal-formed of organic material deposited one layer above the other. Across millions of years, due to physical and chemical changes, oxygen was forced out and was left with carbon-rich deposits.
Hence, the correct option is (B).

33. Koderma is the leading producer of Mica. It is located in the Hazaribagh belt of Jharkhand. Jharkhand, as a whole, is quite rich in minerals. Koderma is recognized as the world's major preserve of mica and was once a lively town along with its neighbourhood town Jhumri Telaiya. Koderma is one of the districts of Jharkhand which is blessed with abundant natural resources and rich mineral deposits throughout the district. Earlier it was famous for the production of world-class mica and was known as the Mica Capital of India or Abrakh-Nagri.
Hence, the correct option is (B).

34. The horizontal strata in Sedimentary rocks are where the minerals are deposited and accumulated. The particles that form a sedimentary rock are known as sediment. Minerals are found in layers or strata in sedimentary rocks. Minerals are accumulated in horizontal strata after being exposed to high heat and pressure for a long period of time. Coal, Iron ore, gypsum, potash salt etc are formed in this way.
Hence, the correct option is (A).

35. Steel Authority Of India Limited (SAIL) is one of the largest state-owned steel-making company which supplies steel for public sector plants. SAIL operates and owns five integrated steel plants at Bhilai, Rourkela, Durgapur, Bokaro and Burnpur (Asansol) and three special steel plants at Salem, Durgapur and Bhadravathi. It also owns a Ferro Alloy plant at Chandrapur. As a part of its global ambition, the company is undergoing a massive expansion and modernisation programme involving upgrading and building new facilities with an emphasis on the state of the art green technology.
Hence, the correct option is (B).

36. Bauxite is used in a lot of industries like the chemical industry, refractory, abrasive, cement, steel, and petrol industry amongst others. In chemical, bauxite along with alumina is used in the manufacturing of aluminium chemicals. In refractory, it is used as a raw material for making several products. Alumina and bauxite are the two main raw materials in the aluminium making process. Aluminium is obtained by the electrolysis of alumina which extracts pure aluminium metal from alumina.
Hence, the correct option is (A).

37. The pipeline transport helps in reducing the transhipment delays and losses.It requires minimal labour. The pipeline is analyzed to be the best mode of trans-shipment. This is because it is situated underground and is not influenced by any delays that might be caused on the roads and the railways.
Hence, the correct option is (B).

38. Vishakhapatnam is the deepest land-locked and well-protected port along the Eastern coast of India. The port which is encircled by land from all sides with a water passage towards the sea or ocean is termed as a land-locked port. It is often called "The Jewel of the East Coast", situated in the state of Andhra Pradesh, located on the eastern shore of India. It is nestled among the hills of the Eastern Ghats and facing the Bay of Bengal to the east.
Hence, the correct option is (D).

39. The Cold Desert of India is located in Ladakh.

- The Cold Desert Cultural Landscape of India is situated in the Himalayas and stretches from Ladakh (in the state of Jammu and Kashmir) in the north to Kinnaur (in the state of Himachal Pradesh) in the south.

- The region constitutes a Cold Desert biome with harsh climatic conditions, which can be attributed to two factors. One is its location on the leeward side of the Himalayas, which makes it a rain-shadow zone inaccessible to the annual southeastern monsoon winds that sweep the rest of the country, thus creating desert conditions with low levels of precipitation.

- Cold desert- They have hot summers but extremely cold winters. These deserts are found in high, flat areas, called plateaus, or mountainous areas in temperate regions of the world. The mean winter temperature is between -2 to 4°C.

Hence, the correct option is (C).

40. Since, the insolation is highest at equator; temperature should be highest at the equator and lowest near the poles, however actually it is not. Highest temperature on earth is recorded at a few degrees north of equator. Altitude is the second major control of temperature of a place. The temperature depends upon albedo of the surface also.
Hence, the correct option is (B).

41. Roaring forties found in the southern hemisphere are strong westerly winds caused by air displaced from the equator to the South Pole and aid yachtsmen in on competitions and voyages. In other words, the strong west-to-east air currents are caused by the combination of air being displaced from the Equator towards the South Pole, the Earth's rotation, and the scarcity of landmasses to serve as windbreaks.
Hence, the correct option is (D).

42. Homospheric layers of the atmosphere include layers where the chemical composition is independent of the molecular weight of gases due to mixing by turbulence. Therefore, the lower layers such as troposphere, ionosphere and mesosphere are

homospheres.
Hence, the correct option is (A).

43. Standard atmospheric pressure is called 1 atm
of pressure and is equal to 760 Torr and 1013.25 Pa. Atmospheric
pressure is also often stated as pounds/square inch (psi).
The atmospheric pressure at sea level is 14.696 psi. It is important
to be able to convert between different units of pressure.

Hence, the correct option is (D).

44. The Karman line lies at an altitude of 100km, between the
atmospheric boundary of the Earth and outer space. The Kármán
line is the altitude where space begins. It is 100 km (about 62
miles) high. It commonly represents the border between the
Earth's atmosphere and outer space. This definition is accepted
by the Fédération Aéronautique Internationale (FAI).
Hence, the correct option is (C).

45. The ionosphere is a secondary layer of the atmosphere that
extends through the mesosphere, thermosphere and exosphere
during day time and is responsible for aurora – natural light
display in the sky in high altitude region. The ionosphere is the
ionized part of Earth's upper atmosphere, from about 48 km (30
mi) to 965 km (600 mi) altitude, a region that includes
the thermosphere and parts of the mesosphere and exosphere.
The ionosphere is ionized by solar radiation.
Hence, the correct option is (D).

46. 'Saving energy and other resources for the future without
sacrificing people's comfort at present' is the definition of
sustainable development. It is the idea that human societies must
live and meet their needs without compromising the ability of
future generations to meet their own needs. The "official"
definition of sustainable development was developed for the first
time in the Brundtland Report in 1987. The 2030 Agenda for
Sustainable Development, adopted by all United Nations
Member States in 2015, provides a shared blueprint for peace
and prosperity for people and the planet, now and into the
future. At its heart are the 17 Sustainable Development Goals
(SDGs), which are an urgent call for action by all countries -
developed and developing - in a global partnership.
Hence, the correct option is (C).

47. Placing of the threatened animals and plants in a special care
unit for protection is called Ex-situ conservation. Ex-situ
conservation sites may be a wild area or within the care of
humans. Showy Indian clover, Wollemi pine are examples of
organisms that are preserved via ex-situ conservation. The most
conventional methods of Ex-situ conservation are in zoos are
botanical gardens. There are approximately 2,107 aquaria and
zoos in 125 countries. There are approximately 2,000 botanical
gardens in 148 countries.
Hence, the correct option is (A).

48. The correct answer is Dachigam: Asiatic lions. Some of the
salient features of Dachigam National Park is:

It was established in 1981 and is home to Kashmiri Stag or
Hangul. Hangul is the state animal of Jammu and Kashmir.

IUCN status: Endangered

Hence, the correct option is (D).

49. Living Planet Report is published every 2 years by WWF. It is a
comprehensive study of trends in global biodiversity and the
health of the planet. The report presents a comprehensive
overview of the state of the natural world through the Living
Planet Index (LPI).
Hence, the correct option is (B).

50. In simpler terms, the greenhouse effect is a process that
occurs when gases in Earth's atmosphere trap the Sun's heat
which increases the temperature. When the Sun's energy reaches
the Earth's atmosphere, some of it is reflected back to space and
the rest is absorbed and re-radiated by greenhouse gases.
Greenhouse gases include water vapor, carbon dioxide, methane,
nitrous oxide, ozone and some artificial chemicals such as
chlorofluorocarbons (CFCs). The absorbed energy warms the
atmosphere and the surface of the Earth. Human activities such
as burning fossil fuels (coal, oil and natural gas), agriculture and
land clearing - are increasing the concentrations of greenhouse
gases. This is the enhanced greenhouse effect, which is
contributed to the global warming of the Earth.
Hence, the correct option is (A).

51. The correct answer is Gir National Park. Asiatic lions belong to
big cat families. It is one of the five major big cats found in India.
Asiatic lions are an endangered species and their availability is
restricted only to the Gir National Park situated in Gujarat, India.
Gir National Park is the world's only place where lions and tigers
coexist. It was declared as a protected area in the early 1900 s.
According to the April 2010 census, the lion count was 411 which
rose to 523 as per the 2015 Asiatic lion census.
Hence, the correct option is (B).

52. Food chain: A food chain shows the feeding relationship
between different organisms in a particular environment and/or
habitat. A food chain shows how energy is passed from the sun
to producers, from producers to consumers, and from consumers
to decomposes such as fungi. They also show how animals
depend on other organisms for food.

The food chain is distributed between Autotrophs, Hetrotrops,
and Decomposers i.e Producers, consumers and decomposers.

Autotrophs produce their own food like plants, trees and some
algae.

Heterotrophs are consumers i.e. animals, man, insects etc.

Decomposers are bacteria, fungi etc.

Therefore correct order is:

$$\text{Grass} \rightarrow \text{Grasshopper} \rightarrow \text{Frog} \rightarrow \text{Snake} \rightarrow \text{Hawk}$$

Hence, the correct option is (B).

53. The central institute of agricultural engineering is located at
Bhopal in Madhya Pradesh. It was established on 15 February
1976. It is a subsidiary body under the ministry of agriculture &
farmer's welfare. It was established with an aim to develop and
popularize technologies for the mechanization of Indian
agriculture. Central Institute of agricultural engineering was
formed during the 5th five-year planning in India. It was
established on the recommendation of a committee headed by
Dr. JS Kanwar.
Hence, the correct option is (A).

54. Water-Borne diseases: These are conditions caused by pathogenic micro-organisms that are transmitted in water. The disease can spread while bathing, washing or drinking water, or by eating food exposed to infected water and can cause severe, life-threatening diseases. Examples are typhoid fever, cholera and Hepatitis A or E. Other microorganisms induce less dangerous diseases such as diarrhoea.

Cholera: Cholera is a waterborne disease and is diarrhoeal in nature.

Diarrhoea: Diarrhoea is one of the most common waterborne diseases that mostly affects children under the age of 5.

Hepatitis A: Another type of waterborne disease is Hepatitis A and it is caused by the Hepatitis A virus, which affects the liver.

Typhoid: It is another disease that gets transmitted by drinking contaminated water that carries 'Salmonellae Typhi bacteria'.
Hence, the correct option is (A).

55. The "NITI Aayog" an agency of the Government of India, has been entrusted with the task of implementing and overseeing the Sustainable Development Goals. NITI Aayog has identified sustainable development goals and plans related to their objectives. Many major government programs, such as 'Swachh Bharat', 'Make in India', 'Skill India' and 'Digital India', are at the core of the Sustainable Development Goals. The United Nations in India these days is helping state governments to achieve sustainable development goals. So that the major challenges of development at the state level can be resolved.
Hence, the correct option is (B).

56. The substance that causes the maximum air pollution is Sulphur dioxide. Sulphur dioxide is the chemical compound with the formula SO_2. It is a toxic gas responsible for the smell of burnt matches. Pungent smelling colourless gas produced from mostly volcanic activities, industrial processes, and production of sulphuric acid. Sulfur dioxide causes a range of harmful effects on the lungs.
Hence, the correct option is (C).

57. Bioremediation as the name suggests is a remedy (solution of a problem) through biological means. Bioremediation is a process in which microorganisms or their enzymes are used to treat pollutants. i.e. the problem is a pollutant and the remedy is micro-organisms. As there are numerous micro-organisms are present on the earth, there are numerous possibilities in which humans can use them. In the future, micro-organisms may solve the problem of plastic pollution too.
Hence, the correct option is (D).

58. Himachal Pradesh, which has obliged all government departments to initiate environmental audits, is on its way to becoming the country's first carbon-free state.

Countries that produce the most emissions are measured in millions of tons of CO_2 in 2019 are:

1. China, with more than 10,065 million tons of CO_2 released.

2. The United States, with 5,416 million tons of CO_2.

3. India, with 2,654 million tons of CO_2.

4. Russia, with 1,711 million tons of CO_2.
Hence, the correct option is (B).

59. Similipal National Park is a National Park and Tiger Reserve, covering 2,750 km² (1,060 sq mi) in the Mayurbhanj district of the Indian state of Odisha. It is part of the Mayurbhanj Elephant Sanctuary, which consists of three protected areas - Similipal Tiger Reserve, Hadgarh Wildlife Sanctuary with 91.06 km² (73.77 sq mi), and Kuldiha Wildlife Sanctuary at 272.75 km² (105.31 sq mi). Simlipal National Park derives its name from the abundance of red silk cotton trees that grow in the region. It is the 7th largest national park in India. The park is home to some beautiful waterfalls such as the Bengal Tiger, Asi Elephant, Gaur, and Chausinga as well as the Joranda and Barhiapani Falls. This protected area is part of UNESCO's World Network of Biosphere Reserves since 2009.
Hence, the correct option is (D).

60. The twenty-first session of the Conference of Parties (COP) and the eleventh session of the Conference of Parties for the Kyoto Protocol (CMP) were held in Paris, France from 30 November to 11 December 2015. "UNFCCC" was adopted during the Rio de Janeiro Earth Summit in 1992. The Paris Agreement provides a way forward to reduce the temperature rise to less than 2 ° C, perhaps even 1.5. The Conference of the Parties is the supreme decision-making body of the UNFCCC. It meets annually to make decisions that will ensure the objectives of achieving the climate. As of December 2020, 194 UNFCCC members have signed the agreement, and 189 have become a party to it. The Paris Agreement is a replacement for the 2005 Kyoto Protocol.
Hence, the correct option is (B).

61. 'Sagarmatha' is the Nepali name for Mount Everest. Mount Everest is the Great Himalayas of southern Asia that lies on the border between Nepal and the Tibet Autonomous Region of China, at $27°59'N\,86°56'E$. Reaching an elevation of 29,035 feet $(8,850$ meters) is the highest mountain in the world. Its most common Tibetan name, Chomolungma, means "Goddess Mother of the World" or "Goddess of the Valley." The Sanskrit name Sagarmatha means literally "Peak of Heaven." Everest is shaped like a three-sided pyramid.
Hence, the correct option is (A).

62. Wular Lake is the largest freshwater lake in India and lies in the Kashmir Valley. Wular Lake is also one of the largest freshwater lakes in Asia. It is sited in the Bandipora district in Jammu and Kashmir, India. The lake basin was formed as a result of tectonic activity and is fed by the Jhelum River. The lake's size varies seasonally from 12 to 100 square miles. Wular Lake is important to fish habitat, the main species being the common carp, rosy barb, mosquitofish, Nemacheilus species, etc.
Hence, the correct option is (D).

63. The largest part of the Gangetic soil is covered by the Bangar soil. It is found in those high plain regions which are free from floodwater. It is not very fertile in nature due to kankars. Kankars are calcareous deposits. It has a low upland covered by laterite deposits. It is old and matured alluvial soil. It is not renewed frequently as compared to the khaddar soil. It is known by various names like clay, sandy, loam. The fertility of the soil has been lost due to the continuous use of this soil for agriculture

since ancient times.
Hence, the correct option is (A).

64. Tehri Dam is the highest hydroelectric power plant in the country. Its total capacity is $2400 MW$. It is located in Uttrakhand. Srisailam Dam, Nathpa Jhaki Dam, and Sardar Sarovar Dam is also among the top five biggest hydroelectric power plant in India. The capacity of Srisailam Dam is $1670 MW$. It is located in Andhra Pradesh. Nathpa Jhakri Dam produces $1530 MW$ of electricity. It is located in Himachal Pradesh. Sardar Sarovar Dam's capacity is $1450 MW$. It is located in Gujarat.
Hence, the correct option is (A).

65. Over 8 Indian states does the Deccan Plateau extend. The Deccan Plateau covers the majority of the southern part of the country. It is located between three mountain ranges and extends over eight Indian states. They are:

Telangana
Maharashtra
Karnataka
Andhra Pradesh
Kerala
Tamil Nadu

It also covers some part of Madhya Pradesh and Chhatisgarh.
Hence, the correct option is (B).

66. An imaginary line running on the globe divides it into two equal parts. This line is called the equator. The northern half of the earth is called the Northern Hemisphere. The southern half is called the Southern Hemisphere. All parallel circles from the equator up to the poles are called parallels of latitudes. Latitudes are measured in degrees. There are four important parallels of latitudes:

The Tropic of Capricorn is in the Southern Hemisphere. Tropic of Cancer is in the Northern Hemisphere. Arctic Circle is in the north of the Equator. Antarctic Circle is in the south of the Equator. Thus, we can say that the Tropic of Capricorn lies in the Southern Hemisphere.
Hence, the correct option is (C).

67. The summer months are a period of excessive heat and falling air pressure in the northern half of the country. Dust storms in the evening are very common during May in Punjab, Haryana, Eastern Rajasthan and Uttar Pradesh. Loo is the hot and dry winds blow in the Northern plains from Punjab to Bihar with higher intensity between Delhi and Patna.
Hence, the correct option is (A).

68. In Punjab the major cause of land degradation is over-irrigation. Over-irrigation leads to water logging which in turn leads to increase in alkalinity and salinity in the soil.
Hence, the correct option is (C).

69. Bhakra Dam is a concrete gravity dam on the Sutlej River in Bilaspur, Himachal Pradesh in northern India. The dam forms the Govind Sagar reservoir. The dam, located at a gorge near the (now submerged) upstream Bhakra village in Bilaspur district of Himachal Pradesh of height 226 m.
Hence, the correct option is (A).

70. Golden Quadrilateral is a high-density traffic corridor that connects four big metro cities of India i.e. Delhi-Mumbai-Chennai-Kolkata. It is designated as one of the longest highways in the world. It was former Prime Minister Atal Bihari Vajpayee's first dream project and is enshrined as the biggest infrastructure intervention in the roadways sector in post-Independent India.
Hence, the correct option is (C).

71. The Arabian Sea lies towards the western side of India. All the rivers that flow into this Sea form the Arabian Sea Drainage system. Examples of the rivers that flow towards the western side of the Arabian Sea are Sabarmati river, Mahi, Luni.

Hence, the correct option is (B).

72. Godavari is known as Dakshina Ganga in India. The Godavari is India's second longest river after the Ganga. Its source is in Triambakeshwar, Maharashtra.
Hence, the correct option is (A).

73. Cold Deserts are deserts having extremely cold winters. These deserts are generally found in mountainous areas. Ladakh is the only cold desert in India, situated in the Himalayas. It doesn't get affected by the monsoon as it lies in the rain shadow region of the Himalayas. The rainfall in this region is as low as 10 cm annually.
Hence, the correct option is (B).

74. The northern part of the west coast of India is known as the Konkan coast. Its rugged and narrow portion is located on the western portion of Western Ghats. It includes the state of Maharashtra, Karnataka and Goa.

Geographically, Konkan is bound by the Arabian Sea to the west, the Deccan plateau to the east.

Hence, the correct option is (A).

75. The Koeppen climate classification system recognizes five major climatic types and each type is designated by a capital letter- A, B, C, D, E, and H. A, C, D, E are considered as Humid whereas B is considered as Dry. H is referred to as the climate of Highland regions.
Hence, the correct option is (D).

76. The herb Himalayan Trillium has numerous uses for human beings thus inviting people to utilize it, paving way for overutilization. In recent years, the plant has become one of the most traded commercial plants of the Himalayan region, due to its high medicinal quality. It is found in temperate and sub-alpine zones of the Himalayas, at an altitude from $2,400 - 4,000$ metres above sea level. Their existence has also been traced across India, Bhutan, Nepal, China, Afghanistan and Pakistan. In India, it is found in four states only- Himachal Pradesh, Jammu and Kashmir, Sikkim, and Uttarakhand. Often called Nagchatri, in local areas this herb grows to a height of $15 - 20\ cm$.
Hence, the correct option is (B).

77. A Himalayan serow has been sighted for the first time in the Himalayan cold desert region. The animal was spotted near Hurling village in Spiti, Himachal Pradesh. Scientific name: The Himalayan serow, or Capricornis sumatraensis thar, is a subspecies of the mainland serow (Capricornis sumatraensis).
Hence, the correct option is (C).

78. Shevaroy Hills are located in Tamil Nadu. The Servarayan hills, with the anglicised name Shevaroy Hills, are a towering mountain range near the city of Salem, in Tamil Nadu state, southern India. It is one of the major hill stations in Tamil Nadu and in the Eastern Ghats. The local Tamil name comes from a local deity, Servarayan.
Hence, the correct option is (D).

79. The Ken-Betwa Link Project (KBLP) is the River interlinking project that aims to transfer surplus water from the Ken river in MP to Betwa in UP to irrigate the drought-prone Bundelkhand region spread across the districts of two states mainly Jhansi, Banda, Lalitpur and Mahoba districts of UP and Tikamgarh, Panna and Chhatarpur districts of MP. Hence, statement 2 is NOT correct. This is the country's first river interlinking project.
Hence, the correct option is (A).

80. A lagoon is a shallow body of water that may have an opening to a larger body of water but is also protected from it by a sandbar or coral reef. Examples: Hilton Lagoon, Hawaii, The Venetian Lagoon, Lake Nokoue, Ganvie, Benin, Lake Piso, Liberia, Lycian Lagoon. The Venetian Lagoon is home to the "Queen of the Adriatic", the city of Venice, Italy.
Hence, the correct option is (A).

81. Rohtang Pass is a high mountain pass on the eastern end of the Pir Panjal Range of the Himalayas around $51\ km$ from Manali. It connects the Kullu Valley with the Lahaul and Spiti Valleys of Himachal Pradesh. It links Manali and Leh by road.
Hence, the correct option is (C).

82. Both the statements are individually true and Statement II is the correct explanation of Statement I.

The interior part of Maharashtra does not receive adequate rain in the summer season because the interior part of Maharashtra lies in the rain shadow of the Western Ghats. Rain shadow is the lee side of a mountain and Western Ghats receives mostly orographic precipitation due to its topography.
Hence, the correct option is (A).

83. The World's largest area of mangrove forests is Sunderbans. The Sundarbans is a UNESCO World Heritage Site and located at the Southeastern tip of the 24 Paraganas district about $110\ km$ from Kolkata. Sunderbans got its name from one of the mangrove plants known as Sundari (Heritiera Minor). Sundarbans are a part of the world's largest delta, formed by the mighty rivers Ganga, Brahmaputra, and Meghna.
Hence, the correct option is (D).

84. The pokkalli variety of rice is known for its saltwater resistance and flourishes in the rice paddies of coastal Alappuzha, Ernakulam, and Thrissur districts of Kerala.
Hence, the correct option is (C).

85. Narmada originates from Amarkantak Plateau in the Anuppur district of Madhya Pradesh. It forms the traditional boundary between North India and South India and flows westwards over a length of 1,312 km (815.2 mi) before draining through the Gulf of Khambhat into the Arabian Sea, 30 km (18.6 mi) west of Bharuch city of Gujarat. Ganga Brahmaputra and Chenab all originate from the Himalayas.
Hence, the correct option is (C).

86. While selecting the site for rain gauge stations the following. points should be considered:

The site should be on level ground and on open space. It should never be on sloping ground. The site should be such that the distance between the gauge station and the objects (like a tree, building, etc) should be at least twice the height of the objects. In the hilly area, where level ground is not available, the site should be so selected that the station may be well shielded from high wind.
Hence, the correct option is (D).

87. Infiltration rate is always equal to or less than the infiltration capacity. Infiltration is the flow of water through the soil surface into a porous medium under gravitational action and pressure effects. The factors that influence the infiltration are the soil type such as texture, structure, hydrodynamic characteristics which influence capillary forces and adsorption, and the soil coverage.

Hence, the correct option is (B).

88. The probability for the annual maximum flood magnitude to

$$\text{occur} = \frac{1}{\text{Return period}}$$

$$\Rightarrow p = \frac{1}{T} = 0.1$$

$$\Rightarrow q = 1 - p = 0.9$$

Probability of flood at least once in next 4 years

$= 1 -$ no flood in next 4 years

$$= 1 - q^4$$

$$= 1 - (0.9)^4 = 0.35$$

Hence, the correct option is (B).

89. Water logging: An agricultural land is said to be waterlogged when the root zone of the crops gets flooded with high water table and become ill-aerated. The productivity gets affected by water logging problem.

Water logging & Salinity: When water table has risen up substantially it comes within the root zone of the crops and the soluble salts present in the water also rise up towards the surface. So, when water is evaporated the salts gets deposited in the root zone, resulting in increased salinity. Therefore, it affects the process of osmosis which in turn results in reduction in water extraction capacity of the roots. Thus, water logging reduces the productivity or yield of the crops.

Control of waterl logging: Water logging can be controlled by provision of efficient drainage to drain away the storm water and excess irrigation water by use of surface and sub-surface drainage. These drainage will check and reduce the water percolating in the soil mass, thus reducing the chances of water logging. But it cannot be eliminated completely as there will be always some water percolation into the soil mass.
Hence, the correct option is (C).

90. Landscape drip irrigation is a method of delivering water slowly, at low pressure, at or near the root zone of the landscape plant material. It is often referred to as targeted or precise watering, because drip irrigation allows to target the precise area.

The highest water saving method for irrigation is drip irrigation. Hence, the correct option is (B).

91. The relation between Duty (D) in ha/cumecs, Delta in meter and Base period (B) in days is given by the following relation:

$$D = \frac{8.64B}{\Delta}$$

$$D = \frac{8.64 \times 10}{8.64 \times 10^{-2}}$$

$\therefore$ Thus, Duty $= 1000$ hectares per cum/s
Hence, the correct option is (D).

92. Evaporation: It is the process in which a liquid change to the gaseous state at the free surface below the boiling point through the transfer of heat energy.

Vapour pressure: Vapour pressure is defined as the pressure exerted by a vapor in thermodynamic equilibrium with its condensed phases (solid or liquid) at a given temperature in a closed system.

Evapotranspiration: It is the process by which water leaves the body of a living plant and reaches atmosphere as water vapour.
Hence, the correct option is (D).

93. Victoria Falls is one of the greatest attractions in Africa and one of the most spectacular waterfalls in the world. Victoria Falls is located on the Zambezi River, the fourth largest river in Africa, which is also defining the border between Zambia and Zimbabwe.

Hence, the correct option is (C).

94. Assumptions in the Unit Hydrograph Theory:

1. Time Invariance: This implies that the direct runoff hydrograph for a given effective rainfall (ER) in a catchment is time-invariant i.e. it is always the same irrespective of when it occurs.

2. Linear Response: The direct runoff response to rainfall excess is assumed to be linear i.e. any change in the input value is linearly reflected in the output value.
Hence, the correct option is (C).

95. Methods use to convert point rainfall values at different rain gauge stations into an average value over a catchment are:

1. Arithmetical mean method

2. Thiessen Polygon method

3. Isohyetal Method
Hence, the correct option is (B).

96. Given that, ϕ index $= 3.2 \; cm/$ hour

The rates of rainfall for successive 20 min period of 140 minutes are $2.5, 2.5, 10, 7.6, 1.25, \; 1.25$ and $5 \; cm/h$. But among these only $10, 7.6$ and $5 \; cm/hour$ rates are greater than phi index. So, only these rate of rainfalls will be considered for calculating runoff (R).

Effective precipitation value, $P = \dfrac{113}{15} \; cm$, and effective duration of rainfall, $T = 1$ hour.

$$\therefore R = \frac{113}{15} - 3.2 \times 1 = 7.533 - 3.2 = 4.333 \; cm.$$
Hence, the correct option is (B).

97. Barrage is a structure similar to weir with the only difference that the crest is kept at a low level and ponding of water is accomplished mainly by means of gates. During floods these gates can be raised above HFL and thus enable the high flood to pass with minimum afflux.

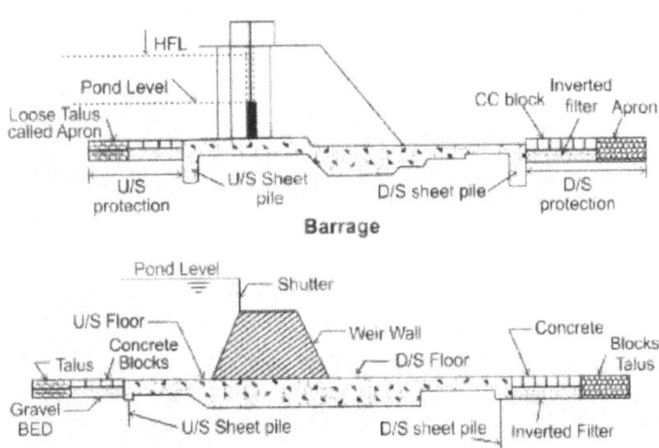

Hence, the correct option is (D).

98. Given: Capacity of well = 4 m³/hour,

$\therefore$ Total discharge from the well for 20 days $= 4 \times 20 \times 20 = 1600 \; m^3$

$\Rightarrow$ Area of Irrigation $= \dfrac{1600}{0.07} = 2.29 \times 10^4 \; m^2$ [$\because$ $Area = \dfrac{Discharge}{Depth}$]

Hence, the correct option is (D).

99. Flood routing: It is the technique of determining outflow patterns or the flood hydrograph at a section of the river or reservoir by utilizing the data of flood flow at one or more upstream sections.

Hydrograph: A hydrograph is a graph or plot that shows the rate of water flow in relation to time, given a specific point or cross section. These graphs are often used to evaluate stormwater runoff on a particular site considering a development project.

Flood discharge: It is the discharge from the catchment area at peak flow. The design of bridges, culvert waterways and spillways and hydraulic structures is done while considering this.

Runoff estimation: Runoff means the draining off of precipitation from a catchment area through a surface channel. The unit hydrograph method is used to determine runoff.

Hence, the correct option is (D).

100. Ogee fall: In this type of fall, the water was gradually led down by providing convex and concave curves as shown in figure below.

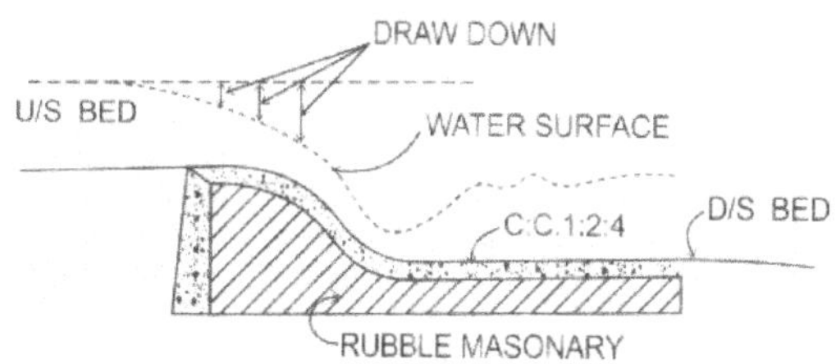

Hence, the correct option is (D).

101. Brahmaputra: It originates under the name of Siang or Dihang, from the Chemayungdung glacier of the Kailash range near the Mansarovar lake. It flows eastwards parallel to the Himalayas. It receives a large number of tributaries in Tibet and flows through India, Bangladesh and china. The first major tributary is the Raga Tsangpo meeting the Tsangpo near Lhatse Dzong. After reaching Namcha Barwa, it takes a "U" turn (also known as Hair Pin turn) and enters India west of Sadiya town in Arunachal Pradesh through the deep Dihang or Siang gorge of Himalayas.
Hence, the correct option is (D).

102. The McMahon Line is a borderline between China (Tibetan region) and India (North-east region). This line is proposed by the Administrator of British colonial Henry McMahon in the Shimla Convention in 1914. It was signed between Tibetan representatives & the British.
Hence, the correct option is (B).

103. Three Indian states and one union territory share a boundary with Pakistan. Indian states/union territory that share borders with Pakistan are:

1. Jammu and Kashmir

2. Rajasthan

3. Gujarat.

4. Punjab.
Hence, the correct option is (D).

104. Lake Baikal is the largest freshwater lake by volume in the world. Lake Baikal is a rift lake located in the southern part of the eastern Siberia region in Russia. Lake Baikal contains one-fifth of the freshwater lake on the earth surface It is the seventh-largest lake by surface area.
Hence, the correct option is (C).

105. Lake Victoria, also called Victoria Nyanza, the largest lake in Africa and the chief reservoir of the Nile, lying mainly in Tanzania and Uganda but bordering on Kenya. It is also the third-largest freshwater lake on Earth.
Hence, the correct option is (C).

106. Fold Mountains is formed due to the compressive forces generated by endogenetic forces (earthquake, landslide, etc.). Examples of fold mountains are the Himalayas, Alps, Andes, Rockies, Atlas, etc. Young/New Fold Mountains: It came into existence after the continental drift. The Himalayas are regarded as the youngest mountains in the world. Old Mountains: They belong to the pre-drift era, then subject to denudation and uplift, e.g., Aravallis (India), etc.
Hence, the correct option is (B).

107. India's longest border is with Bangladesh and the shortest border is with Afghanistan. It shares a 3488 km long border with China along with Ladakh, Himachal Pradesh, Uttarakhand, Sikkim, and Arunachal Pradesh. India- Nepal border is a porous 1051-kilometer border along with the states of Uttarakhand, Uttar Pradesh, Bihar, West Bengal, and Sikkim.
Hence, the correct option is (A).

108. Dresden Line is the new railway line in Prague. Radcliffe Line - This boundary line is between India and Pakistan drew by Sir Cyril Radcliffe in 1947. Durand Line - It is between Pakistan and Afghanistan.
Hence, the correct option is (A).

109. The Guinness Book of World Records has named Majuli as the world's largest river island. The beautiful river island is located on the River Brahmaputra in Assam. It is formed by the Brahmaputra River in the South, and Kherkutia Xuti, an anabranch of Brahmaputra, joined by the Subansiri River in the north. The island is populated by the Mising, Deori, and Sonowal Kachri tribes.
Hence, the correct option is (B).

110. The Strait of Gibraltar connects the Atlantic Ocean with the Mediterranean Sea and separates Spain on the European continent from Morocco on the African continent.
Hence, the correct option is (C).

111. The Narmada and the Tapti are major rivers that drain into the Arabian Sea. The Narmada originates in eastern Madhya Pradesh (India) and flows west across the state, through a narrow valley between the Vindhya Range and spurs of the Satpura Range.
Hence, the correct option is (A).

112. The Palk Strait is a strait between India and Sri Lanka. It connects the Bay of Bengal in the northeast with the Gulf of Mannar in the southwest. This chain extends between Dhanushkodi on Pamban (Rameswaram) Island in Tamil Nadu and Mannar Island in Sri Lanka.
Hence, the correct option is (A).

113. Duncan Passage is a strait in the Indian Ocean. It is about 48 km (30 mils) wide; it separates Rutland Island (part of Great Andaman) to the north and Little Andaman to the south. West of Duncan Passage is the Bay of Bengal; east is the Andaman Sea.
Hence, the correct option is (B).

114. Mauritius country does not have a boundary with India. It is formally the Republic of Mauritius, a Nations on-line country profile of the tiny remote dry land within the ocean in the Japanese Southern continent. The capital is Port Louis.
Hence, the correct option is (C).

115. Ujjain is a district in Madhya Pradesh. It is situated on the Malwa Plateau on the eastern side of the Chambal River tributary, the Sipra (Shipra) River. One of the seven holiest Hindu towns in Ujjain. It takes its name from the Sanskrit Jai. The city was the capital (as Ujjayini) of the Aryan Avanti kingdom (6th-4th centuries BCE), lying on the first meridian of the ancient Hindu geographers.
Hence, the correct option is (A).

116. The exosphere is to be considered as the actual "final frontier" of Earth's gaseous envelope. The "air" in the exosphere is a very thin layer, which makes this layer even more space-like than the outer atmosphere. In fact, the air in the exosphere is constantly - though very gradually - "leaking" out of Earth's atmosphere into outer space.

Hence, the correct option is (B).

117. Geography is divided into two main branches: human geography and physical geography. Human geography or anthropogeography is the branch of geography that is associated and deals with humans and their relationships with communities, cultures, economies, and interactions with the environment by studying their relations with and across locations.
Hence, the correct option is (D).

118. According to Fredrick Ratzel, "Human geography is the synthetic study of the relationship between human societies and earth's surface". Ratzel's father was the head of the household staff of the Grand Duke of Baden. Friedrich attended high school in Karlsruhe for six years before being apprenticed at age 15 to apothecaries. In 1863, he went to Rapperswil on the Lake of Zurich, Switzerland, where he began to study the classics.
Hence, the correct option is (C).

119. Radical school of thought employed Marxian theory to explain the basic cause of poverty, deprivation and social inequality. Contemporary social problems were related to the development of capitalism. Marxian economics is a school of economic thought based on the work of 19th-century economist and philosopher Karl Marx.
Hence, the correct option is (C).

120. As per the population density, Bangladesh is at 1st place, Because Bangladesh's land area is small according to the number of people there. Bangladesh is most densely populated with approximately 1260 Peoples per Square Kilometer. This is almost three times dense of its neighbor country India.
Hence, the correct option is (A).

121. Uttar Pradesh with a population size of 166 million people is the most populous state of India. Uttar Pradesh accounts for about 16.16 per cent of the Country's population.
Hence, the correct option is (C).

122. The most common sort among the calculations of population density is as defined by the number of persons per square kilometre. Calculations of population density depict the concentration of population over certain spatial units, and the Census of India uses number of persons per square kilometre as its principle method with which to measure population density. Jammu and Kashmir has a population density below 100 persons per square kilometre; there was an increase of two persons for every 100 persons in the base population.
Hence, the correct option is (A).

123. According to the records of NITI Aayog Chattisgarh is the state where the population density is below 250 persons per square km. Other states having a population density of less than 250 persons per square km are: Arunachal Pradesh, Himachal Pradesh, Jammu & Kashmir, Madhya Pradesh, Manipur, Meghalaya, Nagaland, Mizoram, Rajasthan Sikkim, and Uttarakhand.
Hence, the correct option is (C).

124. High birth rate is the result of a large proportion of children in a population. The percentage of children and the aged affect the dependency ratio because these groups are not producers.
Hence, the correct option is (C).

125. Death rate is the number of deaths per thousand persons in a year. The main cause of the rate of growth of the Indian population has been the rapid decline in death rates.
Hence, the correct option is (B).

Mock Test 03

Q.1 A level of atmosphere which is composed partly of electrons and positive ions is called-

A. Troposphere   **B.** Ionosphere
C. Stratosphere   **D.** Mesosphere

Q.2 Greywater is ___.
A. Waste water released from kitchen
B. Waste water released from toilets
C. Waste water released from factories
D. Waste water released from hospitals

Q.3 The largest delta in the world is______.
A. Yellow River Delta
B. Ganges-Brahmaputra Delta
C. Mississippi Delta
D. None of these

Q.4 The Palk Strait is a strait between the Tamil Nadu state of India and the ______ district of the Northern Province of the island nation of Sri Lanka.

A. Puttalam   **B.** Chunnakam
C. Mannar   **D.** Chilaw

Q.5 Why the Earth is having its own atmosphere?
A. Winds
B. Clouds
C. Gravity
D. Rotation of the Earth

Q.6 Why is Carbon Monoxide a pollutant?
A. Reacts with hemoglobin
B. It inhibits glycolysis
C. It reacts with Oxygen
D. None of these

Q.7 Which layer of the Earth's atmosphere contains the ozone layer?
A. Troposphere   **B.** Mesosphere
C. Lonosphere   **D.** Stratosphere

Q.8 The outermost range of Himalays is called ___.
A. Himadri   **B.** Shiwaliks
C. Himachal   **D.** Kumaon

Q.9 India shares longest international boundary with which country?
A. Bangladesh   **B.** China
C. Nepal   **D.** Bhutan

Q.10 In Peninsular India, the direction of prevailing summer monsoon wind is-
A. From South-East   **B.** From Southwest
C. From North   **D.** From South

Q.11 Southern Oscillation was discovered by whom?

A. Sir Gilbert Walker   **B.** Flohn
C. Sir Palker   **D.** Sir Thomson

Q.12 Which months are known for retreating monsoons?
A. April and May
B. June and August
C. October and November
D. March and April

Q.13 Soil erosion is caused due to-
A. Erosion by water
B. Erosion by wind
C. Due to plate movement of earth
D. Both A and B

Q.14 Which soil is largest of all soil groups in India?
A. Red Soil   **B.** Alluvial Soil
C. Black Soil   **D.** Desert soil

Q.15 The Kovvada Nuclear Park project is proposed to be setup in which State?
A. Rajasthan   **B.** Uttar Pradesh
C. Andhra Pradesh   **D.** Karnataka

Q.16 The World's largest island is-
A. Greenland   **B.** Iceland
C. New Guinea   **D.** Madagascar

Q.17 Nandadevi peak is located in _________ State.
A. Himachal Pradesh   **B.** Uttarakhand
C. Uttar Pradesh   **D.** Sikkim

Q.18 Which one of the following is not a non-conventional source of energy?
A. Solar Energy   **B.** Natural Gas
C. Wind Energy   **D.** Tidal Power

Q.19 What is dew point?
A. The temperature at which an air becomes unsaturated
B. The temperature at which an air becomes cold from warm
C. The temperature at which an air becomes saturated
D. None of the above

Q.20 Radiation inversion occurs only on ___.
A. Air surface   **B.** Ocean surface
C. Land surface   **D.** None of the above

Q.21 The comparative ratio between humidity of certain area with the maximum limit is called-
A. Relative strength   **B.** Relative humidity
C. Ultra humidity   **D.** Mild humidity

Q.22 Marbles are formed due to change in-
A. Clay   **B.** Limestones
C. Sandstones   **D.** Granite

Q.23 Loess is a-
A. Loss of rocks
B. Animal deposited sediments
C. Water deposited sediments
D. Wind deposited sediments

Q.24 At Barren Island, the only active volcano in India is situated in-
A. Andaman Islands
B. Nicobar Islands
C. Lakshadweep
D. Minicoy

Q.25 The depletion in Ozone layer is caused by __________ .
A. Nitrous oxide
B. Carbon dioxide
C. Chlorofluorocarbons
D. Methane

Q.26 The Himalayas is the example of _______ .
A. Fold mountains
B. Block mountains
C. Ancient mountains
D. Residual mountains

Q.27 Which of the following is the longest river originating in India?
A. Brahmaputra
B. Ganga
C. Yamuna
D. Godavari

Q.28 The Malwa Plateau is not a part of which state?
A. Rajasthan
B. Gujarat
C. Maharashtra
D. Madhya Pradesh

Q.29 Which of the following statement is incorrect?
A. The Sundarban Delta has the world's largest mangrove forest
B. India is the world's largest producer of maize
C. Easter Island is the only region situated on the earth in exactly the opposite direction of India
D. India's largest saltwater lake is located in Gujarat

Q.30 What is the type of Ladang agricultural system of Indonesia?
A. Transplanting
B. Shifting cultivation
C. Mixed farming
D. Gardening

Q.31 In geography who propounded the theory of convectional current hypothesis?
A. Arthur Holmes
B. Carl Ritter
C. Arnaldo Faustini
D. Immanuel Kant

Q.32 On which river is the Babli project being constructed by the Government of Maharashtra?
A. Bhima River
B. Krishna River
C. Godavari River
D. Panganga River

Q.33 Matbhanga river forms the border between which two countries?
A. India and Nepal
B. India and Bangladesh
C. India and Myanmar
D. India and Sri Lanka

Q.34 In which state is the Manikaran hot water source located?

A. Uttarakhand
B. Himachal Pradesh
C. Jammu-Kashmir
D. Gujarat

Q.35 India's 60% of salt is produced by which state?
A. Rajasthan
B. Odisha
C. Gujarat
D. Maharashtra

Q.36 Which of the following is the largest irrigation canal in the world?
A. Panama Canal
B. Sirhind Canal
C. Suez Canal
D. Indira Gandhi Canal

Q.37 When did Arunachal Pradesh get full statehood?
A. 1985
B. 1986
C. 1987
D. 1988

Q.38 The coir industry in India is mainly concentrated in which state?
A. Karnataka
B. Tamil Nadu
C. Kerala
D. Andhra Pradesh

Q.39 What is the ratio between the coastline of peninsular India and the coast of Andaman Nicobar and Lakshadweep?
A. 2:1
B. 2.5:1
C. 3:1
D. 3.5:1

Q.40 Which is the longest National Highway in India?
A. National Highway 4
B. National Highway 7
C. National Highway 8
D. National Highway 10

Q.41 In which state is the thermal power plant located at Talcher?
A. Karnataka
B. Odisha
C. West Bengal
D. Himachal Pradesh

Q.42 Which of the following biomes does not have a tree?
A. Taiga
B. Tundra
C. Chaparral
D. Savannah

Q.43 Which of the following statements is correct in relation to the vast plains of India?
1. India's largest alluvium deposit is found in the world.
2. Bangar has new alluvium as compared to Khadar region.
3. Khadar region is located in low altitude areas.
A. Only 1 and 2
B. Only 2 and 3
C. Only 1 and 3
D. 1, 2 and 3

Q.44 What percentage of the total area of Rajasthan is located in the Thar Desert?
A. 30%
B. 40%
C. 60%
D. 70%

Q.45 The Dampier-Hodges line is related to which of the following?
A. Gulf of Cambay
B. Palk Strait
C. Andaman and Nicobar Islands
D. Sundarbans

Q.46 Helmand province of Afghanistan is famous for whose cultivation?
A. Tobacco
B. Opium
C. Wheat
D. Cotton

Q.47 Consider the following statements:
1. Balearic Island is located in the Mediterranean Sea.
2. Corsica and Sardinia islands are located in the west of Italy.
Which of the above statements is true?
A. Only 1
B. Only 2
C. Both 1 and 2 are correct
D. Both statements are false

Q.48 Pemba and Zanzibar islands of Africa are known for their cultivation and export?
A. Cloves
B. Sugarcane
C. Tobacco
D. Coffee

Q.49 Which of the main rivers of North America originates in the Rocky mountain range?
1. Mississippi
2. Missouri
3. Colorado
4. Rio Grande
5. Colombia
A. 1, 2 and 3
B. 1, 2, 3 and 4
C. 2, 3 and 5
D. All of the above

Q.50 The heat difference is used for which of the following concepts?
A. Monsoon
B. Jet stream
C. Cyclone
D. Desert storm

Q.51 Frontal fogs are produced in the _____.
A. Low latitudes
B. High latitudes
C. Middle latitudes
D. None of these

Q.52 Which rocks are called primary rocks?
A. Sedimentary rocks
B. Metamorphic rocks
C. Igneous rocks
D. None of the above

Q.53 Indian climate is generally influenced by-
A. Presence of Himalayas in the North
B. Indian ocean in the south
C. Both of the above
D. None of the above

Q.54 What is ITCZ?
A. Intra Tropical Convergence Zone
B. Inter Tropical Convergence Zone
C. International Tropical Convergence Zone
D. None of the above

Q.55 El Nino replaces which current?
A. Greenland
B. Kuroshio
C. Atlantic Ocean
D. Humboldt

Q.56 Black soil is also called-
A. Normal soil
B. Wet soil
C. Regur soil
D. Moist soil

Q.57 Which of the following district are common between Jammu & Kashmir and Pakistan Occupied Kashmir?
A. Poonch
B. Kargil
C. Muzaffarabad
D. Jammu

Q.58 The highest peak in South India is-
A. Anamudi
B. Doddabetta
C. Meesapulimala
D. Ooty

Q.59 In which state Kunchikal Falls located?
A. Kerala
B. Karnataka
C. Tamil Nadu
D. Andhra Pradesh

Q.60 The Iguazu Falls is located in which country?
A. Brazil
B. Ghana
C. Argentina
D. None of these

Q.61 Guwahati is situated on the bank of the river-
A. Teesta
B. Brahmaputra
C. Hooghly
D. Sone

Q.62 What is the time difference (in hours) between GMT and IST (Indian Standard Time)?
A. Five
B. Six
C. Six and a half
D. Five and a half

Q.63 Which State in India is called the 'Land of Five Rivers'?
A. Uttar Pradesh
B. Punjab
C. Haryana
D. Bihar

Q.64 Which city in India is called the 'Lake City'?
A. Udaipur
B. Jaipur
C. Raipur
D. Jodhpur

Q.65 'El Nino' associated with the formation of the South West Monsoon of India is-
A. A periodic low pressure center
B. An abnormally warm ocean current
C. A periodic warm air-mass
D. A periodic warm wind

Q.66 In the interior of the Earth-
A. The temperature rises with increasing depth
B. The temperature falls with increasing depth
C. The pressure falls with increasing depth
D. Both temperature and pressure fall with increasing depth

Q.67 The Marine cliffs are formed mainly due to-
A. Ocean Currents
B. Structure of Shall
C. Coast of Sea
D. Depth of The Ocean

Q.68 Hawaiian islands are located in _____.
A. North Atlantic Ocean
B. South Atlantic Ocean
C. North Pacific Ocean
D. South Pacific Ocean

Q.69 Victoria Falls in Africa are located on _____.
A. Niger River
B. Congo River
C. Zambezi River
D. Nile River

Q.70 The Atlantic Ocean routes are busier than the Pacific Ocean routes because Atlantic Ocean _____.
A. Routes are shorter
B. Routes are not so dangerous

C. Is surrounded on both sides by industrialized nations

D. Has better shipping facilities

Q.71 Agents of fog formation do not include _______.

A. High relative humidity

B. Diurnal temperatures of short ranges

C. Winter season

D. Rapid radiation

Q.72 Which one among the following forces is most powerful in determining movement of wind including its velocity?

A. Gravitational force

B. Centrifugal force

C. Frictional force

D. Pressure gradient force

Q.73 Consider the following rivers-

1. Tapi
2. Mahi
3. Damodar

Which of the above mentioned rivers flow through erratic valleys?

A. Only 1 and 2

B. Only 2 and 3

C. 1, 2 and 3

D. Only 1 and 3

Q.74 Which is the warmest layer of the atmosphere?

A. Thermosphere

B. Troposphere

C. Stratosphere

D. Mesosphere

Q.75 The intensity of insolation depends on-

A. Altitude

B. Nature of terrain

C. Wind

D. The angle

Q.76 In India, the state with highest density of population is-

A. Uttar Pradesh

B. Bihar

C. West Bengal

D. Haryana

Q.77 The Growth rate of population means-

A. Difference between the growth of male and female

B. Difference between the population of urban and rural areas

C. No. of births per thousand persons

D. Difference between birth rate and death rate

Q.78 The tribal population in Andaman and Nicobar Islands belongs to the-

A. Astraloids

B. Caucasoids

C. Mongoloids

D. Negroids

Q.79 The largest population of Scheduled Tribes is in _______.

A. Himachal Pradesh

B. Madhya Pradesh

C. Arunachal Pradesh

D. Sikkim

Q.80 Which of the following is mainly responsible for the lack of female population in India?

A. Political Factors

B. Economic Factors

C. Social Factors

D. Superstitions

Q.81 Dykes are especially constructed in _______.

A. Norway

B. Holland

C. France

D. United Kingdom

Q.82 What is the difference between a geyser and a hot spring?

A. Water is ejected explosively in a geyser

B. Water from the geyser may be cold

C. Geysers are found on volcanic mountains

D. Geysers are more common in cold countries

Q.83 The intensity of earthquakes is measured on _______.

A. Beaufort scale

B. Richter scale

C. Secant scale

D. Mercalli scale

Q.84 The narrow strip of land joining two land masses is called as-

A. Cape

B. Isthmus

C. Strait

D. Peninsula

Q.85 Which of the following is/are the correct characteristic(s) of primary seismic wave?

A. It is a longitudinal and compressional wave

B. It is analogous to sound waves

C. It travels with faster speed through solids but slowly through liquids

D. All the above three

Q.86 The transverse, longitudinal and surface waves in an earthquake originate from _______.

A. The focus within the body of the earth

B. The focus on the surface of the earth

C. The epicenter on the surface of the earth

D. The epicenter within the body of the earth

Q.87 The Base Level concept was postulated by-

A. James Hutton

B. J.W. Powell

C. W.M. Davis

D. Walther Penck

Q.88 Who wrote the book ' Geographia'?

A. Thales

B. Strabo

C. Ptolemy

D. Homer

Q.89 Who among the following geographers laid down the foundation of dichotomy of general versus special Geography?

A. Immanuel Kant

B. Bernhard Varenius

C. Peter Apin

D. Sebastian Munster

Q.90 Who among the following was the author of text on classical astronomy entitled 'Almagest'?

A. Strabo

B. Plato

C. Aristotle

D. Ptolemy

Q.91 The technique of cartography in geography refers to-

A. Geo-Informatics

B. Field Survey methods

C. Skill of Map making

D. Statistical Techniques

Q.92 Stalactites and stalagmites are the depositional features related to which type of landforms?

A. Karst topography

B. Running Water

C. Ocean waves

D. None of these

Q.93 Bio-geography is a sub-branch of geography and is closely related to which field of Science.

A. Physics related to Astronomy
B. Botany related to Ecology
C. Mathematics related to Statistics
D. Geology related to Earth Science

Q.94 Which of the following is a metamorphic rock?

[UP Police Sub Inspector, 2017]

A. Basalt
B. Syenite
C. Gneiss
D. Sand Stone

Q.95 When is the longest day in the southern hemisphere?

A. 21 June
B. 23 September
C. 21 March
D. 22 December

Q.96 The World's major commercial fishing grounds are located in the________.

A. Cool waters of the northern hemisphere in comparatively higher latitudes
B. Equatorial water
C. Temperate waters of tropical seas
D. The warm water of seas in the southern hemisphere

Q.97 The islands of Seychelles are located in the________.

A. Arctic Ocean
B. Atlantic Ocean
C. Indian Ocean
D. Pacific Ocean

Q.98 Lateral Planation Theory of pediment formation was proposed by-

A. Lawson
B. Davis
C. Gilbert
D. McGee

Q.99 Which of the following is formed due to tectonic forces?

A. Rift valley
B. Hanging valley
C. Superimposed valley
D. Antecedent valley

Q.100 Which among the following mountains are formed due to the convergence of one oceanic and one continental plate?

A. Urals
B. Alps
C. Andes
D. Appalachians

Q.101 The slope replacement model was propounded by-

A. Wood
B. Davis
C. Walther Penck
D. Strahler

Q.102 Rainshadow area is associated with which type of rainfall?

A. Convectional rainfall
B. Orographic rainfall
C. Cyclonic rainfall
D. Frontal rainfall

Q.103 Which of the following authors is associated with the concept of Geosyn-cline?

A. Penck and Davis
B. Wooldridge and Morgan
C. Hall and Dana
D. Wooldridge and Lapichan

Q.104 At what concentration (in ppm), is nitrogen present in the atmosphere?

A. 780,840
B. 390,420
C. 78,084
D. 900,000

Q.105 In the lower layers of atmosphere, what range of wavelengths of light is predominant?

A. Less than 100 nm
B. Greater than 300 nm
C. Between 100-300 nm
D. All wavelengths are equally present

Q.106 What is the region of mild and irregular wind in the equatorial region known as?

A. Trade winds
B. Westerlies
C. Doldrums
D. Easterlies

Q.107 Kampala is the capital of which of the following African countries?

A. Uganda
B. Zambia
C. Kenya
D. Angola

Q.108 Which planet is known as the "Bright Wandering Star"?

A. Mars
B. Venus
C. Saturn
D. Jupiter

Q.109 Which is the most abundant metal in the Earth's crust?

A. Silicon
B. Iron
C. Aluminium
D. Zinc

Q.110 Which country has a flag with a pointed Red Maple Leaf?

A. Austria
B. Canada
C. Lebanon
D. Australia

Q.111 What is the reason of Venus being the hottest planet of the Solar system?

A. Proximity to Sun
B. Greenhouse gases in the atmosphere
C. High speed of Rotation
D. Presence of powerful magnetic field

Q.112 The Archipelago Sea is the part of which sea?

A. Arabian Sea
B. Mediterranean Sea
C. Baltic Sea
D. Sea of Japan

Q.113 The Amazon Reef is located in which ocean?

A. Pacific Ocean
B. Indian ocean
C. Atlantic Ocean
D. Arctic Ocean

Q.114 Which is the fastest moving glacier in Kyrgyzstan?

A. Batura Glacier
B. Engilchek Glacier
C. Biafo Glacier
D. Byrd Glacier

Q.115 What is the process where the star gets denser and hotter ultimately changing into helium called?

A. Nuclear Fission
B. Radiation
C. Luminosity
D. Nuclear Fusion

Q.116 In which Eon did the formation of the Moon take place?

A. Hadean
B. Archean
C. Phanerozoic
D. Proterozoic

Q.117 The coastal city of Dublin is located in which among the following countries?

A. Sweden   **B.** France

C. New Zealand   **D.** Ireland

Q.118 The Antrim coast is located in which among the following countries?

A. Sweden   **B.** Australia

C. Norway   **D.** Northern Ireland

Q.119 Which among the following peaks is situated in the Alaskan Range?

A. Mountain Whitney   **B.** Mountain Blanc

C. Mountain Mckinley   **D.** Mountain Elbert

Q.120 Which among the following mountains is also known as the 'Yellow Mountain'?

A. Mount Huang   **B.** Aoraki Mount Cook

C. Mount Kinabalu   **D.** Monte Fitz Roy

Q.121 Which among the following plateaus is called as 'Flood Basalt Plateau'?

A. Colorado Plateau

B. Columbia-Snake Plateau

C. Mexican Plateau

D. Tibetan Plateau

Q.122 At which among the following latitudes do Doldrums lie?

A. 10 degree North and 10 degree South latitudes

B. 35 degree North and 35 degree South latitudes

C. 45 degree North and 45 degree South latitude

D. 90 degree North and 90 degree South latitude

Q.123 Which instrument is used to measure the wind direction?

A. Barometer   **B.** Thermometer

C. Weather vane   **D.** Hygrometer

Q.124 Which is the warmest ocean in the world?

A. Pacific   **B.** Atlantic   **C.** Indian   **D.** Southern

Q.125 Which among the following statements is/are correct about the Sub Tropical High Pressure Belt?

1. It extends near the tropics to about 35 degree North and South Latitudes.

2. Most of the deserts are present along this belt, in both hemispheres.

3. They are also known as Horse Latitudes

Select the correct code from the options given below:

A. Only 1   **B.** Only 1 & 2

C. Only 2 & 3   **D.** 1, 2 & 3

// Smart Answer Sheet //

Correct   Indicates percentage of students who answered questions correctly.

Skipped   Indicates percentage of students who skipped questions.

Q.	Ans.	Correct / Skipped	Q.	Ans.	Correct / Skipped	Q.	Ans.	Correct / Skipped	Q.	Ans.	Correct / Skipped	Q.	Ans.	Correct / Skipped
1	B	46.15 % / 0.0 %	17	B	46.15 % / 50.0 %	33	B	9.62 % / 48.07 %	49	C	11.54 % / 50.0 %	65	B	30.77 % / 50.0 %
2	A	7.69 % / 48.08 %	18	B	34.62 % / 48.07 %	34	B	25.0 % / 50.0 %	50	A	26.92 % / 48.08 %	66	A	46.15 % / 48.08 %
3	B	44.23 % / 48.08 %	19	C	38.46 % / 48.08 %	35	C	46.15 % / 48.08 %	51	B	19.23 % / 48.08 %	67	A	19.23 % / 50.0 %
4	C	32.69 % / 50.0 %	20	C	25.0 % / 48.08 %	36	D	48.08 % / 48.07 %	52	C	50.0 % / 48.08 %	68	C	36.54 % / 50.0 %
5	C	40.38 % / 50.0 %	21	B	36.54 % / 48.08 %	37	C	30.77 % / 50.0 %	53	C	38.46 % / 50.0 %	69	C	36.54 % / 50.0 %
6	A	26.92 % / 48.08 %	22	B	36.54 % / 50.0 %	38	C	17.31 % / 48.07 %	54	B	46.15 % / 48.08 %	70	C	42.31 % / 50.0 %
7	D	40.38 % / 50.0 %	23	D	42.31 % / 48.07 %	39	B	25.0 % / 50.0 %	55	D	44.23 % / 48.08 %	71	B	21.15 % / 48.08 %
8	B	34.62 % / 48.07 %	24	A	40.38 % / 50.0 %	40	B	42.31 % / 50.0 %	56	C	44.23 % / 50.0 %	72	D	25.0 % / 48.08 %
9	A	46.15 % / 50.0 %	25	C	46.15 % / 50.0 %	41	B	42.31 % / 48.07 %	57	A	9.62 % / 50.0 %	73	C	19.23 % / 50.0 %
10	B	40.38 % / 48.08 %	26	A	46.15 % / 50.0 %	42	B	28.85 % / 50.0 %	58	A	40.38 % / 48.08 %	74	A	40.38 % / 48.08 %
11	A	38.46 % / 48.08 %	27	B	40.38 % / 48.08 %	43	C	30.77 % / 48.08 %	59	B	23.08 % / 48.07 %	75	D	36.54 % / 50.0 %
12	C	46.15 % / 48.08 %	28	C	21.15 % / 50.0 %	44	C	15.38 % / 50.0 %	60	D	0 % / 100 %	76	B	42.31 % / 48.07 %
13	D	46.15 % / 48.08 %	29	D	38.46 % / 48.08 %	45	D	13.46 % / 48.08 %	61	B	44.23 % / 50.0 %	77	D	26.92 % / 50.0 %
14	B	44.23 % / 48.08 %	30	B	42.31 % / 48.07 %	46	B	42.31 % / 50.0 %	62	D	48.08 % / 48.07 %	78	D	32.69 % / 48.08 %
15	C	26.92 % / 48.08 %	31	A	42.31 % / 48.07 %	47	C	42.31 % / 48.07 %	63	B	48.08 % / 48.07 %	79	B	42.31 % / 48.07 %
16	A	40.38 % / 48.08 %	32	C	13.46 % / 48.08 %	48	A	30.77 % / 50.0 %	64	A	40.38 % / 50.0 %	80	C	40.38 % / 48.08 %

Q.	Ans.	Correct / Skipped
81	A	26.92 % / 48.08 %
82	A	23.08 % / 48.07 %
83	B	34.62 % / 50.0 %
84	B	38.46 % / 48.08 %
85	D	38.46 % / 50.0 %
86	A	30.77 % / 48.08 %
87	B	32.69 % / 50.0 %
88	B	30.77 % / 50.0 %
89	B	34.62 % / 50.0 %

Q.	Ans.	Correct / Skipped
90	D	28.85 % / 50.0 %
91	C	36.54 % / 50.0 %
92	A	42.31 % / 50.0 %
93	B	44.23 % / 48.08 %
94	C	28.85 % / 50.0 %
95	D	36.54 % / 48.08 %
96	A	19.23 % / 48.08 %
97	C	38.46 % / 50.0 %
98	C	25.0 % / 48.08 %

Q.	Ans.	Correct / Skipped
99	A	42.31 % / 48.07 %
100	C	38.46 % / 48.08 %
101	C	34.62 % / 50.0 %
102	B	28.85 % / 50.0 %
103	C	30.77 % / 50.0 %
104	A	19.23 % / 48.08 %
105	B	9.62 % / 50.0 %
106	C	38.46 % / 50.0 %
107	A	32.69 % / 48.08 %

Q.	Ans.	Correct / Skipped
108	D	3.85 % / 50.0 %
109	C	11.54 % / 48.08 %
110	B	25.0 % / 48.08 %
111	B	26.92 % / 48.08 %
112	C	13.46 % / 50.0 %
113	C	42.31 % / 48.07 %
114	B	9.62 % / 50.0 %
115	D	34.62 % / 48.07 %
116	A	15.38 % / 50.0 %

Q.	Ans.	Correct / Skipped
117	D	32.69 % / 48.08 %
118	D	7.69 % / 48.08 %
119	C	34.62 % / 48.07 %
120	A	15.38 % / 48.08 %
121	B	19.23 % / 48.08 %
122	A	42.31 % / 50.0 %
123	C	34.62 % / 48.07 %
124	C	28.85 % / 50.0 %
125	D	36.54 % / 50.0 %

Performance Analysis

Avg. Score (%)	42.59%
Toppers Score (%)	92.71%
Your Score	

//Hints and Solutions//

1. The layer of atmosphere composed of ionic gaseous molecules helping in propagation of radio waves is Ionosphere. It is the 2nd layer from the top. It ranges from 60km. to 1000km. It also protects Earth from meteorites.

Hence, the correct option is (B).

2. Greywater is gently used water from your bathroom sinks, showers, tubs, and washing machines. It is not water that has come into contact with feces, either from the toilet or from washing diapers. Greywater may contain traces of dirt, food, grease, hair, and certain household cleaning products.

Hence, the correct option is (A).

3. Ganges Delta, officially known as Ganges-Brahmaputra or the Bengal Delta, is located in the Bengal region of Indian subcontinent which consists of the Indian state of West Bengal and the country of Bangladesh. The delta is the largest in the world and one of the most fertile regions of the in the world therefore the name the Green Delta.

Hence, the correct option is (B).

4. The Palk Strait is a strait between the Tamil Nadu state of India and the Mannar district of the Northern Province of the island nation of Sri Lanka.

Hence, the correct option is (C).

5. An atmosphere, meaning is a layer of gases surrounding a planet or other material body, that is held in place by the gravity of that body. Earth also has its own environment due to gravity.

Hence, the correct option is (C).

6. Carbon monoxide (CO) is a colorless, odorless, tasteless, and toxic air pollutant. It is produced in the incomplete combustion of carbon-containing fuels, such as gasoline, natural gas, oil, coal, and wood. Breathing the high concentrations of CO leads to reduced oxygen (O_2) transport by hemoglobin.

Hence, the correct option is (A).

7. About 90% of the ozone in the Earth's atmosphere is found in the region called the Stratosphere. This is the atmospheric layer between 16 and 48 km (10 and 30 miles) above the Earth's surface.

Hence, the correct option is (D).

8. The outermost range of Himalayas is called Shiwaliks. The Shiwaliks Hills, also known as Churia Hills.

Hence, the correct option is (B).

9. India shares a 4,096 km international border with Bangladesh. The terrestrial border of India is 15106.7 km which is in 92 districts of 17 territories. India shares the longest terrestrial border with Bangladesh. India's aquatic border is 7516.6 km, which is in 13 states and union territories.

Hence, the correct option is (A).

10. This causes a complete reversal of the direction of winds during summer. Air moves from the high-pressure area over the southern Indian Ocean, in a south-easterly direction, crosses the equator, and turns right towards the low-pressure areas over the Indian subcontinent. These are known as the Southwest Monsoon winds.

Hence, the correct option is (B).

11. Two giants of 20th-century meteorology, Sir Gilbert Walker and Jacob Bjerknes, are usually given credit for discovering the El Nino-Southern Oscillation phenomenon.

Hence, the correct option is (A).

12. During the months of October November, the southwest monsoon winds become weaker and start to retreat from the skies of North India. This phase of the monsoon is known as the retreating monsoon.

Hence, the correct option is (C).

13. Soil erosion is caused due to erosion by wind and water.

Soil erosion is the displacement of the upper layer of soil, it is a form of soil degradation. This natural process is caused by the dynamic activity of erosive agents, that is, water, ice, wind, plants, animals, and humans.

Hence, the correct option is (D).

14. Alluvial soils are formed mainly due to silt deposited by Indo-Gangetic-Brahmaputra rivers. In coastal regions some alluvial deposits are formed due to wave action. Rocks of the Himalayas form the parent material. Thus the parent material of these soils is of transported origin. They are the largest soil group covering about 15 lakh sq km or about 46 percent of the total area.

Hence, the correct option is (B).

15. Kovvada Atomic Power Project is a proposed 6,600 MW nuclear power station in the state of Andhra Pradesh, India. The project is planned over an area of 2067 acres.

Hence, the correct option is (C).

16. Greenland is the worlds largest island with an total area of 836,109 sq miles (2,166,086 sq km).

Hence, the correct option is (A).

17. The NandaDevi National Park, established in 1982, is a national park situated around the peak of Nanda Devi (7816 m) in the state of Uttarakhand in northern India.

Hence, the correct option is (B).

18. Natural Gas is a conventional source of energy and not a non-conventional source of energy.

Hence, the correct option is (B).

19. The dew point is the temperature to which air must be cooled to become saturated with water vapor. When further cooled, the airborne water vapor will condense to form liquid water.

Hence, the correct option is (C).

20. A radiation inversion commonly occurs when the evening air is still and there are no clouds to trap heat. Surface temperature drops as longwave radiation emitted by the Earth escapes to space. Since a land surface radiates more heat than the air, ground is cooled more rapidly than the air at great heights during night time. Consequently the coldest air lies at the ground and is overlaid by warmer air.

Hence, the correct option is (C).

21. Relative humidity is the ratio of the current absolute humidity to the highest possible absolute humidity (which depends on the current air temperature). A reading of 100 percent relative humidity means that the air is totally saturated with water vapor and cannot hold any more, creating the possibility of rain.

Hence, the correct option is (B).

22. Marble is a metamorphic rock that forms when limestone is subjected to the heat and pressure of metamorphism. It is composed primarily of the mineral calcite ($CaCO_3$) and usually contains other minerals, such as clay minerals, micas, quartz, pyrite, iron oxides, and graphite.

Hence, the correct option is (B).

23. Loess is mostly created by wind, but can also be formed by glaciers. When glaciers grind rocks to a fine powder, loess can form. Streams carry the powder to the end of the glacier.

Hence, the correct option is (D).

24. At Barren Island, the only active volcano in India is situated in Andaman Islands. Barren Island is situated in the Andaman Sea, and lies about 138 km (86 miles) northeast of the territory's capital, Port Blair. It is the only active Volcano along the chain from Sumatra to Myanmar and also the only active volcano in India.

Hence, the correct option is (A).

25. The ozone layer is a region of Earth's stratosphere that absorbs most of the Sun's ultraviolet (UV) radiation. The depletion in Ozone layer is caused by Chlorofluorocarbons.

Hence, the correct option is (C).

26. Fold mountains are mountains formed from the folding of the earth's crust. Fold mountains are formed when two plates move together (a compressional plate margin). This can be where two continental plates move towards each other or a continental and an oceanic plate. The Himalayas is the example of Fold mountains.

Hence, the correct option is (A).

27. The Ganges River originates from the Gangotri Glacier in Uttarakhand, with a total length of 2,525 km. Through Bangladesh, it falls in the Bay of Bengal.

Hence, the correct option is (B).

28. The Malwa plateau is spread across Rajasthan, Madhya Pradesh and Gujarat. Its total area is about 81,767 square kilometers. The Malwa plateau is a triangular plateau at the base of the Vindhya hills. It is a lava plateau. To its east lies Bundelkhand and the Aravalli hills in the north-west.

Hence, the correct option is (C).

29. Chilka Lake is the largest saltwater lake in India, the lake is spread over an area of about 1,100 square kilometers. This lake is located in Odisha.

Hence, the correct option is (D).

30. This transfer is shifting cultivation, it is called Milpa in Mexico, Conuco in Venezuela, Roca in Brazil, Masole in Central Africa and Ray in Vietnam.

Hence, the correct option is (B).

31. Arthur Holmes postulated convection current theory in the year 1928–29. It is widely accepted driving mechanism for continental drift(moving apart) which lead to the foundation of modern plate tectonics. His main objective was to find the scientific explanation of origin of the continent and oceans. But it is also widely accepted concept of mountain building.

Hence, the correct option is (A).

32. The Babli project / dam is being built by the Government of Maharashtra on the Godavari River, there is a dispute between Maharashtra, Andhra Pradesh and Telangana over the sharing of water on this project.

Hence, the correct option is (C).

33. The Matbhanga River passes through Krishnaganj in India, this river is divided into several parts.

Hence, the correct option is (B).

34. Manikaran hot water source is located on the banks of river Parvati in Kullu district of Himachal Pradesh, this hot water source is considered useful in the treatment of skin diseases.

Hence, the correct option is (B).

35. India is the third largest salt producer in the world, India produces 160 million tonnes of salt. Gujarat, Rajasthan, Andhra Pradesh and Tamil Nadu are the largest salt producing states in India.

Hence, the correct option is (C).

36. The Indira Gandhi Canal is the longest canal in India and the largest irrigation project in the world. Indira Gandhi Canal is 649 km long and consists of Rajasthan feeder canal and Rajasthan main canal and runs through 167 km in Punjab and Haryana and remaining 492 km in Rajasthan.

Hence, the correct option is (D).

37. On 20 February, 1987, Arunachal Pradesh was accorded full statehood, before which Arunachal Pradesh was a union territory.

Hence, the correct option is (C).

38. It is dependent on coconut from the industry Kerala produces 60% of the world's total production of white coir.

Hence, the correct option is (C).

39. The total coastline of India is 7,517 km. The coastline of peninsular India is 5,423 km while the coastline of Andaman Islands and Lakshadweep is 2,049 km.

Hence, the correct option is (B).

40. National Highway 7 has now been renamed as National Highway 44. The highway starts from Srinagar in Jammu and Kashmir to Kanyakumari in South India. Its total length is 3,745 km.

Hence, the correct option is (B).

41. Talcher Thermal Power Plant is located in Angul district of Odisha. This power plant was commissioned in February 1968. It has a power generation capacity of 460 MW.

Hence, the correct option is (B).

42. The Tundra region is located near the North Pole, due to the extreme cold climate at this place, only a limited number of vegetation is available here.

Hence, the correct option is (B).

43. The vast Gangetic plains in North India are the largest alluvium deposits in the world, fertile soil is deposited on it by rivers flowing from the Himalayas. Khadar region is formed from new aluvium, it is a low altitude area.

Hence, the correct option is (C).

44. 60% of the total area of Rajasthan is located in the Thar Desert.

The Thar Desert is the world's 10 largest desert. This desert is spread over an area of about 2,00,000 sq km in the Indian subcontinent.

Hence, the correct option is (C).

45. The Dampier-Hodges line is a hypothetical line, drawn in 1829-30, which shows the northern boundary of the Sundarbans delta. The line lies parallel to the 24 Parganas district of West Bengal.

Hence, the correct option is (D).

46. Helmand province of Afghanistan is famous for opium cultivation.

Helmand is located in the south of Afghanistan, it is the largest province in Afghanistan by area. The total area of Helmand province is 58,584 sq km. It is the world's largest opium-producing region, 75% of the world's total production of opium is produced in Helmand.

Hence, the correct option is (B).

47. The Balearic Islands is part of Spain, the islands are located in the Mediterranean Sea, its total area is 4,992 sq km. Sardinia is the second largest island in the geo-central sea after Cecily, it is the autonomous region of Italy.

Hence, the correct option is (C).

48. Pemba Island is located in the Swahili coastline in the Indian Ocean. Zanzibar is a semi-autonomous region of Tanzania, famous for the production and export of cloves.

Hence, the correct option is (A).

49. The Missouri River is the longest river in North America, originating in western Montana. The Colorado River is 1,450 kilometers in length, flowing into the United States and Mexico.

The Columbia River originates from British Columbia in Canada, the river flows into the United States and Canada.

Hence, the correct option is (C).

50. The monsoon originates due to uneven temperatures at the site and water area. The air pressure is low due to the high temperature in the site, while the pressure in the aquatic area is relatively high. Air flows from the area of high pressure to the area of low air pressure.

Hence, the correct option is (A).

51. Frontal fog forms near a front when raindrops, falling from relatively warm air above a frontal surface, evaporate into cooler air close to the Earth's surface and cause it to become saturated. The visibility in an ice fog is often considerably worse than that in a water fog containing the same concentration of condensed water.

Hence, the correct option is (B).

52. Igneous rocks are formed from magma, the molten material from the center of the Earth. Igneous rocks begin the rock cycle, and are therefore called primary rocks.

Hence, the correct option is (C).

53. India's climate is strongly influenced by the Oceans, Himalayas and the Thar Desert. The Himalayas act as a barrier to the frigid katabatic winds flowing down from Central Asia keeping the bulk of the Indian subcontinent warmer than most locations at similar latitudes. The climate of India may be broadly described as tropical monsoon type. India's climate is affected by two seasonal winds viz. the north-east monsoon and the south-west monsoon.

Hence, the correct option is (C).

54. The Inter Tropical Convergence Zone, or ITCZ, is a belt of low pressure which circles the Earth generally near the equator where the trade winds of the Northern and Southern Hemispheres come together. It is characterized by convective activity which generates often vigorous thunderstorms over large areas. It is most active over continental land masses by day and relatively less active over the oceans.

Hence, the correct option is (B).

55. The Humboldt Current, also called the Peru Current, is a cold, low-salinity ocean current that flows north along the western coast of South America. Normally, for a period of just a few weeks around Christmas each year, this cold water is replaced by a warm current. This event is called El Nino, also known as "the little boy." Every 2 to 7 years, however, this warm water event lasts much longer and is much more pronounced. Then it is called a major El Nino event.

Hence, the correct option is (D).

56. Black soil is also called Regur soil. It is black in colour and ideal for growing cotton. This type of soil is typical of the Deccan trap (Basalt) region spread over North-West Deccan plateau and is made up of lava flows.

Hence, the correct option is (C).

57. District Poonch or Punch is one of the most remote districts of Jammu and Kashmir. It is bounded by the Line of Control (boundary between Indian and Pakistan-administered Kashmir) on three sides (north, west and south).

Hence, the correct option is (A).

58. Anamudi is the highest peak in the Western Ghats in India, having an elevation of 2,695 meters (8,842 ft). Anamudi is also the highest point in South India.

Hence, the correct option is (A).

59. Kunchikal Falls is located in Nidagodu village near Masthikatte in Shimoga district of state Karnataka. Kunchikal Falls is formed by the River Varahi.

Hence, the correct option is (B).

60. Iguazu Falls, in the Iguazu River, are one of the world's largest waterfalls. They extend over 2,700 m (nearly 2 miles) in a semi-circular shape. Iguazu Falls are on the border between the Brazilian state of Parana and the Argentine province of Misiones.

Hence, the correct option is (D).

61. Guwahati (Pragjyotishpura in ancient Assam, Gauhati in the modern era) is the largest city in the Indian state of Assam and also the largest urban area in Northeast India. A major riverine port city and one of the fastest growing cities in India, Guwahati is situated on the south bank of the Brahmaputra.

Hence, the correct option is (B).

62. GMT stands for Greenwich Mean/Meridian Time and IST stands for Indian Standard Time. India Standard Time (IST) is 5:30 hours (5 hours 30 minutes) ahead of Greenwich Mean Time (GMT+5.5).

Hence, the correct option is (D).

63. It is named so because of the five rivers flowing through this land and these five rivers of Punjab are Sutlej, Beas, Ravi, Chenab and Jhelum.

Hence, the correct option is (B).

64. Udaipur City, formally known as the city of lakes and Venice of East. Udaipur, the capital of the former princely state of Mewar is a beautiful city in Rajasthan, India. Udaipur is also referred to as the "Venice of the East", the "Most Romantic City of India" and the "Kashmir of Rajasthan".

Hence, the correct option is (A).

65. Collectively, El Nino and La Nina are parts of an oscillation in the ocean-atmosphere system called the El Nino-Southern Oscillation. El Nino Southern Oscillation refers to the cycle of warm and cold temperatures, as measured by sea surface temperature, SST, of the tropical central and eastern Pacific Ocean.

Hence, the correct option is (B).

66. Structure of earth's interior is fundamentally divided into three layers – crust, mantle and core. A rise in temperature with increase in depth is observed in mines and deep wells. These evidence along with molten lava erupted from the earth's interior

supports that the temperature increases towards the center of the earth. Just like the temperature, the pressure is also increasing from the surface towards the center of the earth.

Hence, the correct option is (A).

67. The Marine cliffs are formed mainly due to Ocean Currents. Moving water works as degradational agent (erosional). As oceanic currents move constantly in their definite path. They erode away rock against which they strike.

Hence, the correct option is (A).

68. The main Hawaiian Islands are a group of inhabited islands situated in the northern Pacific Ocean.

Hence, the correct option is (C).

69. Victoria Falls is one of the greatest attractions in Africa and one of the most spectacular waterfalls in the world, Victoria Falls is located on the Zambezi River , the fourth largest river in Africa, which is also defining the border between Zambia and Zimbabwe.

Hence, the correct option is (C).

70. The Atlantic Ocean routes are busier than the Pacific Ocean routes because Atlantic Ocean is surrounded on both sides by industrialized nations. The Atlantic ocean is the second largest ocean basin only behind the pacific ocean. Its bounded by North and South Americas in the west and Africa and Europe in the east. It also boasts of being the busiest ocean in the world.

Hence, the correct option is (C).

71. Agents of fog formation do not include Diurnal temperatures of short ranges. Diurnal temperature range (DTR) is defined as the difference between daily maximum and minimum temperature, which describes the within-day temperature variability and reflects weather stability.

Hence, the correct option is (B).

72. Pressure gradient force is most powerful in determining movement of wind including its velocity. Wind is the movement of air across the Earth's surface and is produced by differences in air pressure between one place to another.

Hence, the correct option is (D).

73. Narmada, Tapi, Mahi and Damodar, all these rivers flow through the rift valleys. Hence option C is correct. The Narmada River flows westwards into the Bhrush valley, located between the Satpura and Vindhya ranges. The Damodar River flows through the Bhrush Valley located in the Chota Nagpur Plateau. The Tapti and Mahi rivers also flow through fault basins between different ranges.

Hence, the correct option is (C).

74. The thermosphere is a layer of Earth's atmosphere. The thermosphere is directly above the mesosphere and below the exosphere. It extends from about 90 km (56 miles) to between 500 and 1,000 km (311 to 621 miles) above our planet. Based on the vertical temperature profile in the atmosphere, the thermosphere is the highest layer, located above the mesosphere.

Hence, the correct option is (A).

75. Factors influencing insolation Depending on the level of sunlight at the horizon, insolation depends on solar elevation, or the angle created by solar rays on the horizon. The intensity of insolation on a horizontal surface is inversely proportional to the sine of this angle.

Hence, the correct option is (D).

76. In India, the state with highest density of Population is Bihar. Bihar with 1,106 population persons per sq.km is most thickly populated state followed by West Bengal (1,028) and Kerala (860).

Hence, the correct option is (B).

77. The Growth rate of population means difference between birth rate and death rate. Population can be said to be growing when number of individuals increase in it. It can be best calculated by calculating difference between birth rate and death rate.

Hence, the correct option is (D).

78. The tribal population in Andaman and Nicobar Islands belongs to the Negroids. Negroids is a grouping of human beings historically regarded as a biological taxon. The term has been used by forensic and physical anthropologists to refer to individuals and populations that share morphological and skeletal traits.

Hence, the correct option is (D).

79. The largest population of Scheduled Tribes is in Madhya Pradesh. Madhya Pradesh has the largest Tribal population. It has more than 1.6 crore Schedule Tribe population whom are 21% of state population according to 2011 census.

Hence, the correct option is (B).

80. Social factors are mainly responsible for the lack of female population in India. Social factors such as dowry and patriarchal mindset along with other prejudices are responsible for lack of population of females.

Hence, the correct option is (C).

81. Dykes are especially constructed in Norway. Dike, also called dyke are tabular or sheet like igneous body that is often oriented vertically or steeply inclined to the bedding of pre-existing intruded rocks; similar bodies oriented parallel to the bedding of the enclosing rocks are called sills.

Hence, the correct option is (A).

82. Water is ejected explosively in a geyser. The big difference between a geyser and a hot spring is that a geyser has an obstruction in its hydrothermal plumbing near the surface. In hot springs, water is allowed to circulate to the surface and move freely, giving off steam and heat. In geysers, constrictions keep the boiling water underground.

Hence, the correct option is (A).

83. The intensity of an earthquake is measured on the Richter scale. The Richter scale is a mathematical scale used to measure the intensity of earthquake waves. The simple logarithm of the ratio of the maximum amplitude of the earth's vibration at the time of an earthquake and a random (arbitrary) small amplitude is called the 'Richter scale'. The Richter scale was developed in the 1130s.

Hence, the correct option is (B).

84. The narrow strip of land joining two land masses is called as Isthmus. Isthmus is a narrow strip of land (with water on both sides) connecting two larger land areas. Isthmus of Panama connects South America and North America, while Isthmus of suez connects Asia and Africa.

Hence, the correct option is (B).

85. The characteristic(s) of primary seismic wave are that it is a longitudinal and compressional wave, it is analogous to sound waves and it travels with faster speed through solids but slowly through liquids. Primary waves (P- waves) are compressional waves that are longitudinal in nature.

Hence, the correct option is (D).

86. The transverse, longitudinal and surface waves in an earthquake originate from the focus within the body of the earth. The epicenter of an earthquake sends out waves which are like an object dropped on to a still body of water that sends out ripples. After the stone hits the water ripples move outwards from the center in every direction. An earthquake releases energy as shock waves, the so-called seismic waves, which ripple across the earth's surface.

Hence, the correct option is (A).

87. The first formal statement and naming of the concept was by J. W. Powell in 1875, who wrote "We may consider the level of the sea to be a grand base level, below which the drylands cannot be eroded, but we may also have, for local and temporary purposes, other base levels of erosion, which are the levels of the beds."

Hence, the correct option is (B).

88. The 'Geographia' or Geography, is an encyclopedia of geographical knowledge, consisting of 17 'books', written in Greek and attributed to Strabo, an educated citizen of the Roman Empire of Greek descent.

Hence, the correct option is (B).

89. Bernhard Varenius laid down the foundation of dichotomy of general versus special Geography .In the development of the scientific geographical thought was the work of Bernhard Varenius (1622-1650) who profoundly influenced the content and scope of geography for more than a century. Varenius started work on his famous work Geographia generalis in the fall of 1649 and completed it in the spring of 1650. It is sometimes said that his Geographia generalis was a legitimate successor of Munster's 'Cosmographia Universalis'.

Hence, the correct option is (B).

90. The 'Almagest' is a 2nd-century Greek-language mathematical and astronomical treatise on the apparent motions of the stars and planetary paths, written by Claudius Ptolemy (c. AD 100 – c. 170). One of the most influential scientific texts of all time, it canonized a geocentric model of the Universe that was accepted for more than 1200 years from its origin in Hellenistic Alexandria, in the medieval Byzantine and Islamic worlds, and in Western Europe through the Middle Ages and early Renaissance until Copernicus. It is also a key source of information about ancient Greek astronomy.

Hence, the correct option is (D).

91. Cartography, the art and science of graphically representing a geographical area, usually on a flat surface such as a map or chart. It may involve the superimposition of political, cultural, or other non-geographical divisions onto the representation of a geographical area.

Hence, the correct option is (C).

92. Stalactites and stalagmites are the depositional features related to Karst topography.

Stalactites: It is a type of rock formation produced by the precipitation of minerals from water dripping through the cave ceiling. It hangs from the ceiling of a cave.

Stalagmites: It is a type of rock formation that rises from the floor of a cave due to the accumulation of material deposited on the floor from ceiling drippings.

Karst topography is formed due to excavating effects of underground water on massive soluble limestone. It is usually characterized by barren, rocky ground, caves, sinkholes, underground rivers.

Hence, the correct option is (A).

93. Ecology deals with the mutual relationships and interactions between organisms and their physical environment. The physical factors of the atmosphere, the climate, and the soil affect the physiological functions of the plant in all its manifestations, so that, to a large degree, plant ecology is a phase of plant physiology under natural and uncontrolled conditions.

Hence, the correct option is (B).

94. Gneiss usually forms by regional metamorphism at convergent plate boundaries.

- It is a high-grade metamorphic rock in which mineral grains are recrystallized under intense heat and pressure.
- Basalt is a dark-colored, fine-grained, igneous rock composed mainly of plagioclase and pyroxene minerals. Syenite is an intrusive igneous rock composed of feldspar and a ferromagnesian mineral.
- Chemically, syenites contain a moderate amount of silica, relatively large amounts of alkalies, and alumina.
- Sandstone is a sedimentary rock composed mostly of quartz sand.
- Sandstone that contains more than 90% quartz is called quartzose sandstone.
- When the sandstone contains more than 25% feldspar, it is called arkose or arkosic sandstone.

Hence, the correct option is (C).

95. December 22 is the longest day in the southern hemisphere. This is due to the rays of the Sun falling directly on the Tropic of Capricorn on 22 December. The longest day in the northern hemisphere is on 21 June. This is due to the direct fall of the sun's rays on the Tropic of Cancer on 21 June.

Hence, the correct option is (D).

96. The World's Ocean Fishing grounds are located in the cool waters of the northern hemisphere because in the southern hemisphere commercial ocean fishing is less developed and the best fishing grounds founded above continental shelves.

Hence, the correct option is (A).

97. Seychelles, island republic in the western Indian Ocean, comprising about 115 islands, with lush tropical vegetation, beautiful beaches, and a wide variety of marine life.

Hence, the correct option is (C).

98. The lateral planation theory of pediment formation was proposed by Gilbert. Pediments are highly evident in dry climates. It is essential to know that it has led to an extremely dry climate mechanism.

Hence, the correct option is (C).

99. Rift Valley, in terms of the theory of plate tectonics, occurs in divergence zones where two of the various lithospheric plates that make up the Earth's surface are separating. Numerous submarine rift valleys have been discovered along the crests of the large ridges that run throughout the Earth's oceans.

Hence, the correct option is (A).

100. The Andes were formed by tectonic activity whereby Earth is uplifted as one plate (oceanic crust) subducts under another plate (continental crust). To get such a high mountain chain in a subduction zone setting is unusual, which adds to the importance of trying to figure out when and how it happened. The Andes, running along South America's western side, is among the world's longest mountain ranges.

Hence, the correct option is (C).

101. Slope replacement first proposed by Walther Penck challenging Davis' ideas on slope development. Slope replacement describes an evolution of slopes that is associated with decreasing rates of overall erosion (denudation).

Hence, the correct option is (C).

102. The rainshadow area is associated with Orographic rainfall. When the saturated air is obstructed by a landform barrier such as a mountain, it forced to ascend and as it rises, it expands and the temperature falls. As a result, condensation takes place and rainfall occurs. In this type of presentation, the windward slope of the mountain receives maximum rain and the leeward slope remains generally drier and is known as the rain shadow area.

Hence, the correct option is (B).

103. The Geosyn-cline concept was first conceived by the American geologists James Hall and James Dwight Dana in the mid-19th century, during the classic studies of the Appalachian

Mountains. Emile Haug further developed the geosyncline concept and introduced it to Europe in 1900.

Hence, the correct option is (C).

104. Nitrogen constitutes 78% of the atmosphere. So 78% of one million = 780,840 ppm – is the concentration of nitrogen gas in the atmosphere.

Hence, the correct option is (A).

105. In the lower layers of atmosphere, light of wavelengths greater than 300nm are present and it is because of this reason, there is generally no ozone formation at the ground level.

Hence, the correct option is (B).

106. Doldrums are irregular winds and their exact location is hard to analyze. Ships in the region of doldrums might restrict their movement due to a lack of proper wind.

Hence, the correct option is (C).

107. Kampala is Uganda's national and commercial capital. It borders Lake Victoria, which is Africa's largest lake. Ugandan shilling (UGX) is the currency.

Hence, the correct option is (A).

108. Jupiter is the fourth brightest object in the sky (after the Sun, the Moon and Venus). It has been known since prehistoric times as a "bright wandering star".

Hence, the correct option is (D).

109. Aluminium is the most abundant metal in the earth's crust. Oxygen is the most abundant element in the earth's crust.

Hence, the correct option is (C).

110. Canadian Flag is also known as Maple Leaf Flag. It consists of a red field with a white square at its center having an 11-pointed red maple leaf.

Hence, the correct option is (B).

111. Venus has surface temperatures over 400 °C and it is the hottest planet of Solar system , most likely due to the amount of greenhouse gases in the atmosphere.

Hence, the correct option is (B).

112. The Archipelago Sea is a part of the Baltic Sea and it is the second largest archipelago in the world comprising around 40,000 islands, islets and reefs. It is located between The Gulf of Bothnia, the Gulf of Finland and the Sea of Aland.

Hence, the correct option is (C).

113. The Amazon Reef is located in the Atlantic Ocean, off the coast of French Guiana and Brazil. It is a coral and sponge reef system. It happens to be one of the largest known reef systems in the world.

Hence, the correct option is (C).

114. Engilchek Glacier is the largest and fastest moving glacier in Kyrgyzstan. It is located in the Central Tian Shan Mountains of Issyk-Kul region of northeastern Kyrgyzstan. Also, it is the sixth longest non polar glacier in the world.

Hence, the correct option is (B).

115. When the core of the star is hot enough, Nuclear Fusion takes place. Fusion is the process where two hydrogen atoms combine to form a helium atom, releasing energy.

Hence, the correct option is (D).

116. The formation of the Moon took place in the Hadean Eon (around 4533- 4527 million years ago).

Hence, the correct option is (A).

117. The coastal city, Dublin is the cultural capital of Ireland. It has more green space per kilometer than any other European city. It is famous for the Guinness Brewery.

Hence, the correct option is (D).

118. The Antrim coast is located in Northern Ireland. It is best known for the Giant Causeway, a UNESCO World Heritage site.

Hence, the correct option is (D).

119. Mountain Mckinley is also known as Denali is the highest peak in North America. It is situated in the Alaskan Range in North America.

Hence, the correct option is (C).

120. Mount Huang also known as Huangshan or the 'Yellow Mountain' is located in eastern China. Lotus peak is the tallest peak in the Huangshan mountain range.

Hence, the correct option is (A).

121. The Columbia-Snake Plateau in Washington, Oregon, and Idaho (USA) is formed due to volcanic eruptions with a consequent coating of basalt lave. Hence it is called as 'Flood Basalt Plateau'.

Hence, the correct option is (B).

122. The equatorial low-pressure belt lies between 10 degrees N and 10 degree S latitudes. This belt is also called the Doldrums because of the extremely calm air movements. This belt is the zone of convergence of trade winds from two hemispheres from sub-tropical high-pressure belts. It is characterized by extremely low pressure with calm conditions.

Hence, the correct option is (A).

123. Wind is an air movement having both direction and speed. The direction of the wind is measured by a conventional instrument called weather vane or the wind vane.

Hence, the correct option is (C).

124. The Indian Ocean is the warmest ocean in the world. Long-term ocean temperature records show a rapid, continuous warming in the Indian Ocean, at about 1.2 °C. Human induced greenhouse warming, and changes in the frequency and magnitude of El Nino (or the Indian Ocean Dipole), events are a trigger to this strong warming in the Indian Ocean.

Hence, the correct option is (C).

125. Sub Tropical High Pressure Belt extend near the tropics to about 35 degree North and South Latitudes. The high pressure

along this belt is due to subsidence of air coming from the equatorial region which descends after becoming heavy.

Hence, the correct option is (D).

Q.1 Who first used the term 'Geographica' for geography?
A. Hecataeus
B. Herodotus
C. Eratosthenes
D. Aristotle

Q.2 "Human geography is the study of the interchangeable relations between the floating earth and the fickle human." Whose statement is this?
A. Blache
B. Huntington
C. Alan Sample
D. Humboldt

Q.3 "The present is the key to the past." Which scholar has the statement?
A. Dutton
B. James Hutton
C. Davis
D. Walter Pank

Q.4 Who is the proponent of the ideology of 'Stop and Go Determinism'?
A. A.J. Herbertson
B. George Tatham
C. Hartshorne
D. Griffith Taylor

Q.5 Who is the scholar defining geography as 'human ecology'?
A. Vidal de La Blache
B. Jean Brunhes
C. Hetzner
D. H.H. Barrows

Q.6 "If history presents a scientific study of 'when', then geography makes a scientific and logical study of 'where'." Which of the following scholars is the statement?
A. Carl Seaver
B. N.J. Spykman
C. H.J. Mackinder
D. D.H. Whiteley

Q.7 Who is called the 'father of geography'?
A. Herodotus
B. Aristotle
C. Eratosthenes
D. Hecataeus

Q.8 "Structure is a byproduct of structure, process and condition." Whose statement is this?
A. Walter Pank
B. W.M. Davis
C. L.C. King
D. Peltier

Q.9 Who is considered the father of Geomorphology?
A. Davis
B. Peshal
C. Pank
D. Hutton

Q.10 Which of the following scholars is credited with establishing geography as a separate study scripture?
A. Eratosthenes
B. Hipparchus
C. Hecataeus
D. Herodotus

Q.11 The device that measures the direction and speed of clouds is called:
A. Anemometer
B. Rengage
C. Nephoscope
D. Hygrometer

Q.12 Relative humidity is shown on which of the following graphs?
A. Barograph
B. Climograph
C. Heathergraph
D. Hipsometric graph

Q.13 Which of the following is a geosynchronous satellite?
A. Landset
B. Mitioset
C. IRS
D. Kitset

Q.14 What does a seismograph record?
A. Heartbeat
B. Atmospheric pressure
C. Earthquake intensity
D. None of these

Q.15 Which of the following is measured with a lysometer?
A. Atmospheric humidity
B. Direction and speed of clouds
C. Amount of solar radiation
D. The amount of endocrine water going down through the soil

Q.16 Which is the most extensive geomorphic region of India?
A. Greater Northern Field
B. Great Indian Plateau
C. Greater Himalayas
D. Sea coast

Q.17 The territories determined on the basis of relationship are called:
A. Natural state
B. Nodal state
C. Planning state
D. Developing state

Q.18 Which of the following would be an ideal adjustment for the establishment of an iron-steel industry?
A. Coal power market
B. Coal-iron ore-water
C. Electro-hydro-iron ore
D. Coal-water-cotton

Q.19 Seasonal conditions, net area, crop etc. can be shown simultaneously:
A. At heathergraph
B. At ergograph
C. At climograph
D. At bandgraph

Q.20 The geometry of the sky is measured by which of the blue instruments?
A. Cyanometer
B. Actinometer
C. Clinometer
D. Pyrometer

Q.21 What are the lines that display the salinity of oceans and oceans on a map?
A. Isotherm
B. Isobar
C. Isoheline
D. Isohyte

Q.22 What is the line joining the places coming at the same time of the earthquake?
A. Isosismal
B. Homosomal
C. Isobrant
D. Isogonal

Q.23 What is the line joining the locations of seismic intensity similarities?

A. Isogonal

B. Homosismal

C. Isosismal

D. Isohel

Q.24 Which one of the following earthquakes occurred in India was highly devastating and destructive?

A. Kangra Earthquake of 1905

B. Bihar earthquake of 1934

C. Gujarat earthquake of 2001

D. Koyna earthquake of 1967

Q.25 What is the boundary line classifying places of similar language in a state?

A. Isopaiknik

B. Isonif

C. Contour

D. Isogloss

Q.26 Taking Economic Reforms in India:

I. Towards concentration of economic activities.

II. Towards a growing gap between rich and poor people.

III. Towards a relatively high growth rate of metropolitan areas.

IV. Towards low cost accessibility of urban facilities and services.

A. I and II are correct

B. I, II and III are correct

C. II and IV are correct

D. I, III and IV are correct

Q.27 Lines called isotherms are drawn to represent the locations on the map where:

A. Temperature remains the same

B. Pressure remains the same

C. Have the same salinity

D. Is the same height

Q.28 Who said that according to the action of regeneration, the shield lanes are advanced or flat or concave?

A. Davis

B. Pank

C. Johnson

D. Wood

Q.29 Which of the following theory of plate tectonics is not helpful in clarifying its origin and location?

A. Earthquake

B. Mountains

C. Sea currents

D. Characteristics of Major Sea Levels

Q.30 Which of the following wind falls in the area of Headley Cell?

A. Monsoon winds

B. Trade winds

C. West winds

D. Polar winds

Q.31 The event of a diamond ring occurs:

A. Every full moon day

B. On every new moon day

C. Solar eclipse day

D. Lunar eclipse day

Q.32 If the atmosphere between the Earth and space is considered to be removed, what will be the color of the sky?

A. Blue

B. Red

C. White

D. Black

Q.33 Planets smaller in size than Earth are:

A. Arun and Mangal

B. Varun and Venus

C. Venus and Mars

D. Varun and Mangal

Q.34 Who among the following said for the first time that the Earth is round?

A. Aristotle

B. Copernicus

C. Strabo

D. No one

Q.35 The circumference of the Earth is:

A. 35,000 km

B. 40,075 km

C. 45,000 km

D. 47,050 km

Q.36 The term adiabatic changes in temperature means:

A. Temperature drop after precipitation

B. Heating and cooling of ascending or descending air through compression and expansion

C. Ascending wind heating

D. Descending wind cooling

Q.37 When is the minimum distance between the Sun and the Earth?

A. On 22 December

B. On 21 June

C. On 22 September

D. On 3 January

Q.38 Who first proposed that the Sun is the center of our solar system and the Earth revolves around it?

A. Newton

B. Galileo

C. Panini

D. Copernicus

Q.39 What is the distance of the Earth from the Sun?

A. 149 million km

B. 150 million km

C. 227 million km

D. 300 million km

Q.40 The main gases besides volcanoes in volcanoes are:

A. Nitrogen, oxygen

B. Hydrogen, oxygen

C. Carbon dioxide, hydrogen, nitrogen

D. Sulfur dioxide, carbon dioxide, nitrogen

Q.41 What percentage of the Earth's total volume is found in the mantle?

A. 32%

B. 52%

C. 68%

D. 83%

Q.42 Where is Moho disambiguation located?

A. Between crust and mantle

B. Between mantle and core

C. Between upper mantle and lower mantle

D. Between internal mantle and external mantle

Q.43 What is the rate of increase in temperature with depth when moving from ground to ground?

A. $1°C$ per 165 m

B. $1°C$ per 165 feet

C. $1°C$ per 32 m

D. $1°C$ per 32 feet

Q.44 Which of the following elements predominate in the mantle?

A. Silica and manganese

B. Silica and aluminum

C. Silica and magnesium
D. Silica and iron

Q.45 By whom is the division of geology in the form of sial, boundary and nifa?
A. By Van Dergrat
B. By Deli
C. By Holmes
D. By Sves

Q.46 What is the correct descending order of the quantities of different elements found in the earth's crust?
A. Oxygen, silicon, iron, aluminum
B. Silicon, oxygen, aluminum, iron
C. Iron, silicon, oxygen, aluminum
D. Oxygen, silicon, aluminum, iron

Q.47 What is included in the venue?
A. Upper Terrain Only
B. Both the upper surface and the lower surface
C. Upper surface, lower surface and concrete upper part of mantle
D. None of the above

Q.48 The metamorphic form of Lime Stone is:
A. Marble
B. Slate
C. Granite
D. Quartzite

Q.49 Which of the following is not a flake rock?
A. Gypsum
B. Conglomerate
C. Dolomite
D. Slate

Q.50 What is the source of the most important information regarding the internal structure of the Earth?
A. Unnatural means
B. Seismology
C. Volcanic action
D. Plate tectonics

Q.51 Australia is the highest mountain peak in the continent:
A. Mount Koziasco
B. Mount Vinson massif
C. Mount Mckinley
D. Mount Elbrush

Q.52 Which one of the following is known as 'island continent'?
A. Asia
B. Europe
C. Australia
D. Antarctica

Q.53 Europe is the largest lake on the continent:
A. Onega Lake
B. Ladoga Lake
C. Cyma complex
D. None of these

Q.54 North America is the largest lake on the continent:
A. Superior Lake
B. Huron Lake
C. Michigan Lake
D. Great Bear Lake

Q.55 The highest mountain of the continent of Antarctica is _____ peak:
A. Mount Elbrush
B. Mount Mckinley
C. Mount Acancagua
D. Mount Vinson Massif

Q.56 In which country are Java and Sumatra islands located?

A. The philippines
B. New zealand
C. Indonesia
D. Japan

Q.57 The largest island of Asia is:
A. Borneo
B. Sumitra
C. Java
D. Sri Lanka

Q.58 Which island is called the 'Crossing of the Pacific Ocean'?
A. Fiji
B. Tonga
C. East Timor
D. Hawai Islands

Q.59 The capital of Japan 'Tokyo' is located on which of the following islands?
A. Honshu
B. Shikoku
C. Hokkaido
D. Kyushu

Q.60 On which island is the capital of Indonesia 'Jakarta' located?
A. Sulabesi
B. Java
C. Sumatra
D. Bali

Q.61 According to Wegner, in which era did the fragmentation of Pejia begin?
A. Cambrian
B. Precambrian
C. Carboniferous
D. Permian

Q.62 Which category of reliefs are the continent and ocean?
A. First class
B. Second class
C. Third class
D. Fourth class

Q.63 On what percentage of the earth's surface is the expansion of continents found?
A. 25.5
B. 29.2
C. 35.6
D. 40.7

Q.64 The deepest trough of the world is located at:
A. Near Fiji
B. Near the island of Guam
C. On the east coast of Japan
D. On the east coast of the Philippines

Q.65 How many ocean troughs have been detected in all the oceans of the world so far?
A. 19
B. 32
C. 51
D. 57

Q.66 Which of the following rocks is the oldest in terms of construction?
A. Igneous
B. Metamorphosed
C. Sedentary
D. Adrenaline

Q.67 The igneous rock is called:
A. Hard rock
B. Original rock
C. Secondary rock
D. None of these

Q.68 Which of the following statements regarding igneous rock is false?
A. There is complete absence of layers in igneous rocks
B. Crystals are found in these rocks
C. There is a lack of fossils in these rocks
D. Joints are found in these rocks

Q.69 Which of the following rocks is found on the highest part of the surface?

A. Igneous rock   **B.** Sedimentary rock

C. Metamorphic rock   **D.** None of these

Q.70 There are about 2000 types of minerals found on the earth, but some of these minerals form rocks. What is the number of these minerals?

A. 10   **B.** 20   **C.** 500   **D.** 150

Q.71 Who is the author of 'Anthropogeography' or 'Human Geography'?

A. Ellen Churchill Semple

B. Ratzel

C. Huntington

D. Blache

Q.72 The series of lines connecting the vibrating places at the same time is called:

A. Homoacoustic lines

B. Earthquake lines

C. Covariance lines (coseismal lines)

D. Isosomal lines

Q.73 Which of the following seismic waves causes the most damage?

A. Primary   **B.** Secondary

C. Long surface   **D.** Injurious

Q.74 Focus is the place where-

A. The first knowledge of seismic waves on the ground is

B. Where the earthquake originates

C. From where the earthquake originates, its waves travel back to the place immediately below and return again.

D. None of the above

Q.75 Which soil area is found on two-thirds of Tamil Nadu?

A. Red soil   **B.** Black soil

C. Laterite soil   **D.** Alluvial soil

Q.76 Which of the following is called the face of a volcano?

A. Crater   **B.** Dormant

C. The dead   **D.** Internet

Q.77 What is the molten material beneath the solid rocks of the earth's crust, which sometimes comes to the top of the earth with the origin of the volcano?

A. Magma   **B.** Macus   **C.** Marsh   **D.** Meseta

Q.78 Most active volcanoes of the world are found:

A. In ancient plateau areas

B. In deep ocean plains

C. Newly Folded Mountain Areas

D. In the plains

Q.79 Uttar Pradesh's climate can be referred as __________.

A. Humid Subtropical Climate

B. Temperate Climate

C. Dry Climate

D. Tropical Climate

Q.80 What is a volcano?

A. Hot shell pieces and slag

B. Lava level

C. Non-toxic gas

D. Steam explosive

Q.81 Laterite soil predominates:

A. Malabar coastal region

B. Coromandal in coastal region

C. In Bundelkhand

D. In Baghelkhand

Q.82 Which of the following is called the stable plateau between mountains?

A. Single front plateau

B. Intercontinental plateau

C. Continental plate

D. None of these

Q.83 The Pyrenees Mountains lie between which of the following countries?

A. France and Spain

B. England and Ireland

C. Italy and France

D. Bulgaria and Greece

Q.84 The highest peak of the Andes ranges is:

A. Aconcagua   **B.** Ojos del Celado

C. Chimborajo   **D.** Huella

Q.85 Which soil is formed by the fragmentation of basalt rocks?

A. Black soil   **B.** Red soil

C. Laterite soil   **D.** Alluvial soil

Q.86 In which ocean is the world's widest continental magna coast situated?

A. Pacific Ocean   **B.** Arctic Ocean

C. Atlantic Ocean   **D.** Indian Ocean

Q.87 The length of the Mid Atlantic Ridge located in the Atlantic Ocean is approximately:

A. 11,000 km   **B.** 14,000 km

C. 18,000 km   **D.** 20,000 km

Q.88 The sandstone changes:

A. In nees   **B.** In cyst

C. In quartzite   **D.** In graphite

Q.89 The rocks formed due to the condensation of the earth's liquid substances are called:

A. Igneous   **B.** Sedentary

C. Modified   **D.** No one

Q.90 The remains of animals, flora and micro-organisms are found in which type of rocks?

A. In igneous rocks

B. In sedimentary rocks

C. In metamorphic rocks

D. In epidermal rocks

Q.91 Match these:

	List I (State)		List II (National Park)
A.	Uttar Pradesh	1.	Bandipur
B.	Assam	2.	Dudhwa
C.	Odisha	3.	Simlipal
D.	Karnataka	4.	Manas

A. A-1,B-2,C-3,D-4   **B.** A-2,B-4,C-3,D-1
C. A-4,B-3,C-2,D-1   **D.** A-2,B-3,C-1,D-4

Q.92 Where is the world's highest mountain peak located?
A. India   **B.** Tibet   **C.** Nepal   **D.** Bhutan

Q.93 Which mountain is known as continental watershed?
A. Himalaya
B. Andies
C. Rockies
D. Great dividing range

Q.94 Which of the following types of volcanoes have the shape of a cauliflower?
A. Volcanic equivalent
B. Jaundice equivalent
C. Stromboli equivalent
D. Air equivalent

Q.95 The old alluvial soil of the Gangetic plains is called:
A. Bangar   **B.** Khadar   **C.** Kallar   **D.** Regud

Q.96 Krakatau volcano is located in which of the following islands?
A. Papua New Guinea
B. In the Spratly Islands
C. In Indonesia
D. In the western isles

Q.97 Which of the following gases does not come out during volcanic eruption?
A. Oxygen   **B.** Hydrogen
C. Ammonia   **D.** Carbon dioxide

Q.98 What type of soil is formed from granite and nice rocks?
A. Red clay   **B.** Black clay
C. Alluvial clay   **D.** Laterite clay

Q.99 What is the 'Sal' tree?
A. Tropical evergreen tree
B. Tropical semi-evergreen tree
C. Dry deciduous tree
D. Wet deciduous trees

Q.100 Which of the following boxes fall in the world's most earthquake?
A. Mature ocean belt   **B.** Mid continental box
C. Mid Atlantic box   **D.** Indian Ocean Box

Q.101 Italy's Etna volcano can be placed in which of the following types?
A. Active   **B.** Still
C. The dead   **D.** Dormant

Q.102 Coal is found in which rock?
A. Converted rock   **B.** Flaky rock
C. Abiotic rock   **D.** Igneous rock

Q.103 Environmental degradation means:
A. Complete degradation of environmental properties
B. Reverse change with human activities
C. Ecological imbalance as a result of ecological variation
D. All of the above

Q.104 Petroleum (mineral oil) is found in which rocks?
A. Igneous   **B.** Newly layered
C. Ancient layered   **D.** Converted

Q.105 Acid rain is caused by the following pollution in the environment:
A. Carbon monoxide and carbon Dioxide
B. Carbon dioxide and nitrogen
C. Ozone and carbon Dioxide
D. Nitrous Oxide and Sulfur Dioxide

Q.106 Which of the following is not a modified rock?
A. Slate   **B.** Rhinestone
C. Marble   **D.** Granite

Q.107 Fly ash is an environmental pollutant that is produced by:
A. By thermal power plants
B. By oil purifier factories
C. By fertilizer plants
D. By struepe Manning

Q.108 Soil erosion (erosion) is more when:
A. It rains a lot   **B.** It doesn't rain
C. It rains less   **D.** None of these

Q.109 The instrument used for measuring relative humidity in the air is:
A. Hygrometer   **B.** Hydrograph
C. Pantograph   **D.** Barograph

Q.110 Which of the following two continents gives a mirror image of each other?
A. South America and Australia
B. South America and Africa
C. Eurasia and North America
D. Europe and Australia

Q.111 Africa is the southernmost point of the continent:
A. Asha cape   **B.** Cape Agulhas
C. Cape Town   **D.** Natal

Q.112 Which of the following continents is spread in all the northern, southern, eastern and western hemispheres?
A. Asia   **B.** Europe
C. Africa   **D.** South america

Q.113 The continent with the most countries is:
A. Asia   **B.** Europe
C. North America   **D.** Africa

Q.114 South America is the longest river in the continent?

A. Paraná   **B.** Maderia   **C.** Amazon   **D.** Orinoco

Q.115 Nagasaki city of Japan is located on which island?

A. Honshu   **B.** Shikoku
C. Hokkaido   **D.** Kyushu

Q.116 The smallest island in Japan is:

A. Honshu   **B.** Hokkaido
C. Shikoku   **D.** Kyushu

Q.117 The proponent of continental flow theory is:

A. Pratt   **B.** Wegner   **C.** Holmes   **D.** Gregory

Q.118 Who propounded the theory of plate tectonics?

A. Harry has   **B.** Tailor
C. Jeprise   **D.** Dana

Q.119 According to Wegner, the direction in which continental displacement occurred is:

A. Equator and northern fog
B. Equator and western
C. Equator and South Pole
D. Equator and east

Q.120 Which is the latest theory to explain continental displacement?

A. Taylor's continental displacement hypothesis
B. Wegner's Continental Displacement Theory
C. Tetrahedron hypothesis
D. Plate tectonics theory

Q.121 Which of the following is represented on the Beaufort scale?

A. Speed of seismic waves
B. Wind speed
C. Running water speed
D. All these

Q.122 The highest depth in the ocean is that of the Mariana Trough of the Pacific Ocean, which is:

A. 9,200 m above sea level bottom
B. 10,500 m above sea level bottom
C. 10,500 m above sea level bottom
D. 11,500 m above sea level bottom

Q.123 Syzygy is:

A. The position of the same straight line of the Sun, Earth and Moon
B. Earth's position relative to the Sun and the Moon
C. The position of the sun and the moon on the same side of the earth
D. Right position of Sun, Moon and Earth

Q.124 By which name are the flat top sea mountains known?

A. Monednock   **B.** Guyot
C. Inselberg   **D.** Jugen

Q.125 Which of the following countries has the highest population density?

A. Bangladesh   **B.** Pakistan
C. Sri Lanka   **D.** India

// Smart Answer Sheet //

Correct Indicates percentage of students who answered questions correctly.

Skipped Indicates percentage of students who skipped questions.

Q.	Ans.	Correct	Skipped
1	C	56.67 %	0.0 %
2	C	23.33 %	26.67 %
3	B	30.0 %	26.67 %
4	D	50.0 %	30.0 %
5	D	33.33 %	30.0 %
6	A	30.0 %	26.67 %
7	D	16.67 %	30.0 %
8	B	46.67 %	26.66 %
9	B	6.67 %	30.0 %
10	A	36.67 %	26.66 %
11	C	46.67 %	26.66 %
12	B	13.33 %	26.67 %
13	B	10.0 %	26.67 %
14	C	63.33 %	26.67 %
15	D	30.0 %	26.67 %
16	B	30.0 %	26.67 %
17	B	40.0 %	30.0 %
18	B	50.0 %	26.67 %
19	B	20.0 %	26.67 %
20	A	20.0 %	26.67 %
21	C	63.33 %	26.67 %
22	B	16.67 %	26.66 %
23	C	46.67 %	26.66 %
24	C	43.33 %	30.0 %
25	D	6.67 %	30.0 %
26	D	26.67 %	26.66 %
27	A	56.67 %	26.66 %
28	B	36.67 %	30.0 %
29	C	43.33 %	26.67 %
30	B	53.33 %	26.67 %
31	C	40.0 %	26.67 %
32	D	53.33 %	26.67 %
33	C	46.67 %	26.66 %
34	A	33.33 %	30.0 %
35	B	46.67 %	26.66 %
36	B	60.0 %	26.67 %
37	D	56.67 %	30.0 %
38	D	50.0 %	26.67 %
39	A	36.67 %	30.0 %
40	C	13.33 %	30.0 %
41	D	23.33 %	26.67 %
42	A	53.33 %	30.0 %
43	C	50.0 %	26.67 %
44	C	40.0 %	30.0 %
45	D	40.0 %	26.67 %
46	D	36.67 %	30.0 %
47	C	40.0 %	26.67 %
48	A	50.0 %	30.0 %
49	D	23.33 %	30.0 %
50	B	50.0 %	26.67 %
51	A	26.67 %	26.66 %
52	C	46.67 %	26.66 %
53	B	26.67 %	30.0 %
54	A	53.33 %	26.67 %
55	D	43.33 %	26.67 %
56	C	60.0 %	30.0 %
57	A	30.0 %	30.0 %
58	D	36.67 %	26.66 %
59	A	53.33 %	26.67 %
60	B	33.33 %	26.67 %
61	C	36.67 %	30.0 %
62	A	43.33 %	26.67 %
63	B	56.67 %	26.66 %
64	B	16.67 %	30.0 %
65	D	20.0 %	30.0 %
66	A	43.33 %	26.67 %
67	B	56.67 %	30.0 %
68	D	23.33 %	30.0 %
69	B	36.67 %	30.0 %
70	B	33.33 %	30.0 %
71	B	60.0 %	26.67 %
72	A	10.0 %	26.67 %
73	C	46.67 %	30.0 %
74	B	43.33 %	26.67 %
75	A	30.0 %	30.0 %
76	A	56.67 %	26.66 %
77	A	56.67 %	30.0 %
78	C	50.0 %	26.67 %
79	A	40.0 %	26.67 %
80	A	46.67 %	26.66 %

Q.	Ans.	Correct / Skipped
81	A	43.33 % / 26.67 %
82	B	56.67 % / 26.66 %
83	A	26.67 % / 30.0 %
84	A	43.33 % / 26.67 %
85	A	43.33 % / 30.0 %
86	B	26.67 % / 26.66 %
87	B	30.0 % / 30.0 %
88	C	60.0 % / 30.0 %
89	A	46.67 % / 30.0 %

Q.	Ans.	Correct / Skipped
90	B	56.67 % / 30.0 %
91	B	60.0 % / 30.0 %
92	C	53.33 % / 30.0 %
93	C	13.33 % / 26.67 %
94	A	16.67 % / 30.0 %
95	A	50.0 % / 26.67 %
96	B	10.0 % / 26.67 %
97	A	23.33 % / 30.0 %
98	A	20.0 % / 26.67 %

Q.	Ans.	Correct / Skipped
99	D	26.67 % / 26.66 %
100	A	43.33 % / 26.67 %
101	D	3.33 % / 30.0 %
102	B	36.67 % / 30.0 %
103	A	30.0 % / 30.0 %
104	C	56.67 % / 26.66 %
105	D	53.33 % / 30.0 %
106	D	50.0 % / 30.0 %
107	A	23.33 % / 26.67 %

Q.	Ans.	Correct / Skipped
108	C	23.33 % / 30.0 %
109	A	53.33 % / 26.67 %
110	B	60.0 % / 26.67 %
111	B	33.33 % / 26.67 %
112	C	33.33 % / 30.0 %
113	D	33.33 % / 26.67 %
114	C	60.0 % / 30.0 %
115	D	23.33 % / 26.67 %
116	C	23.33 % / 30.0 %

Q.	Ans.	Correct / Skipped
117	B	46.67 % / 26.66 %
118	A	53.33 % / 26.67 %
119	B	50.0 % / 26.67 %
120	D	43.33 % / 26.67 %
121	B	26.67 % / 26.66 %
122	C	10.0 % / 30.0 %
123	A	53.33 % / 26.67 %
124	B	46.67 % / 30.0 %
125	A	53.33 % / 30.0 %

Performance Analysis

Avg. Score (%)	32.0%
Toppers Score (%)	92.0%
Your Score	

//Hints and Solutions//

1. Eratosthenes (250 BCE) first used the term 'Geographica' for geography and measured the globe. He also indicated the principle of difference of climate with latitude and season and the notion of water flow in the sea and rivers.

Hence, the correct option is (C).

2. According to Alan Sample, "Human geography is the study of the interchangeable relationships between fickle humans and the floating earth." Human geography focuses exclusively on the study of ecological adjustment and field organization of different regions. In this human being is considered as the focal point.

Hence, the correct option is (C).

3. "The present is the key to the past." this statement is from James Hutton.

James Hutton in 1785 proposed the 'Principles of Identityism'. According to this, the geological processes and rules that are working in the present time, he was the only one working in all the geological history, but there was a difference in his activism.

Hence, the correct option is (B).

4. Griffith Taylor is an exponent of the 'Stop and Go Determinism' ideology. First of all, Griffith Taylor amended the deterministic ideology and heralded this new ideology. Griffith Taylor holds that the processes of man and nature are interrelated. Both elements are kinetic. Both are variable and have an impact on each other.

Hence, the correct option is (D).

5. The scholar who defines geography as 'human ecology' is H.H. Barrows. The famous geographer H.H. Barrows supported the development of human geography as a human ecology at the 1922 AD annual session of the Association of American Geographers.

Hence, the correct option is (D).

6. "If history presents a scientific study of 'when', then geography makes a scientific and logical study of 'where'." The following statement is from Carl Seaver. Carl Seaver was a famous American cultural geographer. He took a research degree in Chicago University in 1915. He is called the father of cultural geography.

Hence, the correct option is (A).

7. Hecataeus is called the 'the father of geography'. He considered the site part to be surrounded by seas and gave knowledge of two continents. His famous book was 'Ges-Periods' i.e. 'description of the earth' which was probably published in the late sixth century. 'Ges- Periods' ie 'description of the earth' is the first ordered description of the world and that is why Hecataeus is called the 'the father of geography'.

Hence, the correct option is (D).

8. The 'Geographic Cycle of Erosion', related to the development and transformation of the landscape, W.M. Davis has a concept in which he considers three factors to be important in the development of landforms of a place. These factors are: (i) structure (ii) process (iii) time or phase. These factors were addressed by W.M. Davis is called the Trikuta and expressed in a sentence that "Structure is a byproduct of structure, process and condition."

Hence, the correct option is (B).

9. Peshal is considered to be the originator of geomorphology. Geomorphology is the scientific study of landforms and the processes that shape them; And more broadly, it is the study of the processes that control the reliefs and topography of any planet.

Hence, the correct option is (B).

10. Eratosthenes owes the credit of establishing geography as a separate study of scripture. Eratosthenes was a Greek mathematician, geographer, poet, astronomer and music theorist. Established geography as a separate study of scripture and used the term 'Geographica' for geography. Therefore, he is also called the father of systematic geography. He gave birth to geophysics.

Hence, the correct option is (A).

11. The instrument measuring the direction and speed of the clouds is called nephoscope. The instrument to measure the flow speed and direction of clouds is often used in observations of medium height and higher clouds. It is of many types in which 'bison comb meghampi' is more popular.

Hence, the correct option is (C).

12. Relative humidity is shown on the following climograph. It is a type of diagram in which two climatic elements of a place (eg, humid bulb and dry bulb temperature; heat and precipitation) are displayed face-to-face on a graph. It was first used by Griffith Taylor.

Hence, the correct option is (B).

13. Meteosat is a geosynchronous satellite used to provide weather information. The geosynchronous satellite resembles the figure number eight (8) on observation from a particular position on the ground.

Hence, the correct option is (B).

14. The seismograph (seismometer) records the intensity of the earthquake. Seismograph (seismometer) is a tool to record a component of geometry more accurately than the direct or indirect method. Geotropism can occur due to well-known natural earthquakes, man-made explosions in underground nuclear tests and petroleum exploration etc. and strong winds, sea waves, strong monsoons and micro-waves caused by hurricanes or depression in the sea area.

Hence, the correct option is (C).

15. The amount of endocrine water going down through the soil is measured by a lycometer. The instrument that measures the transpiration of crops or vegetation is called a lysometer.

Hence, the correct option is (D).

16. The largest Indian geographical region of India is the Great Indian Plateau. This plateau extends in a triangular form to the south of the Tapi River. Satpura and Vindhyachal in the northwest; Mahadev and Makalu in the north; The Eastern Ghats in the east and the Western Ghats in the west form its boundaries. It has an average elevation of 600 meters. This plateau is 2000 meters high in the south but in the north, its height is only 500 meters. The slope of this huge plateau with an area of about 2 lakh square kilometers is from west to east.

Hence, the correct option is (B).

17. The territories determined on the basis of the relationship are called nodal states. A planning region is a specific regional unit that has a definite plan for socio-economic development. In a perfect planning state, there is generally a similarity between natural conditions, economic resources, social and economic conditions and political factors.

Hence, the correct option is (B).

18. Coal-iron ore and water would be ideal adjustments for the establishment of iron-steel industry. Coal and iron ore are used as basic raw materials for the establishment of iron and steel industry and water is an essential element for hydroelectricity. In addition, lime is also an essential raw material for the localization of the iron and steel industry.

Hence, the correct option is (B).

19. The blueness of the sky is measured by a cyanometer. De Saucerus is credited with inventing the cyanometer in 1789. The cyanometer of De Saucerus had 53 sections. De Saucerus concluded, that the color of the sky depended on the amount of suspended particles in the atmosphere.

Hence, the correct option is (B).

20. The blueness of the sky is measured by a cyanometer. De Saucerus is credited with inventing the cyanometer in 1789. The cyanometer of De Saucerus had 53 sections. De Saucerus concluded, that the color of the sky depended on the amount of suspended particles in the atmosphere.

Hence, the correct option is (A).

21. The lines that display the salinity of oceans and seas on a map are called isoheline. The line representing places with uniform temperature is called isotherm. The isobar line displays uniform pressure on the map. The isohyte line is called the line joining places with equal rainfall.

Hence, the correct option is (C).

22.

- The line joining the places coming at the same time of the earthquake is called Homosomal.
- The line joining places of uniform intensity of earthquake is called "isosismal".
- The "isobrant line" blends places with storms once upon a time.
- The "isogonal line" combines the locations with the same magnetic inclination.

Hence, the correct option is (B).

23.

- The line joining places with similarities of seismic intensity is called isosismal.
- The "isogonal line" combines the locations with the same magnetic inclination.
- The line joining the places coming at the same time of the earthquake is called Homosismal.
- The "isohel line" combines places with similar sunrays.

Hence, the correct option is (C).

24. The earthquake in Bhuj in Gujarat on 26 January 2001 was very devastating and devastating. Thousands of people died and millions were injured in this earthquake.

Hence, the correct option is (C).

25.

- The boundary line classifying places with similar language in a region is called isogloss.
- The line joining the same mass density is called "isopaiknik".
- The "isonif line" represents places with similar snowfall.
- The "Contour Line" joins places of equal height above sea level.

Hence, the correct option is (D).

26. Economic reforms in India are moving towards concentration of economic activity. At the same time, there is a move towards higher growth rate and lower cost accessibility of urban facilities and services than metropolitan areas.

Hence, the correct option is (D).

27. Lines called isotherms are drawn on the map to represent the locations where the uniform temperature resides.]

Hence, the correct option is (A).

28. Pank stated that according to the action of regeneration, the gradient is the appendage ,plane or concave. German scientist Walter Pank proposed Davis' concept of time dependent topography and the 'morphological system' or 'natural analysis' model to explain the evolution and evolution of topographies, rejecting the geographic cycle. The main purpose of the Pank's theory was to find out the evolution of the surface movement and its reasons based on the exogenous processes and the physical characteristics.

Hence, the correct option is (B).

29. Plate tectonics theory is helpful in clarifying the origin and location of earthquake ,mountain and major sea level features. According to the theory of plate tectonics, when the continental and oceanic plates converge, the oceanic plate goes under the continental plate due to being heavy, causing the volcano to erupt.A prime example of this is the formation of the Andes Mountains by the injection of the Pacific Ocean plate below the South American continental plate. Similarly, sea nits are formed by the middle oceanic cuttack.

Hence, the correct option is (C).

30. Winds from the tropical region (0 ° –5 °) rise and rise above ,again (30 ° –35 °) as the atmospheric pressure rises at latitudes, creating an air circulation in the atmosphere called the Headley Cell. is. These winds are called commercial winds. Hence the trading winds fall in the area of Headley Sale.

Hence, the correct option is (B).

31. The event of diamond ring occurs on the day of solar eclipse. During a total solar eclipse, pieces of light appear on the edge of the sun before the sun sinks into darkness, resembling beads of a rosary. This is called bellybeeds. Only a shiny pearl of bellybeads remains, which looks like a diamond ring. This is called a diamond ring.

Hence, the correct option is (C).

32. If the atmosphere between the earth and space is considered to be removed, then the color of the sky will be black. In space where there is no atmosphere, the sun looks white and the sky black, because there is no light scattering.

Hence, the correct option is (D).

33. Venus and Mars are smaller planets in size than Earth. It is the brightest natural object in the night sky after Venus Moon. Venus is closest to the Earth in both size and distance. Mars is the fourth planet in the solar system from the Sun. It is also known as "Red Planet". Like Earth, Mars is also a terrestrial planet.

Hence, the correct option is (C).

34. Aristotle was a Greek philosopher. He was a disciple of Plato and a master of Alexander. In 340 BCE, Aristotle first said that the Earth is spherical in his book "On the Heaven".

Hence, the correct option is (A).

35. Earth is a planet in the solar system which is also called Vishwa. It is the third planet from the Sun based on distance. It is a planet on which life is found. 71% of its surface is covered by water and 29% is covered by land. The circumference of the Earth is 40,075 km.

Hence, the correct option is (B).

36. Atmospheric density ,volume expansion or contraction, etc. factors also have an effect on the amount of heat in the troposphere. When these factors or their effects change the atmospheric temperature without receiving or releasing them from any external source. Then this change is called adiabatic change. The term temperature change in temperature refers to the heating and cooling of ascending or descending air through compression and expansion.

Hence, the correct option is (B).

37. The Earth remains the lowest distance from the Sun on 3 January on the orbital path, it is called the position of the Upasour. While the Earth is at maximum distance from the Sun on 4 July, it is called the position of Apsaur.

Hence, the correct option is (D).

38. It was first proposed by Copernicus that the Sun is the center of our solar system and the Earth revolves around it. Copernicus was a Polish astronomer and mathematician. He gave this revolutionary formula that the Earth is not in the center of space.

Hence, the correct option is (D).

39. The distance from Sun to Earth is 149 million km. And it takes 8.3 minutes for light to come from the Sun to the Earth. With this optical energy there is an important biochemical reaction called photosynthesis which is the basis of life on Earth.

Hence, the correct option is (A).

40. Many types of gases are released at the time of volcanic eruption. Hydrogen, hydrogen sulfide, nitrogen, carbon dioxide, hydrochloric acid and ammonia chloride are prominent among them. Among gases, water vapor is of the highest importance. 60 to 90% of the gases coming out of the volcano consist of water vapor.

Hence, the correct option is (C).

41. About 83 percent of the Earth's total volume is found in the mantle.

- The internal structure of the Earth is divided into several levels. There are three main parts of the Earth's internal structure – the upper crust, the middle mantle and the inner layer the metallic core. About 0.5 percent of the Earth's total volume is made up of crust, while 83 percent of the mantle is extensive. The remaining 16 percent is core.

- The thickness of the mantle is about 2895 km. It is in a semi-solid state. A transition layer that separates the mantle from the core is called the Gutenberg discontinuity.

Hence, the correct option is (D).

42. The thickness of the crust or crust is assumed to be 8 to 40 km. The lower boundary of this layer is called the Mohorovic disambiguation or the Moho disambiguation. The oceans and continents on Earth are located in this part only. The Moho disambiguation lies between the crust and the mantle.

Hence, the correct option is (A).

43. The geothermal gradient is the amount that the Earth's temperature increases with depth. This explains the reason for the temperature from the warm interior of the Earth to its surface. The rate of temperature increase with depth when moving from ground to geostation is $1°C$ per 32 m.

Hence, the correct option is (C).

44. The mantle is a layer inside the planet that is bordered by a core and bordered by a crust. Volcanic lava from the mantle comes to the Earth's surface through a pillar-like structure. This columnar structure is called mantle plume. Mantle is dominated by silica and magnesium elements.

Hence, the correct option is (C).

45. The geology is divided by Sves in the form of Seal, Seema and Nife. The maximum amount of oxygen in the composition of the earth's crust is oxygen. Sves named it Sial because it is made of silica and aluminum. The third and last layer of earth is found below the boundary layer, which is called the core. It consists of nickel (Ni) and iron (Fe). Hence the name of this layer is NiFe.

Hence, the correct option is (D).

46. The correct descending order of quantities of various elements found in the earth's crust is oxygen, silicon, aluminum, iron.

Quantity of different elements found in the earth's crust:

- Oxygen - (46%),
- Silicon - (28%),
- Aluminum - (8%),
- Iron - (6%)

Hence, the correct option is (D).

47. Lithosphere is the topmost rocky or rock-forming layer of a rocky planet or natural satellite in geography and geology. The terrain includes the upper surface, the lower surface and the solid upper part of the mantle.

Hence, the correct option is (C).

48. Limestone is a sedimentary rock consisting mainly of various crystalline forms of calcium carbonate ($CaCO_3$) such as the mineral calcite or aragonite. Its metamorphosed form is a marble.

Hence, the correct option is (A).

49. The slate is a metamorphic rock with a dull rock. The most common color of slate is gray, but it can also be brown, green, purple, or blue. Slate is formed when a sedimentary rock (shale, mudstone, or basalt) is compacted. Slate is not flaky rock.

Hence, the correct option is (D).

50. The source of the most important information regarding the internal structure of the Earth is seismology. Seismology is a major branch of physical geography, which includes scientific study and factual analysis of earthquakes.

Hence, the correct option is (B).

51. Mount Koziasco is the highest mountain-top of the continent of Australia. The Koziasco Mountains are a mountain in the main range of Snowy Hills in the state of New South Wales, Australia. At 2228 meters (7390 ft) above sea level, this mountain is the highest point in the mainland of Australia.

Hence, the correct option is (A).

52. Australia is officially a country under the Australian Commonwealth continent of the Southern Hemisphere, which is also the world's smallest continent and the world's largest island, with Tasmania and several other islands in the Indian and Pacific oceans. That is why Australia is known as the 'island continent'.

Hence, the correct option is (C).

53. Europe is the largest Ladoga lake on the continent. Lake Ladoga is a freshwater lake located in the regions of Republic of Karelia and Leningrad Oblast in northwestern Russia. It is the largest lake in Europe and the 14th largest freshwater lake in the world by area.

Hence, the correct option is (B).

54. North America is the largest superior lake on the continent. Lake Superior, Huron, Eri, and Ontario are located on the border of the United States and Canada. The water from these lakes is used in equal amounts by both countries.

Hence, the correct option is (A).

55. Mount Vinson Massif is the highest mountain in the continent of Antarctica. Mount Vinson Massif is a large mountain massif located 21 km (13 mi) long and 13 km (8.1 mi) wide in the branch known as the Sentinel Mountains of the Elsworth Hills of Antarctica.

Hence, the correct option is (D).

56. Java and Sumatra islands are in the country of Indonesia. The island of Java is the most populous island in Indonesia. Java is an island in the Republic of Indonesia, which is the best and most famous in the Malaya Islands. Its area is 132174 square miles. It is bounded on the north by Java sea, on the south by the Indian Ocean and on the east by Bali and on the west by the island of Sumatra.

Hence, the correct option is (C).

57. The largest island of Asia is the island of Borneo. Borneo (Indonesian: Kalimantan, Malay: Borneo,) is the world's third largest and Asia's largest island. Geographically it is situated in the north from Java, west of Sulawesi and east of Sumatra. It is divided into Indonesia, Malaysia and Brunei countries.

Hence, the correct option is (A).

58. The island of Hawaii is called the 'Crossroads of the Pacific Ocean'. The Hawaiian Islands are a region of the United States located in the middle of the Pacific Ocean. It is the only province in the United States that consists entirely of islands and most of the islands of the Hawaiian Islands are included in this province.

Hence, the correct option is (D).

59. Japan's capital 'Tokyo' is located on Honshu Island. In 2005, 10.3 crore people were living on Honshu. It has an area of 2,27,962 sq km, which is larger than Britain and smaller than the state of Uttar Pradesh, India. In the Japanese language, 'hone shu' means 'main province'.

Hence, the correct option is (A).

60. Indonesia's capital 'Jakarta' is located on the island of Java. Jakarta is the capital and largest city of Indonesia. Its full name is Batabia. Its total area is 661 km and according to the 2010 census the population here is about 95,80,000.

Hence, the correct option is (B).

61. According to Wegner, the fragmentation of Pejia began in the Carboniferous era. Pangea had three major phases of fragmentation. The first phase began in the early-middle Jurassic period (in the Carboniferous era) when Pangea began to diverge from the Tethys Ocean in the east and the Pacific Ocean in the west, eventually leading to the development of the vast continents Lauresia and Gondwana. The rift that began to form between North America and Africa gave rise to many failed cracks. A rift resulted in the creation of a new ocean, the North Atlantic Ocean.

Hence, the correct option is (C).

62. The elevation is the pattern or pattern formed from the height of the ground. The continent and oceanic basin are included under the first class relief. Mountains, plateaus, plains and lakes etc. are the second class reliefs. The continent and the ocean are first class reliefs.

Hence, the correct option is (A).

63. The continent is an extensive land span that appears distinct from the sea on Earth. There are no clear criteria to express the continent. The continents extend over 29.2 percent of the Earth's surface.

Hence, the correct option is (B).

64. The deepest trough in the world is located near the island of Guam. The Mariana Trough is a major and very deep ocean trough in the world. The island of Guam is the southernmost and largest island in the Mariana Islands, as well as the largest island in the Micronesia territory.

Hence, the correct option is (B).

65. So far, 57 oceanic troughs have been detected in all the oceans of the world. Oceanic troughs are the lowest part of the oceanic basin and their bottom is quite below the average oceanic net. Their status is not found everywhere in scattered form here and there.

Hence, the correct option is (D).

66. The igneous rock is the oldest in terms of construction. The rocks formed by fire, ie the rocks which are formed when the lava, magma and dust particles emanate from the volcano are called igneous rocks.

Hence, the correct option is (A).

67. The igneous rock is called elemental rock. They are also called 'primary rocks' because they were first formed in the origin of the earth's surface. These are the first rocks to be formed from molton rock material, while sedimentary or metamorphic rocks are formed by the breaking of these igneous rocks or changing the shape of heat and pressure effects.

Hence, the correct option is (B).

68. Igneous rocks are formed by the freezing of molten rocky material. It can also be ruddy and without particles or rave. These rocks together with the other two major rocks found on Earth, sedimentary and metamorphic, form three major types of rocks found on Earth. There is a complete lack of layers in igneous rocks.

Hence, the correct option is (D).

69. Sedimentary rock is found on most part of the surface. Avadi rocks are formed from igneous rock. Igneous rocks start to freeze away due to wind and water. From this sedimentary rocks are formed. Sedimentary rocks are formed by layer-by-layer deposition of igneous rock.

Hence, the correct option is (B).

70. There are about 2000 types of minerals found on the earth, but some of these minerals form rocks. The number of these minerals is 20. Mainly in the composition of the rocks, oxygen constitutes 46.6%, silicon 27.7%, aluminum 8.1%, iron 5%, calcium 3.6%, sodium 2.8%, potassium 2.6% and magnesium 2.1%

Hence, the correct option is (B).

71. Ratzel was a prominent geographer. He first published a critique of Darwin's evolutionary book in 1869. From then on, he wrote articles and books on biology, geology, physical, human and political geography. Ratzel is the author of 'Anthropogeography' or 'Human Geography'.

Hence, the correct option is (B).

72. The series of lines connecting the vibrating places at the same time are called homoacoustic lines.

Hence, the correct option is (A).

73. Longer surface seismic waves cause the most damage. The velocity of these waves is the lowest (1.5 to 3 km / s). It reaches at the very end on the ground. It is the most destructive wave whose travel path is convex.

Hence, the correct option is (C).

74. Earthquake-origin is the place from which an earthquake originates. The place where rocks break below the surface of the earth is called the epicenter of the earthquake. According to the established rules of geometry, this place on the surface of the earth is closest to the center of the earthquake, so the intensity or loss of the earthquake shock is relatively high around this place.

Hence, the correct option is (B).

75. Red soil expanse is found on two-thirds of the area of Tamil Nadu. The red soil is red, yellow and chalky colored. In dry and wet climate, the formation of ancient rocky and altered rocks is broken and this soil looks light yellow due to exposure to water. This soil contains more iron, aluminum and lime. It is found in Madhya Pradesh, Chhattisgarh, Jharkhand, West Bengal, Meghalaya, Nagaland, Uttar Pradesh, Rajasthan, Tamil Nadu and Maharashtra.

Hence, the correct option is (A).

76. A volcano is a crack or mouth on the surface of the Earth that brings out hot lava, gas, ash, etc. inside the earth. That mouth is called a crater.

Hence, the correct option is (A).

77. The molten material beneath the solid rocks of the earth's crust, which sometimes comes to the top floor of the earth with the volcano's origin, is called magma. Inside the ground, hot moving matter that is composed of molten silicates, water, steam and other volatile components. This molten rock substance is found under the solid rocks of the earth's crust, and has a very high temperature and also contains gases and other promising substances.

Hence, the correct option is (A).

78. Most of the active volcanoes of the world are found in the newly folded mountainous regions. Active volcanoes are called volcanic mountains, in which eruptions often occur. Prominent among these volcanoes are 'Etna' and 'Stramboli' of Italy. The most active volcanoes are located on the coasts of the Americas and the continent of Asia.

Hence, the correct option is (C).

79. Uttar Pradesh's climate can be referred to as Humid Subtropical Climate. Uttar Pradesh is situated between 23°52′N and 31°28′N latitudes and 77°3′ and 84°39′E longitudes.

A Humid Subtropical Climate generally lies between latitudes 20° and 35°. The Humid Subtropical Climate is a major climate type of the Köppen classification. Humid Subtropical Climate characterized by relatively high temperatures.

Hence, the correct option is (A).

80. Volcanic crust is a natural hole or crack through which the molten material of the earth emits lava, ash, steam and other gases. The lava that comes out and flies into the air soon cools down and turns into small pieces which we call Sender.

Hence, the correct option is (A)

81. Malarite is the predominance of laterite soil in the coastal region. This soil is usually found in those tropical regions where there is rain. The color of this soil is red, but it is different from 'red soil'.

Hence, the correct option is (A)

82. The stable plateau between the mountains is called the intercontinental plateau. The construction of such plateaus is completed with the formation of high mountain ranges as a result of the internal forces of geology and they are surrounded by mountains from all around.

Hence, the correct option is (B)

83. The Pyrenees Mountains lie between the country of France and Spain. The Pyrenees Mountains are a range located on the border of Spain and France in southwestern Europe. It separates the Iberia Peninsula from other parts of the continent of Europe.

Hence, the correct option is (A)

84. The highest peak of the Andes ranges is Ekankagua. Acancagua is the highest mountain in the Andes Mountains of South America. Acancagua lies on the outskirts of Chile and Argentina, although its summit falls on the land of Argentina.

Hence, the correct option is (A)

85. Black soil is formed by the fragmentation of basalt rocks. Black soil is a mature soil found mainly in the lava region of the southern peninsular plateau. It is formed from two classes of rocks, the Deccan Trap and the Lohmay Nees and Schist.

Hence, the correct option is (A)

86. The world's widest continental submerged coast is located in the Arctic Ocean. The Arctic Ocean is located in the northern hemisphere of the Earth. It extends mostly into the Arctic North Polar region. It is the smallest and shallowest ocean among the five major marine divisions of the world, ie, five oceans.

Hence, the correct option is (B)

87. Located in the Atlantic Ocean, the length of the Middle Atlantic Ridge is about 14,000 km. The Atlantic Ocean is the name of the vast watershed that separates the continents of Europe and Africa from the continents of the New World.

Hence, the correct option is (B)

88. The sandstone converts to quartzite. Sandstone is such a hard rock which is formed mainly due to freezing of sand particles and is attached to some additive. Like sand, its composition can contain many substances in different amounts, but it contains most of the crystals.

Hence, the correct option is (C)

89. The rocks formed due to the condensation of the earth's liquid substances are called igneous. They are also called 'primary rocks' because of the first formation of igneous rocks in the origin of the earth's surface. It is also said that these are the first rocks to be formed from molten rock, while sedimentary or metamorphic rocks are formed by the breaking of these igneous rocks or by changing the shape of heat and pressure effects.

Hence, the correct option is (A).

90. The remains of animals, flora and micro-organisms are found in sedimentary type rocks. Small rocks formed by factors of nature accumulate at some place and later form into layer-like solid form due to chemical reaction or other reasons. These are called sedimentary rocks.

Hence, the correct option is (B)

91.

	List I (State)		List II (National Park)
A.	Uttar Pradesh	1.	Dudhwa
B.	Assam	2.	Manas
C.	Odisha	3.	Simlipal
D.	Karnataka	4.	Bandipur

Hence, the correct option is (B)

92. The highest mountain peak in the world is located in Nepal. Which is named Mount Everest. And the height is 8,850 meters. Earlier it was known as XV.

Hence, the correct option is (C)

93. The Rockies Mountains are known as continental aquifers. The Rockies Mountains or Rockies is the name of a range extending from the western part of North America, usually in the north-south direction, from Alska to northern Numéxico. The mountains range in height from 1,000 feet to 14,431 feet, and the terrestrial spread of the ranges is just over 4,000 miles.

Hence, the correct option is (C)

94. The volcanic equivalent volcano has the shape of a cauliflower. The lava emanating from the volcanic-like volcano is viscous and viscous. Which soon blocks the passage at the entrance of the volcano. When a large amount of gas accumulates below. So she removes the above barrier with extreme power.

Hence, the correct option is (A)

95. The old alluvial soil of the gangetic plains is called bangar. Sand and pebbles are found in the soil of bangar. Bangar is the highest ground in the plain. They were built in the middle and upper plastocene times.

Hence, the correct option is (A)

96. Krakatau volcano is located in the Spratly Islands. These volcanoes are located near Sunda, between Sumatra and Java islands. It is located in the Indian Ocean, it is the Javalamukhi, the Pilian Tulay.

Hence, the correct option is (B)

97. Oxygen gases do not leave at the time of the volcanic eruption. Several types of gases are released during volcanic eruptions, among which hydrogen sulfide, carbon dioxide, hydrochloric acid, and ammonia chloride are the main ones. Among gases, water vapor is of the highest importance. 60 to 90% of the gases coming out of the volcano consist of water vapor.

Hence, the correct option is (A)

98. Red clay is formed from granite and fine rocks. The red soil is red, yellow, and chalky colored. In dry and wet climates, the formation of ancient rocky and altered rocks is broken and this soil looks light yellow due to exposure to water. This soil contains more iron, aluminum, and lime.

Hence, the correct option is (A)

99. The 'Sal' tree is a dicot tree multivariate tree. Its wood is used in building works. Its wood is very hard, heavy, strong, and brown in color. The 'Sal' tree is a humid deciduous tree.

Hence, the correct option is (D)

100. Most of the world's earthquake waves fall in the ocean belt. About 63 percent of the world's earthquakes occur in this box. This box is located in the islands and continents like the circumference of a circle around the Pacific Ocean. Here the four major seas of the earthquake are found in the ocean and land meeting area, the New Valley Mountains area, the volcanic zone, the destructive plate, the boundary erosion zone.

Hence, the correct option is (A)

101. Volcanoes from which lava, gas, and various types of substances are released continuously, such volcanoes are called active volcanoes. There are about 500 such volcanoes in the world. Etna and Stromboli of Italy are prominent among such volcanoes.

Hence, the correct option is (D)

102. Coal is a solid organic material that is used as a fuel. Coal is very important as a major source of energy. Coal is found in the flaky rock. Other combustible and useful substances are also obtained from coal. Among other sources of energy, petroleum and its product name are paramount. Different types of coal have varying amounts of carbon.

Hence, the correct option is (B)

103. Environmental degradation refers to the complete degradation of environmental properties, adverse changes from human activities, and ecological imbalance as a result of ecological variation. Environmental degradation involves all

changes in the environment that are undesirable and threaten life and sustainability in a particular area or on the whole earth. Hence, pollution, climate change, erosion of biodiversity and other natural disasters are included in this.

Hence, the correct option is (A)

104. Petroleum (mineral oil) is found in ancient layered rocks. The word petroleum derives from petra (rock) and oleum (oil) because it is extracted from the middle of the rocks below the ground. These fuels are derived from natural sources.

Hence, the correct option is (C)

105. Acids in acid years come from two types of air pollutants: Sulfur Dioxide (SO_2) and Nitrous Dioxide (NO_2), these pollutants are initially emitted into the atmosphere by the burning of factory chimneys, buses, and automated vehicles.

Hence, the correct option is (D)

106. Granite is not a metamorphic rock. Granite is a granular granular rock, with its major components being rhinestones and feldspars. It is an igneous stone. The term granite was first used by ancient Italian collectors. Its first reference is found in a description of Rome's craftsman Flaminius Veca.

Hence, the correct option is (D)

107. Fly ash is a by-product produced by the burning of coal in thermal power plants.

- Fly ash is a pollutant, often produced by coal-fired power plants, that is carried by exhaust gases from the combustion chamber.

- It is collected from the exhaust gases by electrostatic precipitators or bag filters.

- Fly ash contains substantial amounts of silicon dioxide (SiO_2), aluminum oxide (Al_2O_3), ferric oxide (Fe_2O_3) and calcium oxide (CaO).

Hence, the correct option is (A)

108. Soil erosion (erosion) is more when there is more rainfall. The action of land particles moving away from their original place and collecting at another place is called soil erosion or soil erosion.

Hence, the correct option is (C)

109. The instrument used for relative humidity measurement in air is a hygrometer. The hygrometer is a weather instrument used to measure the amount of humidity in the atmosphere. There are two main types of hygrometers - a dry and wet bulb psychometer and a mechanical hygrometer.

Hence, the correct option is (A)

110. The continents of South America and Africa provide a mirror image of each other. South America is a continent in the western hemisphere located to the southeast of North America. The continent of Africa is the world's largest continent after Asia. It is situated between 37 ° 14 'north latitude to 34 ° 50' south latitude and 17 ° 33 'western longitude (longitude) to 51 ° 23' east longitude (longitude).

Hence, the correct option is (B)

111. Cape Agulhas is the southernmost point of the continent of Africa. Cape Agulhas is a rocky archway located in the Western Cape, the state of South Africa. Geographically it is the southern tip of Africa and officially the dividing point of the dark ocean and the Indian Ocean.

Hence, the correct option is (B)

112. The continent of Africa extends across all the northern, southern, eastern and western hemispheres. Africa is the world's largest continent after Asia. It is situated between 37 ° 14 'north latitude to 34 ° 50' south latitude and 17 ° 33 'west longitude to 51 ° 23' east longitude.

Hence, the correct option is (C)

113. The continent with the most countries is Africa. Africa is the world's largest continent after Asia. In the north of Africa are the Mediterranean Sea and the continent of Europe, the dark ocean in the west, the South Ocean in the south and the Arabian Sea and the Indian Ocean in the east. The continent has vast deserts, extremely dense forests, vast grasslands, large rivers and lakes and bizarre wild animals.

Hence, the correct option is (D)

114. South America is the longest Amazon river in the continent. The Amazon River is a river flowing through South America. It is the world's largest by volume and second by length in terms of volume. It flows through Brazil, Peru, Bolivia, Colombia and Ecuador.

Hence, the correct option is (C)

115. Nagasaki City of Japan is located on the island of Kyushu. The island of Kyushu is the third largest of the four main islands in Japan and the southwestern island. The total area of Kyushu is 35680 sq km and its population in 2006 was 1,32,31,995. It is located to the southwest of the Honshu and Shikoku islands.

Hence, the correct option is (D)

116. Japan consists of some 3800 islands. Of these, only 340 islands are larger than 1 square kilometer. Japan is often called the country of four large islands. These islands are Hokkaido, Honshu, Shikoku and Kyushu. Japan's smallest island is Shikoku.

Hence, the correct option is (C)

117. The proponent of continental flow theory is Wegner.

Wegner was a polar researcher, geophysicist, and meteorologist from Germany. He gave the theory of continental flow in 1912. His life span was from 1880 to 1930. Continental flow was a theory that explained how continents shift position on Earth's surface.

Hence, the correct option is (B).

118. The theory of plate tectonics was formulated by Harry Hass. Plate tectonics theory is the study of the nature and flow of plates. This theory was formulated in the 1960s. Scholars like Harry Hayes, Wilson, Morgan, McKenzie and Parker contributed significantly in this direction.

Hence, the correct option is (A)

119. According to Wegner, the direction in which continental displacement occurred is the equator and the west. Continental displacement is the moving of the continents of the earth in relation to each other. If seen in geographical epochs of millions of years, then it seems that the continents and their parts are lying on the floor of the sea and flowing in some direction.

Hence, the correct option is (B)

120. The latest theory to explain continental displacement is the theory of plate tectonics. Plate tectonics theory is the study of the nature and flow of plates. According to this theory, the Earth's plane is mainly divided into six large and six small plates and these plates are moving continuously.These plates are moving continuously in reference to each other and in terms of the Earth's rotation-axis.

Hence, the correct option is (D)

121. Wind speed is shown on the Beaufort scale. The scale was drawn in 1805 by the Irish hydrographist Francis Beaufort. The Beaufort scale was increased in 1946 when 13 to 17 forces were added.

Hence, the correct option is (B)

122. The highest depth in the ocean is that of the Mariana Trough of the Pacific Ocean, which is 10,500 m above sea level. is down. Mariana troughs are one of the major and very deep ocean troughs in the world. It is located 200 kilometers (124 mi) east of the Mariana Islands in the western Pacific Ocean.

Hence, the correct option is (C)

123. Syzygy is a simple linear configuration of three celestial bodies in a gravitational system. This position is called Syzygy when the Sun, Earth and Moon are in a straight line. In the Syzygy position, the Moon is either in conjunction with the Sun or is opposite to the Sun. Solar eclipse and lunar eclipse occur at the time of Syzygy.

Hence, the correct option is (A)

124. The flat top marine mountains are known as Guyot. In the oceans, the Guyot or Nimgan islands are like mountain peaks. The peak of the Guyot is flat. Most of the coral growth occurs over the Guyot.

Hence, the correct option is (B).

125. Among the given options, Bangladesh has the highest population density.

Country	Density
Bangladesh	1179
Sri Lanka	333
Pakistan	225
India	382

Hence, the correct option is (A).

Mock Test 05

Q.1 Consider the following:

1. The sun, the moon, and the earth are in a straight line.

2. Moon's orbit is closest to the Earth.

3. The tidal range is greater than normal.

The above-given conditions define which of the following tides?

A. Apogean Spring tides

B. Perihelion Spring tides

C. Perigean Spring tides

D. Aphelion Spring tides

Q.2 Which of the following is/are favorable conditions for the faster decomposition of the organic matter in the soil?

1. Lack of oxygen

2. Detritus rich in nitrogenous substances

3. Cold temperatures

Select the correct answer using the code given below.

A. 2 only **B.** 1 and 2 only

C. 2 and 3 only **D.** 1, 2 and 3

Q.3 Which of the following are/are the components of Bharatmala Pariyojana?

1. Development of economic corridors.

2. Development of border and international connectivity roads.

3. Development of port connectivity roads.

4. Development of expressways

Select the correct answer using the code given below.

A. 1 and 3 only **B.** 2 and 4 only

C. 1, 2, 3 and 4 **D.** 1, 2 and 3 only

Q.4 Which of the following statements is/are correct regarding the igneous rocks?

1. They can form beneath as well as on the surface of the earth.

2. They are devoid of fossils.

3. Quartzite and granite are igneous rocks.

Select the correct answer using the code given below.

A. 1 and 2 only **B.** 2 and 3 only

C. 1 only **D.** 1, 2 and 3

Q.5 These cool temperate western margins are under the permanent influence of the Westerlies all around the year. They are also regions of much cyclonic activity. Summers are never very warm here. The natural vegetation of this climatic type is a deciduous forest like oak, elm, ash, birch, beech, poplar, and hornbeam.

Which of the following climatic types is described in the passage given above?

A. Mediterranean Climate

B. British Type Climate

C. Steppe Climate

D. Natal climate

Q.6 Which of the following correctly describes the phenomenon of 'Break in the Monsoon'?

A. A rain deficient situation in any area when the mean annual rainfall is less than 75% of the normal rainfall.

B. When rain falls to occur for one or more weeks during the south-west monsoon period after having rained for a few days.

C. Bifurcation of monsoon winds into Arabian Sea branch and Bay of Bengal branch.

D. Sudden onset of the moisture-laden winds associated with violent thunder and lightning.

Q.7 Which of the following evidence supports the Continental Drift Theory proposed by Alfred Wegner?

1. Jig Saw fit of South American and African coastlines.

2. The occurrence of rich placer deposits of gold on the Ghana coast despite the absence of source rocks.

3. Distribution of identical fossils across oceans.

Select the correct answer using the code given below.

A. 1 and 2 only **B.** 2 and 3 only

C. 1 and 3 only **D.** 1, 2 and 3

Q.8 Consider the following statements with respect to ocean trenches:

1. They are located along divergent plate boundaries.

2. They are associated with active volcanoes and strong earthquakes.

3. Tonga trench and Mariana trench are located in the Pacific Ocean.

Which of the statements given above is/are correct?

A. 2 only **B.** 1 and 3 only

C. 2 and 3 only **D.** 1, 2 and 3

Q.9 Consider the following statements regarding Latitudes and Longitudes:

1. Latitude is measured as the angular distance of a point on the earth's surface north or south of the equator.

2. Both the latitude and the longitude of a place are measured from the centre of the earth.

Which of the statements given above is/are correct?

A. 1 only **B.** 2 only

C. Both 1 and 2 **D.** Neither 1 nor 2

Q.10 In the context of geomorphology, the term playas refer to:

A. Shallow lakes in the depressions of plains found in desert regions.

B. Unassorted coarse and fine debris dropped by melting glaciers.

C. Large-sized angular blocks plucked from land by glaciers.

D. Small round shallow depressions formed on limestone surfaces.

Q.11 Which of the following statements is/are correct with reference to the Western Disturbances?

1. They are shallow cyclonic depressions originating over the eastern Mediterranean Sea.

2. Their arrival in India is characterized by a sudden drop in the prevailing night temperature.

3. It is highly beneficial for rabi crops in Northern India.

Select the correct answer using the code given below.

A. 1 and 2 only   **B.** 2 only

C. 1 and 3 only   **D.** 1, 2 and 3

Q.12 With reference to the earth's gravity(g), consider the following statements:

1. It is influenced by the distribution of mass of material within the earth.

2. It is greater near the poles than at the equator.

Which of the statements given above is/are correct?

A. 1 only   **B.** 2 only

C. Both 1 and 2   **D.** Neither 1 nor 2

Q.13 Which of the following is/are proof(s) of the sphericity of the Earth?

1. Possible circumnavigation of the earth without a steep fall.

2. Different times of sunrise and sunset at different places on earth.

3. Shape of earth's shadow during a lunar eclipse.

Select the correct answer using the code given below.

A. 1 and 2 only   **B.** 1 and 3 only

C. 2 only   **D.** 1, 2 and 3

Q.14 With reference to River Luni, which of the following statements is correct?

A. It is formed by two streams, the Saraswati and Sabarmati.

B. It flows through the states of Madhya Pradesh, Rajasthan, and Gujarat.

C. It drains into Gulf of Khambhat.

D. It is cut twice by the Tropic of Cancer.

Q.15 The Western Ghats are locally known by different names. In this context, consider the following pairs:

Local name	Region
1. Sahyadri	Maharashtra
2. Nilgiri	Tamil Nadu
3. Anamalai	Karnataka

Which of the pairs given above is/are correctly matched?

A. 1 and 2 only   **B.** 1 and 3 only

C. 1 only   **D.** 2 and 3 only

Q.16 Which of the following statements is correct in the context of the Lakshadweep Islands?

A. The entire island group is built of coral deposits.

B. Narcondam is a small volcanic island in the Lakshadweep group.

C. Saddle peak is the highest peak in Lakshadweep islands.

D. An eleven-degree channel separates Lakshadweep from Maldives.

Q.17 Which of the following are the effects of the Himalayan Mountains on the Indian climate?

1. It protects the subcontinent from the cold northern winds.

2. It traps the monsoon winds, forcing them to shed their moisture within the subcontinent.

3. It creates different air pressure zones causing a reversal in the direction of monsoon winds.

Select the correct answer using the code given below.

A. 1 and 2 only   **B.** 2 and 3 only

C. 1 and 3 only   **D.** 1, 2 and 3

Q.18 In the context of Indian geography, Karewas are:

A. Thick deposits of glacial clay and other materials found in the Kashmir Himalayas.

B. Alluvial fans formed by the tributaries of Indus in the Northwest region of India

C. Ill-drained, damp, and thickly forested narrow tracts at the foothills of Himalayas

D. Oases in the Thar desert

Q.19 It is a unique rice variety in the coastal areas of Alappuzha, Ernakulam, and Thrissur districts. The salt water-resistant variety grows tall, flourishes under flood-like conditions, and grows entirely on leftovers from half a year of fish culture in fields. The cycle is called 'one fish and one rice' in which fish is grown up to April 15 after which fields are drained before the first bout of rains get them rid of salt. The season goes up to October when they are brought under fish culture again.

Which of the following varieties of rice is being described in the above passage?

A. Pokkali   **B.** Damodar

C. Porteresia   **D.** IR-8

Q.20 With reference to the structure of the earth, consider the following statements:

1. The outer core is in a liquid state while the inner core is in solid-state

2. The outer core is the main source of magma that finds its way to the surface during volcanic eruptions.

Which of the statements given above is/are correct?

A. 1 only   **B.** 2 only

C. Both 1 and 2   **D.** Neither 1 nor 2

Q.21 In which of the following plate boundaries, new crust formation takes place?

1. Convergent Boundaries

2. Divergent Boundaries

3. Transform Boundaries

Select the correct answer using the code given below.

A. 1 and 2 only   **B.** 2 only

C. 1 and 3 only   **D.** 1, 2 and 3

Q.22 In the context of Indian physiography, Malda fault separates:

A. The Vindhyas from the Satpura ranges.

B. The Delhi ridge from the Aravallis.

C. The Eastern Ghats from the Western Ghats.

D. Meghalayan plateau from the Peninsular plateau.

Q.23 Which of the following weather phenomenon are observed during the winter season in India?

1. Development of high pressure in the region lying to the north of the Himalayas.

2. The inflow of dry surface winds from Central Asia.

3. The onset of an easterly jet stream over peninsular India.

Select the correct answer using the code given below.

A. 1 and 2 only

B. 2 and 3 only

C. 1 and 3 only

D. 1, 2 and 3

Q.24 Consider the following statements in the context of Central Highlands (or the Madhya Bharat Plateau):

1. The general slope of the highlands is towards the south and south-east.

2. Musi river basin forms the majority part of the region.

Which of the statements given above is/are correct?

A. 1 only

B. 2 only

C. Both 1 and 2

D. Neither 1 nor 2

Q.25 Consider the following local winds:

1. Sirocco

2. Mistral

3. Foehn

4. Chinook

Which of the winds mentioned above blow over the Mediterranean region?

A. 1 and 2 only

B. 2 and 3 only

C. 3 and 4 only

D. 1 and 3 only

Q.26 Which of the following vertebrates first originated in the course of geological time scale?

A. Amphibians

B. Fish

C. Reptiles

D. Mammals

Q.27 Barchukki Falls are located in which state of India?

A. Karnataka

B. Andhra Pradesh

C. Telangana

D. Tamil Nadu

Q.28 The Sankosh river forms the boundary between which two states?

A. Bihar and West Bengal

B. Assam and Arunachal Pradesh

C. Assam and West Bengal

D. Bihar and Jharkhand

Q.29 Which of the following statements is incorrect?

A. The Khasi and Mizo hills are part of the Patkai Range

B. Fangpui is the highest place of Mizo Hill

C. Khasi hills are called Lushai hills in the local language

D. All the above statements are correct

Q.30 How many countries share India's terrestrial border?

A. 6

B. 7

C. 8

D. 9

Q.31 Arrange the ports given from south to north direction:

A. Cochin → Thiruvananthapuram → Calicut → Mangalore

B. Calicut → Thiruvananthapuram → Cochin → Mangalore

C. Thiruvananthapuram → Cochin → Calicut → Mangalore

D. Thiruvananthapuram → Calicut → Mangalore → Cochin

Q.32 Match List-I with List-11 and select the correct answer from the given below:

List-I (Book)	List-II (Author)
A. Periplus	1. Eratosthenes
B. The Guide to Geography	2. Ptolemy
C. Historical Memoir	3. Hecateaus
D. The Ekumene	4. Stabo

A. A-3, B-4, C-1, D-2

B. A-1, B-4, C-2, D-3

C. A-3, B-2, C-1, D-4

D. A-3, B-2, C-4, D-1

Q.33 The Environment presents a range of opportunities and man is free to choose between them. This basic premise in geography is known as:

A. Determinism

B. Neo-determinism

C. Possibilism

D. Probabilism

Q.34 Who, amongst the following, defined Geography as a chorological science ?

A. Ptolemy

B. Richthofen

C. Hettner

D. P.E. James

Q.35 Stop and go determinism was postulated by whom?

A. Humbold

B. Jean Brunhes

C. Griffith Taylor

D. Ratzel

Q.36 Who defined Geography as human ecology?

A. Schaefer

B. Barrows

C. Hartshorne

D. Ellen Semple

Q.37 Match List-I with List-II and select the correct answer from the codes given below.

List-I (Taxon)	List-II (Authors)
I. Cycle of Erosion	A. Freidrich Ratzel
II. The Origin of Species	B. Oscar Peschel
III. Originator of Dualism between Physical & Human Geography	C. Davis
IV. Theory of Social Darwinism	D. Charles Darwin

A. I-B, II-C, III-A, IV-D

B. I-C, II-D, III-B, IV-A

C. I-D, II-A, III-C, IV-B

D. I-A, II-B, III-D, IV-C

Q.38 Who among the following geographers laid down the foundation of the dichotomy of general versus special Geography?

A. Immanuel Kant

B. Bernhard Varenius

C. Peter Apin

D. Sebastian Munster

Q.39 Kotla Lake is situated in which of the following place?

A. Gurugram

B. Faridabad

C. Nuh

D. Hisar

Q.40 On which river is the Ranjit Sagar Dam river valley project located?

A. Ravi

B. Sutlej

C. Jhelum

D. Indus

Q.41 Where is the origin of Indus river?

A. Dal Lake

B. Mansarovar Lake

C. Sheshnag Lake

D. Wullar Lake

Q.42 On which river is the "Jawahar Sagar" dam located?

A. Krishna **B.** Chambal **C.** Betwa **D.** Sutlej

Q.43 Which is the longest coastline state of India?

A. Kerala

B. Goa

C. Gujarat

D. Andhra Pradesh

Q.44 Which of the following is/are the aims of National Forest Policy 1988?

1. Bringing 33 percent of the geographical area under forest cover.

2. Reduction of floods and droughts.

3. Creating people's movement to encourage the planting of trees.

Select the correct answer using the code given below.

A. 1 only

B. 2 and 3 only

C. 1 and 3 only

D. 1, 2 and 3

Q.45 Consider the following statements regarding the Solar System:

1. All the planets have more than one natural satellite.

2. All the planets rotate on their own axis in the west to east direction.

3. Saturn is the only planet to have a ring system around itself.

Which of the statements given above is/are correct?

A. 1 only

B. 2 and 3 only

C. 1 and 3 only

D. None

Q.46 Consider the following statements regarding the Earthquake:

1. All the natural earthquakes take place in the lithosphere

2. The point where the energy is released is called the epicenter.

Which of the statements given above is/are correct?

A. 1 only

B. 2 only

C. Both 1 and 2

D. Neither 1 nor 2

Q.47 Which of the following are not major tectonic plate?

1. Antarctica plate

2. Cocos plate

3. Arabian plate

4. South American plate

Select the correct answer using the code given below.

A. 1, 2 and 4 only

B. 2 and 3 only

C. 3 and 4 only

D. 2, 3 and 4 only

Q.48 Why people do not sink in the Dead Sea?

A. The presence of marine animals in the sea.

B. The low temperature in the dead sea makes swimmers more buoyant.

C. The high salt concentration in the dead sea increases the density of the water.

D. The depth of the thermocline is located near the surface of the Dead sea.

Q.49 Rattans or Lianas are the common types of vegetation found in which of the following climatic regions of the world?

A. Hot desert regions

B. Temperate grasslands

C. Arctic region

D. Equatorial regions

Q.50 Which of the following statements correctly describes the term river regime?

A. It is the dividing area between two rivers

B. It is the pattern of flow of water in a river channel over a year

C. It is a raised landform formed by a river near its banks due to the deposition of sediments

D. It refers to the origination or source of a river

Q.51 The movement of ocean currents is influenced by

1. Movement of planetary winds

2. The salinity of the ocean

3. Earth's rotation

4. Landmass distribution

5. Gravity

Select the correct answer using the code given below

A. 1, 3 and 4 only

B. 2, 3 and 5 only

C. 1 and 4 only

D. 1, 2, 3, 4 and 5

Q.52 Consider the following statements with respect to temperature distribution in the oceans:

1. The highest surface oceanic temperature is recorded at the equator.

2. The temperature decreases at a uniform rate with increasing oceanic depth.

3. The oceans in the northern hemisphere record relatively higher temperatures than in the southern hemisphere.

Which of the statements given above is/are correct?

A. 3 only

B. 2 only

C. 1 and 2 only

D. 2 and 3 only

Q.53 Known to be the land of rolling mountains, the region is accompanied by the formation of foreland basins (valley-like depressions) which run parallel to the mountains, these depressions are accumulated vastly with soft unconsolidated deposits forming a molasses basin.

Which Indian state is being described in the above passage?

A. Assam

B. Manipur

C. Himachal Pradesh

D. Mizoram

Q.54 Which of the following conditions is/are responsible for the formation of a China type of climate?

1. Intense heating in the continental interiors of Asia in summers.

2. The steep pressure gradient between the cold interiors of Mongolia and Siberia, and the warmer Pacific coastlands in winters.

Select the correct answer using the code given below.

A. 1 only

B. 2 only

C. Both 1 and 2

D. Neither 1 nor 2

Q.55 Which of the following statements correctly describes Agro-forestry?

A. Raising trees on public land such as pasture and temple land, roadside, etc.

B. Raising and management of trees on public and private land.

C. Raising of trees for commercial and noncommercial purposes on their farmlands.

D. Raising of trees and agriculture crops on the same land inclusive of the waste patches.

Q.56 These are smooth oval-shaped ridge-like depositional features composed mainly of glacial till with some masses of gravel and sand. One end of them facing the glacier called the stoss end is blunter and steeper than the other end called the tail. They give an indication of the direction of the glacier movement.

Which of the following landforms is described in the passage given above?

A. Moraines   **B.** Eskers

C. Drumlins   **D.** Serrated ridges

Q.57 With reference to the Western Coastal plains, which of the following statements is/are correct?

1. They are spread out in five Indian states.

2. They are broader in the middle and get narrower towards North and South.

3. The Malabar stretch of the western coastal plains has backwaters called Kayals.

Select the correct answer using the code given below.

A. 1 only   **B.** 1 and 3 only

C. 2 only   **D.** 3 only

Q.58 Consider the following statements with regard to River Vamsadhara:

1. It is an east-flowing river between Rushikulya and Godavari.

2. The river passes through Andhra Pradesh and Odisha.

3. Boddepalli Rajagopala Rao Project was constructed on it to meet the irrigation needs.

Which of the statements given above is/ are correct?

A. 1 only   **B.** 1 and 3 only

C. 2 and 3 only   **D.** 1, 2 and 3

Q.59 Red and Yellow soils are widely prevalent in the Deccan Plateau. With reference to these soils, consider the following statements:

1. They develop on crystalline igneous rocks in areas of low rainfall.

2. The reddish color of the soil is due to the diffusion of Iron.

Which of the statements given above is/are correct?

A. 1 only   **B.** 2 only

C. Both 1 and 2   **D.** Neither 1 nor 2

Q.60 Consider the following statements with respect to continental shelf, a division of ocean floor:

1. It is the shallowest part of the ocean.

2. The width of the continental shelves varies from one ocean to another.

3. Rich fishing grounds are located on continental shelves due to the availability of planktons.

Which of the statements given above are correct?

A. 1 and 2 only   **B.** 2 and 3 only

C. 1 and 3 only   **D.** 1, 2 and 3

Q.61 Which of the following are Atlantic Ocean currents?

1. Benguela current

2. Canary current

3. Alaska current

4. Humboldt current

5. Labrador current

Select the correct answer using the code given below.

A. 1, 2 and 5 only   **B.** 2, 4 and 5 only

C. 1, 3 and 5 only   **D.** 1, 2, 3 and 4 only

Q.62 Consider the following statements regarding black soil:

1. It is widespread in the northern and eastern plains.

2. It is generally clayey, deep, and impermeable.

3. They are also known as regur soil.

Which of the statements given above is/are correct?

A. 1 and 3 only   **B.** 2 and 3 only

C. 3 only   **D.** 2 only

Q.63 Which of the following causes the complete reversal of North Indian Ocean currents between summer and winter?

A. Coriolis force

B. Thermohaline circulation

C. Movement of the counter equatorial current

D. Monsoon winds

Q.64 Which of the following UNESCO Biosphere Reserve is located between the Narmada and the Tapi river valleys?

A. Pachmarhi

B. Achanakmar-Amarkantak

C. Agasthyamalai

D. Similipal

Q.65 Which of the following statements is correct with respect to the salinity in the oceans?

A. Salinity in equatorial waters is higher than the average ocean water salinity.

B. In the zone of Halocline, salinity rapidly decreases with increasing depth.

C. Sodium Chloride constitutes more than 75% of the dissolved mineral water in the oceans.

D. The Arabian Sea shows lower salinity trends than the Bay of Bengal.

Q.66 Which of the following is/are the impacts of the occurrence of El-Nino?

1. Distortion of equatorial atmospheric circulation.

2. Delay in the onset of southwest monsoon over the Indian subcontinent.

3. Reduction in the number of fish in the sea along the Peruvian coast.

Select the correct answer using the code given below.

A. 1 and 2 only   **B.** 2 only

C. 2 and 3 only   **D.** 1, 2 and 3

Q.67 Which of the following regions can be best described by the term "Bush-veld" landscape?

A. Steppe grasslands

B. Mediterranean region

C. Savannah grasslands

D. Hot deserts

Q.68 Consider the following statements with reference to River Yamuna:

1. It is the westernmost tributary of the River Ganga.

2. It has its source on the western slopes of the Banderpunch range in Uttarakhand.

3. It passes through four states and one Union territory of India.

Which of the statements given above is/ are correct?

A. 1 and 3 only   **B.** 2 and only

C. 1 and 2 only   **D.** 1, 2 and 3

Q.69 These are dome-shaped granitic bodies formed from the cooled portion of magma chambers. They appear on the surface only after the denudational processes remove the overlying materials. They cover large areas, and at times, assume depth that may be several kilometers.

Which of the following volcanic landform is described in the above passage?

A. Phacolith   **B.** Lapolith

C. Dyke   **D.** Batholiths

Q.70 "This type of climate is experienced along the eastern coasts of tropical lands, receiving steady rainfall from the Trade Winds all the time. The rainfall is both orographic as well as convectional. There is no month without any rainfall."

Which type of climate is being referred to in the above passage?

A. The Hot, Wet Equatorial climate

B. Tropical Marine Climate

C. Tropical Monsoon Climate

D. The Sudan Climate

Q.71 Consider the following pairs:

Desert	Country
1. Patagonian Desert	Saudi Arabia
2. Mojave Desert	United States of America
3. Gibson Desert	Turkey

Which of the pairs given above is/are correctly matched?

A. 1 only   **B.** 1 and 3 only

C. 2 only   **D.** 1, 2 and 3

Q.72 Which of the following process of rock formation is being described in the below passage?

When the rocks of the earth's surface area exposed to denudational agents, they are broken up into various sizes of fragments. Such fragments are transported by different exogenous agencies and deposited. These deposits through compaction turn into rocks. It is a process of porosity destruction through compaction and fermentation.

Select the correct answer using the code given below.

A. Recrystallisation   **B.** Foliation

C. Lithification   **D.** Exfoliation

Q.73 Consider the following pairs:

Water Channels	Between
1. 10 degrees Channel	Andaman and Nicobar Islands
2. Duncan passage	Middle Andaman and Little Andaman
3. Coco Strait	Great Nicobar and Sumatran Island

Which of the pairs given above is/are correctly matched?

A. 1 and 2 only   **B.** 2 and 3 only

C. 1 and 3 only   **D.** 1 only

Q.74 Which of the following families of modern Indian languages has the highest number of speakers in India?

A. Austric   **B.** Dravidian

C. Sino-Tibetan   **D.** Indo-European

Q.75 Consider the following statements:

1. Sugar Industry is a seasonal industry.

2. India is the largest producer of sugarcane in the world.

3. The crop yield of sugarcane is higher in Northern India than in Southern India.

Which of the statements given above is/are correct?

A. 1 only   **B.** 2 and 3 only

C. 1 and 3 only   **D.** 1, 2 and 3

Q.76 Which of the statements given below is correct regarding the cotton industry?

A. Cotton is a non-weight-losing raw material.

B. Cotton industries are mostly market-based industries

C. Maharashtra, Gujarat and Andhra Pradesh are leading producers of cotton

D. All the statements are correct

Q.77 Which of the following activities are called gold-collar professions?

A. Quinary activities

B. Quaternary activities

C. Secondary activities

D. Primary activities

Q.78 With reference to the growth trends of the global population, consider the following statements:

1. The doubling time of the world population has been increasing in the last century.

2. At the beginning of the twentieth century, the world population was less than half of its current levels.

Which of the statements given above is/are correct?

A. 1 only   **B.** 2 only

C. Both 1 and 2   **D.** Neither 1 nor 2

Q.79 Consider the following statements about sedimentary basins in India:

1. In India they are located only along with the offshore areas.

2. They are an important source of oil, natural gas, and petroleum.

Which of the statements given above is/are not correct?

A. 1 only   **B.** 2 only

C. Both 1 and 2   **D.** Neither 1 nor 2

Q.80 Consider the following statements:

1. The maximum percentage of surface water in India is utilized by the industrial sector.

2. The maximum percentage of groundwater in India is utilized by the agriculture sector.

Which of the statements given above is/are correct?

A. 1 only   **B.** 2 only

C. Both 1 and 2   **D.** Neither 1 nor 2

Q.81 Which of the following factors play a role in determining the nature of rural settlements in India?

1. Nature of terrain

2. Caste and ethnicity of people

3. Availability of water

Select the correct answer using the code given below.

A. 1 and 2 only   **B.** 2 and 3 only

C. 1 and 3 only   **D.** 1, 2 and 3

Q.82 Which of the following are metallic minerals?

1. Copper

2. Graphite

3. Bauxite

4. Limestone

Select the correct answer using the code given below.

A. 1 and 2 only   **B.** 1 and 3 only

C. 3 only   **D.** 1, 2 and 4 only

Q.83 Which of the following are identified shale gas basins for exploration?

1. Cambay

2. K-G Basin

3. Assam-Arakan

4. Indus River Basin

Select the correct answer using the code given below.

A. 1 and 4 only   **B.** 1, 2 and 3 only

C. 2, 3 and 4 only   **D.** 1, 2, 3 and 4

Q.84 Consider the following pairs:

Nuclear Plant	State
1. Tarapur	Maharashtra
2. Rawatbhata	Rajasthan
3. Kalpakkam	Karnataka
4. Kaiga	Tamil Nadu

Which of the pairs given above is/are correctly matched?

A. 1, 2 and 3 only   **B.** 1 and 4 only

C. 1 and 2 only   **D.** 2 and 3 only

Q.85 Consider the following :

This stage in the demographic transition theory is marked by a high birth rate but lowering death rates resulting in a natural increase in the population. Countries like Kenya and Sri Lanka are currently said to be in this stage.

Which of the following stages of the demographic transition theory is being described in the above passage?

A. Stage I   **B.** Stage II   **C.** Stage III   **D.** None

Q.86 Consider the following pairs:

Settlement	Region
1. Dispersed	Himachal Pradesh
2. Clustered	Bundelkhand
3. Hamleted	Lower Ganga Plains

Which of the pairs given above is/are correctly matched?

A. 1 only   **B.** 2 and 3 only

C. 1, 2 and 3   **D.** None

Q.87 Which of the following statements best describes truck farming?

A. It is farming in which farmers specialise in vegetables.

B. It is farming in which animals are transported from one place to another for trading.

C. It is farming in which heavy machinery is used for harvesting crops.

D. It is a part of dairy farming in which trucks are used for transporting milk from one place to another.

Q.88 Consider the following statements regarding Iron and Steel Industries:

1. All the raw materials used in the iron and steel industry are non-weight-losing raw materials.

2. In India, all steel plants are located near the sites of raw material.

Which of the statements given above is/are correct?

A. 1 only   **B.** 2 only

C. Both 1 and 2   **D.** Neither 1 nor 2

Q.89 Consider the following statements about the Human Development Index:

1. It is issued every year by the World Bank.

2. It is calculated as a geometric mean of Health, Education & Standard of Living Indicators.

Which of the statements given above is/are correct?

A. 1 only   **B.** 2 only

C. Both 1 and 2   **D.** Neither 1 nor 2

Q.90 With respect to agriculture in the Mediterranean region, consider the following statements:

1. The Mediterranean lands are known as the world's orchard lands.

2. Viticulture is a traditional occupation of the Mediterranean region.

3. In mountainous regions transhumance is widely practiced.

Which of the statements given above is/are correct?

A. 1 only   **B.** 1 and 3 only

C. 2 and 3 only   **D.** 1, 2 and 3

Q.91 With reference to the Demographic Transition Theory, consider the following statements:

1. According to the theory, the population of a given region changes from high births and high deaths to low births and low deaths.

2. During a complete demographic cycle, rural agrarian societies are transformed into urbanized and industrial economies.

Which of the statements given above is/are correct.

A. 1 only
B. 2 only
C. Both 1 and 2
D. Neither 1 nor 2

Q.92 Arrange the following religions in increasing order of the number of people practicing them in India?

1. Sikhs
2. Christians
3. Muslims
4. Buddhists

Select the correct answer using the code given below.

A. 2-1-3-4 **B.** 3-1-2-4 **C.** 3-2-1-4 **D.** 1-2-3-4

Q.93 Consider the following statements about Quinary Activities:

1. The highest level of decision-makers or policymakers perform quinary activities.
2. Banking and Legal Advisory are prime examples of quinary activities.

Which of the statements given above is/are correct?

A. 1 only
B. 2 only
C. Both 1 and 2
D. Neither 1 nor 2

Q.94 Which of the following regions are major industrial regions in India?

1. Mumbai-Pune Region
2. Vishakhapatnam-Guntur Region
3. Chhotanagpur Region
4. Ambala-Amritsar Region

Select the correct answer using the code given below.

A. 1, 2 and 3 only
B. 1 and 3 only
C. 2 and 4 only
D. 1, 2, 3 and 4

Q.95 In the Himalayas, some tribes like Gujjars, Bakarwals, Gaddis, and Bhotiyas migrate from plains to the mountains in summers and to the plains from the high altitude pastures in winters in every season.

Which of the following practice is described in the above statement?

A. Jhuming
B. Transhumance
C. Gathering
D. Pastoralism

Q.96 Consider the following statements:

1. Coal accounts for more than half of India's energy needs.
2. Most of India's coal reserves are of non-cooking grade.

Which of the statements given above is/are correct?

A. 1 only
B. 2 only
C. Both 1 and 2
D. Neither 1 nor 2

Q.97 Consider the following pairs:

Crop/Tree	Leading producer Country
1. Palm oil	Indonesia
2. Jute	Bangladesh
3. Teak	India

Which of the pairs given above is/are correctly matched?

A. 1 only
B. 2 and 3 only
C. 1 and 2 only
D. 1, 2 and 3

Q.98 Consider the following statements:

1. Migration takes place only when people move from rural to urban areas in search of employment.
2. In India, intra-state rural to rural migration by place of last residence is dominated by females.

Which of the statements given above is/are correct?

A. 1 only
B. 2 only
C. Both 1 and 2
D. Neither 1 nor 2

Q.99 Consider the following activities:

1. Hunting and gathering
2. Pastoral activities
3. Fishing
4. Forestry
5. Mining and quarrying

Which of the activities mentioned above are considered primary activities?

A. 3 and 4 only
B. 1, 2 and 3 only
C. 2, 4 and 5 only
D. 1, 2, 3, 4 and 5

Q.100 Which of the following factors contribute to 'Population Ageing'?

1. Declining fertility rates
2. Increase in life expectancy
3. Increase in the proportion of the working-age population.

Select the correct answer using the code given below.

A. 1 and 2 only
B. 2 and 3 only
C. 1 and 3 only
D. 1, 2 and 3

Q.101 Consider the following pairs:

Inland Waterway	Origin Country
1. The Rhine Waterway	Germany
2. The Danube Waterway	France
3. The Volga Waterway	Russia

Which of the pairs given above is/are correctly matched?

A. 1 only
B. 1 and 3 only
C. 3 only
D. 2 and 3 only

Q.102 Consider the following statements:

1. North America has the highest road density in the world.
2. Africa has the highest length of inland waterways in the world.

Which of the statements given above is/are correct?

A. 1 only
B. 2 only
C. Both 1 and 2
D. Neither 1 nor 2

Q.103 With reference to the Census of India (2011), consider the following statements:

1. Urban areas accommodating more than 10 million persons are known as megacities.
2. Over 40% of India's Population resides in cities and urban areas.

Which of the statements given above is/are correct?

A. 1 only
B. 2 only
C. Both 1 and 2
D. Neither 1 nor 2

Q.104 The Hazira-Vijaipur-Jagdishpur Pipeline system, which is India's first cross-state gas pipeline, passes through which of the following Indian states?

1. Madhya Pradesh
2. Maharashtra
3. Gujarat
4. Uttar Pradesh

Select the correct answer from the codes given below:

A. 1, 3 and 4 only
B. 1 and 3 only
C. 2, 3 and 4 only
D. 2 and 4 only

Q.105 Consider the following statements:

1. Coal has the most widely distributed reserves among all fossil fuels.
2. The United States of America is the leading producer of coal in the world.

Which of the statements given above is/are correct?

A. 1 only
B. 2 only
C. Both 1 and 2
D. Neither 1 nor 2

Q.106 Which of the following are the characteristics of the footloose industry?

1. They are dependent on a specific raw material.
2. They are generally non-polluting industries.

Select the correct answer using the code given below.

A. 1 only
B. 2 only
C. Both 1 and 2
D. Neither 1 nor 2

Q.107 Consider the following statements:

1. India is the largest producer of coffee in the world.
2. India mostly produces arabica coffee.
3. Kerala is the largest coffee-producing state in India.

Which of the statements given above is/are correct?

A. 2 only
B. 1 and 3 only
C. 1 and 2 only
D. All statements are wrong

Q.108 Which of the following is/are 'Push Factors' responsible for the mass exodus of the migrant laborers from urban areas?

1. Better living conditions in rural areas.
2. Epidemics in urban areas.
3. Lack of employment opportunities inrural areas.

Select the correct answer using the code given below.

A. 1 and 2 only
B. 2 only
C. 1 and 3 only
D. 1, 2 and 3

Q.109 Consider the following pairs:

Cropping Season	Crop
1. Kharif Season	Wheat
2. Rabi Season	Cotton
3. Zaid Season	Cucumber

Which of the pairs given above is/are correctly matched?

A. 1 and 2 only
B. 2 and 3 only
C. 3 only
D. 1, 2 and 3

Q.110 Consider the following pairs:

Tribes	Regions
1. Pygmies	Malaysia
2. Indian	Amazon Basin
3. Orang Asli	Congo Basin

Which of the pairs given above is/are correctly matched?

A. 1 only
B. 1 and 2 only
C. 2 and 3 only
D. 2 only

Q.111 Consider the following statements:

1. Primitive human society was highly influenced by the strong forces of nature.
2. Level of technological development was low and humans were afraid of fury of nature.
3. Ellen Semple was a proponent of this school of Human Geography.

Which of the following schools of Human Geography do the above statements refer to?

A. Possibilism
B. Environmental Determinism
C. Cultural Determinism
D. Neo Determinism

Q.112 What is common to the sites of Mayurbhanj, Kudremukh and Bailadila?

A. They are important oil fields
B. They are iron ore belts in India
C. They are well known sites of nuclear power plants
D. They are one of the largest sites of copper mines

Q.113 In a given time period, which of the following best describes the term 'Actual Growth of Population' of a given region?

A. It is the total increase in the number of new births
B. It is the net increase in the population of a region after accounting only for new births and deaths
C. It refers to the change in number of inhabitants of a region due to births, deaths as well as migration
D. It refers to the change in the fertility rates of a population

Q.114 Consider the following pairs in the context of shifting cultivation:

Local name	Region
1. Milpa	India
2.Taungiya	Myanmar
3. Ladang	Malaysia

Which of the pairs given above are correctly matched?

A. 1 and 2 only
B. 2 and 3 only
C. 1 and 3 only
D. 1, 2 and 3

Q.115 Arrange the following Executive Capital cities of the states of India from north to south:

1. Bengaluru
2. Vishakhapatnam
3. Raipur
4. Thiruvananthapuram

Select the correct answer using the code given below.

A. 3-2-4-1
B. 3-2-1-4
C. 2-3-1-4
D. 2-3-4-1

Q.116 Which of the following is/are considered 'Urban Agglomerations'?

1. A town and its adjoining urban outgrowths.
2. Two or more contiguous towns with or without their outgrowths.
3. A city and one or more adjoining towns with their outgrowths together forming a contiguous spread.

Select the correct answer using the code given below.

A. 3 only
B. 1 and 2 only
C. 2 and 3 only
D. 1, 2 and 3

Q.117 With reference to population statistics, which of the following statements is not correct?

A. The population of India is larger than the total population of North America

B. The population density of India has more than doubled since Independence

C. West Bengal is the state with highest population density in India

D. Arunachal Pradesh has the lowest density of population among the states in India

Q.118 Global Forest Resource Assessment 2020, recently seen in news, has been published by:

A. Global Green Growth Institute
B. International Panel on Climate Change
C. United Nations Food and Agriculture Organization
D. United Nations Environment Program

Q.119 In the context of economic geography, what are the Ports of Call?

A. Ports that act as collection centers where the goods are brought from different countries for export

B. Ports that are concerned with the transportation of passengers and mail across water bodies covering short distances

C. Ports that serve warships and have repair workshops for them

D. Ports developed on main sea routes where ships anchor for refueling, watering and taking food items

Q.120 Which of the following industries are most likely to be located near their raw material producing areas?

1. Pulp Industries
2. Copper Smelting
3. Pig Iron Industries
4. Synthetic Nitrogen Manufacturing Industries

Which of the statements given above is/are correct?

A. 1 and 2 only
B. 1, 3 and 4 only
C. 1, 2 and 3 only
D. 2 and 4 only

Q.121 Consider the following pairs:

Tribes	Dwellings
1. Bindibu	Zeriba
2. Tuaregs	Wurlies
3. Gobi Mongols	Yurts

Which of the pairs given above is/are correctly matched?

A. 1 and 2 only
B. 2 and 3 only
C. 3 only
D. 1, 2 and 3

Q.122 Which of the following conditions are favorable for the cultivation of Tea?

1. Moderate Temperatures.
2. Medium Rainfall
3. Well-drained highland slopes.

Select the correct answer using the code given below.

A. 1 and 2 only
B. 2 and 3 only
C. 1 and 3 only
D. 1, 2 and 3

Q.123 Which of the following are pass that connects India and Nepal?

1. Lipulekh
2. Nathu La
3. Jelep La
4. Zoji La

Select the correct answer using the codes given below.

A. 1 and 2 only
B. 1, 3 and 4 only
C. 1 only
D. 2, 3 and 4 only

Q.124 Arrange the following continents in increasing order of their population density.

1. Asia
2. Africa
3. Europe

Select the correct answer using the code given below.

A. 2-1-3
B. 2-3-1
C. 1-2-3
D. 1-2-3

Q.125 Which of the following states in India issetting up the first observatory formammals?

A. Odisha
B. Uttar Pradesh
C. Bihar
D. West Bengal

// Smart Answer Sheet //

Correct   Indicates percentage of students who answered questions correctly.

Skipped   Indicates percentage of students who skipped questions.

Q.	Ans.	Correct / Skipped
1	C	40.0 % / 3.33 %
2	A	33.33 % / 33.34 %
3	C	46.67 % / 33.33 %
4	A	26.67 % / 36.66 %
5	B	33.33 % / 36.67 %
6	B	50.0 % / 33.33 %
7	D	40.0 % / 36.67 %
8	C	20.0 % / 36.67 %
9	C	43.33 % / 36.67 %
10	A	46.67 % / 33.33 %
11	C	16.67 % / 33.33 %
12	C	43.33 % / 36.67 %
13	D	53.33 % / 33.34 %
14	A	20.0 % / 36.67 %
15	A	43.33 % / 33.34 %
16	A	56.67 % / 33.33 %

Q.	Ans.	Correct / Skipped
17	A	6.67 % / 36.66 %
18	A	53.33 % / 36.67 %
19	A	53.33 % / 30.0 %
20	A	36.67 % / 33.33 %
21	B	36.67 % / 33.33 %
22	D	40.0 % / 36.67 %
23	A	16.67 % / 30.0 %
24	D	3.33 % / 36.67 %
25	A	30.0 % / 36.67 %
26	B	23.33 % / 36.67 %
27	A	40.0 % / 33.33 %
28	B	36.67 % / 36.66 %
29	C	6.67 % / 33.33 %
30	B	46.67 % / 33.33 %
31	C	33.33 % / 33.34 %
32	D	30.0 % / 33.33 %

Q.	Ans.	Correct / Skipped
33	C	23.33 % / 30.0 %
34	C	26.67 % / 36.66 %
35	C	46.67 % / 33.33 %
36	B	40.0 % / 33.33 %
37	B	40.0 % / 36.67 %
38	B	53.33 % / 33.34 %
39	C	33.33 % / 36.67 %
40	A	26.67 % / 36.66 %
41	B	56.67 % / 33.33 %
42	B	40.0 % / 36.67 %
43	C	53.33 % / 33.34 %
44	D	40.0 % / 36.67 %
45	D	46.67 % / 33.33 %
46	A	26.67 % / 36.66 %
47	B	60.0 % / 33.33 %
48	C	56.67 % / 36.66 %

Q.	Ans.	Correct / Skipped
49	D	23.33 % / 36.67 %
50	B	26.67 % / 33.33 %
51	D	33.33 % / 33.34 %
52	A	40.0 % / 33.33 %
53	D	26.67 % / 36.66 %
54	C	50.0 % / 33.33 %
55	D	20.0 % / 33.33 %
56	C	26.67 % / 36.66 %
57	B	43.33 % / 36.67 %
58	D	56.67 % / 33.33 %
59	C	50.0 % / 33.33 %
60	D	60.0 % / 33.33 %
61	A	46.67 % / 36.66 %
62	B	50.0 % / 33.33 %
63	D	50.0 % / 33.33 %
64	A	33.33 % / 36.67 %

Q.	Ans.	Correct / Skipped
65	C	40.0 % / 36.67 %
66	D	46.67 % / 33.33 %
67	C	33.33 % / 36.67 %
68	D	23.33 % / 36.67 %
69	D	40.0 % / 36.67 %
70	B	26.67 % / 36.66 %
71	C	46.67 % / 30.0 %
72	C	26.67 % / 33.33 %
73	D	13.33 % / 36.67 %
74	D	36.67 % / 33.33 %
75	A	33.33 % / 36.67 %
76	D	53.33 % / 33.34 %
77	A	33.33 % / 36.67 %
78	B	13.33 % / 33.34 %
79	A	20.0 % / 30.0 %
80	B	33.33 % / 33.34 %

Q.	Ans.	Correct	Skipped
81	D	56.67 %	33.33 %
82	B	43.33 %	33.34 %
83	B	30.0 %	36.67 %
84	C	40.0 %	33.33 %
85	B	50.0 %	36.67 %
86	C	23.33 %	33.34 %
87	A	43.33 %	36.67 %
88	D	13.33 %	36.67 %
89	B	33.33 %	36.67 %

Q.	Ans.	Correct	Skipped
90	D	56.67 %	36.66 %
91	C	50.0 %	36.67 %
92	C	33.33 %	36.67 %
93	C	40.0 %	33.33 %
94	A	20.0 %	36.67 %
95	B	56.67 %	33.33 %
96	C	53.33 %	33.34 %
97	A	10.0 %	36.67 %
98	B	43.33 %	33.34 %

Q.	Ans.	Correct	Skipped
99	D	53.33 %	33.34 %
100	A	26.67 %	33.33 %
101	C	10.0 %	36.67 %
102	A	26.67 %	36.66 %
103	A	33.33 %	36.67 %
104	A	46.67 %	33.33 %
105	A	26.67 %	36.66 %
106	C	20.0 %	36.67 %
107	D	46.67 %	33.33 %

Q.	Ans.	Correct	Skipped
108	B	36.67 %	36.66 %
109	C	46.67 %	33.33 %
110	D	23.33 %	33.34 %
111	B	53.33 %	30.0 %
112	B	56.67 %	36.66 %
113	C	43.33 %	33.34 %
114	B	40.0 %	36.67 %
115	B	60.0 %	33.33 %
116	D	40.0 %	36.67 %

Q.	Ans.	Correct	Skipped
117	C	56.67 %	33.33 %
118	C	16.67 %	36.66 %
119	C	33.33 %	33.34 %
120	C	40.0 %	33.33 %
121	C	16.67 %	33.33 %
122	C	16.67 %	36.66 %
123	C	40.0 %	33.33 %
124	C	23.33 %	36.67 %
125	C	23.33 %	36.67 %

Performance Analysis

Avg. Score (%)	32.47%
Toppers Score (%)	85.65%
Your Score	

//Hints and Solutions//

1. The periodical rise and fall of the sea level, once or twice a day, mainly due to the attraction of the sun and the moon, is called a tide. The moon's gravitational pull to a great extent and to a lesser extent the sun's gravitational pull, are the major causes for the occurrence of tides. Another factor is centrifugal force, which is the force that acts to counter the balance the gravity. Together, the gravitational pull and the centrifugal force are responsible for creating the two major tidal bulges on the earth.

The position of both the sun and the moon in relation to the earth has a direct bearing on tide height. When the sun, the moon and the earth are in a straight line, the height of the tide will be higher. These are called spring tides and they occur twice a month, one on full moon period and another during new moon period.

Once in a month, when the moon's orbit is closest to the earth (perigee), unusually high and low tides occur. During this time the tidal range is greater than normal. Two weeks later, when the moon is farthest from Earth, the moon's gravitational force is limited and the tidal ranges are less than their average heights.

If a lunar perigee falls near a new or full moon (spring tides occur), then perigean spring tides of a greater tidal range occur. Hence, the correct option is (C).

2. Oxygen accelerates the process of decomposition. Since major organisms depend on oxygen for respiration and reproduction, they can not multiply in hypoxic conditions i.e. lack of enough oxygen levels.

Decomposition will be faster if the detritus is rich in nitrogen and water-soluble substances like sugars and it will be slower if the detritus is rich in lignin and chitin.

Cool temperatures inhibit the decomposition and piling up of the organic content in the soil takes place. Warm temperature makes the microorganisms active and faster will be the decomposition. Hence, the correct option is (A).

3. Bharatmala Pariyojana is an umbrella project for the highways sector with Phase I from 2017 to 2022. A total of around 24,800 km are being considered in Phase I. In addition, Phase I also includes 10,000 km of balance road works under National Highways Development Project. Bharatmala Pariyojana subsumes all existing highway projects including the flagship National Highways Development Project (NHDP), launched in 1998. Bharatmala Pariyojana consists of 6 components:

- Economic corridors development
- Inter-corridor & feeder roads
- National Corridors Efficiency improvements:
- Border & International connectivity roads
- Coastal & port connectivity roads
- Expressways

Hence, the correct option is (C).

4. Igneous rocks form out of magma and lava from the interior of the earth, so they are known as primary rocks. The igneous rocks (Ignis – in Latin means 'Fire') are formed when magma cools and solidifies. When magma in its upward movement cools and turns into a solid form it is called igneous rock. The process of cooling and solidification can happen in the earth's crust (plutonic rocks) or on the surface of the earth (volcanic rocks).

Igneous rocks are devoid of any fossils. This is because any fossils in the original rock will have melted when the rock melted to form magma.

Metamorphic Rocks are formed out of existing rocks undergoing recrystallization. Gneissoid, granite, syenite, slate, schist, marble, quartzite, etc. are some examples of metamorphic rocks. Hence, the correct option is (A).

5. The Cool Temperate Western Margin (British Type) Climate:

- The cool temperate western margins are under the permanent influence of the Westerlies all around the year.
- They are also regions of much cyclonic activity, typical of Britain, and are hence named British type of climate.

Spatial spread:

- Britain, lowlands North-West Europe, northern and western France, Belgium, the Netherlands, Denmark, western Norway and also north-western Iberia.
- In the southern hemisphere, southern Chile, Tasmania, and most parts of New Zealand.

Temperature:

- The mean annual temperatures are usually between 5°C and 15°C. The annual range of temperature is small. Summers are, in fact, never very warm.

Precipitation:

- The British type of climate has adequate rainfall throughout the year with a tendency towards a slight winter or autumn maximum from cyclonic sources
- Since the rain-bearing winds come from the west, the western margins have the heaviest rainfall. The amount decreases eastwards with increasing distance from the sea.

Natural Vegetation:

- The natural vegetation of this climatic type is deciduous forest. The trees shed their leaves in the cold season, for protecting themselves against the winter snow and frost.
- The common species include oak, elm, ash, birch, beech, poplar, and hornbeam.
- Unlike the equatorial forests, the deciduous trees occur in pure stands and have greater lumbering value from the commercial point of view.
- The deciduous hardwoods are excellent for both fuel and industrial purposes.

Economy:

- The region differs from many others in its unprecedented industrial advancement.

Hence, the correct option is (B).

6. If rain fails to occur for one or more weeks during the southwest monsoon period after having rained for a few days. These breaks in the different regions are due to different reasons:

- In northern India, rains are likely to fail if the rain-bearing storms are not very frequent along the monsoon trough or the ITCZ over this region.

- Over the west coast, the dry spells are associated with days when winds blow parallel to the coast.

Hence, the correct option is (B).

7. Evidence in Support of the Continental Drift:

The shorelines of Africa and South America facing each other have a remarkable and unmistakable match. It may be noted that a map produced using a computer programme to find the best fit of the Atlantic margin was presented by Bullard in 1964. It proved to be quite perfect. The match was tried at 1,000- fathom line instead of the present shoreline.

The radiometric dating methods developed in the recent period have facilitated correlating the rock formation from different continents across the vast ocean. The belt of ancient rocks 2,000 million years from Brazil's coast matches with those from western Africa. The earliest marine deposits along the coastline of South America and Africa are of the Jurassic age. This suggests that the ocean did not exist prior to that time.

The occurrence of rich placer deposits of gold on the Ghana coast and the absolute absence of source rock in the region is an amazing fact. The gold-bearing veins are in Brazil and it is obvious that the gold deposits of Ghana are derived from the Brazil plateau when the two continents lay side by side.

When identical species of plants and animals adapted to living on land or in fresh water are found on either side of the marine barriers, a problem arises regarding accounting for such distribution. The observations that Lemurs occur in India, Madagascar and Africa led some to consider a contiguous landmass "Lemuria" linking these three landmasses. Mesosaurus was a small reptile adapted to shallow brackish water. The skeletons of these are found only in two localities: the Southern Cape province of South Africa and Traver formations of Brazil. The two localities presently are 4,800 km apart with an ocean in between them.
Hence, the correct option is (D).

8. Ocean trenches are long, narrow depressions on the seafloor. They are the deepest parts of the oceans. The trenches are relatively steep-sided, narrow basins. They are some 3-5 km deeper than the surrounding ocean floor.

Ocean trenches are a result of tectonic activity, which describes the movement of the Earth's lithosphere. In particular, ocean trenches are a feature of convergent plate boundaries, where two or more tectonic plates meet. At many convergent plate boundaries, dense lithosphere melts or slides beneath less-dense lithosphere in a process called subduction, creating a trench.

They occur at the bases of continental slopes and along island arcs and are associated with active volcanoes and strong earthquakes. That is why they are very significant in the study of plate movements. As many as 57 deeps have been explored so far; of which 32 are in the Pacific Ocean; 19 in the Atlantic Ocean and 6 in the Indian Ocean.

The deepest known trench is the Mariana trench near Guam Island which is more than 36,000 feet deep. Other notable ocean deeps include Tonga trench, Japanese trench, Mindanao deep, etc., all located in the Pacific Ocean.
Hence, the correct option is (C).

9. Latitude can be thought of as the angular distance of a point (on the surface of the earth) north or south of the equator. Since the plane of the equator is the reference plane for measuring latitudes, the equator is at 0° latitude. It is parallel to a line, the equator, which lies midway between the poles. These lines are therefore called parallels of latitude, and on a globe are actually circles, becoming smaller polewards. The equator represents 0° and the North and South Poles are 90°N and 90°S.

Longitude is an angular distance, measured in degrees along the equator east or west of the prime meridian. On the globe, longitude is shown as a series of semi-circles that run from pole to pole passing through the equator. Such lines are also called Meridians.
Hence, the correct option is (C).

10. Plains are by far the most prominent landforms in the deserts. In basins with mountains and hills around and along, the drainage is towards the center of the basin, and due to the gradual deposition of sediment from basin margins, a nearly level plain forms at the center of the basin.

Sometimes the water collected in the depression does not completely disappear by evaporation or seepage covering the depression or plain with a shallow water body. Such types of shallow lakes are called playas where water is retained only for a short duration due to evaporation and quite often the playas contain heavy deposition of salts. Thus these are landforms formed by the action of water in deserts. The playa plain covered up by salts is called alkali flats.

Small round shallow depressions formed on limestone surfaces through solution are called Swallow holes, a common erosional feature of karst topography. Unassorted coarse and fine debris dropped by melting glaciers is called Glacial till.
Hence, the correct option is (A).

11. They are shallow cyclonic depressions (weak temperate cyclones) originating over the eastern Mediterranean Sea and travelling eastwards across West Asia, Iran, Afghanistan and Pakistan before they reach the northwestern parts of India.

They are steered in India by Westerly Jet Streams. On their way, the moisture content gets augmented from the Caspian Sea in the north and the Persian Gulf in the south. Although the amount of rainfall caused by them is meager, it is highly beneficial for rabi crops.

It sustains the flow of water in the Himalayan rivers during the summer months. An increase in the prevailing night temperature generally indicates an advance in the arrival of these cyclones disturbances.
Hence, the correct option is (C).

12. The gravitation force (g) is not the same at different latitudes on the surface. The reading of the gravity at different places is influenced by many other factors including the uneven distribution of mass of material within the earth influences this value. The gravity values also differ according to the mass of the material. It is greater near the poles and less at the equator. This is because of the distance from the centre at the equator being greater than that at the poles. These readings differ from the expected values. Such a difference is called a gravity anomaly. Gravity anomalies give us information about the distribution of mass of the material in the crust of the earth. Hence, the correct option is (C).

13. All observations from telescopes reveal that the planetary bodies, the Sun, Moon, satellites, and stars have circular outlines from whichever angle they are seen. They are strictly spheres. Earth, by analogy, cannot be the only exception. The first voyage around the world by Ferdinand Magellan and his crew, from 1519 to 1522 proved beyond doubt that the Earth is a sphere. No traveler going around the world by land or sea has encountered an abrupt edge, over which he would fall.

The distant horizon viewed from the deck of a ship at sea, or from a cliff on land always and everywhere is circular in shape. This circular horizon widens with increasing altitude and could only be seen on a spherical body. The sunsets and rises at different times at different places. As the earth rotates from west to east, places in the east see the sun earlier than those in the west. If the earth were flat, the whole world would have sunrise and sunset at the same time.

During the lunar eclipse, the shadow cast by the earth on the moon is always circular. It takes the outline of an arc of a circle. Only a sphere can cast such a circular shadow. Hence, the correct option is (D).

14. Luni is the largest river system of Rajasthan, west of Aravalli. It originates near Pushkar in two branches, i.e. the Saraswati and the Sabarmati, which join with each other at Govindgarh. From here, the river comes out of Aravalli and is known as Luni. It flows towards the west till Telwara and then takes a southwest direction to join the Rann of Kutch. During its total course of 495 km, the Luni river passes through the states of Rajasthan and Gujarat. The entire river system is ephemeral.

Mahi River is the only river in India that cuts the Tropic of Cancer twice, first in Madhya Pradesh from where it flows towards Rajasthan and enters Gujarat where it cuts for the second time. Hence, the correct option is (A).

15. The Western Ghats are locally known by different names such as Sahyadri in Maharashtra, Nilgiri hills in Karnataka, and Tamil Nadu and Anaimalai hills, and Cardamom hills in Kerala. The Western Ghats are comparatively higher in elevation and more continuous than the Eastern Ghats. Their average elevation is about 1,500 m with the height increasing from north to south. 'Anaimudi' (2,695 m), the highest peak of the Peninsular plateau is located on the Anaimalai Hills of the Western Ghats followed by Dodabetta (2,637 m) on the Nilgiri hills. Most of the Peninsular rivers have their origin in the Western Ghats. Hence, the correct option is (A).

16. The islands of the Arabian sea include Lakshadweep and Minicoy. The entire group of islands is broadly divided by the Eleventh-degree channel, north of which is the Amini Island and to the south of the Cannanore Island.

The entire island group is built of coral deposits. Hence, the correct option is (A).

17. Himalayan mountain range Protecting the subcontinent from the cold northern winds blowing from as far as Siberia. Trapping the monsoon winds, forcing them to shed their moisture within the subcontinent. Differential heating of land and sea and the shift of ITCZ is responsible for creating different air pressure zones causing a reversal in the direction of monsoon winds. Hence, the correct option is (A).

18. Karewas are the thick deposits of glacial clay and other materials embedded with moraines. To be more precise, Karewas are lacustrine deposits. According to geographers, the Karewa Formation is glacial- fluvial-lacustrine and aeolian loess of PlioPleistocene age. Hence, the correct option is (A).

19. Pokkali is a unique rice variety in the coastal areas of Alappuzha, Ernakulam, and Thrissur districts. The salt water-resistant variety grows tall, flourishes under flood-like conditions, and grows entirely on leftovers from half a year of fish culture in fields. The cycle is called 'one fish and one rice' in which fish is grown up to April 15 after which fields are drained before the first bout of rains get them rid of salt. The season goes up to October when they are brought under fish culture again. Hence, the correct option is (A).

20. The structure of the earth is divided into three major components: the crust, the mantle, core.

Crust is the outermost solid part of the earth. It is brittle in nature. The thickness of the crust varies under the oceanic and continental areas. Oceanic crust is thinner as compared to continental crust. The mean thickness of the oceanic crust is 5 km whereas that of the continental is around 30 km. The continental crust is thicker in the areas of major mountain systems. It is as much as 70 km thick in the Himalayan region.

The portion of the interior beyond the crust is called the mantle. The mantle extends from Moho's discontinuity to a depth of 2,900 km. The upper portion of the mantle is called the asthenosphere. The word astheno means weak. It is considered to be extending up to 400 km. It is the main source of magma that finds its way to the surface during volcanic eruptions. The crust and the uppermost part of the mantle are called the lithosphere. Its thickness ranges from 10-200 km. The lower mantle extends beyond the asthenosphere. It is in a solid-state.

The core-mantle boundary is located at the depth of 2,900 km. The outer core is in a liquid state while the inner core is in a solid state. The core is made up of very heavy material mostly constituted by nickel and iron. It is sometimes referred to as the nife layer. Hence, the correct option is (A).

21. Divergent Boundaries: Where a new crust is generated as the plates pull away from each other. The sites where the plates move away from each other are called spreading sites. The best-known example of divergent boundaries is the Mid-Atlantic Ridge. At this, the American Plate(s) is/are separated from the Eurasian and African Plates.
Hence, the correct option is (B).

22. The northeastern parts are separated by the Malda fault in West Bengal from the Chotanagpur plateau. The Malda fault broadly separates the Meghalayan Plateau from the peninsular plateau.
Hence, the correct option is (D).

23. The Winter season in India extends roughly from November to March. Winter Season is characterized by the following weather phenomenon:

- Development of high pressure in the region lying to the north of the Himalayas.

- This centre of high pressure gives rise to the flow of air at the low level from the north towards the Indian subcontinent, south of the mountain range. The surface winds blowing out of the high-pressure centre over Central Asia reach India in the form of a dry continental air mass.

- All of Western and Central Asia remains under the influence of westerly jet streams winds along with an altitude of 9-13 km from west to east. The southern branch of the jet stream exercises an important influence on the winter weather in India.

- The western cyclonic disturbances enter the Indian subcontinent from the west and the northwest during the winter months.

- Tropical cyclones originate over the Bay of Bengal and the Indian ocean.

- An easterly jet stream flows over the southern part of the Peninsula in the Summer month of June.

Hence, the correct option is (A).

24. Central Highlands also called the Madhya Bharat Pathar or Madhya Bharat Plateau. It is to the east of the Marwar or Mewar Upland and the north of the Narmada river. It covers the major portion of the Malwa plateau. Most of the plateau comprises the basin of the Chambal river which flows in a rift valley. The Kali Sindh, flowing from Rana Pratap Sagar, The Banas flowing through the Mewar plateau, and The Parwan and the Parbati flowing from Madhya Pradesh are Chambal's main tributaries. It is a rolling plateau with rounded hills composed of sandstone. Thick forests grow here. To the north are the ravines or badlands of the Chambal river and Satpura ranges, to the south, is the Deccan plateau, and to the west are Aravalli ranges. It slopes towards the north and northeastern directions.
Hence, the correct option is (D).

25. Sirocco and Mistral are the local winds of the Mediterranean Climate.

Sirocco is a hot, dry dusty wind that originates in the Sahara Desert. It may occur at any time of the year but is most frequent in spring. It blows outwards in a southerly direction from the desert interiors into the cooler Mediterranean Sea. It is known by different names in different countries around the Mediterranean.

Mistral is a cold wind from the north, rushing down the Rhone valley in France over to the Mediterranean sea. Foehn and Chinook are the local winds of the Temperate Continental Climate. The Foehn in Switzerland and the Chinook on the eastern slopes of the Rockies have a considerable effect on the local pastures. They are hot winds and may raise the temperature by about 4 to 5 degrees Celcius, thus melting the snow in winter or early spring and is beneficial for agriculture. Warm moist air moves from the Mediterranean region and brings precipitation on the southern slopes of the Alps. This air becomes warm due to an adiabatic rise in temperature, loses its original characteristics, and descends on the northern slopes of the Alps in Switzerland, Germany, and Austria. This dry warm air is called Foehn.
Hence, the correct option is (A).

26. The geologic time scale (GTS) is a system of chronological dating that relates geological strata (stratigraphy) to time. It is used by geologists, paleontologists, and other Earth scientists to describe the timing and relationships of events that have occurred during Earth's history. Devonian Period, in geologic time, an interval of the Paleozoic Era that follows the Silurian Period and precedes the Carboniferous Period, spanning between about 419.2 million and 358.9 million years ago. The Devonian Period is sometimes called the "Age of Fishes" because of the diverse, abundant, and, in some cases, bizarre types of these creatures that swam Devonian seas.
Hence, the correct option is (B).

27. Bharchukki Falls are located 130 km from Bangalore. In fact, this waterfall is only a part of Shivanasamudram Falls.
Hence, the correct option is (A).

28. The Sankosh river originates from northern Bhutan, in Assam it joins the Brahmaputra. This river forms the border between Assam and Arunachal Pradesh.
Hence, the correct option is (B).

29. The Mizo hills are called Lushai in the local language. The Mizo Hills are located in Mizoram and Tripura. It is situated at an altitude of 2,157 meters above sea level.
Hence, the correct option is (C).

30. India has a total terrestrial border of 15,106 km, comprising 92 districts and 17 states. India's terrestrial border is Pakistan, Bangladesh, China, Nepal, Myanmar, Bhutan and Afghanistan.
Hence, the correct option is (B).

31. The correct sequence from the south to north direction of the above ports would be: Thiruvananthapuram → Cochin → Calicut → Mangalore.
Hence, the correct option is (C).

32.

List-I (Book)	List-II (Author)
A. Periplus	3. Hecateaus
B. The Guide to Geography	2. Ptolemy
C. Historical Memoir	4. Stabo
D. The Ekumene	1. Eratosthenes

Hence, the correct option is (D).

33. Possibilism is the philosophy introduced by Fabvre, to explain man and environment relationship in a different way of determinism, taking man as an active agent in the environment; which asserts that the natural environment provides options, the number of which increases as the knowledge and technology of a culture group.
Hence, the correct option is (C).

34. German geographer Hettner defined geography as a chronological science. He was of the view that geography should be studied as a chronological science, which studies diverse phenomena existing together in regions of the earth's space.
Hence, the correct option is (C).

35. A geographer, Griffith Taylor introduced another concept which reflects a middle path (Madhyam Marg) between the two ideas of environmental determinism and possibilism. He termed it as Neodeterminism or stop and go determinism.
Hence, the correct option is (C).

36. The doctrine was further strengthened by Barrows in 1922 when in his presidential address before the American Association of Geographers he emphasized that in geography human ecology is the guiding concept. In the words of Barrows (1923) – "Thus defined, geography is the science of human ecology.
Hence, the correct option is (B).

37.

List-I (Taxon)	List-II (Authors)
I. Cycle of Erosion	C. Davis
II. The Origin of Species	D. Charles Darwin
III. Originator of Dualism between Physical & Human Geography	B. Oscar Peschel
IV. Theory of Social Darwinism	A. Freidrich Ratzel

Hence, the correct option is (B).

38. Bernhard Varenius s laid down the foundation of the dichotomy of general versus special Geography.

In brief, general geography deals with the whole world as a unit. It was, however, mainly restricted to physical geography which could be understood through natural laws. On the contrary, special geography was primarily intended as a description of individual countries and world regions.
Hence, the correct option is (B).

39. Kotla lake at the foothills of Aravalli Range in Nuh District of Haryana. The length of this lake is 5 kilometers and the breadth is 4 kilometers. It is one of the largest lakes of Haryana. Kotla lake lies across Nuh and Ferozpur Jhirka tehsils. Kotla Lake is drained by November to make the land available for cultivation.

Hence, the correct option is (C).

40. Ranjit Sagar Dam, also known as Thim Dam, is a hydroelectric project constructed by the Government of Punjab on the border of the state of Punjab and Jammu and Kashmir. 60% of this lake is located in Jammu and Kashmir. Work on the project began in 1981, and was completed in 2001. It has a production capacity of 600 MW.
Hence, the correct option is (A).

41. The Indus River is one of the longest rivers in Asia. It flows through Pakistan, India (Jammu and Kashmir) and China (Western Tibet). The origin of the Indus River, near Mansarovar in Tibet, is believed to be a stream called Sin-Ka-Bab.
Hence, the correct option is (B).

42. The "Jawahar Sagar" dam is situated on the Chambal river.

The Chambal River is a tributary of the Yamuna River in central India. This river originates from the "Janapav mountain" Bachu Pite Mhow. Its ancient name is "Charamvati". Its tributaries are Shipra, Sindh (Sindh), Kali Sindh and Kunu River. Four hydroelectric projects - Gandhi Sagar, Rana Sagar, Jawahar Sagar and Kota Barrage (Kota) - are running on this river.
Hence, the correct option is (B).

43. The total terrestrial range of India is 15200 km while the coastal length of the mainland of India is 6100 km and the total coastal length including the islands is 7516.6 km.

The state with the longest coastline among the given options is Gujarat.
Hence, the correct option is (C).

44.

- The Government of India adopted the nationwide Forest Conservation Policy in 1952, which was further modified in 1988. The forest policy aimed at:
- Bringing 33% of the geographical areas under forest cover, through social forestry and afforestation on degraded land.
- Maintaining environmental stability and restoring forests where ecological balance was disturbed.
- Conserving the natural heritage of the country, its biological diversity, and genetic pool.
- Checks soil erosion, an extension of the desert lands, and reduction of floods and droughts.
- Increasing the productivity of forests to make timber, fuel, fodder, and food available to rural population dependent on forests, and encourage the substitution of wood.
- Creating a massive people's movement involving women to encourage the planting of trees, stop the felling of trees, and thus, reduce pressure on the existing forest.

The government has also enacted the Forest Conservation Act in 1980 and has set up a National Forest Commission in 2003, for the assessment and integrated development of forests in India.
Hence, the correct option is (D).

45. Many planets in our solar system have more than one moon. Mars has two moons, Jupiter has 67, Saturn 62, Uranus 27, Neptune 14. Those numbers keep changing and updating. Of the inner planets, Mercury and Venus have no natural satellites; Earth has one large natural satellite, known as the Moon; and Mars has two tiny natural satellites, Phobos and Deimos.

Venus is one of just two planets that rotate from east to west. Only Venus and Uranus have this "backward" rotation. It completes one rotation in 243 Earth days — the longest day of any planet in our solar system, even longer than a whole year on Venus. Uranus orbits the sun quite unusually, being the only planet whose equator is nearly at a right angle to its orbit, with a tilt of 97.77 degrees. Because of this, it rotates in the opposite direction than most planets, from East to West.

A ring system around a planet is also known as a planetary ring system. The most prominent and most famous planetary rings in the Solar System are those around Saturn, but the other three giant planets (Jupiter, Uranus, and Neptune) also have ring systems.
Hence, the correct option is (D).

46. All-natural earthquakes take place in the lithosphere. The release of energy occurs along a fault. A fault is a sharp break in the crustal rocks. Rocks along a fault tend to move in opposite directions. As the overlying rock strata press them, the friction locks them together. However, their tendency to move apart at some point in time overcomes the friction. As a result, the blocks get deformed and eventually, they slide past one another abruptly. This causes a release of energy, and the energy waves travel in all directions.

The point where the energy is released is called the focus of an earthquake, alternatively, it is called the hypocentre. The energy waves traveling in different directions reach the surface.
Hence, the correct option is (A).

47. A tectonic plate (also called a lithospheric plate) is a massive, irregularly-shaped slab of solid rock, generally composed of both continental and oceanic lithosphere. Plates move horizontally over the asthenosphere as rigid units.

The major plates are as follows:

- Antarctica and the surrounding oceanic plate
- North American Plate (with western Atlantic floor separated from the South American plate along with the Caribbean islands)
- South American Plate (with western Atlantic floor separated from the North American plate along with the Caribbean islands)
- Pacific plate
- India-Australia-New Zealand plate
- Africa with the eastern Atlantic floor plate
- Eurasia and the adjacent oceanic plate.

Hence, the correct option is (B).

48. The Dead Sea is landlocked. All the minerals of the surrounding countryside get washed into one pool, which in turn gets baked by the sun. This makes water in the Dead sea very high in salt concentration.

The concentration of salt reaches 34%. The extremely high concentration of dissolved mineral salts in the water causes the water to be denser than that of plain fresh water. Since our body weight is lighter (less dense) than the density of the water, our body is more buoyant in the Dead Sea, making it easy to float.
Hence, the correct option is (C).

49. High temperatures and abundant rainfall in the hot and wet equatorial regions support a mix of luxuriant types of vegetation

-the tropical rain forest. The growing season here is all year round and hence the forests are evergreen.

Amazon tropical rain forests, for their lush green and broad leaves, are known as Selvas. The region's vegetation comprises a multitude of evergreen trees that yield tropical hardwood, e.g. mahogany, ebony, greenheart, cabinet wood. There are also small palm trees and climbing plants like Lianas or Rattans, which are epiphytic (A plant that grows on another plant and depends on it for support but not food). Under the trees, they also grow a wide variety of ferns, orchids, and Lalang. This leads to a distinct layer arrangement in the forests, with tall trees and their dense canopy at the top, smaller trees forming the next layer and then the ground is covered with herbaceous ferns and shrubs. Trees of single species are very scarce in such vegetation. and hence commercial exploitation of tropical timber is most difficult.
Hence, the correct option is (D).

50. The pattern of flow of water in a river channel over a year is known as its regime. The north Indian rivers originating from the Himalayas are perennial as they are fed by glaciers through snowmelt and also receive rainfall water during the rainy season. The rivers of South India do not originate from glaciers and their flow pattern witnesses fluctuations. The flow increases considerably during monsoon rains. Thus, the regime of the rivers of South India is controlled by rainfall which also varies from one part of the Peninsular plateau to the other.
Hence, the correct option is (B).

51. The primary forces that influence the currents are:

Heating by solar energy causes the water to expand. That is why near the equator, the ocean water is about 8 cm higher in level than in the middle latitudes. This causes a very slight gradient and water tends to flow down the slope. Wind blowing on the surface of the ocean pushes the water to move. Friction between the wind and the water surface affects the movement of the water body in its course.

Gravity tends to pull the water down to pile and create gradient variation. The Coriolis force intervenes and causes the water to move to the right in the northern hemisphere and to the left in the southern hemisphere. These large accumulations of water and the flow around them are called Gyres. These produce large circular currents in all the ocean basins.

Differences in water density affect the vertical mobility of ocean currents. Water with high salinity is denser than water with low salinity and in the same way cold water is denser than warm water. Denser water tends to sink, while relatively lighter water tends to rise.

Cold-water ocean currents occur when the cold water at the poles sinks and slowly moves towards the equator. Warm-water currents travel out from the equator along the surface, flowing towards the poles to replace the sinking cold water. The topography and shape of ocean basins and nearby landmasses also influence ocean currents.
Hence, the correct option is (D).

52. The maximum temperature of the oceans is always at their surfaces because they directly receive the heat from the sun and the heat is transmitted to the lower sections of the oceans through the process of conduction. It results in a decrease in temperature with the increasing depth, but the rate of decrease is not uniform throughout. The temperature structure of oceans can be described as a three-layer system. The first layer (Top layer) is about 500m thick with temperatures ranging between 20 to 25°c. The second layer (Thermocline) is characterized by a rapid decrease in temperature with increasing depth. It is about 500m-1000m thick. The third layer is very cold and extends up to the deep ocean floor. Here temperature change with the depth is very slight.

The average temperature of surface water of the oceans is about 27°C and it gradually decreases from the equator towards the poles. The oceans in the northern hemisphere record relatively higher temperatures than in the southern hemisphere. The highest temperature is not recorded at the equator but slightly towards the north of it. The average annual temperatures for the northern and southern hemispheres are around 19°C and 16°C respectively. This variation is due to the unequal distribution of land and water in the northern and southern hemispheres. Hence, the correct option is (A).

53. Mizoram is known as the land of rolling mountains as it has a huge number of mountains, the formation of most mountains is accompanied by the formation of a foreland basin or in simple terms valley-type depression which runs parallel to mountains. These depressions get accumulated with unconsolidated deposits known as molasses basin. hence it is also known as the molasses basin of India.
Hence, the correct option is (D).

54. The China Type of climate is also called the temperate monsoon climate. The great landmass of the Asiatic continent with its mountainous interior induces great pressure changes between summer and winter. Intense heating in 'the heart of Asia' sets up a region of low pressure in summer that draws in the tropical Pacific air stream as the rain-bearing South-East Monsoon. In winter, a steep pressure gradient is set up between the cold interiors of Mongolia and Siberia, and the warmer Pacific coastlands. The continental polar air stream flows outwards as the North-West Monsoon. There is little rain but considerable snow on the windward slopes of certain regions.
Hence, the correct option is (C).

55. Agro-forestry is the raising of trees and agriculture crops on the same land inclusive of the waste patches. Most agro-forestry systems aim to increase or maintain the production and productivity of farming systems; reduce agricultural inputs and thus production costs; and diversify production by the use of trees or other woody perennials to produce, for example, food, fodder, lumber, building materials and wood fuel.

Hence, the correct option is (D).

56. Drumlins are depositional landforms of glaciation. These are smooth oval-shaped ridge-like features composed mainly of glacial till with some masses of gravel and sand. The long axes of drumlins are parallel to the direction of ice movement. One end of the drumlins facing the glacier called the stoss end is blunter and steeper than the other end called the tail. The stoss end gets blunted due to pushing by moving ice. Drumlins give an indication of the direction of the glacier movement.
Hence, the correct option is (C).

57. Indian coastal plains can be broadly divided into two: (i) the western coastal plains; (ii) the eastern coastal plains.

Western Coastal plains an example of submerged coastal plains. Because of this submergence, it is a narrow belt and provides natural conditions for the development of ports and harbors. Extending from the Gujarat coast in the north to the Kerala coast in the south i.e., in five Indian states ((Maharashtra, Goa, Karnataka Kerala, and Gujarat). They are narrow in the middle and get broader towards the north and south. The Malabar coast has got certain distinguishing features in the form of 'Kayals' (backwaters), which are used for fishing, inland navigation, and also due to its special attraction for tourists.
Hence, the correct option is (B).

58. River Vamsadhara is an east-flowing river between Rushikulya and Godavari, in Odisha and Andhra Pradesh. It is an east-flowing river that originates in the Kalahandi district of Odisha, flows in Odisha, along its boundary with Andhra Pradesh, and finally joins the Bay of Bengal at Kalingapatnam, Andhra Pradesh. It is the main river of the north-eastern Andhra region and the Boddepalli Rajagopala Rao Project was constructed on it to meet the irrigation needs of the region.
Hence, the correct option is (D).

59. Red soil develops on crystalline igneous rocks in areas of low rainfall in the southern and eastern parts of the Deccan Plateau. A long stretch of area is occupied by red loamy soil, along the piedmont zone of Western Ghat. Yellow and red soils are also found in parts of Chhattisgarh and Odisha and in the southern parts of the middle Ganga plain.

Due to a wide diffusion of iron in crystalline and metamorphic rocks, the soil develops a reddish color. When it occurs in a hydrated form, it looks yellow. The fine-grained red and yellow soils are normally fertile, whereas in dry upland areas the soil has poor fertility due to coarse-grained structure. They are generally poor in humus, phosphorus, and nitrogen.
Hence, the correct option is (C).

60. The continental shelf is the extended margin of each continent occupied by relatively shallow seas and gulfs. It is the shallowest part of the ocean showing an average gradient of 1° or even less. The shelf typically ends at a very steep slope, called the shelf break.

The width of the continental shelves varies from one ocean to another. The average width of continental shelves is about 80 km. The shelves are almost absent or very narrow along some of the margins like the coasts of Chile, the west coast of Sumatra, etc. On the contrary, the Siberian shelf in the Arctic Ocean, the largest in the world, stretches to 1,500 km in width.

The continental shelves are of great geographic significance. Their shallowness enables sunlight to penetrate through the water. It encourages the growth of planktons on which many surfaces and bottom-feeding fishes thrive. The continental shelves are therefore homes to the world's riches fishing grounds. E.g.: Grandbanks of Newfoundland
Hence, the correct option is (D).

61. Atlantic ocean currents include the below-given currents:

- North Equatorial Current (warm)

- Gulf Stream (warm)
- Florida Current (Warm)
- Canary Current (Cold)
- Labrador Current (Cold)
- Brazilian Current (Warm)
- Falkland Current (Cold)
- South Atlantic Drift (Cold)
- Benguela Current (Cold)

Hence, the correct option is (A).

62. Black soil covers most of the Deccan Plateau which includes parts of Maharashtra, Madhya Pradesh, Gujarat, Andhra Pradesh and some parts of Tamil Nadu. In the upper reaches of the Godavari and the Krishna, and the northwestern part of the Deccan Plateau, the black soil is very deep. These soils are also known as the 'Regur Soil' or the 'Black Cotton Soil'. The black soils are generally clayey, deep and impermeable. They swell and become sticky when wet and shrink when dried. So, during the dry season, this soil develops wide cracks. Thus, there occurs a kind of 'self ploughing'. Because of this character of slow absorption and loss of moisture, the black soil retains the moisture for a very long time, which helps the crops, especially, the rain-fed ones, to sustain even during the dry season. Chemically, the black soils are rich in lime, iron, magnesia and alumina. They also contain potash. But they lack in phosphorous, nitrogen and organic matter. The color of the soil ranges from deep black to grey.
Hence, the correct option is (B).

63. In the North Indian Ocean, there is a complete reversal of the direction of currents between summer and winter, due to the changes of monsoon winds. In summer from June to October, when the dominant wind is the South-West Monsoon, the currents are blown from a south-westerly direction as the South West Monsoon Drift. This is reverse in winter beginning from December when the North-East Monsoon blows the currents from the north-east as the North-East Monsoon Drift. The currents of the North Indian Ocean, demonstrate most convincingly the dominant effects of winds on the circulation of ocean currents.
Hence, the correct option is (D).

64. The Pachmarhi Biosphere Reserve is located in the Satpura Range of Madhya Pradesh. The Satpura range forms the watershed between the river Narmada to the north and river Tapi to the south. UNESCO designated it a biosphere reserve in 2009. It includes three wildlife conservation units: Bori Sanctuary, Pachmarhi Sanctuary, and Satpura National Park.
Hence, the correct option is (A).

65. Seawater contains a large amount of dissolved mineral matter of which Sodium Chloride alone constitutes more than 77 percent. The other important compounds include magnesium, calcium, potassium salts.
Hence, the correct option is (C).

66. El-Nino is merely an extension of the warm equatorial current which gets replaced temporarily by cold Peruvian current or Humbolt current. This current increases the temperature of the water on the Peruvian coast by 10 degrees Celcius. This results in:

- The distortion of equatorial atmospheric circulation.
- Irregularities in the evaporation of seawater.
- Reduction in the number of planktons further reduces the number of fish in the sea.

El-Nino is used in India for forecasting long-range monsoon rainfall.
Hence, the correct option is (D).

67. Savannah grasslands are typified by tall grasses and short trees. Hence, it is misleading to call the savannah 'tropical grassland', because trees are always present with luxuriant tall grass. The terms "Parkland" and "bush-veld" describe the landscape better.

Savannah climate is confined within the tropics and is best developed in Sudan, hence its name the Sudan Climate. It is a transitional type of climate found between the equatorial rainforests and hot deserts.
Hence, the correct option is (C).

68. The Yamuna, the westernmost tributary and the longest tributary of Ganga. The Yamuna has its source in the Yamunotri glacier on the western slopes of the Banderpunch range (6316 km) in Uttarakhand. Whereas the Ganga rises In the Gangotri glacier near Gurmukh. The Yamuna defines the state borders between Himachal Pradesh and Uttarakhand, and between Haryana, Delhi, and Uttar Pradesh.
Hence, the correct option is (D).

69. Batholiths are dome-shaped granitic bodies formed from the cooled portion of magma chambers. They appear on the surface only after the denudational processes remove the overlying materials. They cover large areas, and at times, assume depth that may be several km.
Hence, the correct option is (D).

70. The Hot, Wet Equatorial Climate, is a climate of great uniformity of temperature throughout the year. It is found between 5 degrees and 10 degrees north and south of the equator, in the lowlands of Amazon, the west coast of Africa, Malaysia, and the Indonesian islands. Though the precipitation is well distributed throughout the year, there are two periods of maximum rainfall, which occur shortly after the equinoxes. Precipitation is mainly of convectional type due to intense evaporation.

The Tropical Marine Climate is experienced along the eastern coast of tropical lands in Central America, West Indies, north-eastern Australia, eastern Africa, etc. They receive steady rainfall from the Trade Winds all the time. The rainfall is both orographic where the moist trades meet upland masses as in eastern Brazil, and convectional due to intense heating during the day and in summer. There is no month without any rainfall.
Hence, the correct option is (B).

71. Patagonian desert is also known as the Patagonian Steppe is the largest desert in Argentina.

Mojave desert is an arid rain-shadow desert and the driest desert in North America.

Gibson desert is the arid zone in the interior of Western Australia.
Hence, the correct option is (C).

72. Rocks (igneous, sedimentary and metamorphic) of the earth's surface area exposed to various denudational agents and are broken up into various sizes of fragments. Such fragments are transported by different exogenous agencies and deposited. These deposits through compaction turn into rocks.

Lithification is a process of porosity destruction through compaction and fermentation. In many sedimentary rocks, the layers of deposits retain their characteristics even after lithification. So, we see a number of layers of varying thickness in sedimentary rocks like sandstone, shale, etc.
Hence, the correct option is (C).

73. The Ten Degree Channel is a channel that separates the Andaman Islands and the Nicobar Islands from each other in the Bay of Bengal. The two sets of islands together form the Indian Union Territory (UT) of Andaman and Nicobar Islands.

The Coco Strait is between the North Andaman Islands and the Coco Islands of Myanmar.

South Andaman (Great Andaman) and Little Andaman are separated by Duncan Passage.

The Grand Channel is between the Great Nicobar Islands and the Sumatra islands of Indonesia.
Hence, the correct option is (D).

74. Indo-European language has the highest number of speakers in India. It is the biggest of the language groups in India and accounts for about 73% of the total Indian population. It comprises all the principal languages of northern and western India such as Hindi, Bengali, Marathi, Gujarati, Punjabi, Sindhi, Rajasthani, Assamese, Oriya, Pahari, Bihari, Kashmiri, Urdu, and Sanskrit.
Hence, the correct option is (D).

75. The sugar industry is the second most important agro-based industry in the country. Brazil is the top country with sugar cane production in the world. As of 2018, sugar cane production in Brazil was 746 million tonnes that account for 39.20% of the world's sugar cane production. The top 5 countries (others are India, China, Thailand, and Pakistan) account for 73.70% of it.

The sugar industry is a seasonal industry because of the seasonality of raw materials. Uttar Pradesh is the second-largest producer of sugar. The sugar factories are concentrated in two belts – the Ganga-Yamuna doab and the Tarai region. The crop yield is low in Northern India than in Southern India. Uttar Pradesh's yield is low, but in Maharashtra, Karnataka, and Tamil Nadu the yield is high.
Hence, the correct option is (A).

76. Cotton is a "pure" raw material that does not lose weight in the manufacturing process. So other factors, like, the power to drive the looms, labor, capital, or market may determine the location of the industry. At present, the trend is to locate the industry at or close to markets, as it is the market that decides what kind of cloth is to be produced. Also, the market for the finished products is extremely variable, therefore, it becomes important to locate the mills close to the market.

The cotton textile industry is one of the traditional industries of India. In ancient and medieval times, it used to be only a cottage industry. India was famous worldwide for the production of muslin, a very fine variety of cotton cloth, calicos, chintz, and other different varieties of fine cotton cloth. The development of this industry in India was due to several factors. One, it is a tropical country and cotton is the most comfortable fabric for a hot and humid climate. Second, a large quantity of cotton was grown in India. Abundant skilled labor required for this industry was available in this country. In fact, in some areas, the people were producing cotton textiles for generations and transferred the skill from one generation to the other and in the process perfected their skills.

There are three cotton-growing areas, i.e. parts of Punjab, Haryana and northern Rajasthan in the northwest, Gujarat and Maharashtra in the west and plateaus of Andhra Pradesh, Karnataka and Tamil Nadu in the south. Leading producers of this crop are Gujarat, Maharashtra and Telangana per hectare output of cotton is high under irrigated conditions in the north-western region of the country. Its yield is very low in Maharashtra where it is grown under rainfed conditions.

Initially, the British did not encourage the development of the indigenous cotton textile industry. They exported raw cotton to their mills in Manchester and Liverpool and brought back the finished products to be sold in India. This cloth was cheaper because it was produced at a mass scale in factories in the U.K. as compared to the cottage-based industries of India. In 1854, the first modern cotton mill was established in Mumbai.
Hence, the correct option is (D).

77. Quinary activities are services that focus on the creation, re-arrangement and interpretation of new and existing ideas; data interpretation and the use and evaluation of new technologies.

Often referred to as 'gold collar' professions, they represent another subdivision of the tertiary sector representing special and highly paid skills of senior business executives, government officials, research scientists, financial and legal consultants, etc.
Hence, the correct option is (A).

78. The doubling time is the time it takes for a population to double in size. The population of the world has been doubling at a faster pace, reducing the doubling in the last century.

At the beginning of the twentieth century (the 1900s), the population of the world was less than 2 billion whereas the current world population stands at 7 billion. Hence, at the beginning of the twentieth century, the world population was less than half of its current levels.
Hence, the correct option is (B).

79. India has 26 sedimentary basins covering an area of 3.14 million square kilometers. The sedimentary basins of India, on land and offshore up to the 200m isobaths, have an area extent of about 1.79 million sq. km. In the deepwater beyond the 200m isobath, the sedimentary area has been estimated to be about 1.35 million sq. km. Thus, the total works out to 3.14 million sq. km. They are spread across on land, offshore and deepwater areas.

Over the last twelve years, there have been significant forward steps in exploring the hydrocarbon potential of the sedimentary basins of India. The unexplored area has come down to 15% which was 50% in 1995-96. They are an important source of

Natural Gas, CBM and Shale Gas along with Oil, Petroleum.
Hence, the correct option is (A).

80. Agriculture accounts for most of the surface and groundwater utilization, it accounts for 89 percent of the surface water and 92 percent of the groundwater utilization. While the share of the industrial sector is limited to 2 percent of the surface water utilization and 5 percent of the groundwater, the share of the domestic sector is higher (9 percent) in surface water utilization as compared to groundwater. The share of the agricultural sector in total water utilization is much higher than in other sectors.

Rain-fed areas contributed significantly to the country's food production. They account for 89 percent of millet production, 88 percent of pulses, 73 percent of cotton, 69 percent of oilseeds, and 40 percent of rice production in the country. Besides, rain-fed areas support 64 percent of cattle, 74 percent of sheep, and 78 percent of the goat population in the country. About 61 percent of India's farmers rely on rain-fed agriculture and 55 percent of the gross cropped area is under rain-fed farming. India ranks first in rain-fed agriculture, both in the area and the value of produce.
Hence, the correct option is (B).

81. In India compact or clustered village of a few hundred houses is a rather universal feature, particularly in the northern plains. However, there are several areas, which have other forms of rural settlements. There are various factors and conditions responsible for having different types of rural settlements in India.

These include:

Physical features – nature of terrain, altitude, climate and availability of water

Cultural and ethnic factors – social structure, caste and religion

Security factors – defence against thefts and robberies
Hence, the correct option is (D).

82. On the basis of chemical and physical properties, minerals may be grouped under two main categories of metallics and non-metallics. Metallic minerals are the sources of metals. Iron ore, copper, gold produce metal and are included in this category. Metallic minerals are further divided into ferrous and non-ferrous metallic minerals. All those minerals which have iron content are ferrous such as iron ore itself and those which do not have iron content are non-ferrous such as copper, bauxite, etc.

Non-metallic minerals are either organic in origins such as fossil fuels also known as mineral fuels which are derived from the buried animal and plant life such as coal and petroleum. Other types of nonmetallic minerals are inorganic in origin such as mica, limestone, and graphite, etc.
Hence, the correct option is (B).

83. Shale gas & oil is defined as natural gas & oil from shale formations. Shale gas is an unconventional source of energy found in non-porous rocks. The shale acts as both the source and the reservoir for these unconventional hydrocarbons. Older shale wells were vertical while more recent wells are primarily horizontal and need artificial stimulation, like hydraulic fracturing, to produce. Only shale formations with certain characteristics will produce gas and oil.

The Government of India has carried out studies through various national and international agencies for the identification of shale oil and gas resources in the country. Based on the data available from conventional oil/gas exploration in the country for the last so many years, the country holds promising reserves of Shale Gas & Oil resources, and the following sedimentary basins are considered prospective from Shale oil and gas point of view:

- Cambay Basin
- Gondwana Basin
- KG Basin
- Cauvery Basin
- Indo-Gangetic Basin
- Assam-Arakan Basin

Hence, the correct option is (B).

84. Nuclear energy has emerged as a viable source in recent times. Important minerals used for the generation of nuclear energy are uranium and thorium. Uranium deposits occur in the Dharwar rocks.

The important nuclear power projects are Tarapur (Maharashtra), Rawatbhata near Kota m(Rajasthan), Kalpakkam (Tamil Nadu), Narora (Uttar Pradesh), Kaiga (Karnataka), and Kakarapara (Gujarat).
Hence, the correct option is (C).

85. The first stage has high fertility and high mortality because people reproduce more to compensate for the deaths due to epidemics and variable food supply. The population growth is slow and most of the people are engaged in agriculture where large families are an asset. Life expectancy is low, people are mostly illiterate and have low levels of technology. Two hundred years ago all the countries of the world were in this stage.

Fertility remains high at the beginning of the second stage but declines with time. This is accompanied by a reduced mortality rate. Improvements in sanitation and health conditions lead to a decline in mortality. Because of this gap, the net addition to the population is high. In the last stage, both fertility and mortality decline considerably. The population is either stable or grows slowly. The population becomes urbanized, literate and has the high technical know-how, and deliberately controls the family size.
Hence, the correct option is (B).

86. The dispersed or isolated settlement pattern in India appears in the form of isolated huts or hamlets of few huts in remote jungles, or on small hills with farms or pasture on the slopes. Extreme dispersion of settlement is often caused by the extremely fragmented nature of the terrain and land resource base of habitable areas. Many areas of Meghalaya, Uttaranchal, Himachal Pradesh and Kerala have this type of settlement.

The clustered rural settlement is a compact or closely built-up area of houses. In this type of village, the general living area is distinct and separated from the surrounding farms, barns and pastures. The closely built-up area and its intervening streets present some recognisable pattern or geometric shape, such as rectangular, radial, linear, etc. Such settlements are generally found in fertile alluvial plains and in the northeastern states.

Sometimes, people live in compact village for security or defence reasons, such as in the Bundelkhand region of central India and in Nagaland. In Rajasthan, scarcity of water has necessitated compact settlement for maximum utilization of available water resources.

Sometimes a settlement is fragmented into several units physically separated from each other bearing a common name. These units are locally called Panna, para, Palli, nagla, Dhani, etc. in various parts of the country. This segmentation of a large village is often motivated by social and ethnic factors. Such villages are more frequently found in the middle and lower Ganga plain, Chhattisgarh and lower valleys of the Himalayas.
Hence, the correct option is (C).

87. In the regions where farmers specialize in vegetables, the farming is known as truck farming. The distance of truck farms from the market is governed by the distance that a truck can cover overnight, so the name truck farming.
Hence, the correct option is (A).

88. The raw materials besides iron ore and coking coal, essential for the iron and steel industry are limestone, dolomite, manganese, and fire clay. All these raw materials are gross (weight losing), therefore, the best location for the iron and steel plants is near the source of raw materials.

New steel plants that were set up in the Fourth Plan period are away from the main raw material sources. All three plants are located in South India. The Vizag Steel Plant, in Vishakhapatnam in Andhra Pradesh, is the first port-based plant that started operating in 1992. Its port location is of advantage. Apart from major steel plants, there are more than 206 units located in different parts of the country. Most of these use scrap iron as their main raw material and process it in electric furnaces.
Hence, the correct option is (D).

89. The Human Development Index (HDI) is a summary measure of average achievement in key dimensions of human development: a long and healthy life, being knowledgeable, and have a decent standard of living. The HDI is the geometric mean of normalized indices for each of the three dimensions.

The Human Development Index (HDI) provides a single index measure to capture three key dimensions of human development: a long and healthy life, access to knowledge, and a decent standard of living.
Hence, the correct option is (B).

90. The warm, bright summers and cool, moist winters enable the cultivation of a wide range of citrus fruits such as oranges, lemons, limes, citrons, and grapefruit in this region. The Mediterranean lands account for 70 percent of the world's export of citrus fruits. Hence, this region is known as the world's orchard lands.

In the Mediterranean region, 85 percent of the grapes cultivated are used for the production of wine and it amounts to three-quarters of the world's production. Here, traditionally commercial viticulture is practiced. The inferior grapes are preserved as dried grapes and exported.

The summers being mostly warm and dry, some pastures can be found in the mountainous areas with a comparatively cooler climate that supports a few sheep, goats, and sometimes cattle, and transhumance is widely practiced.
Hence, the correct option is (D).

91. Demographic transition theory can be used to describe and predict the future population of any area. The theory tells us that population of any region changes from high births and high deaths to low births and low deaths as society progresses from rural agrarian and illiterate to urban industrial and literate society. These changes occur in stages which are collectively known as the demographic cycle.

The first stage has high fertility and high mortality because people reproduce more to compensate for the deaths due to epidemics and variable food supply. The population growth is slow and most of the people are engaged in agriculture where large families are an asset. Life expectancy is low, people are mostly illiterate and have low levels of technology. Two hundred years ago all the countries of the world were in this stage. Fertility remains high in the beginning of the second stage but it declines with time. This is accompanied by a reduced mortality rate. Improvements in sanitation and health conditions lead to a decline in mortality. Because of this gap, the net addition to population is high. In the last stage, both fertility and mortality decline considerably. The population is either stable or grows slowly. The population becomes urbanized, literate and has the high technical know-how and deliberately controls the family size.
Hence, the correct option is (C).

92. As per the adjoining figure, the correct order of given religions in increasing order of their population is Muslims-Christians-Sikhs-Buddhists.
Hence, the correct option is (C).

93. The highest level of decision-makers or policymakers performs quinary activities. These are subtly different from the knowledge-based industries that the quinary sector in general deals with.

Quinary activities are services that focus on the creation, re-arrangement, and interpretation of new and existing ideas; data interpretation, and the use and evaluation of new technologies. Often referred to as 'gold collar' professions, they represent another subdivision of the tertiary sector representing special and highly paid skills of senior business executives, government officials, research scientists, financial and legal consultants, etc. Their importance in the structure of advanced economies far outweighs their numbers.

Examples of KPOs include research and development (R and D) activities, e-learning, business research, intellectual property (IP) research, the legal profession, and the banking sector.
Hence, the correct option is (C).

94. Major industrial regions of the country are given below:

- Mumbai-Pune Region
- Hugli Region
- Bengaluru-Tamil Nadu Region
- Gujarat Region
- Chotanagpur Region

- Vishakhapatnam-Guntur Region
- Gurugram-Delhi-Meerut Region, and
- Kollam-Thiruvananthapuram Region

Hence, the correct option is (A).

95. The process of migration from plain areas to pastures on mountains during summers and again from mountain pastures to plain areas during winters is known as transhumance.

In mountain regions, such as Himalayas, Gujjars, Bakarwals, Gaddis and Bhotiyas migrate from plains to the mountains in summers and to the plains from the high altitude pastures in winters.
Hence, the correct option is (B).

96. Coal is the most important and abundant fossil fuel in India. It accounts for 55% of the country's energy needs. Hard coal deposit spread over 27 major coalfields are mainly confined to eastern and south-central parts of the country. A cumulative total of 2,93,497 million tones of geological resources of Coal up to a depth of 1200 meters have so far been estimated in the country.

Bituminous coal or black coal is relatively soft coal containing a tar-like substance called bitumen. It is of higher quality than lignite coal but of poorer quality than anthracite. The carbon content of bituminous coal is around 60-80%; the rest is composed of water, air, hydrogen, and sulfur. About 80 percent of the coal deposits in India are of a bituminous type and is of non-coking grade.
Hence, the correct option is (C).

97. Indonesia is the largest producer of palm oil, followed by Malaysia.

India is the world's largest producer of raw jute and jute goods, contributingto over 50 percent and 40 percent respectively of global production.

Myanmar is the leading producer of teak in the world.

Hence the correct option is (A).

98. Migration may be permanent, temporary or seasonal. It may take place from rural to rural areas, rural to urban areas, urban to urban areas and urban to rural areas.

The distribution of male and female migrants in different streams of intra-state and inter-state both types of migration. Contrary to this, men predominate the rural to an urban stream of inter-state migration due to economic reasons.
Hence, the correct option is (B).

99. Primary activities are directly dependent on the environment as these refer to the utilization of earth's resources such as land, water, vegetation, building materials and minerals. It, thus includes hunting and gathering, pastoral activities, fishing, forestry, agriculture, and mining, and quarrying.
Hence, the correct option is (D).

100. Population aging is the process by which the share of the older population becomes proportionally larger. This is a new phenomenon of the twentieth century. In most of the developed countries of the world, the population in the higher age groups has increased due to increased life expectancy. With a reduction in birth rates, the proportion of children in the population has declined.

Demographic dividend, as defined by the United Nations Population Fund (UNFPA) means, "the economic growth potential that can result from shifts in a population's age structure, mainly when the share of the working-age population (15 to 64) is larger than the non-working-age share of the population (14 and younger, and 65 and older). Therefore an increase in the proportion of the working population does not contribute to population ageing.
Hence, the correct option is (A).

101. The Rhine river flows through Netherlands and Germany and is navigable for 700 km from Rotterdam, in the Netherlands to Basel in Switzerland. It connects the industrial areas of Switzerland, Germany, France, Belgium, and the Netherlands with the North Atlantic Sea Route.

The Danube river rises in the Black Forest of Germany and flows eastwards through many countries. It is navigable up to Taurna Severin, Romania.

Volga Waterway starts in Russia, it provides a navigable waterway of 11,200 km and drains into the Caspian Sea. The Volga-Moscow canal connects it with the Moscow region and the Volga-Don Canal with the Black Sea.
Hence, the correct option is (C).

102. Road transport is the most economical for short distances. The world's total motorable road length is only about 15 million km, of which North America accounts for 33 percent. The highest road density and the highest number of vehicles are registered in this continent.

Railways are a mode of land transport for bulky goods and passengers over long distances. Europe has one of the densest rail networks in the world. Belgium has the highest density of 1 km of railways for every 6.5 sq km area.

Rivers, canals, lakes, and coastal areas are important waterways. The development of inland waterways is dependent on the navigability width and depth of the channel, continuity in the water flow, and transport technology in use. Asia with major rivers like the Ganga-Brahmaputra river system, Beijing-Hangzhou Grand Canal, etc. have the highest length of inland waterways.
Hence, the correct option is (A).

103. As per the census 2011, there are very large Urban Areas with more than 10 million persons in the country. These are known as Megacities. These are Greater Mumbai UA, Delhi UA, and Kolkata UA. The growth in population in the Mega Cities has slowed down considerably during the last decade. Greater Mumbai UA, which had witnessed 30.47% growth in population during 1991- 2001 has recorded 12.05% during 2001-2011. Similarly, Delhi UA (from 52.24% to 26.69% in 2001-2011) and Kolkata UA (from 19.60% to 6.87% in 2001-2011) have also slowed down considerably.

The level of urbanization is measured in terms of the percentage of urban population to the total population. The level of urbanization in India in 2001 was 28 percent. The total urban population in the country as per Census 2011 is more than 377

million constituting 31.16% of the total population.
Hence, the correct option is (A).

104. HVJ an abbreviation for Hazira-Vijaipur-Jagdishpur (also known as HBJ where B stands for Bijeypur, another name of Vijaipur) is India's first cross-state gas pipeline. The project was started in 1986 after the incorporation of GAIL (India) Limited to supply gas to the fertilizer plants located in the state of Uttar Pradesh. It passed through Gujarat, Madhya Pradesh, and Uttar Pradesh. The first phase of the project consisting of a non-branched 1,750-kilometer grid was commissioned in 1997. Later on, the system was expanded with additional branches to supply gas for industrial and domestic use in the states of Rajasthan, Haryana, and NCT, which increased the total grid length to 3,474 km. In the year 1998, the newly established Indraprastha Gas Limited took control of the Delhi branch of the pipeline to set up a citywide gas grid.
Hence, the correct option is (A).

105. Of the three fossil fuels (petroleum, natural gas, and coal), coal has the most widely distributed reserves; coal is mined in over 100 countries, and on all continents except Antarctica. The largest proved reserves are found in the United States, Russia, China, Australia, and India. Coal is found majorly in the forms of Lignite and Anthracite.

In terms of production, China is the top coal producer since 1983. In 2011 China produced 3,520 million tones (mt) of coal – 49.5% of 7,695 million tones world coal production. In 2011 other large producers were United States (993 mt), India (589 mt), European Union (576 mt), and Australia (416 mt).
Hence, the correct option is (A).

106. The footloose industry is a general term for an industry that can be placed and located at any location without effect from factors such as resources or transport. The reason for the growth of footloose industries lies in the rapid development of highly sophisticated products requiring a great deal of scientific research and development. Footloose industries enable quick product improvement of their products to suit the market demand. Characteristic features of footloose Industries which favor the free choice of location:

- Light industries often do not use raw materials but component parts.

- Power requirements, usually only electricity — available from the national grid

- The end product is small and often cheaper and easier to move.

- Employs a small labor force

- Non-polluting industries that can be located near residential areas.

Hence, the correct option is (C).

107. All statements are wrong because:

- Brazil is the largest coffee producer in the world. For example, in 2016 it is thought that 2,595,000 metric tons of coffee beans were produced in Brazil alone.

- The production of Robusta coffee in India is almost double to that of Arabica; while notably, both share

equal cropped area i.e. Robusta 52% and Arabica 48%. Further, while Karnataka and Kerala produce more Robusta.

- Coffee production in India occurs in the mountainous regions of South Indian states, with Karnataka accounting for 71 percent, followed by Kerala and Tamil Nadu.

Hence, the correct option is (D).

108. The Push factors make the place of origin seem less attractive for reasons like unemployment, poor living conditions, political turmoil, unpleasant climate, natural disasters, epidemics, and socio-economic backwardness. Epidemics in urban areas is, therefore, a Push factor.

The Pull factors make the place of destination seem more attractive than the place of origin for reasons like better job opportunities and living conditions, peace and stability, the security of life and property, and pleasant climate. Therefore better-living conditions in rural areas is a 'Pull factor'.

Lack of employment opportunities in rural areas is a 'push factor' for rural to urban migration but not for the mass exodus of migrant laborers from urban to rural areas.
Hence, the correct option is (B).

109. The Kharif season largely coincides with Southwest Monsoon under which the cultivation of tropical crops, such as rice, cotton, jute, jowar, bajra, and tur is possible.

The rabi season begins with the onset of winter in October-November and ends in March-April. The low-temperature conditions during this season facilitate the cultivation of temperate and subtropical crops such as wheat, gram, and mustard.

Zaid is a short duration summer cropping season beginning after harvesting of rabi crops. The cultivation of watermelons, cucumbers, vegetables and fodder crops during this season is done on irrigated lands.
Hence, the correct option is (C).

110. In the Amazon basin the Indian tribes collect wild rubber, in the Congo basin the Pygmies gather nuts and in the jungles of Malaysia, the Orang Asli make all sorts of cane products and sell them to people in villages and towns. With the cultivation of plantation crops like rubber, cocoa, sugar, coffee, tea, etc. many tribes have begun to lead a settled life.

The recent Amazon fires have destroyed the habitat of the uncontacted Indian tribes and they are now at risk as some of their last forest refuges are being consumed by flames.
Hence, the correct option is (D).

111. Environmental Determinism is a school of thought which believes that all the activities of humans are controlled by nature. The primitive humans were greatly influenced by their interactions with the natural environment. The level of technology was very low and humans listened to Nature, was afraid of its fury and worshipped it. Proponents of this theory were Ratzel, Ellen Semple, etc.
Hence, the correct option is (B).

112. The major iron ore belts in India are:

Odisha-Jharkhand belt: In Odisha high grade hematite ore is found in Badampahar mines in the Mayurbhanj and Kendujhar districts. In the adjoining Singbhum district of Jharkhand haematite iron ore is mined in Gua and Noamundi.

Durg-Bastar-Chandrapur belt lies in Chhattisgarh and Maharashtra. Very high grade hematites are found in the famous Bailadila range of hills in the Bastar district of Chhattisgarh. The range of hills comprise of 14 deposits of super high grade hematite iron ore. It has the best physical properties needed for steel making. Iron ore from these mines is exported to Japan and South Korea via Vishakhapatnam port.

Ballari-Chitradurga-Chikkamagaluru-Tumakuru belt in Karnataka has large reserves of iron ore. The Kudremukh mines located in the Western Ghats of Karnataka are a 100 percent export unit. Kudremukh deposits are known to be one of the largest in the world. The ore is transported as slurry through a pipeline to a port near Mangaluru.
Hence, the correct option is (B).

113. Growth Rate of Population is the change of population expressed in percentage.

Natural Growth of Population - This is the population increased by the difference between births and deaths in a particular region between two points of time.

- Natural Growth = Births – Deaths
- Actual Growth of Population = Births – Deaths + In Migration – Out Migration.

Hence, the correct option is (C).

114. Shifting cultivation is so widely practiced amongst indigenous peoples that different local names are used in different countries.

Region	Local Name
Malaysia	Ladang
Sri Lanka	Chena
Myanmar	Taungiya
Thailand	Tamrai
Java	Humah
Philippines	Caingin
Africa & Central America	Milpa
North East India	Jhum

Hence, the correct option is (B).

115. Though most of the states in India have only one state capital, however Maharashtra (Mumbai and Nagpur) and Himachal Pradesh (Shimla and Dharmshala) have two capitals each and Andhra Pradesh has three capitals (Amaravati - Legislative capital, Visakhapatnam - Executive capital and Kurnool - Judicial capital).

Among the given cities the correct order in the North to South direction is Raipur-Vishakhapatnam Bengaluru-Thiruvananthapuram.
Hence, the correct option is (B).

116. The majority of metropolitan and mega cities are urban agglomerations. An urban agglomeration may consist of any one of the following three combinations: (i) a town and its adjoining urban outgrowths, (ii) two or more contiguous towns with or without their outgrowths, and (iii) a city and one or more adjoining towns with their outgrowths together forming a contiguous spread.

Examples of urban outgrowth are railway colonies, university campuses, port areas, military cantonments, etc. located within the revenue limits of a village or villages contiguous to the town or city. According to census 2011, an urban agglomeration is a continuous urban spread constituting a town and its adjoining outgrowths (OGs), or two or more physically contiguous towns together with or without outgrowths of such towns.
Hence, the correct option is (D).

117. Among the northern Indian States, Bihar (1106), West Bengal (1028) and Uttar Pradesh (829) have higher densities, while Kerala (860) and Tamil Nadu (555) have higher densities among the peninsular Indian states. States like Assam, Gujarat, Andhra Pradesh, Haryana, Jharkhand, Odisha have moderate densities.
Hence, the correct option is (C).

118. The Global Forest Resource Assessment is released by the United Nations Food and Agriculture Organization (FAO). The FRA 2020 is based on the assessment of more than 60 forest-related variables in 236 countries and territories in the period of 1990–2020. According to this, the rate of forest loss has declined in the period of 1990-2020.
Hence, the correct option is (C).

119. Ports of Call are stock replenishment ports where ships anchor for refueling, watering and taking food items. eg. Aden, now developed as a commercial port.
Hence, the correct option is (C).

120. Industries using weight-losing raw materials are located in the regions where raw materials are located. Sugar mills in India are located near sugarcane producing areas. Similarly, the locations of the pulp industry, copper smelting, and pig iron industries are located near their raw materials. In iron and steel industries, iron ore and coal both are weight-losing raw materials. Therefore, an optimum location for iron and steel industries should be near raw material sources. This is why most of the iron and steel industries are located either near coalfields (Bokaro, Durgapur, etc.) or near sources of iron ore (Bhadravati, Bhilai, and Rourkela). Similarly, industries based on perishable raw materials are also located close to raw material sources.

Power provides the motive force for machines, and therefore, its supply has to be ensured before the location of any industry. However, certain industries, like aluminum and synthetic nitrogen manufacturing industries tend to be located near sources of power because they are power-intensive and require huge quantum of electricity.
Hence, the correct option is (C).

121. The Bindibu or Aborigines of Australia live in wurlies, simple shelters made of branches and tufts and grass.

The Tuaregs of the Sahara dwell in zeriba made up of grass.

The Gobi Mongols live in portable yurts (a kind of tent).
Hence, the correct option is (C).

122. Tea originated in China and is still an important crop there. but as it requires moderate temperatures (above 18 degree Celcius), heavy rainfall (over 60 inches) and well-drained highland slopes (stagnant water is injurious to its roots) it thrives well in the tropical monsoon zone, at a higher altitude. Tea is a shade-loving plant and develops more vigorously when planted along with shady trees. Thus, it grows best along the Himalayan foothills of India and Bangladesh, the central highlands of Sri Lanka and western Java. China is the leading producer and exporter of tea in the world followed by India.
Hence, the correct option is (C).

123. Lipulekh Pass also known as Lipu-Lekh Pass/Qiangla or Tri-Corner is a high altitude mountain pass situated in the western Himalayas with a height of 5,334 metre or 17.500 feet. It is an International mountain pass between India, China, and Nepal.

Zoji La is a high mountain pass located in the Kargil district of Ladakh. The pass links Leh and Srinagar and provides an important link between the Union Territories of Ladakh and Kashmir.

Jelep La connects Sikkim with Bhutan. It passes through Chumbi Valley. It is an important link between Sikkim and Lhasa (Capital of Tibet).

Nathu La connects Sikkim with Tibet. It forms part of an offshoot of the ancient Silk Route and also an important trade route between India and China.
Hence, the correct option is (C).

124. Patterns of population distribution and density help us to understand the demographic characteristics of any area. Broadly, 90 percent of the world population lives in about 10 percent of its land area. The 10 most populous countries of the world contribute about 60 per cent of the world's population. Of these 10 countries, 6 are located in Asia.

The correct order of increasing population density is Asia (144 P/Km^2), Africa (42 P/Km^2) followed by Europe (33 P/Km^2).
Hence, the correct option is (C).

125. Bihar government is setting up India's first observatory for the mammals in Bhagalpur district at the Vikramshila Gangetic Dolphin Sanctuary (VGDS). The observatory is being built on the Sultanganj-Aguwani Ghat bridge over the Ganga, it will be in the middle of the river, where the bridge's width will be nearly 100 feet.
Hence, the correct option is (C).

Q.1 Name one of the important tribal groups of Japan.

A. Hottentot   **B.** Eskimo

C. Fula   **D.** Ainu

Q.2 The winter snow house of Eskimos are called:

A. Yurt   **B.** Igloo   **C.** Kayak   **D.** Toupic

Q.3 Consider the following statements and select the correct answer from the codes given below:

Assertion (A): There are disparities in regional development globally and within each country.

Reason (R): Such disparities are mainly due to the lack of adequate skilled labour.

Codes:

A. Both A and R are true and R is the correct explanation of A.

B. Both A and R are true, but R is not the correct explanation of A.

C. A is true, but R is false.

D. A is false, but R is true.

Q.4 The Groups of people inhabiting Asiatic Tundra is known as:

A. Vedda   **B.** Kirghiz

C. Samoyed   **D.** Gaucho

Q.5 Which one of the following pairs is not correctly matched?

A. Berber-Morocco

B. Incites-Canada

C. Semsangs-Indonesia

D. Veddas-Sri Lanka

Q.6 Lapland is a cultural region largely within the Arctic Circle in the north of the Scandinavian Peninsula. Who inhabited the Lapland?

A. Sami people   **B.** Padaung people

C. Hamar people   **D.** Himba people

Q.7 Tuareg is a pastoral nomad living in the desert of:

A. Kalahari   **B.** Sahara

C. Arabia   **D.** Patagonia

Q.8 To which of the following racial groups, the natives of North America belong?

A. Austric   **B.** Caucasoid

C. Mongoloid   **D.** Negroid

Q.9 In describing the process of spatial interaction, geographers are most concerned with-

A. Density and Dispersion

B. Diffusion and Pattern

C. Accessibility and Connectivity

D. Pedestrian Cities

Q.10 British Isles, the Balearic Islands of the Mediterranean and also those of the Aegean Sea are the example of:

A. Individual islands   **B.** Island groups

C. Festoons   **D.** Volcanic Islands

Q.11 Consider the following statements about the Oceanic Islands.

1. These are normally small and are located in the midst of oceans.

2. Their former connection with the neighbouring mainland can be traced from the similar physical structure.

3. Remoteness from the major trading centres of the world is a feature of these Islands.

Which of these statements is/are correct?

A. 1 and 2 only   **B.** 2 and 3 only

C. 1 and 3 only   **D.** All of them

Q.12 Consider the following statements about the Coral Islands.

1. Unlike the volcanic islands, the coral islands are very much lower and emerge just above the water surface.

2. Mauritius and Reunion Islands of the Indian Ocean are the examples.

Which of these statements is/are correct?

A. 1 only   **B.** 2 only

C. Both of them   **D.** Neither of them

Q.13 Consider the following statements by Coral Polyps.

1. They secrete calcium carbonate with their tiny cells.

2. Under favourable conditions, they grow in great profusion just below the water level.

3. Each polyp resides in a tiny cup of Coral and helps to form coral reefs.

Which of these statements is/are correct?

A. 1 and 2 only   **B.** 2 and 3 only

C. 1 and 3 only   **D.** All of them

Q.14 Which of these are correctly matched?

1. Precious corals - Pacific Ocean

2. Red coral - Mediterranean

Choose from the following options.

A. 1 only   **B.** 2 only

C. Both of them   **D.** Neither of them

Q.15 Water that rises to the surface as a result of Ocean Upwelling is typically:

A. Colder and poor in nutrients

B. Warmer and poor in nutrients

C. Colder and rich in nutrients

D. Warmer and rich in nutrients

Q.16 Sea level rise at specific locations may be more or less than the global average due to many factors. Which of these factors can create differences between local sea level and global sea level?

1. Local land subsidence

2. Ocean currents

3. Variations in land height

Choose the correct option.

A. 1 only

B. 2 only

C. 2 and 3 only

D. All of the above

Q.17 In an open ocean, the higher the wind speed and the longer the distance of open water across which the wind blows and waves will be:

A. The deeper the waves will be and possess lesser and lesser energy

B. The waves will be larger and possess more energy

C. The waves will be progressively smaller and possess less energy

D. Any of the above depending on the geographical profile of the water body

Q.18 Consider the following statements:

Assertion (A): Seamounts tend to be found on oceanic crust near mid-ocean ridges and island arcs.

Reason (R): Most seamounts are volcanic in origin.

In the context of the above, which of these is correct?

A. A is correct, and R is an appropriate explanation of A.

B. A is correct, but R is not an appropriate explanation of A.

C. A is correct, but R is incorrect.

D. Both A and R are incorrect.

Q.19 Consider the following statements about the lower or Plain Course of the river.

1. The river moving downstream across a broad, level plain is heavy with debris brought down from the upper course.

2. Vertical corrasion has almost ceased through lateral corrasion still goes on to erode its banks further.

3. The work of the river is mainly deposition, building up its bed and forming extensive flood plains.

Which of these statements is/are correct?

A. 1 and 2 only

B. 2 and 3 only

C. 1 and 3 only

D. All of them

Q.20 Consider the following statements.

1. During annual or sporadic floods, the hard materials are spread over the low-lying adjacent areas, a layer of sediment is thus deposited during each flood, gradually building up levees.

2. When the river normally flows its bed is raised through the accumulation of deposits and material is also dropped on the sides forming raised banks called a flood plain.

Which of these statements is/are correct?

A. 1 only

B. 2 only

C. Both of them

D. Neither of them

Q.21 Consider the following statements.

1. When a river reaches the sea, the fine materials it has not yet dropped are deposited at its mouth, forming a fan-shaped alluvial area called a Delta.

2. Due to the obstruction caused by the deposited alluvium, the river may discharge its water through several channels called tributaries.

Which of these statements is/are correct?

A. 1 only

B. 2 only

C. Both of them

D. Neither of them

Q.22 Which of the following are the cold Atlantic Currents?

A. Cayenne Current

B. California Current

C. Kuroshio Current

D. Peruvian Drift

Q.23 Consider the following statements about the river course.

1. A negative movement occurs when there is an uplift of land or a fall in sea level.

2. This will steepen the slope so that active down-cutting is renewed.

3. A fall in sea level leaves the flood-plain at an increased altitude above the sea level.

Which of these statements is/are correct?

A. 1 and 2 only

B. 2 and 3 only

C. 1 and 3 only

D. All of them

Q.24 Which one of the following is the correct sequence of passes when one travels along the Himalayas from Kashmir to Sikkim?

A. Zozila-Nathula-Shipkila

B. Nathula-Shipkila-Zozila

C. Nathula-Zozila-Shipkila

D. Zozila-Shipkila-Nathula

Q.25 Which one of the following experiences the least annual range of temperature?

A. Equator

B. Tropic of Cancer

C. Tropic of Capricorn

D. Arctic Circle

Q.26 Which one of the following States of India is the largest producer of lignite coal?

A. Maharashtra

B. Gujarat

C. Madhya Pradesh

D. Tamil Nadu

Q.27 Which one of the following is the origin of the Brahmaputra river?

A. Milam

B. Gangotri

C. Yamunotri

D. Chemayungdung

Q.28 Which National Highway is called Shershah Suri Marg?

A. National Highway No. 3

B. National Highway No. 8

C. National Highway No. 7

D. National Highway No. 1

Q.29 Lakshadweep Islands are located in the:

A. Indian Ocean

B. Arabian Sea

C. Bay of Bengal

D. South China Sea

Q.30 Consider the following statements regarding the characteristics of Terrestrial Planets.

1. The terrestrial planets were formed in the close vicinity of the parent star where it was too warm for gases to condense to solid particles.

2. The terrestrial planets are larger than Jovian planets and their lower gravity could hold the escaping gases.

Choose the correct statement.

A. Only 1
B. Only 2
C. Both 1 and 2
D. None of the above

Q.31 Which of the following statements are incorrect regarding formation of stars?

A. A galaxy (large number of stars) starts to form by accumulation of helium gas.

B. The formation of stars is believed to have taken place some 5-6 million years ago.

C. The initial density difference in early universe is the core reason for star formation.

D. Both (A) and (B)

Q.32 What are 'planetesimals' associated with theories of planet formations?

A. They are formed by cohesion of small rounded bodies of condensed gas cloud with the matter around the core.

B. They are a combined object formed around the comets and meteorites.

C. Large number of dwarf planets form one planetesimal.

D. None of the above

Q.33 The most important process in the glacial erosion is:

A. Ablation
B. Abrasion
C. Frosting
D. None of the above

Q.34 Which one of the following is not correctly method?

A. Mayurakshi Dam - Subarnrekha
B. Indira Gandhi - Beas River Canal Project
C. Pochampad Project - Godavari River
D. Tehri Dam - Bhagirathi

Q.35 Which one of the following mines has the thickest coal-seam?

A. Kargali
B. Panchet
C. Damuda
D. Talcher

Q.36 Which one of the following has the largest reserves of coal?

A. Jharkhand
B. Madhya Pradesh
C. Orissa
D. West Bengal

Q.37 Which one of the following is not correctly matched?

A. Bongaigaon - Assam
B. Koyli - Gujarat
C. Kochi - Karnataka
D. Haldia - West Bengal

Q.38 The northern boundary of the Indian Plate coincides with the southern margin of:

A. Karakoram
B. Tibet
C. Tien Shan
D. Zanskar

Q.39 The logical and physical classification of geographical phenomena was given by:

A. Kant
B. Humboldt
C. Ritter
D. Varenius

Q.40 The wall maps are generally reduced with the help of:

A. Camera Lucida
B. Ediograph
C. Pantograph
D. Square method

Q.41 Which one of the following states had the highest density of population according to 2001 census?

A. Bihar
B. Punjab
C. Uttar Pradesh
D. West Bengal

Q.42 Which one of the following is not correctly matched?

A. TISCO - Jamshedpur
B. IISCO - Burnpur
C. HSL - Coimbatore
D. VSP - Vishakhapatnam

Q.43 The Binary Star Hypothesis about the origin of the earth was propounded by:

A. H. N. Russell
B. R. A. Lyttelton
C. O. Schimdt
D. Von Weizsacker

Q.44 The concept of 'Base-Level' was developed by:

A. C.E. Dutton
B. G.K. Gilbert
C. J.W. Powell
D. W.M. Davis

Q.45 The theory of Isostasy was developed by:

A. C.E. Dutton
B. G.K. Gilbert
C. J.W. Powell
D. Pratt

Q.46 The concept of spherical Earth was denied by:

A. Firmanus
B. Heidelus
C. Pomponius
D. Solinus

Q.47 "Indian Ocean is a closed sea". This statement was made by:

A. Eratosthenes
B. Hecataeus
C. Herodotus
D. Ptolemy

Q.48 Who out of the following paid attention to the deflection of wind direction resulting from the Earth's rotation?

A. Humboldt
B. Kant
C. Ritter
D. Varenius

Q.49 The Paithan (Jayakwadi) Hydro-electric project, completed with the help of Japan, is on the river:

A. Ganga
B. Cauvery
C. Narmada
D. Godavari

Q.50 The per cent of irrigated land in India is about:

A. 48
B. 65
C. 35
D. 25

Q.51 The southernmost point of peninsular India, that is, Kanyakumari, is:

A. North of Tropic of Cancer
B. South of the Equator
C. South of the Capricorn
D. North of the Equator

Q.52

The pass located at the southern end of the Nilgiri Hills in south India is called:

A. The Palghat gap
B. The Bhorghat pass
C. The Thalgat pass
D. The Bolan pass

Q.53

The principal copper deposits of India lie in which of the following places?
A. Hazaribag and Singbhum of Bihar
B. Khetri and Daribo areas of Rajasthan
C. Anantapur in Andhra Pradesh
D. Siwaliks in Uttar Pradesh and in Karnataka

Q.54 The Yarlung Tsangpo river, in India, is known as:
A. Ganga
B. Indus
C. Brahmaputra
D. Mahanadi

Q.55
The Salal Project is on the river:
A. Chenab
B. Jhelum
C. Ravi
D. Sutlej

Q.56 The only zone in the country that produces gold is also rich in iron is:
A. North-eastern zone
B. North-western zone
C. Southern zone
D. None of the above

Q.57
The percentage of earth surface covered by India is:
A. 2.4
B. 3..4
C. 4.4
D. 5.4

Q.58 The present forest area of India, according to satellite data, is:
A. Increasing
B. Decreasing
C. Static
D. Decreasing in open forest area but increasing in closed forest area

Q.59 India's highest annual rainfall is reported at:
[UPSSSC Rajasva Lekhpal, 2015]
A. Namchi, Sikkim
B. Churu, Rajasthan
C. Mawsynram, Meghalaya
D. Chamba, Himachal Pradesh

Q.60
With reference to the humid subtropical climate consider the following statements:
1. This climate is found from the Cancer and Capricorn line towards the poles.
2. Similar climate is found in the plains of the south part of China.
Which of the above statements is/are true?
A. only 1
B. only 2
C. Both 1 and 2
D. Neither 1 nor 2

Q.61 What is the predominant type of Indian agriculture?
A. Commercial agriculture
B. Extensive agriculture
C. Plantation agriculture
D. Subsistence agriculture

Q.62 The Radcliffe line is a boundary between:
A. India and Pakistan
B. India and China
C. India and Myanmar
D. India and Afghanistan

Q.63 Which of the following has a potential for harnessing of tidal energy in India?
A. Gulf of Cambay
B. Gulf of Mannar
C. Backwaters of Kerala
D. Chilka lake

Q.64 Which of the following is not chemical weathering?
A. Oxidation
B. Hydrolysis
C. Freezing
D. Carbonization

Q.65 Fog is a phenomenon indicating:
A. Low average temperature
B. Normal lapse of temperature
C. Inversion of temperature
D. High average temperature

Q.66 Which one of the following local winds is different from the other three?
A. Sirocco
B. Khamsin
C. Foehn
D. Mistral

Q.67 Thunderstorms are associated with:
A. Cumulus clouds
B. Cumulonimbus clouds
C. Cirrus clouds
D. Stratus clouds

Q.68 A hot local wind blowing in Sahara desert is known as:
A. Haboob
B. Karaburan
C. Jooran
D. Harmattan

Q.69 Atmospheric layer which reflects radio weaves is called:
A. Exosphere
B. Ionosphere
C. Stratosphere
D. Troposphere

Q.70 The layer of the atmosphere which contains dust particles and water vapour is called:
A. Stratosphere
B. Troposphere
C. Ionosphere
D. Mesosphere

Q.71 Tropopause separates:
A. Troposphere and Ozonosphere
B. Stratosphere and Troposphere
C. Stratosphere and Ionosphere
D. Troposphere and Ionosphere

Q.72 Jet stream is westerlies in upper part of Troposphere:
A. Fast blowing
B. Ocean current
C. Monsoon winds
D. None of these

Q.73 Tropical cyclones in Australia are called:
A. Willy willy
B. Hurricanes
C. Easterly waves
D. Typhoons

Q.74 Consider the following statements
1. The Himalayas are spread over only five states in India.
2. The Western Ghats are spread over only five states.

3. Pulicat Lake is spread only in two states.

Which of the statements given above is/are correct?

A. 1 and 2 only
B. Only 3
C. 2 and 3 only
D. 1 and 3 only

Q.75 Which is the correct sequence of hills given below, starting from north to south?

A. Nallamalai Hills - Nilgiri Hills - Jawadi Hills - Annamalai Hills

B. Annamalai Hills - Jawadi Hills - Nilgiri Hills - Nallamalai Hills

C. Nallamalai Hills - Jawadi Hills - Nilgiri Hills - Annamalai Hills

D. Annamalai Hills - Nilgiri Hills - Jawadi Hills - Nallamalai Hills

Q.76 In which state is the Nelang Valley located?

A. Himachal Pradesh
B. Sikkim
C. Jammu and Kashmir
D. Uttarakhand

Q.77 In North India, the plain, supported by the sub-Himalayan region, is called-

A. Lowland
B. Doon
C. Khadar
D. Bhabhar

Q.78 Consider the following statements

1. Silent Valley National forest is in Nallamalai category.

2. It is proposed to construct a Patharakkadavu hydroelectric project near the Silent Valley National Forest.

3. The Kunti River originates from the rain-rich forests of the Silent Valley.

Which of the statements given above is/are correct?

A. 1 and 3
B. Only 2
C. 2 and 3
D. 1, 2 and 3

Q.79 In which state is the Guru Shikhar mountain peak located?

A. Rajasthan
B. Gujarat
C. Madhya Pradesh
D. Maharashtra

Q.80 Which of the following shores of India is situated between Krishna delta and Cape Comorin?

A. Coromandel Coast
B. Northern government
C. Malabar Coast
D. Konkan Coast

Q.81 Which one of the pairs of the following islands is separated by a Ten degree waterway?

A. Andaman and Nicobar
B. Nicobar and Sumatra
C. Maldives and Lakshadweep
D. Sumatra and Java

Q.82 The snow line in the Himalayas ranges between:

A. 4300 to 6000 m east
B. 4000 to 5800 m west
C. 4500 to 6000 m west
D. None of the above

Q.83 Archaeological results provided from India indicate which side in the past is the Indian landlocked government?

A. To the north
B. To the south
C. To the east
D. To the west

Q.84 In how many parts has Koppen classified the climate?

A. 4
B. 5
C. 7
D. 9

Q.85 It is suspected that the recent floods in Australia were due to La-Nina. How is La-Nina different from El-Nino?

1. La-Nina is characterized by the exceptionally cold temperatures of the ocean in the equatorial Indian Ocean, while El-Nino is characterized by the exceptionally warm temperatures of the ocean in the equatorial Pacific Ocean.

2. El-Nino has an adverse effect on the southwest monsoon of India, but La-Nina has no effect on the monsoon climate.

Which of the statements given above is/are correct?

A. Only 1
B. Only 2
C. 1 and 2
D. Neither 1 nor 2

Q.86 Consider the following statements regarding the hot humid climate.

1. The average temperature is above 18°C each month.

2. It rains throughout the year.

Choose the truth statements from the above-

A. Only 1
B. Only 2
C. 1 and 2
D. Neither 1 nor 2

Q.87 Consider the following statements-

1. According to Koppen, the Indian peninsula has a tropical monsoon climate.

2. In the Mediterranean climate, summers are hot and dry and winters are soft and rainy.

3. Tundra is a region of permanent frost.

Choose the truth statements from above:

A. 1 and 2
B. 2 and 3
C. 1 and 3
D. 1, 2 and 3

Q.88 Consider the following statements-

1. Tropical humid climate is found near the equator.

2. Sedimentary forests are found in tropical humid climatic zones.

Choose the truth statements from above:

A. Only 1
B. Only 2
C. 1 and 2
D. Neither 1 nor 2

Q.89 Consider the following statements-

1. In the Mediterranean regions, the year is divided into four main seasons.

2. In the Mediterranean Sea, there is more rainfall in summer.

3. Climate like China receives rainfall throughout the year.

4. Tropical highlands exhibit vertical classification of different climates.

Which of the following statements are correct?

A. 1, 2, 3 and 4
B. 1, 2 and 3
C. 1, 2 and 4
D. 3 and 4

Q.90 The Kurinji species of the Nilgiris Biosphere Reserve gregariously flowers once in:

A. 4 years   **B.** 8 years   **C.** 12 years   **D.** 16 years

Q.91 The term 'underwater tropical rain forests' is associated with which of the following biosphere reserves?

A. Sundarbans   **B.** Gulf of Kachchh
C. Great Nicobar   **D.** Gulf of Mannar

Q.92 The Biosphere Reserves Programme was launched by the UNESCO in:

A. 1970   **B.** 1971   **C.** 1974   **D.** 1976

Q.93 Environment and ecology experts have divided India into how many 'biogeographic regions?

A. 6   **B.** 8   **C.** 10   **D.** 16.6

Q.94 In which of the following Mahi River falls?

A. Gulf of Kachchh   **B.** Ranna of Kachchh
C. Gulf of Khambat   **D.** Gulf of Munnar

Q.95 Which state of India does not touch the India- China border?

A. Uttarakhand   **B.** Uttar Pradesh
C. Himachal Pradesh   **D.** Sikkim

Q.96 Which one of the following states does not touch the Indo-Nepal border?

A. West Bengal   **B.** Himachal Pradesh
C. Uttarakhand   **D.** Uttar Pradesh

Q.97 Which state of India does not share international border with Bangladesh?

A. Manipur   **B.** Meghalaya
C. Mizoram   **D.** Tripura

Q.98 The Pacific Islands from New Guinea south-eastwards to Fiji Islands group is called:

A. Polynesia   **B.** Melanesia
C. Micronesia   **D.** Australasia

Q.99 Generally, there is a decrease in temperature as the altitude increases from the Earth's surface, because-

1. The atmosphere can be warmer only above the surface of the earth.
2. The humidity in the upper atmosphere is high.
3. The air in the upper atmosphere is less dense.

Choose the correct answer based on the following codes-

A. Only 1   **B.** 2 and 3 only
C. 1 and 3 only   **D.** 1, 2 and 3

Q.100 Which of the following reflects more sunlight than the other three?

A. Sand desert   **B.** Paddy Crop
C. Snow covered land   **D.** Prairie land

Q.101 When does the distance between the sun and the earth become shortest?

A. 21 June   **B.** 22 September
C. 22 December   **D.** 4 January

Q.102 Consider the following statements-

1. The annual temperature in the Pacific Ocean is higher than the Atlantic Ocean.

2. The annual temperature variation is higher in the Northern Hemisphere than in the Southern Hemisphere.

Which of the statements given above is/are correct?

A. Only 1   **B.** Only 2
C. Both 1 and 2   **D.** Neither 1 nor 2

Q.103 Reference to the atmosphere which one of the following statements is correct?

A. The atmosphere has definite upper limits, but it gradually becomes sparse, until it becomes indistinguishable.
B. The atmosphere has no fixed upper limits, but it gradually becomes sparse, until it becomes indistinguishable.
C. The atmosphere has definite upper limits, but it gradually becomes dense, until it becomes indistinguishable.
D. The atmosphere has no fixed upper limits, but it gradually becomes dense, until it becomes indistinguishable.

Q.104 What is the atmospheric layer found near the Earth?

A. Troposphere   **B.** Stratosphere
C. Ionosphere   **D.** Exosphere

Q.105 La Nina has a massive tendency to trigger:

A. Tropical floods   **B.** Tropical droughts
C. Tropical cyclones   **D.** Tropical landslides

Q.106 Natural gas is usually found in:

A. Ganga- Yamuna basin
B. Narmada-Tapi basin
C. Krishna- Godavari basin
D. Mahanadi- Godavari basin

Q.107 The southwestern monsoons in India arrive through:

A. The Bay of Bengal   **B.** The Arabian Sea
C. Both (A) and (B)   **D.** Neither (A) nor (B)

Q.108 Alluvial soil is rich in:

A. Sulphuric acid   **B.** Phosphoric acid
C. Nitric acid   **D.** Citric acid

Q.109 Under Pradhan Mantri Kisan Mandhan Yojana, each farmer shall receive a monthly pension of ____.

A. Rs. 3000   **B.** Rs. 4000   **C.** Rs. 5000   **D.** Rs. 6000

Q.110 What is the drainage pattern of the Chotanagpur Plateau?

A. Cyclic   **B.** Circular
C. Radial   **D.** Cylindrical

Q.111 Andaman and Nicobar constitute how many islands?

A. 472   **B.** 485   **C.** 572   **D.** 585

Q.112 In between which of the two following ranges does the Deccan Plateau lie?

A. Shivaliks and Vindhyas
B. Aravallis and Satpuras
C. Satpuras and Himadris
D. Vindhyas and Satpuras

Q.113 Which water body separates the Andaman from Nicobar islands?

A. Eight Degree Channel
B. Nine Degree Channel
C. Ten Degree Channel
D. Eleven Degree Channel

Q.114 Which of the following forest types feature in Lakshadweep Islands?

A. Evergreen forests
B. Tropical rainforests
C. Alpine forests
D. Temperate dry forests

Q.115 Which animal population comprises the largest presence in the Western Ghats?

A. Leopards
B. Lions
C. Giraffes
D. Tigers

Q.116 Which state has the longest coastline in India?

A. Tamil Nadu
B. Gujarat
C. Andhra Pradesh
D. West Bengal

Q.117 Karakoram Highway connect which of the following two countries?

A. India-Nepal
B. China-India
C. China-Pakistan
D. India-Bangladesh

Q.118 Which of the following latitudes passes through India?

A. Equator
B. Tropic of Capricorn
C. Arctic Circle
D. Tropic of Cancer

Q.119 India shares the longest international boundary with which one of the following countries?

A. Bangladesh
B. China
C. Nepal
D. Bhutan

Q.120 Which is the largest southern most single Island in India?

A. Minicoy Island
B. Car Nicobar Island
C. Great Nicobar Island
D. None of these

Q.121 Which is the smallest state by area?

A. Nagaland
B. Goa
C. Sikkim
D. Meghalaya

Q.122 Which of the following countries is not larger than India in terms of geographical area?

A. Australia
B. Brazil
C. Canada
D. Indonesia

Q.123 Which of the following states is India's largest Bauxite producer?

A. Orissa
B. Jharkhand
C. Rajasthan
D. Karnataka

Q.124 Range that rises in eastern Gujarat state near the Arabian Sea coast, running east through Maharashtra and Madhya Pradesh to Chhattisgarh?

A. Vindhya Range
B. Aravalli Range
C. Toba Kakar Range
D. Satpura Range

Q.125 Large deposits of natural uranium, which promises to be one of the top 20 of the world's reserves, have been found in the Tummalapalle belt in which among the following states of India?

A. Kerala
B. Tamil Nadu
C. Andhra Pradesh
D. Odisha

// Smart Answer Sheet //

Correct Indicates percentage of students who answered questions correctly.

Skipped Indicates percentage of students who skipped questions.

Q.	Ans.	Correct / Skipped
1	D	36.36 % / 6.06 %
2	B	45.45 % / 48.49 %
3	C	9.09 % / 48.49 %
4	C	30.3 % / 48.49 %
5	C	21.21 % / 48.49 %
6	A	27.27 % / 48.49 %
7	B	15.15 % / 48.49 %
8	C	24.24 % / 48.49 %
9	C	30.3 % / 48.49 %
10	B	27.27 % / 48.49 %
11	C	15.15 % / 48.49 %
12	A	12.12 % / 48.49 %
13	D	39.39 % / 45.46 %
14	C	39.39 % / 48.49 %
15	C	36.36 % / 48.49 %
16	D	30.3 % / 48.49 %

Q.	Ans.	Correct / Skipped
17	B	24.24 % / 48.49 %
18	A	21.21 % / 48.49 %
19	D	42.42 % / 39.4 %
20	D	0 % / 100 %
21	A	18.18 % / 45.46 %
22	A	30.3 % / 48.49 %
23	D	36.36 % / 39.4 %
24	D	39.39 % / 48.49 %
25	A	27.27 % / 48.49 %
26	D	39.39 % / 48.49 %
27	D	45.45 % / 45.46 %
28	D	36.36 % / 48.49 %
29	B	45.45 % / 45.46 %
30	A	33.33 % / 48.49 %
31	D	36.36 % / 48.49 %
32	A	36.36 % / 48.49 %

Q.	Ans.	Correct / Skipped
33	B	18.18 % / 42.43 %
34	A	15.15 % / 48.49 %
35	D	33.33 % / 48.49 %
36	A	42.42 % / 48.49 %
37	C	42.42 % / 48.49 %
38	B	33.33 % / 48.49 %
39	A	6.06 % / 48.49 %
40	A	21.21 % / 48.49 %
41	D	36.36 % / 45.46 %
42	C	12.12 % / 48.49 %
43	A	36.36 % / 48.49 %
44	C	39.39 % / 48.49 %
45	A	24.24 % / 45.46 %
46	A	6.06 % / 48.49 %
47	D	24.24 % / 48.49 %
48	B	9.09 % / 48.49 %

Q.	Ans.	Correct / Skipped
49	D	24.24 % / 48.49 %
50	A	30.3 % / 48.49 %
51	D	42.42 % / 48.49 %
52	A	42.42 % / 48.49 %
53	A	6.06 % / 48.49 %
54	C	45.45 % / 48.49 %
55	A	33.33 % / 48.49 %
56	C	39.39 % / 48.49 %
57	A	42.42 % / 48.49 %
58	B	6.06 % / 48.49 %
59	C	48.48 % / 48.49 %
60	C	27.27 % / 48.49 %
61	D	45.45 % / 48.49 %
62	A	45.45 % / 48.49 %
63	A	39.39 % / 48.49 %
64	C	45.45 % / 48.49 %

Q.	Ans.	Correct / Skipped
65	C	42.42 % / 48.49 %
66	D	30.3 % / 48.49 %
67	B	36.36 % / 48.49 %
68	D	33.33 % / 48.49 %
69	B	45.45 % / 48.49 %
70	B	42.42 % / 48.49 %
71	B	42.42 % / 42.43 %
72	A	45.45 % / 48.49 %
73	A	45.45 % / 18.19 %
74	B	9.09 % / 48.49 %
75	C	36.36 % / 48.49 %
76	D	18.18 % / 48.49 %
77	D	18.18 % / 48.49 %
78	C	9.09 % / 48.49 %
79	A	42.42 % / 42.43 %
80	A	45.45 % / 48.49 %

Q.	Ans.	Correct / Skipped
81	A	42.42 % / 45.46 %
82	A	27.27 % / 48.49 %
83	A	30.3 % / 48.49 %
84	B	39.39 % / 48.49 %
85	D	12.12 % / 48.49 %
86	C	36.36 % / 48.49 %
87	D	39.39 % / 48.49 %
88	C	39.39 % / 48.49 %
89	D	27.27 % / 48.49 %

Q.	Ans.	Correct / Skipped
90	C	24.24 % / 48.49 %
91	D	15.15 % / 48.49 %
92	B	18.18 % / 48.49 %
93	C	24.24 % / 45.46 %
94	C	30.3 % / 48.49 %
95	B	45.45 % / 48.49 %
96	B	33.33 % / 48.49 %
97	A	30.3 % / 48.49 %
98	B	21.21 % / 48.49 %

Q.	Ans.	Correct / Skipped
99	C	21.21 % / 48.49 %
100	C	45.45 % / 48.49 %
101	D	18.18 % / 48.49 %
102	B	21.21 % / 48.49 %
103	B	18.18 % / 48.49 %
104	A	48.48 % / 48.49 %
105	C	12.12 % / 48.49 %
106	C	27.27 % / 48.49 %
107	C	36.36 % / 48.49 %

Q.	Ans.	Correct / Skipped
108	B	36.36 % / 48.49 %
109	A	24.24 % / 45.46 %
110	C	39.39 % / 48.49 %
111	C	30.3 % / 42.43 %
112	D	21.21 % / 48.49 %
113	C	39.39 % / 45.46 %
114	B	27.27 % / 48.49 %
115	D	18.18 % / 48.49 %
116	B	39.39 % / 48.49 %

Q.	Ans.	Correct / Skipped
117	C	18.18 % / 42.43 %
118	D	45.45 % / 48.49 %
119	A	48.48 % / 42.43 %
120	C	18.18 % / 48.49 %
121	B	45.45 % / 45.46 %
122	D	42.42 % / 48.49 %
123	A	48.48 % / 48.49 %
124	D	18.18 % / 48.49 %
125	C	18.18 % / 48.49 %

Performance Analysis

Avg. Score (%)	35.29%
Toppers Score (%)	91.29%
Your Score	

//Hints and Solutions//

1. Ainu is one of the important tribal groups of Japan.

The Ainu or the Aynu, also known as the Ezo in historical Japanese texts, are an East Asian ethnic group indigenous to northern Japan, the original inhabitants of Hokkaido and some of its nearby Russian territories.

Hence, the correct option is (D).

2. An Igloo is a winter snow house or snow hut built when the snow can be easily compacted.

Although igloos are often associated with all Inuit and Eskimo peoples, they were traditionally used only by the people of Canada's Central Arctic and Greenland's Thule area. Other Inuit tended to use snow to insulate their houses, which were constructed from whalebone and hides. Snow is used because the air pockets trapped in it make it an insulator. On the outside, temperatures may be as low as −45 °C (−49 °F), but on the inside, the temperature may range from −7 to 16 °C (19 to 61 °F) when warmed by body heat alone.

Hence, the correct option is (B).

3. Disparities in regional development on a global scale are not mainly due to the lack of adequate skilled labour.

Causes of Regional Disparity

- Historical Factor.
- Geographical Factors.
- Location Specific Advantages.
- Early Mover Advantage.
- Failure of Planning Mechanism.
- Restricted Success of Green Revolution.
- Law and Order Problem.
- Higher resource transfers from the Centre to the Backward States

Hence, the correct option is (C).

4. The group of people inhabiting Asiatic Tundra is known as Samoyed. The Samoyedic people are those groups that speak Samoyedic languages, which are part of the Uralic family. They are a linguistic grouping, not an ethnic or cultural one.

Hence, the correct option is (C).

5. The Semang are a Negrito ethnic group of the Malay Peninsula. They are found in Perak, Kedah and Pahang of Malaysia. During the colonial British administration, Orang Asli living in the northern Malay Peninsula were classified as Sakai.

Hence, the correct option is (C).

6. The Sami people are indigenous Finno-Ugric people inhabiting the Arctic area of Sapmi, which today encompasses parts of far northern Norway, Sweden, Finland, the Kola Peninsula of Russia, and the border area between south and middle Sweden and Norway.

Hence, the correct option is (A).

7. The Tuareg is a pastoral nomad living in the desert of Sahara. They are found in Algeria, Mali Burkina Faso and Niger.

Tuaregs are found in Sahara desert of North Africa. They in habit the area stretching from far southwestern Libya to southern Algeria, Niger, Mali and Burkina Faso. They are about 2 million nomadic people and are mostly Muslims.

Hence, the correct option is (B).

8. Natives of North America belong to the Mongoloid race.

Mongoloid is an outdated historical grouping of various people indigenous to large parts of Asia, Polynesia, and the Americas. In the past, other terms such as "yellow", "Asiatic" and "Oriental" have been used as synonyms.

The concept of dividing humankind into three races called Caucasoid, Mongoloid, and Negroid was introduced in the 1780s by members of the Göttingen School of History and further developed by Western scholars in the context of "racist ideologies" during the age of colonialism.

Hence, the correct option is (C).

9. Spatial interaction is a dynamic flow process from one location to another. In describing the process of it, geographers are most concerned with Accessibility and Connectivity.

Spatial interaction is the general term for any movement of people, goods, or information over space that results from a decision-making process.

Hence, the correct option is (C).

10. Archipelagoes or island groups. These comprise groups of islands of varying sizes and shapes, such as the British Isles, the Balearic Islands of the Mediterranean, and those of the Aegean Sea.

An archipelago is an area that contains a chain or group of islands scattered in lakes, rivers, or the ocean.

Hence, the correct option is (B).

11. Oceanic islands:

These islands are normally small and are located in the midst of oceans. They have no connection with the mainland, which may be hundreds or thousands of miles away.

They have flora and fauna unrelated to those of the continents. The Galapagos Islands have many unique species of animals.

Due to their remoteness from the world's major trading centres, most of the oceanic islands are very sparsely populated.

Hence, the correct option is (C).

12. Coral islands: Unlike the volcanic islands, the coral islands are much lower and emerge just above the water surface. These islands, built up by coral animals of various species, are found both near the mainland and in the midst of oceans.

Hence, the correct option is (A).

13. Coral Reefs:

Many kinds of coral animals and marine organisms such as coral polyps, calcareous algae, shell-forming creatures, and lime-secreting plants live in large colonies in tropical seas.

Though they are very tiny creatures, their ability to secrete calcium carbonate within their tiny cells has given rise to a particular marine landform type. They exist in numerous species of many forms, colours and shapes.

Under favourable conditions, they grow in great profusion just below the water level. Taking coral animals as a whole, the polyps are the most abundant and also the most important.

Hence, the correct option is (D).

14. There are also non-reef- building species such as the "precious corals' of the Pacific Ocean and the 'red coral of the Mediterranean which may survive in the colder and even the deeper waters. As a rule, they thrive well only in the warmer tropical seas.

Hence, the correct option is (C).

15. Winds blowing across the ocean surface push water away. Water then rises from beneath the surface to replace the water that was pushed away. This process is known as 'upwelling'. Upwelling occurs in the open ocean and along coastlines.

Water that rises to the surface as a result of upwelling is typically colder and is rich in nutrients. These nutrients 'fertilise' surface waters, meaning that these surface waters often have high biological productivity. Therefore, good fishing grounds typically are found where upwelling is common.

Hence, the correct option is (C).

16. Global sea level trends and relative sea-level trends are different measurements.

This is due to many local factors: subsidence, ocean currents, variations in land height, and whether the land is still rebounding from the compressive weight of Ice Age glaciers.

For example, land subsidence involves gradual settling or sudden sinking of the Earth's surface. This can cause short-term changes in local sea levels.

Hence, the correct option is (D).

17. The wind not only produces currents, it creates waves.

As the wind blows across the smooth water surface, the friction or drag between the air and the water tends to stretch the surface. As waves form, the surface becomes rougher and it is easier for the wind to grip the water surface and intensify the waves.

Hence, the correct option is (B).

18. The uplifting of the ocean floor occurs when convection currents rise in the mantle beneath the oceanic crust and create magma where two tectonic plates meet at a divergent boundary.

Seamounts are found close to these ridges. Seamounts can be found in every ocean basin in the world, distributed extremely widely both in space and in age.

A seamount is technically defined as an isolated rise in elevation of 1,000 m or more from the surrounding seafloor, and with a limited summit area, of conical form.

Hence, the correct option is (A).

19. The river moving downstream across a broad, level plain is heavy with debris from the upper course.

Vertical corrasion has almost ceased through lateral corrasion still goes on to erode its banks further.

The work of the river is mainly deposition, building up its bed and forming extensive flood plains.

The volume of water is greatly swelled by the additional tributaries that join the mainstream.

Coarse materials are dropped, and the finer silt is carried down towards the mouth of the river.

Hence, the correct option is (D).

20. Rivers in their lower course cry large quantities of sediments. During annual or sporadic floods, these materials are spread over the low-lying adjacent areas.

A layer of sediment is thus deposited during each flood, gradually building up a fertile flood plain.

When the river normally flows its bed is raised through the accumulation of deposits and material, it also drops on the sides, forming raised banks called levees.

It will not be long before the water level flows dangerously close to the top of the levees.

Hence, the correct option is (D).

21. Due to the obstruction caused by the deposited alluvium, the river may discharge its water through several channels called distributaries. Some deltas are enormous. For instance, the Ganges delta is almost as big as the whole of West Malaysia. Deltas extend sideways and seawards at an amazing rate.

Hence, the correct option is (A).

22. In the North Atlantic Ocean, the Cayenne current is joined and reinforced by the North Equatorial Current.

This current heads north-westwards as a large mass of equatorial water into the Caribbean sea.

This current is further split into two currents: The Florida current and The Gulf Stream.

All of these currents are warm currents.

Hence, the correct option is (A).

23. A negative movement occurs when there is an uplift of land or a sea-level fall. This will steepen the slope so that active down-cutting is renewed.

A fall in sea level leaves the flood-plain at an increased altitude above the sea level. The river with its renewed vigour cuts into the former flood-plain, leaving behind terraces on both sides of the river.

There is also a break in the river's graded profile, often marked by a series of rapids.

Hence, the correct option is (D).

24. Zozila is a high mountain pass in India, Kashmir, located on the Indian National Highway 1D between Srinagar and Leh. Shipkila is a mountain pass and border post on the India-China border. Nathula is a mountain pass in the Himalayas. It connects the Indian state of Sikkim with China's Tibet Autonomous Region.

Hence, the correct option is (D).

25. The Sun oscillates between the two tropics which are located at 23.43° north and south of the equator and since the equatorial region lies between the two tropics, the Sun remains more or less overhead throughout the year. And the circle of illumination always passes through the equator. This is why the annual range of temperature is small in the equatorial region.

Hence, the correct option is (A).

26. Coal is available in four forms: Lignite, bituminous, anthracite and sub- bituminous. Anthracite is the highest-ranked coal with a carbon percentage of above 87%. The carbon content in lignite is 60-70%. Tamil Nadu is the largest producer of lignite coal.

Hence, the correct option is (D).

27. The Brahmaputra also called Tsangpo-Brahmaputra, is a trans-boundary river and one of the major rivers of Asia.

With its origin in the Chemayungdung glacier, located on the northern side of the Himalayas in Burang County of Tibet as theYarlungTsangpo River, it flows across southern Tibet to break through the Himalayas in great gorges (including the YarlungTsangpo Grand Canyon) and into Arunachal Pradesh (India), where it is known as Dihang or Siang.

Hence, the correct option is (D).

28. National Highway No. 1 is a National Highway in Northern India that links the national capital New Delhi to the town of Attari in Punjab near the India–Pakistan border. This was a part of the historical Grand Trunk Road (Shershah Suri Marg), that ran from Bengal to Kabul, built on earlier roads that existed from time immemorial.

Hence, the correct option is (D).

29. Lakshadweep is a tropical archipelago of 36 atolls and coral reefs in the Arabian Sea, off the coast of Kerala, India. Not all of the islands are inhabited, and only a few are open to visitors (permits required). With coconut trees, secluded beaches, lagoons and coral reefs, the islands are known for their scuba diving, snorkeling, kayaking and fishing.

Hence, the correct option is (B).

30. The first four planets are called Terrestrial, meaning earth-like as they are made up of rock and metals, and have relatively high densities. The rest four are called Jovian or Gas Giant planets. Jovian means Jupiter-like. Most of them are much larger than the terrestrial planets and have thick atmosphere, mostly of helium and hydrogen.

(i) The terrestrial planets were formed in the close vicinity of the parent star where it was too warm for gases to condense to solid particles. Jovian planets were formed at quite a distant location.

(ii) The solar wind was most intense nearer the sun; so, it blew off lots of gas and dust from the terrestrial planets. The solar winds were not all that intense to cause similar removal of gases from the Jovian planets.

(iii) The terrestrial planets are smaller and their lower gravity could not hold the escaping gases.

Hence, the correct option is (A).

31. The distribution of matter and energy was not even in the early universe. These initial density differences gave rise to differences in gravitational forces and it caused the matter to get drawn together. These formed the bases for development of galaxies. A galaxy contains a large number of stars. Galaxies spread over vast distances that are measured in thousands of light-years. A galaxy starts to form by accumulation of hydrogen gas in the form of a very large cloud called nebula. Eventually, growing nebula develops localized clumps of gas. These clumps continue to grow into even denser gaseous bodies, giving rise to formation of stars. The formation of stars is believed to have taken place some 5-6 billion years ago.

Hence, the correct option is (D).

32. Development of planets:

(i) The stars are localized lumps of gas within a nebula. The gravitational force within the lumps leads to the formation of a core to the gas cloud and a huge rotating disc of gas and dust develops around the gas core.

(ii) In the next stage, the gas cloud starts getting condensed and the matter around the core develops into small rounded objects. These small-rounded objects by the process of cohesion develop into what is called planetesimals. Larger bodies start forming by collision, and gravitational attraction causes the material to stick together. Planetesimals are a large number of smaller bodies.

(iii) In the final stage, these large number of small planetesimals accrete to form a fewer large bodies in the form of planets.

Hence, the correct option is (A).

33. Abrasion: Glacial abrasion is the surface near achieved by individual clasts or rocks of various sizes contained within ice or subglacial sediments.

Glaciers are primarily of two types:

1. Continental
2. Alpine

Hence, the correct option is (B).

34. Mayurakshi Reservoir Project was taken up for execution in 1951 on river Kopai.

This Project has been completed in all respects in the year 1985. The irrigation potential created through completion of this project comes to 2,50,860 ha. in the districts of Birbhum, Murshidabad and Burdwan.

Irrigation water is also supplied to the state of Jharkhand from this reservoir to an area of about 6,000 ha. This Project is adjudged to be one of the best performing irrigation projects in India.

Hence, the correct option is (A).

35. A coal seam is a dark brown or black banded deposit of coal that is visible within layers of rock. These seams are located underground and can be mined using either deep mining or strip mining techniques depending on their proximity to the surface.

The Talcher coal mines are a 61.83 million tonne-per-annum (MTPA) network of mines, operated by Mahanadi Coalfields Limited, a subsidiary of Coal India, on the Talcher coalfield in Angul, Odisha state, India.

Hence, the correct option is (D).

36. Coal formed millions of years ago when the earth was covered with huge swampy forests where plants - giant ferns, reeds, and mosses - grew. Coal is a nonrenewable fossil fuel that is combusted and used to generate electricity. Mining techniques and combustion are both dangerous to miners and hazardous to the environment.

Jharkhand- Located in north-east India, the state of Jharkhand top the list of India's coal reserves — at more than 26% — and production. The state's main coal-mining centres are Jharia, Bokaro, Auranga, Giridh, Dhanbad, Ramgarh, Karanpur and Hutar. Most of these coal fields are located in a narrow belt that runs east to west. The Jharia coalfield, which is located south of Dhanbad, is India's oldest and richest coalfield with the best of bituminous coal in its reserves. The total coal reserves in Jharkhand are estimated to be 83.15 billion tonnes.

Hence, the correct option is (A).

37. The BPCL Kochi Refinery, embarked on its journey in 1966 with a capacity of 50,000 barrels per day.

Formerly known as Cochin Refineries Limited, the refinery was originally established as a joint venture in collaboration with Phillips Petroleum Corporation, USA.

Kochi Refinery is located at Ambalamugal, near Kochi in Kerala.

Hence, the correct option is (C).

38. The northern boundary of the Indian Plate coincides with the southern margin of Tibet. The timing of the collision between India and Asia is the key boundary condition in all models for the evolution of the Himalaya -Tibetan orogenic system. It profoundly affects the interpretation of the rates of a multitude of associated geological processes ranging from Tibetan Plateau uplift through continental extrusion across eastern Asia, as well as our understanding of global climate change during the Cenozoic.

Hence, the correct option is (B).

39. The systematic geography approach is the same as that of general geography. This approach was introduced by Alexander Von Humboldt. Regional geography approach was developed by another German geographer and a contemporary of Humboldt, Karl Ritter (1779-1859).

Hence, the correct option is (A).

40. The instruments which are basically designed for the change in the scale of the original map are known as a pantograph, eidograph, and camera lucida.

Pantograph is based on the principle of similar triangles.

Eidograph is constructed with two parallel bars, with one support.

Camera lucida is based on the principle of optics and photography.

Hence, the correct option is (A).

41. West Bengal state had the highest density of population.

Population density (2001) of the given states are:

- Bihar: 881
- Punjab: 484
- Uttar Pradesh: 690
- West Bengal: 903

All the data in the table as per the census 2011.

Hence, the correct option is (D).

42. Hindustan Shipyard Limited (HSL) is a shipyard located in Visakhapatnam on the east coast of India. It was built by industrialist Walchand Hirachand as a part of The Scindia Steam Navigation Company Ltd. The first ship to be constructed fully in India after independence was built at the Scindia Shipyard and named Jal Usha. It was launched in 1948 by Jawaharlal Nehru.

Hence, the correct option is (C).

43. The binary star hypothesis about the origin of Earth was given by Russel in 1937. R.A. Lyttelton worked on and improved upon theory.

The most widely accepted theory of planetary formation is the Nebular hypothesis of Immanuel Kant. Pierre-Simon Laplace gave a similar theory in 1796.

According to the hypothesis - Russel said that the primitive sun had two stars in the universe. In the beginning, the 'shared star' was revolving around the primitive sun.

Hence, the correct option is (A).

44. The concept of 'Base-Level' was given by J.W. Powell. The Geomorphology base level is the lower unit for an erosion process. The term was given by Powell in 1875.

Hence, the correct option is (C).

45. The theory of Isostasy explains the tendency of Earth's crust to attain equilibrium and distribution of the material in Earth's crust. This theory is based on the opposing influence of buoyancy and gravity. This was coined by C.E. Dutton in 1889.

Hence, the correct option is (A).

46. Firmanus (260-340 A.D.), one of the leading protagonists of Christianity, denied the concept of a spherical earth. Firmanus visited Ethiopia, the Indian Ocean, Socotra, Persian Gulf, and Ceylon. About the shape of the earth, he deduced that it was flat, bounded on all sides by high walls.

Hence, the correct option is (A).

47. Ptolemy promulgated the concept of Terra-Australis-Incognita declaring that the Indian Ocean is a closed sea. Ptolemy was one of those geniuses who developed sound principles of mathematical geography. His writings inspired the geographers and explorers of the Great Age of Discovery (14th, 15th century A.D.) to explore the Terra-Incognita (unknown land).

Hence, the correct option is (D).

48. Immanuel Kant was a German philosopher. He developed the nebular hypothesis in 1755. This hypothesis considered that the planets were formed out of a cloud of material associated with a youthful sun, which was slowly rotating. In 1754, while contemplating a prize question by the Berlin Academy about the problem of Earth's rotation, he argued that the Moon's gravity would slow down Earth's spin. He put forth the argument that gravity would eventually cause the Moon's tidal locking to coincide with the Earth's rotation.

Hence, the correct option is (B).

49. Jayakwadi dam is an earthen dam located on Godavari river at the site of Jayakwadi village in Paithan taluka of Aurangabad district in Maharashtra, India. The harsh project is one of the largest irrigation projects in the Indian state of Maharashtra.

Hence, the correct option is (D).

50. About 80 per cent of the current water use is drawn by agriculture. Irrigated area accounts for nearly 48.8 per cent of the 140 million hectare (mha) of agricultural land in India. The remaining 51.2 per cent is rainfed. The increasing gap also impacts rainfed production in the country.

Hence, the correct option is (A).

51. Kanyakumari is located north of equator and south of the tropic of cancer and North of the tropic of Capricorn.

The peninsular tip of Kanyakumari is bordered on three sides by the Laccadive Sea. It is located at the confluence of the Western Coastal Plains and Eastern Coastal Plains. Kanyakumari is at the southern tip and is the southernmost point of the contiguous Indian Subcontinent.

Hence, the correct option is (D).

52. The pass located at the southern end of the Nilgiri Hills in south India is called the Palghat gap.

Palakkad Gap or Palghat Gap is a low mountain pass in the Western Ghats between Coimbatore in Tamil Nadu and Palakkad in Kerala. It has an average elevation of 140 metres (460 ft) with a width of 24–30 kilometres (15–19 mi). The pass is located between the Nilgiri Hills to the north and Anaimalai Hills to the south.

Hence, the correct option is (A).

53. India's copper ore reserves have been estimated at 400 million tonnes, with a metal content of 5 million tones. The principal copper belt of India lies in Singhbhum and Hazaribagh in Jharkhand. The mining centres are located at Mosabani, Ghatsila, Thobani and Badia of Singbhum, Hazaribagh of Bihar, the Khetri and Dariba areas of Rajasthan, and Agnigundala of Andhra Pradesh. Total production is 2.6 million tones.

Hence, the correct option is (A).

54. The Brahmaputra, called Yarlung Tsangpo in Tibet, Siang/Dihang River in Arunachal Pradesh and Luit, Dilao in Assam, is a trans-boundary river which flows through Tibet, India and Bangladesh. It is the 9th largest river in the world by discharge, and the 15th longest.

Hence, the correct option is (C).

55. Salal power station is run-of-the-river scheme with an installed capacity of 690 MW to harnesses the Hydropower potential of river Chenab. It is located in Reasi district of Union Territory of Jammu & Kashmir.

Hence, the correct option is (A).

56. The southern zone is the only zone in the country that produces gold and is also rich in iron.

Three sectors Southern Sector, Kerala & Karnataka sector, and Western Sector are under the administrative/operational jurisdiction of South Zone i.e., Tamilnadu, Telangana, Andhra Pradesh and Pondicherry under Southern Sector, Kerala and Karnataka under K K Sector and Maharashtra, Gujarat, Goa, Diu, Daman & Nagar Haveli (U.T) under Western Sector.

Hence, the correct option is (C).

57. India occupies 2.4 percent of the total land area of the world, but supports 16.7 percent of the world population.

Hence, the correct option is (A).

58. The present forest area of India, according to satellite data, is decreasing.

Based on satellite data analysis, the biennial assessment – conducted by the Forest Survey of India (FSI) and released by the Ministry of Environment, Forest and Climate Change (MoEFCC) – has put the total forest and tree cover at around 802,088 square km, which is approximately 24.39 percent of the geographical area of the country.

Hence, the correct option is (B).

59. Mawsynram is a town in the East Khasi Hills district of Meghalaya state in northeastern India, Around 60.9 kilometres from Shillong. Mawsynram receives the highest rainfall in India.

Hence, the correct option is (C).

60. Statement (1) is true. The humid subtropical climate is found from the Tropic of Cancer (northern latitude) in the Northern Hemisphere and from the Tropic of Capricorn (southern latitude) in the Southern Hemisphere.

Statement (2) is true. The humid subtropical climate is found in the northern plains of India including the plains of the southern part of China.

It is worth mentioning that the humid subtropical climate is similar to the tropical humid and dry climate. But, exceptionally, there is temperate in winter.

Hence, the correct option is (C).

61. The predominant type of Indian agriculture is subsistence agriculture. Subsistence agriculture occurs when farmers grow

food crops to meet the needs of themselves and their families on smallholdings. Subsistence agriculturalists target farm output for survival and for mostly local requirements, with little or no surplus.

Hence, the correct option is (D).

62. The Radcliffe Line was the boundary demarcation line between the Indian and Pakistani portions of the Punjab and Bengal provinces of British India. It was named after its architect, Sir Cyril Radcliffe, who, as the joint chairman of the two boundary commissions for the two provinces, received the responsibility to equitably divide 175,000 square miles (450,000 km²) of territory with 88 million people.

Hence, the correct option is (A).

63. Gulf of Cambay has a potential for harnessing of tidal energy in India.

The Gulf of Khambhat, also known as the Gulf of Cambay, is a bay on the Arabian Sea coast of India, bordering the state of Gujarat right north of city of Mumbai. The Gulf of Khambhat is about 200 km (120 mi) long, about 20 km (12 mi) wide in the north and up to 70 km (43 mi) wide in the south. Major rivers draining Gujarat are the Narmada, Tapti, Mahi and Sabarmati that form estuaries in the gulf.

Hence, the correct option is (A).

64. Physical weathering is caused by the effects of changing temperature on rocks, causing the rock to break apart. The process is sometimes assisted by water.

There are two main types of physical weathering:

Freeze-thaw occurs when water continually seeps into cracks, freezes and expands, eventually breaking the rock apart.

Exfoliation occurs as cracks develop parallel to the land surface a consequence of the reduction in pressure during uplift and erosion.

Hence, the correct option is (C).

65. Under stable nighttime conditions, long-wave radiation is emitted by the ground; this cools the ground, which causes a temperature inversion. In turn, moist air near the ground cools to its dew point.

Hence, the correct option is (C).

66. Mistral the local wind is different from the others. The mistral is a strong, cold and usually dry regional wind in France, coming from the north or northwest, which accelerates when it passes through the valleys of the Rhone and the Durance Rivers to the coast of the Mediterranean around the Camargue region.

Hence, the correct option is (D).

67. Cumulonimbus (from Latin cumulus, "heaped" and nimbus, "rainstorm") is a dense, towering vertical cloud, forming from water vapor carried by powerful upward air currents. If observed during a storm, these clouds may be referred to as thunderheads. Cumulonimbus can form alone, in clusters, or along cold front squall lines. These clouds are capable of producing lightning and other dangerous severe weather, such as tornadoes and

hailstones. Cumulonimbus progress from overdeveloped cumulus congestus clouds and may further develop as part of a supercell.

Hence, the correct option is (B).

68. A hot local wind blowing in Sahara desert is known as Harmattan. The Harmattan is a dry and dusty West African trade wind. This northeasterly world blows from the Sahara into the Gulf of Guinea between the end of November and the middle of March. The temperatures can be as low as 3 degrees Celsius.

Hence, the correct option is (D).

69. Atmospheric layer which reflects radio waves is called Ionosphere. The ionosphere is a region of the upper atmosphere, from about 85 km (53 mi) to 600 km (370 mi) altitude, and includes the thermosphere and parts of the mesosphere and exosphere. It is distinguished because it is ionized by solar radiation. It plays an important part in atmospheric electricity and forms the inner edge of the magnetosphere. It has practical importance because, among other functions, it influences radio propagation to distant places on the Earth.

Hence, the correct option is (B).

70. Troposphere contains dust particles and water vapour. This is the most important layer of the atmosphere because all kinds of weather changes take place only in this layer. The air never remains static in this layer. Therefore this layer is called 'changing sphere' or troposphere.

Hence, the correct option is (B).

71. The tropopause is the boundary in the Earth's atmosphere between the troposphere and the stratosphere. It is a thermodynamic gradient stratification layer, marking the end of the troposphere. It lies, on average, at 17 kilometres above equatorial regions, and about 9 kilometres over the polar regions.

Hence, the correct option is (B).

72. Jet stream is fast blowing westerlies in upper part of troposphere. Jet streams are fast flowing, narrow air currents found in the atmospheres of some planets, including Earth. The main jet streams are located near the tropopause, the transition between the troposphere (where temperature decreases with altitude) and the stratosphere (where temperature increases with altitude).

Hence, the correct option is (A).

73. Tropical cyclones in Australia are called Willy-willy. Willy willy is a small windstorm that mostly occurs in dry, outback areas. The term Willy Willy is of Aboriginal origin. Willy willies are normally tropical cyclones.

Hence, the correct option is (A).

74. The Himalayas currently extend into two union territories of India, Jammu and Kashmir and Ladakh, and in Himachal Pradesh, Uttarakhand, Sikkim, Arunachal Pradesh, and partly in the states of Bengal, Assam, Nagaland, Manipur, Mizoram and Tripura. So, it is clear that statement - 1 is not correct.

The Western Ghats, the second longest mountain in India, is spread over the states of Gujarat, Maharashtra, Goa, Karnataka,

Kerala, Tamil Nadu. It is known as Sahyadri. Therefore, it is clear that statement-2 is also not true.

Pulicat lake is spread in the border of Andhra Pradesh and Tamil Nadu states. The island named Sri Harikota separates this lake from the ocean and gives it the form of a lagoon. So, statement-3 is true.

Hence, the correct option is (B).

75. The wide hills in the Eastern Ghats are important in terms of natural beauty, tourism and economic. In Andhra Pradesh, the north to south order of broad hills is Nallamalai, Velikonda, Palakonda and Nagari respectively, while in Tamil Nadu the north to south order of wide hills are Jawadi, Shevaroy, Panchamalai, and Sirumalai respectively. Nilgiri, Annamalai and Kamam (Cardamom) and Nagercoil are respectively the north to south sequence of broad hills in Kerala-Tamil Nadu. It is, therefore, clear that the answer to the above question will be.

Hence, the correct option is (C).

76. The major valleys of India are as follows-

Jammu and Kashmir	Kashmir Valley, Markha Valley, Nubra Valley, Suru Valley
Himachal Pradesh	Kangra Valley, Kinnaur Valley, Parvati Valley, Sangla Valley, Malna Valley, Kullu Valley, Pangi Valley, Spiti Valley, Lahul Valley, Chamba Valley
Uttarakhand	Doon Valley, Johar Valley, Valley of Flowers, Dharma Valley, Tire Valley, Nelang Valley
Bengal	Nyora Valley
Sikkim	Chumbi Valley, Yuthang Valley
Nagaland	Juku Valley
Andhra Pradesh	Araku Valley
Tamil Nadu	Kambam Valley
Kerala	Quiet Valley

Hence, the correct option is (D).

77. The northern plains are anatomically broad as Bhabhar, Terai and alluvial plains (Bangar and Khadar) to the south of Shivalik.

Bhabhar - 8-10 km wide from Indus to Teesta river in Giripad region of Shivalik. The wide band is called Bhabhar. Here the rivers originating from the Himalayan mountain ranges collect heavy water loads like large rocks, shells, and sediments. And sometimes they disappear in themselves.

Tarai - A 10–20 km wide strip south and parallel to Bhabar is called Tarai. In this strip, the rivers again flow out of the earth and flow to the surface. Bangar - The old alluvial plains are called Bangar. They are located above the flood plains and are less fertile than Khadar.

Khadar - The new alluvial plains are called Khadar. They are usually located in flood plains. Here alluvial deposits are renewed by rivers every year. These are the most fertile alluvial plains.

Hence, the correct option is (D).

78. Silent Valley National Forest Area is located on the Nilgiri Hills in Kerala. The Nallamalai hills are spread over Telangana and Andhra Pradesh states and not in Kerala. Hence statement - 1 is wrong. The Patharkkadavu hydroelectric project has been

constructed by the Government of Kerala in Silent Valley National Park. The Kunthi River originates from the Silent Valley forest area. It flows southwest and falls into the Arabian Sea. Therefore, it is clear that statement-2 and statement-3 are correct, so the answer to the above question will be.

Hence, the correct option is (C).

79. Guru Shikhar (1722 m) situated on Mount Abu Mountains in Rajasthan is the highest peak of the Aravali mountain range. The famous Jain religious place, Dilwara Jain Temple, is located in Mount Abu.

Hence, the correct option is (A).

80. The coastal plains have developed here due to the southern part of India being peninsular. Erosion and deposition by rivers played an important role in the construction of these coastal plains. is. The coastal plains are divided into two parts on the basis of location. The western coastal plains - Gujarat, from the state to the state of Kerala, the plains between the Arabian Sea and the Western Ghats are known as the West Coastal Plains. The west coastal plains are locally divided into the following 3 parts-

1.	Gujarat to Goa	Konkan Coast
2.	Goa to Mangalore	Kannada coast
3.	Mangalore to Kerala	Malabar Coast

Eastern Coastal Plains - The plains between the Bay of Bengal and the Eastern Ghats from the state of Bengal to Kanyakumari (Tamil Nadu) are called the Eastern Coastal Plains. The east coast plains are also locally divided into 3 parts-

Bengal to Godavari Coast	Utkal / Northern Government Coast
Godavari to Krishna Delta	Golconda Beach
Krishna delta to Kanyakumari	Coromandel Coast

Hence, the correct option is (A).

81. The Ten Degree Channel is a strait separating the small Andaman Islands in the Andaman and Nicobar archipelago of India from the island of Car Nicobar, which is located 10 latitudes north.

Hence, the correct option is (A).

82. Snow Line - Snow Line refers to the boundary between the snow-capped and snow-free surface. This is the limit above which snow always rests. The average elevation of the Himalayas in the Himalayan mountain region is 4300 to 6000 m. The height of the snow line decreases as it rises from east to west in the Himalayan mountain region. The average elevation of the snow line in the eastern Himalayas is 3500 m. It is the same, in the Western Himalayas it is reduced to 2500 m It is done. This difference in the elevation of the snow line is due to high latitudes and rainfall. Rainfall is comparatively less in the Western Himalayas and occurs mostly in the form of snowfall. In the eastern Himalayas, rainfall is more and mostly in the form of watercourses.

Hence, the correct option is (A).

83. According to the continental displacement theory propounded by Alfred Wegner (Germany), the Indian landmass is part of the ancient Gondwana terrain. In the Jurassic era, the attraction of the Moon in the Gondwana-Territory, and the gravity and polar leaking force of the Earth, led to the fragmentation of South, America, Africa, Madagascar, Peninsular India and Australia. Later, there was a northward flow into Africa, Eurasia and Peninsular India, resulting in the formation of new mountain ranges, such as the Atlas, Alps and the Himalayas.

Hence, the correct option is (A).

84. German meteorologist Vladimir Koppen classified the world climate into 5 parts around 1900 AD, which are indicated by five capital letters (ABCDE) of the English alphabet. Koppen has established a close relationship between the distribution of vegetation and climate in his classification of climate. Its classification is mainly based on the annual and monthly mean of temperature and precipitation.

The Koppen climate classification divides climates into five main climate groups, with each group being divided based on seasonal precipitation and temperature patterns. The five main groups are A (tropical), B (dry), C (temperate), D (continental), and E (polar)The classification of world climate by Koppen is generally the simplest and most effective.

Hence, the correct option is (B).

85. In the month of December every year by marine fishermen of South American countries Peru and Ecuador. The rise in temperature of the surrounding Pacific Ocean was called El-Nino. That is, El-Nino is a phenomenon of the warming of the coastline near Peru in the Pacific Ocean.

La Nina is the process of freezing water in the Pacific Ocean, so it is also known as Anti-El-Nino. This event usually occurs after El-Nino.

In El-Nino, the sea surface temperature rises very high whereas in La-Nina the sea surface temperature is very low.

For India, El-Nino has adverse effects on the southwest monsoon. On the other hand, La-Nina is beneficial for the monsoon of India. In India, al-Nino causes drought conditions, while La-Nina causes excessive rainfall.

Hence, the correct option is (D).

86. According to Koppen's climate classification and their analysis, the average temperature in each month of the year exceeds 18°C in a hot humid climate.

There is a lack of winter in this climate. Here rainfall is always more than evaporation throughout the year.

Hence, the correct option is (C).

87. According to the climatic classification of Koppen, the Indian peninsula has a tropical monsoon climate. In this climate, torrential rains occur in summer and winters are dry. The same climate is also found in the northern part of Australia, the north-eastern part of South America.

The Mediterranean climate is found along the western coast of the continents around the Mediterranean Sea and between 30° to 40° latitudes from the subtropics.

The specialty of this type of climate is that summers are hot and dry and winters are normal and rainy. Central California, central

Chile and the southeastern and southwestern coasts of Australia are examples of this.

Tundra is a region of permanent frost. Where there is constant snow in the site part too. Small vegetation like moss, lichen and flowering plants are found in tundra climatic regions.

Hence, the correct option is (D).

88. The tropical humid climate is found near the equator (latitude 0°). The main regions of this climate are the islands of South East Asia, the Amazon Basin of South America, western equatorial Africa, and so on.

Tropical sedimentary forests with very dense, large and wide biodiversity are found in this climate region. In fact, these climatic regions receive torrential rain with lightning after noon in almost the entire year. The temperature is uniformly high and the annual temperature is negligible.

Hence, the correct option is (C).

89. In the Mediterranean regions, there are mainly two seasons, summer and winter.

Most of the rainfall in the Mediterranean climate occurs in the winter, but it is not high, while it is dry in summer. During winters, the sun is strong, which helps in ripening of fruits.

Climate similar to China is found in northern or southern spheres of latitudes from 30° to the middle, east coast of continents. Although the rainfall here is year-round, the amount of rainfall in winter is less while most of the rainfall is in summer.

A wide variety of climatic conditions can be seen in tropical high mountain regions, ranging from tropical to temperate and tropical. Thus this climatic zone can be classified as vertical.

Hence, the correct option is (D).

90. Strobilanthes kunthiana, known as Kurinji or Neelakurinji in Tamil, is a shrub that is found in the shola forests of the Western Ghats in Kerala and Tamil Nadu. Nilgiri Hills, which literally means the blue mountains, got their name from the purplish blue flowers of Neelakurinji that blossoms only once in 12 years.

Hence, the correct option is (C).

91. The term 'underwater tropical rain forests' is associated with Gulf of Mannar.

The Gulf of Mannar is a large shallow bay forming part of the Laccadive Sea in the Indian Ocean with an average depth of 5.8 m (19 ft).

Hence, the correct option is (D).

92. Man and the Biosphere Programme (MAB) is an intergovernmental scientific program, launched in 1971 by UNESCO, that aims to establish a scientific basis for the improvement of relationships between people and their environments.

Hence, the correct option is (B).

93. There are 10 biogeographic zones in India. They are as follows,

a) Trans Himalayan zone,

b) Himalayan zone,

c) Desert zone,

d) Semiarid zone,

e) Western ghat zone,

f) Deccan plateau zone,

g) Gangetic plain zone,

h) North east zone,

i) Coastal zone,

j) Islands present near the shore line.

Hence, the correct option is (C).

94. Mahi River is one of the major interstate west flowing rivers, along with Tapti River and the Narmada River, of India. The total length of Mahi is 583 km. It originates in the Mahi Kanta hills, from the northern slopes of Vindhyas at an altitude of 500 m near village Bhopawar, Sardarpur tehsil in Dhar district of Madhya Pradesh. Initially the river flows Northwards through Dhar and Jhabua districts of M.P. and then turns left and passes through the Ratlam district of M.P., then turning to North – West, it enters the Banswara district of Rajasthan and flows in South – West directions and thereafter enters the Panchmahal district of Gujarat state. Then the river continuously flows in the same direction through Kheda district of Gujarat and finally falls into the Gulf of Khambat in Arabian Sea.

Hence, the correct option is (C).

95. In between Uttar Pradesh and India's border with China, there is Uttarakhand.

It borders the Tibet Autonomous Region of China to the north; the Sudurpashchim Pradesh of Nepal to the east; the Indian states of Uttar Pradesh to the south and Himachal Pradesh to the west and north-west.

Hence, the correct option is (B).

96. In between Himachal Pradesh and Indo-Nepal border, there is Uttarakhand.

On 9 November, 2000 Uttarakhand was formed and became the 27th State of India. The State shares international boundaries with China (Tibet) in the north and Nepal in the east. To the north-west, it is bounded with Himachal Pradesh.

Hence, the correct option is (B).

97. In between Manipur and Indo-Bangladesh border there is Silchar district of Assam.

Manipur Indian states does not have a common international border with Bangladesh. India enjoys close relations with Bangladesh and shares a 4,096-km-long border which touches Assam, Tripura, Mizoram, Meghalaya and West Bengal.

Hence, the correct option is (A).

98. Melanesia region consists of the four countries of Vanuatu, Solomon Islands, Fiji, and Guinea. It is a sub-region of Oceania extending from the western end of the Pacific Ocean to the Arafura Sea, and eastward to Fiji. Besides these independent countries, Melanesia also includes New Caledonia, Maluku Islands, and West Papua.

Hence, the correct option is (B).

99. The distribution of sunset in the world is the main factor controlling the distribution of temperature. Particles in the atmosphere absorb the heat of the sun and make us feel it because these particles are heavier so they have more presence in the lower layers of the air. This is why the lowest layer of air is warmer.

The surface is heated due to the absorption of sunlight and this also makes the air in contact with the surface warm, so the temperature decreases as the altitude increases. In the upper atmosphere, there is a lack of air and humidity.

In the case of rising above sea level, the temperature decreases gradually. This decrease in temperature is usually up to about 1°C at an altitude of 165 m. Although this rate varies according to the time, weather and different conditions of the place.

Hence, the correct option is (C).

100. The solar radiation energy that reaches the Earth from the Sun is called Suryatap. This energy reaches the Earth from the Sun in the form of short wavelengths. The ratio between the amount of sunset that a surface receives and the amount of sunset that is reflected from the same surface is called Albedo.

The average Albedo of the Earth is 33–35 percent, while the highest Albedo is 65 to 85 percent of newly covered snow cover. The Albedo in the sand desert ranges from 20 to 25 percent and the Albedo 3–15 percent of the paddy crop land and the Albedo 18–22 percent of the prairie land.

Hence, the correct option is (C).

101. The distance between the Sun and the Earth is shortest on January 4.

- The point which is closest to the sun is called subsolar.
- Winter occurs in the Northern Hemisphere when the Earth is closest to the Sun.
- At that time it is summer in the Southern Hemisphere.
- The point which is farthest from the Sun is called Apsour.
- Apsour happens on the 4th of July.

Hence, the correct option is (D).

102. This difference between the highest and lowest temperatures is called the 'temperature difference'. The annual temperature of the ocean is inversely proportional to it. As the size of the Atlantic Ocean is comparatively smaller than the Pacific Ocean, the Atlantic Ocean is found to have a greater warming than the Pacific Ocean.

The site is warmer and faster than water. In the same way, they also cool down faster than water. This feature of water and land has a great influence on the temperature of that place. Because of the terrestrial part in the northern roundness while there is an excess of the aquatic part in the southern hemisphere. Thus, the

annual temperature range is higher in the Northern Hemisphere than in the Southern Hemisphere.

Hence, the correct option is (B).

103. The study of the upper layer of the atmosphere is called the study of aerodynamics and the study of the lower layer as meteorology. About half of the total load of the atmosphere is found at an altitude of 5500 km above ground level. It is clear from modern research that the final height or expansion of the atmosphere is between 16 thousand km to 32 thousand km. It is also clear from a variety of studies that the atmosphere has no fixed upper limits, but it gradually becomes sparse.

Hence, the correct option is (B).

104. The vast amount of air circulating around the Earth is called the atmosphere. The atmosphere is divided into a total of 5 layers, with the lowest layer of the atmosphere called the troposphere or troposphere. This division is called convection because the convection currents are confined to the boundary of this circle.

Key facts troposphere

This is the lowest layer of the atmosphere, so this mantle is also called the subsoil.

Its height is 8 kilometers at the poles and about 18 kilometers at the equator.

All major atmospheric events such as clouds, thunderstorms and rainfall etc. occur in this division.

The rate of temperature drop in the troposphere is 1 degree Celsius per 165 m elevation or 6.4 degree Celsius at 1 km altitude.

Hence, the correct option is (A).

105. It was found that the wind direction in the Pacific changed during La Nina time resulting in an increase in the speed of winds blowing from Africa to Indonesia during the cyclone season. This increased speed led to piling up warmer water in Indonesia and made the Bay of Bengal warmer. With the ocean getting heated up the intensity of the cyclones increased." Now it is clear that intensity of heat in the ocean will also increase the intensity of cyclones," he said. Apart from observing pronounced tropical cyclone activity during La Nina, the scientists found that the genesis location shifted to 87 degrees East in the Bay of Bengal. The study showed that La Nina had a greater tendency to trigger intense tropical cyclones than the El Nino.

Hence, the correct option is (C).

106. Krishna Godavari Basin is a peri-cratonic passive margin basin in India. It is spread across more than 50,000 square kilometres in the Krishna River and Godavari River basins in Andhra Pradesh. The site is known for the D-6 block where Reliance Industries discovered the biggest natural gas reserves in India in 2003.

Hence, the correct option is (C).

107. The southwest monsoon arrives in two branches called the Bay of Bengal branch and the Arabian Sea branch. The Arabian Sea side monsoon of the southwest monsoon first hits the western ghats of Kerala, India. It moves northwards providing rain to the coastal areas of the Western Ghats.

Hence, the correct option is (C).

108. Alluvial soils are rich in humus, phosphoric acid, and lime. They are, however, deficient in potash.

Hence, the correct option is (B).

109. The Pradhan Mantri Kisan Maan-Dhan Yojana (PM-KMY) provides for an assured monthly pension of Rs. 3000/- to all landholding Small and Marginal Farmers (SMFs), whether male or female, on their attaining the age of 60 years.

Hence, the correct option is (A).

110. The old folded mountains of the Singhbhum (Chotanagpur Plateau) have drainage of trellis pattern.

Types of drainage patterns found in India:

1. Antecedent or Inconsequent Drainage
2. Consequent Rivers
3. Subsequent Rivers
4. Superimposed, Epigenetic (Discordant) or Superinduced Drainage
5. Dendritic Drainage
6. Trellis Drainage
7. Barbed Pattern
8. Rectangular Drainage
9. Radial Pattern
10. Annular Pattern
11. Parallel Drainage
12. Deranged Pattern

Hence, the correct option is (C).

111. Andaman and Nicobar Islands is a union territory of India consisting of 572 islands, of which 38 are inhabited, at the juncture of the Bay of Bengal and the Andaman Sea.

Hence, the correct option is (C).

112. The Satpura Range is a range of hills in central India. The range rises in eastern Gujarat state running east through the border of Maharashtra and Madhya Pradesh to the east till Chhattisgarh. The range parallels the Vindhya Range to the north, and these two east-west ranges divide Indian Subcontinent into the Indo-Gangetic plain of northern India and the Deccan Plateau of the south.

Hence, the correct option is (D).

113. The Ten Degree Channel is a channel that separates the Andaman Islands and Nicobar Islands from each other in the Bay of Bengal. The two sets of islands together form the Indian Union Territory (UT) of Andaman and Nicobar Islands.

Hence, the correct option is (C).

114. Tropical rainforests are only found in the rainy parts of India, i.e., the Western Ghats and the island groups of Lakshadweep, and the Andaman and Nicobar Island. These types of forests grow bushy in areas that receive more than 200 cm of rainfall and experience a short dry season.

Hence, the correct option is (B).

115. The largest population of tigers is in the Western Ghats, where there are seven populations with an estimated population size of 1200 individuals occupying about 21,435 km² of forest in three major landscape units spread across Karnataka, Tamil Nadu, and Kerala.

Hence, the correct option is (D).

116. Estimated length of coastline in India 2019 by state. The islands of Andaman and Nicobar had the longest coastline in India, amounting to a little over 1,900 kilometers, followed by Gujarat. The state with the smallest coastline during the measured time period was the union territory of Daman and Diu.

Hence, the correct option is (B).

117. The Karakoram Highway connects China-Pakistan. The Karakoram Highway connects China and Pakistan across the Karakoram mountain range, through the Khunjerab Pass, at an elevation of about 4,693 meters (15,397 ft) above sea level. The road is one of the scariest and hair-raising jeep trips in the world.

Hence, the correct option is (C).

118. The important parallel of latitude that passes through India is the Tropic of Cancer (23.4° north of Equator). This latitude passes through eight states of India, namely, Gujarat, Mizoram, Tripura, Madhya Pradesh, Rajasthan, Jharkhand, West Bengal and Chattisgarh.

Hence, the correct option is (D).

119. India and Bangladesh share one of the longest borders in the world and it covers an area of 1,43,998 sq km and along with a coastline of 580 km.

Hence, the correct option is (A).

120. Great Nicobar is the southern most and largest of the Nicobar Islands of India, north of Sumatra.

Great Nicobar Island was severely affected by the 2004 Indian Ocean earthquake tsunami with many deaths, and was cut off from all outside contact for more than a day.

Hence, the correct option is (C).

121. Goa is smallest according to Area with about 3,702 Sq. km area.

Goa is a state on the southwestern coast of India within the region known as the Konkan, and geographically separated from the Deccan highlands by the Western Ghats.

Hence, the correct option is (B).

122. In terms of area, India ranks seventh in the world after Russia, Canada, US, China, Australia and Brazil.

Hence, the correct option is (D).

123. Orissa is the largest bauxite producing state accounting for more than half of the total production of India. The total recoverable reserves in the state are estimated at about 1,370.5

million tonnes. The main bauxite belt is in Kalahandi and Koraput districts and extends further into Andhra Pradesh.

Hence, the correct option is (A).

124. The Satpura range parallels the Vindhya Range to the north, and these two east-west ranges divide Indian Subcontinent into the Indo-Gangetic plain of northern India and the Deccan Plateau of the south. Satpura range rises in eastern Gujarat state near the Arabian Sea coast, running east through the border of Maharashtra and Madhya Pradesh to the east till Chhattisgarh.

Hence, the correct option is (D).

125. The Tummalapalle Mine is a uranium mine in Tumalapalli village located in Kadapa of the Indian state of Andhra Pradesh. Results from a research conducted by the Atomic Energy Commission of India in 2011 made the analysts conclude that this mine might have one of the largest reserves of uranium in the world. This finding substantially increased India's capability of producing energy from nuclear plants.

Hence, the correct option is (C).

Q.1 As per the theory of Plate tectonics, the cycle of convection cell is responsible for the movement of the plates. The sources of heat within the earth responsible for this cycle of convection cells are:

1. Radioactive decay

2. Residual heat from Earth's formation

3. Solar radiation

Select the correct answer using the code given below.

A. 2 only

B. 1 only

C. 1 and 2 only

D. 1, 2 and 3

Q.2 Which of the following soil types exhibits the characteristic of self-ploughing?

A. Alluvial soil

B. Black soil

C. Laterite soil

D. Peaty soil

Q.3 Consider the following pairs:

National Park	State
1. Chandoli	Tamil Nadu
2. Bannerghatta	Chhattisgarh
3. Kudremukh	Karnataka
4. Nameri	Assam

Which of the pairs given above are correctly matched?

A. 1 and 2 only

B. 2 and 3 only

C. 3 and 4 only

D. 1 and 4 only

Q.4 The drainage pattern of an area depends upon which of the following factors:

1. geological time period

2. structure of rocks

3. amount of water flowing

4. periodicity of the flow

Select the correct answer using the code given below.

A. 1, 2 and 4 only

B. 1 and 3 only

C. 2, 3 and 4 only

D. 1, 2, 3 and 4

Q.5 With reference to the distribution of rainfall in India, which of the following statements is/are correct?

1. The intensity and amount of rainfall in India vary with the oscillation of the axis of the monsoon trough.

2. The rains over the North Indian plains show a declining trend from the southeast towards the northwest.

Select the correct answer using the code given below.

A. 1 only

B. 2 only

C. Both 1 and 2

D. Neither 1 nor 2

Q.6 'October Heat', in the context of Indian climate, refers to:

A. Heat caused due to heavy rain spells in eastern peninsular India

B. Warm and humid conditions during retreating monsoons

C. Cloudy skies and resulting temperature inversion in northern plains

D. Increase in smog and pollution over northern India due to stubble burning

Q.7 Which of the following statements best describes a 'hydrological drought'?

A. A prolonged period of inadequate rainfall along with maldistribution of rainfall over time and space.

B. Drastic reduction in the availability of water in storages and reservoirs.

C. Soil moisture stress-causing crop failure.

D. Decrease in productivity of the ecosystem due to a shortage of water.

Q.8 Steep-sided tabular masses dissected by rivers and winds are referred to as:

A. Mesas

B. Loess

C. Horsts

D. Tuyas

Q.9 Which of the following reasons may be attributed to excessive cold in North India during the winter season?

1. Continentality of the north Indian region

2. Snowfall in the Himalayan ranges

3. Cold winds coming from the Caspian Sea

4. Early-onset of easterly jet streams

Select the correct answer using the code given below.

A. 1, 2 and 3 only

B. 2 and 3 only

C. 1, 3 and 4 only

D. 2 and 4 only

Q.10 This is a vertical cloud with a rounded top and horizontal base, typical of humid tropical regions, associated with up-rising convectional currents. Its great white globular masses may look grey against the sun but it is a fair-weather cloud.

Which of the following types of clouds is described in the above passage?

A. Cirrus

B. Cumulus

C. Nimbostratus

D. Cumulonimbus

Q.11 Consider the following statements regarding igneous rocks:

1. These are formed as a result of the recrystallization and reorganisation of materials within rocks.

2. The texture of these rocks is dependent on the rate and depth of formation.

3. Gabbro and pegmatite belong to the category of igneous rocks.

Which of the statements given above is/are correct?

A. 1 only

B. 2 only

C. 2 and 3 only

D. 1, 2 and 3

Q.12 With reference to the Himalayan and the Peninsular Rivers, consider the following statements:

1. Himalayan Rivers are perennial while Peninsular Rivers are seasonal in nature.

2. Himalayan Rivers are old and mature while Peninsular Rivers are youthful inactivity.

3. Unlike Peninsular Rivers, Himalayan Rivers show meandering activity in the plains.

Which of the statements given above is/are correct?

A. 1 only
B. 2 and 3 only
C. 1 and 3 only
D. 1, 2 and 3

Q.13 In the context of Indian monsoons, which of the following correctly describes 'Southern Oscillation'?

A. Fluctuation of atmospheric pressure over the northern and southern pacific oceans.

B. Variations in the salinity levels between Darwin and Tahiti.

C. Fluctuation of atmospheric pressure over the tropical Indo-Pacific region.

D. Oscillatory movement of ocean currents in the Southern hemisphere.

Q.14 Consider the following passage:

"These are the largest of all the volcanoes on the earth. These are mostly made up of basalt and hence are not steep. Conventionally characterized by low explosivity, however, they become explosive if somehow water gets into the vent."

Which of the following type of volcanoes is being referred to in the above passage?

A. Caldera
B. Mid-ocean ridge volcanoes
C. Shield volcanoes
D. Composite volcanoes

Q.15 Which of the following can induce an earthquake?

1. Sliding of tectonic plates along a fault plane
2. The collapse of roofs of underground mines
3. Volcanic eruption
4. Tsunami

Select the correct answer using the code given below.

A. 1, 2 and 3 only
B. 2 and 3 only
C. 1, 2 and 4 only
D. 1, 3 and 4 only

Q.16 Consider the following rivers:

1. Ganga
2. Indus
3. Godavari
4. Brahmaputra

Which of the following is the correct increasing order of catchment area (in India) of the rivers given above?

A. 4-3-2-1
B. 3-4-2-1
C. 1-2-3-4
D. 3-2-4-1

Q.17 Which of the following constitute(s) as direct source(s) of information about the interior of the Earth?

1. Volcanic eruption
2. Meteors
3. Earthquakes

Select the correct answer using the code given below.

A. 1 only
B. 1 and 3 only
C. 2 only
D. 1, 2 and 3

Q.18 Consider the following tributaries of the river Indus:

1. Jhelum
2. Sutlej
3. Chenab
4. Beas

Which of the following is the correct order from south to north of the tributaries given above?

A. 2-3-4-1
B. 2-4-3-1
C. 1-3-4-2
D. 2-4-1-3

Q.19 Which of the following best describes the term "Gravity Anomaly"?

A. It refers to regions on Earth's surface where the value of gravity is zero

B. It refers to the declining value of gravity on approaching the center of the Earth

C. It refers to the increasing value of gravity on approaching the center of the Earth

D. It refers to the difference between the observed value of gravity and the expected value of gravity

Q.20 Consider the following statements with reference to the structure of the atmosphere:

1. Thickness of the troposphere is greatest at the equator.
2. The air temperature at the tropopause over the equator is less than that at the poles.
3. The temperature within the mesosphere increases with the increase in altitude.

Which of the statements given above is/are correct?

A. 1 and 2 only
B. 3 only
C. 1 only
D. 1, 2 and 3

Q.21 Why is there a complete change in the direction of ocean currents between summer and winter in the Indian Ocean?

A. Coriolis force is stronger in the Indian Ocean
B. There is a complete reversal in wind direction
C. The Indian Ocean is landlocked and smaller than other oceans
D. The salinity variation is greater

Q.22 Which of the following statements is/are correct with reference to Karst topography?

1. It is a result of the action of groundwater through the processes of solution and deposition.
2. It is a dominant feature of the limestone regions.

Select the correct answer using the code given below.

A. 1 only
B. 2 only
C. Both 1 and 2
D. Neither 1 nor 2

Q.23 Consider the following statements:

1. The east coast of India is a low sedimentary coast while the west coast is a high rocky coast.
2. Erosional landforms dominate the east coast of India while depositional landforms dominate the west coast.

Which of the statements given above is/are correct?

A. 1 only
B. 2 only
C. Both 1 and 2
D. Neither 1 nor 2

Q.24 Consider the following statements regarding differences between Richter and Mercalli Scale:

1. While the Richter Scale is used for measuring the intensity of an earthquake, the Mercalli Scale is used for measuring the magnitude of an earthquake.

2. While the Richter Scale has no upper limit for measurement, there is a limit for the Mercalli Scale.

Which of the statements given above is/are correct?

A. 1 only
B. 2 only
C. Both 1 and 2
D. Neither 1 nor 2

Q.25 With reference to differential heating of land and water, consider the following statements:

1. As compared to land, water heats up or cools down slowly.

2. Differential heating of land and sea is responsible for the reversal in the direction of monsoon winds.

Which of the statements given above is/are correct?

A. 1 only
B. 2 only
C. Both 1 and 2
D. Neither 1 nor 2

Q.26 Consider the following pairs:

Ocean Current	Adjacent Coast
1. Agulhas Current	Eastern coast of Africa
2. Irminger Current	Coast of Alaska
3. Humboldt Current	The western coast of South America

Which of the pairs given above are correctly matched?

A. 1 and 2 only
B. 2 and 3 only
C. 1 and 3 only
D. 1, 2 and 3

Q.27 Consider the following mountain ranges:

1. Zaskar range

2. Ladakh range

3. Pir Panjal range

4. Karakoram range

Arrange the above ranges from North to South.

A. 1-2-3-4 **B.** 1-3-2-4 **C.** 4-2-3-1 **D.** 4-2-1-3

Q.28 The Big Splat event is associated with the formation of:

A. Moon
B. Sun
C. Planets
D. Earth's atmosphere

Q.29 Consider the following pairs of layers of earth and their composition:

Layer	Composition
1. Continental Crust	Silicon and Iron
2. Oceanic Crust	Silicon and Alumina
3. Mantle	Olivine
4. Core	Nickel and Iron

Which of the pairs given above are correctly matched?

A. 1 and 2 only
B. 2, 3 and 4 only
C. 3 and 4 only
D. 1, 2, 3 and 4

Q.30 Consider the following countries sharing a land boundary with India:

1. Bangladesh

2. China

3. Pakistan

Arrange the above in the decreasing order of land boundary with India?

A. Bangladesh > China > Pakistan
B. Bangladesh > Pakistan > China
C. China > Bangladesh > Pakistan
D. Pakistan > China > Bangladesh

Q.31 Consider the following statements regarding western coastal plains:

1. The western coastal plains are narrow in the middle and get broader towards the north and south.

2. The rivers flowing through western coastal plains do not form any delta.

Which of the statements given above is/are correct?

A. 1 only
B. 2 only
C. Both 1 and 2
D. Neither 1 nor 2

Q.32 Consider the following statements with respect to Kuroshio's current.

1. It begins off the coast of Japan and flows northwards.

2. It transports warm, tropical water northwards towards the Polar region.

3. It is a part of the North Pacific Ocean gyre.

Which of the statements given above is/are correct?

A. 2 only
B. 1 and 3 only
C. 2 and 3 only
D. 1, 2 and 3

Q.33 Consider the following statements:

1. In India, the Chhota Nagpur Plateau is spread over two states only.

2. The Eastern Ghats are spread over three states only.

Which of the statements given above is/are correct?

A. 1 only
B. 2 only
C. Both 1 and 2
D. Neither 1 nor 2

Q.34 Consider the following statements:

1. The lowermost layers of the atmosphere are heated primarily by the process of conduction.

2. The process of convective transfer of energy is mainly confined to the troposphere.

3. The process of advection is responsible for diurnal variations in daily weather in the middle latitudes.

Which of the statements given above is/are correct?

A. 2 only
B. 3 only
C. 1 and 3 only
D. 1, 2 and 3

Q.35 With reference to the pattern of wind circulation in the Indian Subcontinent, during summers, which of the following statements are correct?

1. The wind circulation undergoes a complete reversal at the lower as well as the upper atmospheric levels.

2. The westerly jet stream withdraws from the Indian region.

3. The Inter-Tropical Convergence Zone (ITCZ) shifts northwards.

Select the correct answer using the code given below.

A. 1 and 2 only
B. 2 and 3 only
C. 1 and 3 only
D. 1, 2 and 3

Q.36 Which of the following can reduce the incidence of landslides?

1. Large scale afforestation
2. Construction of Terraces and bunds
3. Jhum cultivation

Select the correct answer using the code given below.

A. 1 only
B. 1 and 2 only
C. 2 and 3 only
D. 1, 2 and 3

Q.37 Consider the following statements regarding the Nebular Hypothesis:

1. According to the hypothesis, the planets were formed out of a cloud of materials associated with a slowly rotating youthful Sun.
2. It helps in explaining the origin of the solar system.
3. The major contributors to this theory include Immanuel Kant and Laplace.

Which of the statements given above are correct?

A. 1 and 2 only
B. 1 and 3 only
C. 2 and 3 only
D. 1, 2 and 3

Q.38 Consider the following statements regarding asthenosphere:

1. It refers to the upper portion of the mantle along with the lower layer of the crust.
2. It is a part of the lithosphere and acts as the main source of magma during volcanic eruptions.

Which of the statements given above is/are correct?

A. 1 only
B. 2 only
C. Both 1 and 2
D. Neither 1 nor 2

Q.39 Consider the following statements:

1. Increase in the salinity of soil is the result of high temperature.
2. Salinity decreases the porosity of soil and the water-holding capacity of the soil.
3. Estuaries have greater salinity than open oceans.

Which of the statements given above is/are correct?

A. 1 and 2 only
B. 2 only
C. 1 and 3 only
D. 1, 2 and 3 only

Q.40 A geographic region has the following distinct characteristics:

1. No distinct winter season and uniform temperature range throughout the year.
2. Cloudiness and heavy precipitation with high levels of humidity throughout the year.
3. Mahogany and Ebony trees are important vegetation.

The above features are distinct characteristics of which of the following regions?

A. Mediterranean region
B. Central Asian region
C. Equatorial region
D. Atlantic Coast of North America

Q.41 Consider the following statements with reference to the incoming solar radiation:

1. The insolation received by the earth is more at the aphelion than at the perihelion.
2. The equator receives comparatively less insolation than the tropics.
3. At the same latitude, the insolation received is more over the oceans than over the continents.

Which of the statements given above is/are correct?

A. 2 and 3 only
B. 1 and 2 only
C. 1 only
D. 2 only

Q.42 The terms Roaring Forties, Furious Fifties and Shrieking Sixties are used in relation to:

A. Ocean currents
B. Jet streams
C. Easterly winds
D. Westerly winds

Q.43 Consider the following countries:

1. Lebanon
2. Morocco
3. Croatia
4. Jordan
5. Tunisia

Which of the countries given above share border with the Mediterranean sea?

A. 1, 2 and 3 only
B. 2, 3, 4 and 5 only
C. 1, 4 and 5 only
D. 1, 2, 3 and 5

Q.44 These are the most widespread forests in India. They spread over regions that receive rainfall between 70-200 cm. On the basis of the availability of water, these forests are further divided into moist and dry. Teak, sal, shisham, Tendu, palas, and sandalwood are the main species of these forests.

The above passage describes which of the following?

A. Semi Evergreen Forests
B. Tropical Deciduous Forest
C. Thorn Forest
D. Montane Forest

Q.45 Arrange the following sections of the ocean relief as they occur from the coast to the deep sea.

1. Continental Slope
2. Continental Rise
3. Abyssal plain
4. Continental Shelf

Select the correct answer using the code given below.

A. 4-2-1-3
B. 4-1-2-3
C. 2-4-1-3
D. 2-1-4-3

Q.46 Vagaries in the Indian monsoon can lead to which of the following?

1. Soil erosion
2. Floods
3. Damage to winter crops.

Select the correct answer using the code given below.

A. 1 and 2 only
B. 2 and 3 only
C. 2 only
D. 1, 2 and 3

Q.47 Consider the following pairs:

Ocean relief	Characteristics
1. Guyot	Flat-topped seamounts
2. Mid Oceanic Ridges	Chains of mountains at the sea-bottom
3. Trenches	Narrow and steepsided depressions

Which of the pairs given above are correctly matched?

A. 1 and 2 only

B. 2 and 3 only

C. 1 and 3 only

D. 1, 2 and 3

Q.48 Consider the following statements:

1. Western Ghats are more continuous than Eastern Ghats.

2. Western Ghats are higher in elevation as compared to Eastern Ghats.

3. Sahyadris in Maharashtra are part of Western Ghats.

Which of the statements given above are correct?

A. 1 and 2 only

B. 2 and 3 only

C. 1 and 3 only

D. 1, 2 and 3

Q.49 Consider the following statements regarding the Jhelum river valley:

1. Srinagar lies on the banks of Jhelum river.

2. Meandering is one of the main features of the Jhelum river.

Which of the statements given above is/are correct?

A. 1 only

B. 2 only

C. Both 1 and 2

D. Neither 1 nor 2

Q.50 The Tropic of Cancer divides the country into almost two equal halves. It passes through which of the following states?

1. Gujarat

2. Rajasthan

3. Tripura

4. Meghalaya

Select the correct answer using the code given below.

A. 1 and 2 only

B. 1, 2 and 3 only

C. 3 and 4 only

D. 1, 2, 3 and 4

Q.51 Local storms of a hot weather season in India assist in the growth of which of the following crops?

1. Mangoes

2. Coffee

3. Tea

4. Jute

5. Mustard

Select the correct answer using the code given below.

A. 1, 2 and 3 only

B. 4 and 5 only

C. 1, 2, 3 and 4 only

D. 1, 2, 3, 4 and 5

Q.52 Consider the following statements:

1. Among all the continents of the world, Africa has the maximum number of countries through which the equator passes.

2. Africa is the only continent in the world through which a river passes through the Tropic of Capricorn twice.

Which of the statements given above is/are correct?

A. 1 only

B. 2 only

C. Both 1 and 2

D. Neither 1 nor 2

Q.53 Why most parts of India do not receive rainfall during winter monsoons?

1. Winter monsoons have low moisture content.

2. Anticyclonic circulation on land.

3. The prevailing low temperature in North India.

Select the correct answer using the code given below.

A. 1 only

B. 2 and 3 only

C. 1 and 2 only

D. 1, 2 and 3

Q.54 With reference to the Brahmaputra river, consider the following statements:

1. The Brahmaputra river originates from the Mansarovar lake in Tibet.

2. It enters India west of Sadiya town in the state of Assam.

3. The origin of this river is situated at an altitude of 5,150 above sea level.

Which of the statements given above are correct?

A. 1 and 2 only

B. 2 and 3 only

C. 1 and 3 only

D. 1, 2 and 3

Q.55 Which of the following statements is/are correct with reference to the anti-cyclones?

1. They have high pressure at the centre.

2. They are characterized by clear skies and calm air.

3. Winds in anti-cyclones blow anticlockwise in the northern hemisphere and clockwise in the southern hemisphere.

Select the correct answer using the code given below.

A. 1 and 3 only

B. 2 only

C. 1 and 2 only

D. 1 only

Q.56 Consider the following pairs:

Name of Strait	Between countries
1. Hormuz	Iran and the United Arab Emirates
2. Bab-el Mandeb	Syria and Turkey
3. Bosphorous	Saudi Arabia and Sudan
4. Magellan	Colombia and Argentina

Which of the pairs given above is/are correctly matched?

A. 1 only

B. 1 and 4 only

C. 1 and 2 only

D. 3 and 4 only

Q.57 Which of the following can be attributed to the passing of the Tropic of Cancer roughly through the central part of India?

1. India experiences tropical as well as temperate climatic zones.

2. As compared to northern India, southern India experiences high temperatures throughout the year with a small daily and annual range.

3. Entire India observes the overhead sun on the summer solstice of the northern hemisphere.

Select the correct answer using the code given below.

A. 1 and 2 only

B. 2 and 3 only

C. 1 and 3 only

D. 1, 2 and 3

Q.58 Arrange the following Indian cities from west to east :

1. Raipur

2. Bhopal

3. Lucknow

4. Jaipur

Select the correct answer using the code given below:

A. 2-4-3-1   **B.** 2-4-1-3   **C.** 1-3-2-4   **D.** 4-2-3-1

Q.59 In the context of an earthquake, consider the following statements regarding P-Waves and S Waves:

1. While P-Waves create troughs and crests in the material through which they pass, S-waves lead to stretching and squeezing of the material.

2. While P-Waves can travel through gases, liquids, and solids, S-Waves can only travel through solids and liquids.

Which of the statements given above is/are correct?

A. 1 only   **B.** 2 only

C. Both 1 and 2   **D.** Neither 1 nor 2

Q.60 Consider the following statements:

1. The sun is vertically overhead at the equator only on two days each year.

2. The longest day in the northern and southern hemispheres falls on the 22nd December and 21st June summer solstices respectively.

3. The Arctic and Antarctic circles mark the limits of the overhead sun.

Which of the statements given above is/are not correct?

A. 1 only   **B.** 1 and 3 only

C. 2 and 3 only   **D.** 1, 2 and 3

Q.61 Consider the following statements regarding continental drift theory:

1. It was introduced by Arthur Holmes in 1912.

2. According to the theory, all the continents formed a single continental mass with a mega ocean surrounding it.

3. It failed to give an account of the forces responsible for drifting of the continents.

Which of the statements given above is/are correct?

A. 1 only   **B.** 2 only

C. 2 and 3 only   **D.** 1, 2 and 3

Q.62 Which of the following statements is/are correct with reference to the inversion of temperature?

1. Cloudy nights with turbulent winds are ideal for inversion.

2. Dense fogs in winter mornings are caused due to temperature inversion.

3. It is a feature of plains and is not observed on hilly terrains.

Select the correct answer using the code given below.

A. 1 and 3 only   **B.** 2 only

C. 2 and 3 only   **D.** 1, 2 and 3

Q.63 Consider the following passes in the North Eastern region of India:

1. Jelap La

2. Bomdi La

3. Bum La

What is the correct sequence of the above-mentioned passes from West to East?

A. 1-2-3   **B.** 2-3-1   **C.** 1-3-2   **D.** 2-1-3

Q.64 The air is said to be completely saturated when:

A.   Absolute humidity is 100gm/m^3

B.   Relative humidity is 100%

C.   Vapors condense into clouds

D.   It begins to rain

Q.65 This National Park is located along the Western Ghats in the Idukki district of Kerala in India. It is designated as UNESCO World Heritage Site. Anaimudi, the highest peak in south India is inside this park.

The above passage describes which of the following national parks?

A.   Periyar National Park

B.   Pampadum Shola National Park

C.   Eravikulam National Park

D.   Nagarhole National Park

Q.66 Consider the following features of China type of climatic region:

1. Year-round influence of onshore trade winds.

2. Fairly uniform annual distribution of rainfall.

3. It is also referred to as a gulf type of climate.

Which of the statements given above is/are correct?

A. 1 and 2 only   **B.** 2 and 3 only

C. 3 only   **D.** 1, 2 and 3

Q.67 Which of the following atmospheric parameters increase as we move up in the mountains?

1. Temperature

2. Density of air

3. Pressure

Select the correct answer using the code given below.

A. 2 and 3 only   **B.** 2 only

C. 1 and 3 only   **D.** None

Q.68 Which of the following are erosional landforms under the geomorphic regime of a glacier?

1. Cirques

2. Horns

3. Eskers

Select the correct answer using the code given below.

A. 1 and 2 only   **B.** 2 and 3 only

C. 1 and 3 only   **D.** 1, 2 and 3

Q.69 In the context of geomorphic processes, consider the following statements:

1. While orogeny is a continental building process, epeirogeny is a mountain building process.

2. While the energy for orogeny comes from within the earth, the energy for epeirogeny comes from the sun.

Which of the statements given above is/are not correct?

A. 1 only   **B.** 2 only

C. Both 1 and 2   **D.** Neither 1 nor 2

Q.70 Continental Shelves are rich in which of the following resources?

1. Hydrocarbons
2. Placer deposits
3. Fishing resources

Select the correct answer using the code given below.

A. 1 and 2 only
B. 2 and 3 only
C. 1 and 3 only
D. 1, 2 and 3

Q.71 Which of the following disasters is/are classified as Aquatic hazards?

1. Drought
2. Thunderstorms
3. Storm Surge
4. Blizzards

Select the correct answer using the code given below.

A. 1 and 2 only
B. 1, 2 and 4 only
C. 3 only
D. 1, 2, 3 and 4

Q.72 River Ganges passes through which of the following states?

1. Uttar Pradesh
2. Madhya Pradesh
3. Jharkhand
4. West Bengal

Select the correct answer using the code given below.

A. 1 and 4 only
B. 1, 3 and 4 only
C. 1, 2 and 3 only
D. 2, 3 and 4 only

Q.73 As the tsunami waves move from deep water towards coasts, which of the following parameters increase?

1. Speed of wave
2. Wavelength
3. Wave height

Select the correct answer using the code given below.

A. 1, 2 and 3
B. 2 and 3 only
C. 1 and 2 only
D. 3 only

Q.74 Which of the following may be the effects of a flood?

1. Destruction of physical infrastructure
2. Increase in the incidence of water-borne diseases
3. Increase in the fertility of agricultural fields

Select the correct answer using the code given below.

A. 1 and 2 only
B. 1 and 3 only
C. 2 and 3 only
D. 1, 2 and 3

Q.75 Consider the following statements:

1. Temperate Grasslands of the midlatitude region are the best-suited climatic regions for the production of wheat.
2. The harvesting of wheat is most advantageous during warm and sunny summer.

Which of the statements given above is/are correct?

A. 1 only
B. 2 only
C. Both 1 and 2
D. Neither 1 nor 2

Q.76 With reference to various trends of population growth across the world, consider the following statements:

1. The population of the world has more than tripled in the last century.
2. Asia has the highest rate of population growth during the last decade.
3. Currently the annual population growth rate in India is above 2%.

Which of the statements given above is/are correct?

A. 2 only
B. 2 and 3 only
C. 1 only
D. 1 and 2 only

Q.77 Consider the following major ports of India:

1. Kandla
2. Vishakhapatnam
3. Marmagao
4. Paradwip

Which of the following is the correct sequence of the above ports as we travel from North to South?

A. 1-2-3-4
B. 1-3-2-4
C. 4-1-2-3
D. 1-4-2-3

Q.78 Consider the following pairs:

Dam Projects	Rivers
1. Indiranagar	Beas
2. Krishnarajasagar	Krishna
3. Mettur	Kaveri

Which of the pairs is/are correctly matched?

A. 1 and 2 only
B. 2 and 3 only
C. 3 only
D. None of these

Q.79 Consider the following statements regarding the Natural Gas Reserves in India:

1. India has both on-shore and off-shore Natural Gas reserves.
2. Natural Gas Reserves are mainly concentrated in Western India.

Which of the statements given above is/are correct?

A. 1 only
B. 2 only
C. Both 1 and 2
D. Neither 1 nor 2

Q.80 Which of the following parameters of a population is/are an indicator of its socio-economic development?

1. Literacy rate
2. Occupational structure
3. Rural-urban composition

Select the correct answer using the code given below.

A. 2 only
B. 2 and 3 only
C. 1 and 3 only
D. 1, 2 and 3

Q.81 Which of the following statements is not correct regarding 'population ageing'?

A. It is a recent phenomenon observed in the twentieth century
B. The share of the older population becomes proportionally larger
C. It is mostly observed in developed countries
D. It is observed due to a decrease in life expectancy

Q.82 If you travel by road from Srinagar to Kolkata, what is the minimum number of States within India through which you can travel, including the origin and the destination?

A. 5 **B.** 6 **C.** 7 **D.** 8

Q.83 Rain-water harvesting can lead to:

1. Dilution of contaminants like fluorides and nitrates in groundwater

2. Prevention of soil erosion

3. Reduction in the saltwater intrusion in coastal areas

Select the correct answer using the code given below.

A. 1 and 2 only **B.** 2 and 3 only
C. 1 and 3 only **D.** 1, 2 and 3

Q.84 Consider the following statements regarding the mineral resources:

1. Khetri and Bhilwara are famous for Copper mines.

2. Amarkantak and Koraput are famous for Bauxite extraction.

Which of the statements given above is/are correct?

A. 1 only **B.** 2 only
C. Both 1 and 2 **D.** Neither 1 nor 2

Q.85 Which of the following cities in India are among the top ten largest megacities based on population?

1. New Delhi

2. Mumbai

3. Kolkata

4. Chennai

Select the correct answer using the code given below.

A. 1 and 2 only **B.** 1 and 3 only
C. 2 and 3 only **D.** 1, 2, 3 and 4

Q.86 Which of the following metallic minerals belongs to the category of ferrous minerals?

1. Manganese

2. Copper

3. Bauxite

Select the correct answer using the code given below.

A. 1 only **B.** 1 and 3 only
C. 2 and 3 only **D.** None of these

Q.87 Consider the following statements with respect to Census in India:

1. The first complete Census was conducted in the first decade of the 20th century.

2. Population in India has steadily and continuously increased in the last century.

Which of the statements given above is/are correct?

A. 1 only **B.** 2 only
C. Both 1 and 2 **D.** Neither 1 nor 2

Q.88 "Aus", "Aman" and "Boro" are terms used to denote which of the following?

A. These are hybrid seeds developed to overcome nutritional deficiencies in children.

B. These are high-yielding varieties of wheat used in a green revolution.

C. They are names of local winds in the north-eastern region during the pre-monsoon period.

D. These are crops of rice grown by farmers in West Bengal.

Q.89 'Human beings can conquer nature by obeying it' is a concept proposed under which of the following?

A. Environmental determinism

B. Possibilism

C. Neodeterminism

D. Humanism

Q.90 Which of the following are essential raw materials for the Iron and Steel Industry?

1. Coking coal

2. Limestone

3. Fire clay

Select the correct answer using the code given below.

A. 1 and 2 only **B.** 2 and 3 only
C. 1 and 3 only **D.** 1, 2 and 3

Q.91 Consider the following statements regarding the 'Green Revolution' in India:

1. It was limited to a few crops only.

2. Initially, it led to regional disparities in agricultural development in the country.

3. It made the country self-reliant in food grain production.

Which of the statements given above are correct?

A. 1 and 2 only **B.** 2 and 3 only
C. 1 and 3 only **D.** 1, 2 and 3

Q.92 Consider the following pairs:

Inland Waterways	Continent located in
1. Rhine waterways	Europe
2. Great Lakes - St. Lawrence seaway	North America
3. Volga waterway	Australia

Which of the pairs given above is/are correctly matched?

A. 1 only **B.** 1 and 2 only
C. 2 and 3 only **D.** 1, 2 and 3

Q.93 Which of the following shapes of an age-sex pyramid is/are correctly matched with population growth trends?

The shape of the Pyramid	Population Growth Trend
1. Bell-shaped	Constant population
2. Triangular-shaped	Expanding population
3. Inverted Pyramid	Declining population

Select the correct answer using the code given below

A. 1 and 2 only **B.** 1 and 3 only
C. 2 only **D.** 1, 2 and 3

Q.94 Which of the following characterize Plantation agriculture?

1. Large capital investments

2. Multi crop specialization

3. Scientific methods of cultivation

4. Highly-paid skilled workforce

Select the correct answer using the code given below.

A. 1, 2 and 3 only
B. 1 and 3 only
C. 2 and 4 only
D. 1, 2, 3 and 4

Q.95 Which of the following statements best describes the Malthusian view of population growth and development?

A. Population growth is potentially exponential while the growth of the resources is linear.

B. In the absence of a capitalist system, population growth should lead to greater wealth.

C. Populations grow along with predictable phases in line with the economic development of a country.

D. The problems arising out of population growth can be solved by investing in Research and Development.

Q.96 In the context of human geography, Sherms and Wurlies are:

A. Local winds providing relief from extreme weather conditions

B. Tea varieties cultivated across the world

C. Milk yielding buffalo varieties

D. Places of shelters made by tribes

Q.97 Consider the following statements regarding the Sugarcane crop in India:

1. India is the largest producer of Sugarcane in the world.

2. Yield of Sugarcane crop is higher in Northern India as compared to Southern India.

Which of the statements given above is/are correct?

A. 1 only
B. 2 only
C. Both 1 and 2
D. Neither 1 nor 2

Q.98 With respect to India's population growth, consider the following pairs:

Period	The phase of population growth
1. 1901-1921	The stagnant phase of growth
2. 1921-1951	The phase of population explosion
3. 1951-1981	The phase of Steady population growth

Which of the pairs given above is/are correctly matched?

A. 1 only
B. 3 only
C. 1 and 3 only
D. 2 and 3 only

Q.99 The Girmit Act enacted during colonial period was related to:

A. Contracts of indentured labourers

B. Measures to limit the growth of population

C. Exports of cotton

D. Administration of tribal lands

Q.100 Consider the following pairs:

Type of worker	Associated Activity
1. Blue Collar	Primary Activities
2. Gold Collar	Quinary Activities
3. Red Collar	Workers in industries

Which of the pairs given above is/are correctly matched?

A. 1 and 3 only
B. 2 only
C. 2 and 3 only
D. 1, 2 and 3

Q.101 Rural settlements which are extended on both sides of a river and connected by a bridge are known as:

A. T-shaped settlements
B. Double villages
C. Linear pattern settlements
D. Cruciform settlements

Q.102 As per the classification of industries by output, which of the following are basic industries?

1. Iron and steel industry

2. Copper refining

3. Mobile manufacturing

4. A cottage industry of soapmaking

Select the correct answer using the code given below.

A. 1, 2 and 3 only
B. 3 and 4 only
C. 1 and 2 only
D. 1, 2, 3 and 4

Q.103 Panama Canal is one of the vital man-made navigation canals in the world. It has shortened the distance between

1. East Coast and West Coast of USA

2. Western Europe and the West coast of the USA

3. The north-eastern USA and South-East Asia

Select the correct answer using the code given below.

A. 1 and 2 only
B. 2 only
C. 1 and 3 only
D. 1, 2 and 3

Q.104 Which of the following most appropriately defines the concept of 'Human Development?

A. Elimination of poverty in a country

B. Economic growth witnessed in a country

C. Enlargement of people's choices

D. Availability of multiple facilities

Q.105 "The tribes are nomadic herders and food gatherers roaming around in Kalahari Desert with weapons like spear, bows and poisoned arrows to safeguard themselves and hunt their prey. They do not domesticate animals nor do they engage in agricultural activities."

The above passage best describes which of the following tribes?

A. Bushmen
B. Bindibu
C. Bedouin
D. Tuaregs

Q.106 Which of the following practices lead to sustainable development?

1. Shelterbelt plantation

2. Warabandi system

3. Intensive agriculture

Select the correct answer using the code given below.

A. 1 and 2 only
B. 1 and 3 only
C. 2 and 3 only
D. 1, 2 and 3

Q.107 Which of the following settlement types reflects discrimination prevalent in rural areas with people of lower strata?

A. Clustered Settlements
B. Dispersed Settlements
C. Unified Settlements
D. Semi-Clustered Settlements

Q.108 In the context of employment, 'working-age population' is best defined as:

A. People above 18 years of age

B. Persons aged between 18 to 60 years

C. Persons below 65 years of age

D. People aged 15 to 59 years

Q.109 Which of the following statements best describes Crop intensity?

A. It refers to using high amount of fertilizers to increase the production of a particular crop.

B. It refers to the raising of a number of crops from the same field during one agriculture year.

C. It refers to reserving an area of arable land for a particular crop

D. It refers to increasing net sown area to increase overall production of grains.

Q.110 Which of the following is/are the characteristic features of Small Scale Manufacturing?

1. Use of local raw material

2. Power-driven machines

3. Semi-skilled labor

Select the correct answer using the code given below.

A. 1 and 3 only

B. 2 and 3 only

C. 1 only

D. 1, 2 and 3

Q.111 Which of the following is/are economic activities of the Mediterranean region?

1. Orchard Farming

2. Wine production

3. Transhumance

Select the correct answer using the code given below.

A. 1 only

B. 2 and 3 only

C. 1, 2 and 3

D. 3 only

Q.112 Consider the following pairs.

Land type	Description
1. Permanent pastures	Land used to grow grasses or other herbaceous forage that is not included in the crop rotation
2. Current fallow	Land without cultivation for one or less than one agricultural year
3. Culturable WasteLand	Land without cultivation for more than a year but less than five years

Which of the pair/s given above is/are correctly matched?

A. 1 and 2 only

B. 2 only

C. 3 only

D. 1, 2 and 3

Q.113 Ports which are used as collection centres where the goods are brought from different countries for export are known as:

A. Ferry ports

B. Entrepot ports

C. Out ports

D. Ports of calls

Q.114 Consider the following statements regarding 'Hamleted Settlements':

1. It consists of several units physically separated from each other.

2. These settlements can be frequently found in the middle and lower Ganga plain.

Which of the statements given above is/are correct?

A. 1 only

B. 2 only

C. Both 1 and 2

D. Neither 1 nor 2

Q.115 Consider the following pairs:

Canal	Associated region
1. Sirhind Canal	Uttar Pradesh
2. Sharda Canal	Punjab
3. Malaprabha Canal	Karnataka

Which of the pairs given above is/are correctly matched?

A. 1 and 3 only

B. 3 only

C. 1 and 2 only

D. 1, 2 and 3

Q.116 In which of the following aspects, surface mining is different from underground mining?

1. Surface mining is a cheaper way of mining minerals that occur close to the earth's surface.

2. Surface mining is riskier due to the occurrence of poisonous gases, fires, floods, and cavings.

Select the correct answer using the code given below.

A. 1 only

B. 2 only

C. Both 1 and 2

D. Neither 1 nor 2

Q.117 'This region has been one of the major industrial regions of Europe for a long time. Coal and iron and steel have been the basis of its economy. This region is responsible for 80 percent of Germany"s total steel production'.

Which of the following region is being described in the above passage?

A. Upper Silesia

B. Pittsburgh

C. Ruhr Region

D. Kuznetsk Region

Q.118 Which of the following crops fall under the category of Kharif Crops?

1. Mustard

2. Cotton

3. Tur

Select the correct answer using the code given below.

A. 1 and 2 only

B. 2 and 3 only

C. 1 only

D. 1, 2 and 3

Q.119 The Diamond Quadrilateral project of the Indian Railways aims to connect which of the following cities?

1. Delhi

2. Bengaluru

3. Mumbai

4. Kolkata

Select the correct answer using the code given below.

A. 1 and 3 only

B. 1, 3 and 4 only

C. 2 and 4 only

D. 1, 2, 3 and 4

Q.120 Consider the following passage:

"This steel plant was established with Russian collaboration and started production in 1959. The iron ore for the plant comes from the Dalli-Rajhara mine, coal comes from Korba and

Kargali coal fields. The water for the plant comes from the Tanduladam and the power from the Korba Thermal Power Station. This plant also lies on the Kolkata Mumbai railway route."

Which of the following steel plants is being referred to in the above passage?

A. Rourkela Steel Plant

B. Bhilai Steel Plant

C. Durgapur Steel Plant

D. Bokaro Steel Plant

Q.121 Which of the following statements best describes the term command area?

A. Area served by a canal system through supply of water for irrigation

B. Area of land, where the surface water from rainfall, snowmelt, or ice flow into a lower elevation to form a single body of water

C. A unit of elevated land that separates waters flowing to different rivers, basins, or seas

D. An area of land that contains a common set of streams and rivers that all drain into a single larger body of water

Q.122 Which of the following reasons can be attributed to the rapid growth of the service sector in developed economies?

1. Increasing per capita income

2. Ageing population

3. Demand for skills at the workplace

Select the correct answer using the code given below.

A. 1 and 2 only   **B.** 2 and 3 only

C. 1 and 3 only   **D.** 1, 2 and 3

Q.123 Which of the following most appropriately describes transhumance?

A. It is a cyclical pattern of migration between two thermally contrasting regions

B. It is the practice of raising herds of animals on large tracts of land

C. It is the movement of people from one country to another with the intentions of settling permanently

D. It is the gradual demographic transition of the human population towards old age

Q.124 "It refers to a large area of urban development that resulted from the merging of originally separate towns or cities. Greater London, Manchester, Chicago and Tokyo are examples of it".

Does the above passage best describe which of the following?

A. Megalopolis   **B.** Conurbation

C. Million City   **D.** Town

Q.125 Arabica, Robusta, and Liberica are varieties of which of the following crop?

A. Tea   **B.** Cotton   **C.** Jute   **D.** Coffee

// Smart Answer Sheet //

Correct — Indicates percentage of students who answered questions correctly.

Skipped — Indicates percentage of students who skipped questions.

Q.	Ans.	Correct	Skipped
1	C	59.45 %	1.69 %
2	B	42.02 %	1.72 %
3	C	10.64 %	4.19 %
4	D	67.29 %	2.0 %
5	C	27.32 %	3.36 %
6	B	88.77 %	0.0 %
7	B	78.94 %	0.0 %
8	A	68.27 %	1.65 %
9	A	10.6 %	4.32 %
10	B	80.04 %	0.0 %
11	C	32.37 %	3.03 %
12	C	64.27 %	1.64 %
13	C	53.92 %	1.55 %
14	C	58.35 %	1.81 %
15	A	56.6 %	1.33 %
16	A	40.17 %	1.22 %
17	A	85.92 %	0.0 %
18	B	64.74 %	1.02 %
19	D	76.83 %	0.0 %
20	A	50.82 %	1.27 %
21	B	51.02 %	1.81 %
22	C	17.7 %	3.03 %
23	A	62.05 %	1.49 %
24	B	32.31 %	3.93 %
25	C	57.73 %	1.48 %
26	C	24.43 %	3.32 %
27	D	83.03 %	0.0 %
28	A	85.58 %	0.0 %
29	C	67.16 %	1.91 %
30	A	44.49 %	1.08 %
31	C	30.3 %	4.0 %
32	C	14.49 %	4.18 %
33	D	32.16 %	4.71 %
34	D	53.96 %	1.0 %
35	D	16.54 %	4.94 %
36	B	61.02 %	1.82 %
37	D	56.11 %	1.91 %
38	D	40.88 %	1.79 %
39	A	18.28 %	4.06 %
40	C	29.56 %	3.76 %
41	D	57.75 %	1.97 %
42	D	81.96 %	0.0 %
43	D	16.66 %	4.23 %
44	B	56.3 %	1.75 %
45	B	52.49 %	1.44 %
46	D	60.85 %	1.11 %
47	D	57.42 %	1.58 %
48	D	11.71 %	3.57 %
49	C	30.65 %	4.34 %
50	B	77.89 %	0.0 %
51	C	16.41 %	4.25 %
52	C	13.65 %	4.7 %
53	C	10.67 %	3.63 %
54	D	15.62 %	4.65 %
55	C	13.63 %	3.38 %
56	A	31.9 %	3.75 %
57	A	47.85 %	1.14 %
58	D	80.83 %	0.0 %
59	D	11.89 %	3.49 %
60	C	59.69 %	1.81 %
61	B	64.27 %	1.21 %
62	B	15.48 %	4.63 %
63	C	14.63 %	3.43 %
64	B	85.75 %	0.0 %
65	C	41.97 %	2.0 %
66	B	26.11 %	3.98 %
67	D	43.1 %	1.27 %
68	A	22.48 %	3.08 %
69	C	42.04 %	2.0 %
70	D	12.31 %	3.83 %
71	C	62.46 %	1.23 %
72	B	78.79 %	0.0 %
73	D	40.39 %	1.96 %
74	D	54.53 %	1.81 %
75	C	29.47 %	3.54 %
76	C	63.01 %	1.77 %
77	D	82.47 %	0.0 %
78	C	30.32 %	4.75 %
79	A	11.0 %	4.05 %
80	D	47.81 %	1.67 %

Q.	Ans.	Correct		Q.	Ans.	Correct		Q.	Ans.	Correct		Q.	Ans.	Correct		Q.	Ans.	Correct
		Skipped				Skipped				Skipped				Skipped				Skipped
81	D	68.63 % 1.95 %		90	D	57.18 % 1.01 %		99	A	85.11 % 0.0 %		108	D	77.87 % 0.0 %		117	C	43.08 % 1.67 %
82	A	81.54 % 0.0 %		91	D	57.16 % 1.88 %		100	B	82.68 % 0.0 %		109	B	25.57 % 4.09 %		118	B	57.51 % 1.23 %
83	D	32.09 % 4.99 %		92	B	27.15 % 4.99 %		101	B	78.12 % 0.0 %		110	D	65.86 % 1.21 %		119	B	61.85 % 1.73 %
84	C	30.61 % 3.91 %		93	A	67.11 % 1.55 %		102	C	24.07 % 4.1 %		111	C	56.17 % 1.18 %		120	B	64.1 % 1.15 %
85	A	83.99 % 0.0 %		94	B	12.1 % 3.92 %		103	D	49.29 % 1.01 %		112	A	25.14 % 4.67 %		121	A	86.26 % 0.0 %
86	A	48.47 % 1.22 %		95	A	85.95 % 0.0 %		104	C	83.17 % 0.0 %		113	B	80.31 % 0.0 %		122	D	17.98 % 4.68 %
87	D	60.58 % 1.96 %		96	D	47.87 % 1.05 %		105	A	41.11 % 1.19 %		114	C	14.49 % 4.06 %		123	A	83.03 % 0.0 %
88	D	80.87 % 0.0 %		97	D	17.96 % 3.14 %		106	A	13.48 % 4.6 %		115	B	48.04 % 1.63 %		124	B	44.64 % 1.47 %
89	C	44.06 % 2.0 %		98	A	69.55 % 1.99 %		107	D	51.82 % 1.71 %		116	A	17.51 % 3.78 %		125	D	85.94 % 0.0 %

Performance Analysis

Avg. Score (%)	50.12%
Toppers Score (%)	64.94%
Your Score	

//Hints and Solutions//

1. As per the Plate tectonic theory, the surface of the earth and the interior are not static and motionless but are dynamic. The mobile rock beneath the rigid plates is believed to be moving in a circular manner.

The heated material rises to the surface, spreads and begins to cool, and then sinks back into deeper depths. This cycle is repeated over and over to generate what scientists call a convection cell or convective flow. Heat within the earth comes from two main sources: radioactive decay and residual heat.

The radioactive decay of naturally occurring chemical elements - most notably uranium, thorium, and potassium - releases energy in the form of heat, which slowly migrates toward the Earth's surface. Residual heat is gravitational energy left over from the formation of the Earth - 4.6 billion years ago - by the "falling together" and compression of cosmic debris.
Hence, the correct option is (C).

2. The black soils are generally clayey, deep, and impermeable. They swell and become sticky when wet and shrink when dried. So, during the dry season, these soils develop wide cracks. Thus, there occurs a kind of 'self ploughing'. Because of this character of slow absorption and loss of moisture, the black soil retains the moisture for a very long time, which helps the crops, especially, the rain-fed ones, to sustain even during the dry season.
Hence, the correct option is (B).

3. Chandoli National Park is located in the Sangli, Satara, Kolhapur, and Ratnagiri districts of the state of Maharashtra.

Bengaluru Bannerghatta National Park is located about 22 Kms south of Bengaluru city of the state of Karnataka.

Kudremukh National Park is a beautiful place, located in the Dakshina Kannada, Udupi and Chikmagalur districts of the state of Karnataka.

Nameri National Park is located in the foothills of the Eastern Himalayas in the Sonitpur District of Assam.
Hence, the correct option is (C).

4. The flow of water through well-defined channels is known as 'drainage' and the network of such channels is called a "drainage system'. The drainage pattern of an area is the outcome of the geological time period, nature and structure of rocks, topography, slope, amount of water flowing and the periodicity of the flow.
Hence, the correct option is (D).

5. There are two rain-bearing systems in India.

- First originates in the Bay of Bengal causing rainfall over the plains of north India.

- Second is the Arabian Sea current of the southwest monsoon which brings rain to the west coast of India.

As the axis of the monsoon trough oscillates, there are fluctuations in the track and direction of these depressions, and the intensity and the amount of rainfall vary from year to year.

The rain which comes in spells displays a declining trend from west to east over the west coast, and from the southeast towards the northwest over the North Indian Plain and the northern part of the Peninsula.
Hence, the correct option is (C).

6. The retreating southwest monsoon season is marked by clear skies and a rise in temperature. The land is still moist. Owing to the conditions of high temperature and humidity, the weather becomes rather oppressive. This is commonly known as the 'October heat'.
Hence, the correct option is (B).

7. Hydrological Drought results when the availability of water in different storages and reservoirs like aquifers, lakes, reservoirs, etc. falls below what the precipitation can replenish.
Hence, the correct option is (B).

8. Dissected plateaus are formed as a consequence of the continual process of weathering and erosion by running water and winds where high and extensive plateaus are gradually worn down, and their surfaces made irregular.

In drier countries, vertical corrasion by rivers and abrasion by winds will dissect the plateau into steep-sided tabular masses which are termed as Mesas and Buttes, intersected by deep canyons. Buttes were once part of flat, elevated areas of land known as mesas or plateaus. In fact, the only difference between a mesa and a butte is its size. Most geographers say a butte is taller than it is wide, while a mesa is a much larger, slightly less elevated feature. This is a common feature of arid and semi-arid areas. For e.g. In the South-Western USA.
Hence, the correct option is (A).

9. There are three main reasons for the excessive cold in north India during the winter season:

- States like Punjab, Haryana and Rajasthan being far away from the moderating influence of sea experience continental climate.

- The snowfall in the nearby Himalayan ranges creates a cold wave situation.

- Around February, the cold winds coming from the Caspian Sea and Turkmenistan bring cold waves along with frost and fog over the northwestern parts of India.

- The easterly jet stream sets in along 15°N latitude only after the western jet stream has withdrawn itself from the region i.e., around the month of June. This easterly jet stream is held responsible for the burst of the monsoon in India. It does not play a role in an excessive cold climate in North India during the winter season.

Hence, the correct option is (A).

10. Cumulus is a vertical cloud with a rounded top and horizontal base, typical of humid tropical regions, associated with up-rising convectional currents. Its great white globular masses may look grey against the sun but it is a fair-weather cloud.
Hence, the correct option is (B).

11. Igneous rocks form out of magma and lava from the interior of the earth and known as primary rocks. The igneous rocks are formed when magma cools and solidifies. When magma in its upward movement cools and turns into a solid form it is called igneous rock. The process of cooling and solidification can happen in the earth's crust or on the surface of the earth.

Igneous rocks are classified based on texture. The texture depends upon the size and arrangement of grains or other physical conditions of the materials. If molten material is cooled slowly at great depths, mineral grains may be very large. Sudden cooling (at the surface) results in small and smooth grains. Intermediate conditions of cooling would result in intermediate sizes of grains making up igneous rocks. Granite, gabbro, pegmatite, basalt, volcanic breccia, and tuff are some of the examples of igneous rocks.
Hence, the correct option is (C).

12. Himalayan rivers originate from the lofty Himalayan ranges while Peninsular Rivers originate in the Peninsular Plateau. Himalayan rivers have large basins and catchment areas while Peninsular rivers have small basins and catchment areas.

The Himalayan rivers are perennial in nature, i.e., water flows throughout the year in these rivers. These rivers receive water both from the monsoons and snow-melt. While the Peninsular rivers receive water only from rainfall and water flows in these rivers in the rainy season only. Therefore, these rivers are seasonal or non-perennial.

Himalayan rivers flow across the young fold mountains and are still in a youthful stage, while Peninsular rivers have been flowing in one of the oldest plateaus of the world and have reached maturity.

When Himalayan rivers enter the plains, there is a sudden reduction in the speed of flow of water which forms meanders and shifts their beds. While, in the case of Peninsular rivers, the hard rock surface and non-alluvial character of the plateau permit little scope for the formation of meanders. As such, the rivers of the Peninsular Plateau follow more or less straight courses.
Hence, the correct option is (C).

13. Southern Oscillation is a coherent interannual fluctuation of atmospheric pressure over the tropical Indo-Pacific region. It is the atmospheric component of a single large-scale coupled interaction called the El Niño/SouthernOscillation (ENSO). The phase of the Southern Oscillation at a given point in time may be understoodusing the Southern Oscillation Index (SOI), which compares the difference in atmospheric pressure overAustralia and Indonesia with that of the eastern South Pacific.
Hence, the correct option is (C).

14. Barring the basalt flows, the shield volcanoes are the largest of all the volcanoes on the earth. The Hawaiian volcanoes are the most famous examples. These volcanoes are mostly made up of basalt, a type of lava that is very fluid when erupted. For this reason, these volcanoes are not steep. They become explosive if somehow water gets into the vent; otherwise, they are characterized by low explosivity. The upcoming lava moves in the form of a fountain and throws out the cone at the top of the vent and develops into a cinder cone.
Hence, the correct option is (C).

15. The most common ones are tectonic earthquakes. These are generated due to the sliding of rocks along a fault plane. A special class of tectonic earthquakes is sometimes recognized as volcanic earthquakes. However, these are confined to areas of active volcanoes. In the areas of intense mining activity, sometimes the roofs of underground mines collapse causing minor tremors. These are called collapse earthquakes. Ground shaking may also occur due to the explosion of chemical or nuclear devices. Such tremors are called explosion earthquakes. The earthquakes that occur in the areas of large reservoirs are referred to as reservoir-induced earthquakes. A tsunami is the effect of an earthquake, not a cause of it.
Hence, the correct option is (A).

16. The correct ascending order of the catchment area (in India) of the given rivers will be - Brahmaputra, Godavari, Indus, Ganga.

A catchment is an area of land where water collects when it rains, often bounded by hills. As the water flows over the landscape it finds its way into streams and down into the soil, eventually feeding the river. Some of this water stays underground and continues to slowly feed the river in times of low rainfall.
Hence, the correct option is (A).

17. The sources of information about the interior of the earth are divided into direct sources and indirect sources.

In, Direct sources the most easily available solid earth material is surface rock or the rocks we get from mining areas. Gold mines in South Africa are as deep as 3 - 4 km. Volcanic eruption forms another source of obtaining direct information. As and when the molten material (magma) is thrown onto the surface of the earth, during volcanic eruption it becomes available for laboratory analysis.
Hence, the correct option is (A).

18. The order of rivers (tributaries of India) from south to north is:

- Sutlej
- Beas
- Ravi
- Chenab
- Jhelum

Hence, the correct option is (B).

19. The gravitation force (g) is not the same at different latitudes on the surface. It is greater near the poles and less at the equator. This is because of the distance from the centre at the equator being greater than that at the poles. The gravity values also differ according to the mass of the material. The uneven distribution of mass of material within the earth influences this value. The reading of gravity at different places is influenced by many other factors. These readings differ from the expected values. Such a difference is called a gravity anomaly.
Hence, the correct option is (D).

20. The troposphere is the lowermost layer of the atmosphere. Its average height is 13 km and extends roughly to a height of 8 km near the poles and about 18 km at the equator. The thickness of the troposphere is greatest at the equator because heat is transported to great heights by strong convectional currents. This layer contains dust particles and water vapor. All changes in climate and weather take place in this layer. The temperature in this layer decreases at the rate of 1°C for every 165 m of height. This is the most important layer for all biological activity.

The zone separating the troposphere from the stratosphere is known as the tropopause. The air temperature at the tropopause is about minus 800 degrees C over the equator and about minus 45 degrees C over the poles. The temperature here is nearly constant, and hence, it is called tropopause. The stratosphere is found above the tropopause and extends up to a height of 50 km. One important feature of the stratosphere is that it contains the ozone layer. This layer absorbs ultraviolet radiation and shields life on the earth from intense, harmful forms of energy.

The mesosphere lies above the stratosphere, which extends up to a height of 80 km. In this layer, once again, the temperature starts decreasing with the increase in altitude and reaches up to minus 100°C at the height of 80 km. The upper limit of the mesosphere is known as menopause.
Hence, the correct option is (A).

21. The current systems of the Indian Ocean are largely controlled and modified by landmasses and monsoon winds. The Indian Ocean is surrounded by the Indian subcontinent, Africa and Australia. This location does not present the most favorable conditions for the development of a consistent system of ocean currents. The currents in the northern Indian Ocean change their flow direction twice a year due to northeast and south-west monsoon winds.

In summer from June to October, when the dominant wind is the South-West Monsoon, the currents are blown from a south-westerly direction as the SouthWest Monsoon Drift. This is reversed in winter, beginning from December, when the North-East Monsoon blows the currents from the north-east as the North-East Monsoon Drift. The currents of the North Indian Ocean, demonstrate most convincingly the dominant effects of winds on the circulation of ocean currents.
Hence, the correct option is (B).

22. Physical or mechanical removal of materials by moving groundwater is insignificant in developing landforms. That is why the results of the work of groundwater cannot be seen in all types of rocks.

But in rocks like limestones or dolomites rich in calcium carbonate, the surface water as well as groundwater through the chemical process of solution and precipitation deposition develop varieties of landforms. These two processes of solution and precipitation are active in limestones or dolomites occurring either exclusively or interbedded with other rocks.

Any limestone or dolomitic region showing typical landforms produced by the action of groundwater through the processes of solution and deposition is called Karst topography after the typical topography developed in limestone rocks of the Karst region in the Balkans adjacent to the Adriatic sea.
Hence, the correct option is (C).

23. The west coast of our country is a high rocky retreating coast. Erosional forms dominate in the west coast. The east coast of India is a low sedimentary coast. Depositional forms dominate in the east coast.
Hence, the correct option is (A).

24. The earthquake events are scaled either according to the magnitude or intensity of the shock. The magnitude scale is

known as the Richter scale. The magnitude relates to the energy released during the quake. The intensity scale is named after Mercalli, an Italian seismologist. It takes into account the visible damage caused by the event. The effect of an earthquake on the Earth's surface is called the intensity. The intensity scale consists of a series of certain key responses such as people awakening, movement of furniture, damage to chimneys, and finally - total destruction.

In theory, the Richter scale has no upper limit, but, in practice, no earthquake has ever been registered on the scale above magnitude 8.6 (That was the Richter magnitude for the Chile earthquake of 1960). The range of intensity (Mercalli) scale is from 1-12.
Hence, the correct option is (B).

25. India is flanked by the Indian Ocean on three sides in the south and girdled by a high and continuous mountain wall in the north. As compared to the landmass, water heats up or cools down slowly. This differential heating of land and sea creates different air pressure zones in different seasons in and around the Indian subcontinent. The difference in air pressure causes a reversal in the direction of monsoon winds.
Hence, the correct option is (C).

26. The Agulhas Current is the western boundary current of the South-West Indian Ocean. It flows down the east coast of Africa.

The Irminger Current is a north Atlantic ocean current setting westward off the southwest coast of Iceland.

The Humboldt Current, also called the Peru Current, is a cold, low-salinity ocean current that flows north along the western coast of South America.
Hence, the correct option is (C).

27. The correct sequence of above-mentioned ranges from north to south will be - Karakoram Range, Ladakh Range, Zaskar Range, Pirpanjal Range.

Karakoram Range is a large mountain range spanning the borders between Pakistan, India and China, located in the regions of Gilgit-Baltistan (Pakistan), Ladakh (India), and Xinjiang (China). It is the northwestern extension of the Himalayas.

Ladakh Range lies to the north of the Leh and is an important part of the Trans-Himalayan range that merges with the Kailash range in Tibet.

Zaskar/Zanskar Range covers an area of some 7,000 square kilometres (2,700 square miles), at a height of between 3,500 and 7,000 metres. High mountain ranges lie on both sides of the Doda and Kurgiakh valleys, which run north-west to south-east.

Pir Panjal Range is a group of mountains in the inner Himalayan region, running from east-southeast (ESE) to west-northwest (WNW) across the Indian states of Himachal Pradesh and Jammu and Kashmir and Pakistan administered Kashmir.
Hence, the correct option is (D).

28. The moon is the only natural satellite of the earth. There have been several attempts to describe the origin of the moon. In 1838, Sir George Darwin suggested that initially, the earth and the moon formed a single rapidly rotating body. The whole mass became a dumb-bell-shaped body and eventually, it broke. It was also suggested that the material forming the moon was separated from what we have at present the depression occupied by the Pacific Ocean. However, these explanations came under severe scrutiny. This led to the proposal of —the big splatll theory in the 1970s.

According to this theory, an object with the mass of Mars delivered a glancing blow to Earth, launching large amounts of rock into an orbiting ring that coalesced to form the Moon. Most of the Moon would have been made of material from the impactor's mantle. The angle of the impact gave the Earth-Moon system its current angular momentum.
Hence, the correct option is (A).

29. The Earth is made up of several concentric layers. The outer layer is called Crust which comprises of two distinct parts - Continental and Oceanic Crust. The Continental Crust consists of Granitic rocks and its main mineral contents are Silicon and Alumina. Thus, it is collectively referred to as Sial.

The Oceanic Crust is a continuous Zone of denser basaltic rocks forming the Ocean floors, comprising mainly Silica, iron and magnesium. Thus, it is referred to as Sima.

The layer below the Crust is called Mantle. It is composed of very dense rocks rich in Olivine. The interior layer is the Core and is mainly made up of iron and some nickel, and is called nife.
Hence, the correct option is (C).

30.

Name of the country	Length of the border (in km)
Bangladesh	4,096.7
China	3,488
Pakistan	3,323
Nepal	1,751
Myanmar	1,643
Bhutan	699
Afghanistan	106

Hence, the correct option is (A).

31. The western coastal plains are narrow in the middle and get broader towards north and south. The rivers flowing through this coastal plain do not form any delta. On the East Coast, There are well-developed deltas here, formed by the rivers flowing eastward into the Bay of Bengal. These include the deltas of the Mahanadi, the Godavari, the Krishna, and the Kaveri.

Deltas are wetlands that form as rivers empty their water and sediment into another body of water, such as an ocean, lake, or another river. Although very uncommon, deltas can also empty into the land. A river moves more slowly as it nears its mouth or end. This causes sediment, solid material carried downstream by currents, to fall to the river bottom.

The hard nature of rocks of Western ghat doesn't facilitate Western flowing rivers to widen their mouth into sea, so these rivers form Estuaries. On the Other hand, Eastern rivers usually flow by breaking through hills and mountain ranges and flow with less velocity before entering into sea. Subsequently, the accumulated silt and sediments which they have been carrying along are deposited before entering into the sea, thus

Deltas are more prominent on the east coast.
Hence, the correct option is (C).

32. The Kuroshio Current is the warm western boundary current of the North Pacific's subtropical gyre. The Kuroshio Current begins off the east coast of the Philippines and Taiwan and flows northeastward past Japan, where it merges with the easterly drift of the North Pacific Current. It is analogous to the Gulf Stream in the Atlantic Ocean. Its warm waters are carried polewards as the North Pacific Drift keeping the ports of the Alaskan coast ice-free in winter.
Hence, the correct option is (C).

33. Chota Nagpur plateau represents the northeastern projection of the Indian Peninsula. It covers an area of over 87 thousand sq km. It covers much of Jharkhand state as well as adjacent parts of Odisha, West Bengal, Bihar, and Chhattisgarh. Son river flows in the northwest of the plateau and joins the Ganga. The average elevation of the plateau is 700 meters above sea level.

The Eastern Ghats, also known as Mahendra Parvatam in the south, is a discontinuous range of mountains along India's eastern coast. Starting at West Bengal, Eastern Ghats pass through states like Orissa, Andhra Pradesh, Telengana, and Tamil Nadu to the south passing through some parts of Karnataka. They are eroded and cut through by the four major rivers of peninsular India, known as the Godavari, Mahanadi, Krishna, and Kaveri.
Hence, the correct option is (D).

34. Conduction takes place when two bodies of unequal temperature are in contact with one another; there is a flow of energy from the warmer to a cooler body. The transfer of heat continues until both the bodies attain the same temperature or the contact is broken. Conduction is important in heating the lower layers of the atmosphere.

The air in contact with the earth rises vertically on heating in the form of currents and further transmits the heat of the atmosphere. This process of vertical heating of the atmosphere is known as convection. The convective transfer of energy is confined only to the troposphere.

The transfer of heat through the horizontal movement of air is called advection. The horizontal movement of the air is relatively more important than the vertical movement. In middle latitudes, most diurnal (day and night) variations in daily weather are caused by advection alone. In tropical regions particularly in northern India during the summer season, local winds called _loo' is the outcome of the advection process.
Hence, the correct option is (D).

35. As the summer sets in and the sun shift northwards, the wind circulation over the subcontinent undergoes a complete reversal at both, the lower as well as the upper levels. By the middle of July, the low-pressure belt nearer the surface [termed as Inter-Tropical Convergence Zone (ITCZ)] shifts northwards, roughly parallel to the Himalayas between 20° N and 25° N.

By this time, the westerly jet stream withdraws from the Indian region. The interrelationship between the northward shift of the equatorial trough (ITCZ) and the withdrawal of the westerly jet stream from over the North Indian Plain. It is generally believed that there is a cause-and-effect relationship between the two. The

ITCZ being a zone of low pressure attracts an inflow of winds from different directions. The maritime tropical airmass (mT) from the southern hemisphere, after crossing the equator, rushes to the low-pressure area in the general southwesterly direction. It is this moist air current that is popularly known as the southwest monsoon.
Hence, the correct option is (D).

36. It is always advisable to adopt area-specific measures to deal with landslides. Restriction on the construction and other developmental activities such as roads and dams, limiting agriculture to valleys and areas with moderate slopes, and control on the development of large settlements in the high vulnerability zones, should be enforced. This should be supplemented by some positive actions like promoting large-scale afforestation programs and the construction of bunds to reduce the flow of water. Terrace farming should be encouraged in the north-eastern hill states where Jhumming(Slash and Burn/Shifting Cultivation) is still prevalent. Jhumming is often considered responsible for causing soil erosion, triggering landslides, flash floods and thereby degrading the primary land resource.
Hence, the correct option is (B).

37. A large number of hypotheses were put forth by different philosophers and scientists regarding the origin of the earth. One of the earlier and popular arguments was by German philosopher Immanuel Kant. Mathematician Laplace revised it in 1796. It is known as the Nebular Hypothesis. The hypothesis considered that the planets were formed out of a cloud of material associated with a youthful sun, which was slowly rotating. Nebular Hypothesis is used for explaining the origin of the Solar system.
Hence, the correct option is (D).

38. The upper portion of the mantle is called the asthenosphere. The word 'astheno' means weak. It is a layer of solid rock that has so much pressure and heat the rocks can flow like a liquid. It is considered to be extending up to 400 km. It is the main source of magma that finds its way to the surface during volcanic eruptions. It has a density higher than the crust's (3.4 g/cm³). The crust and the uppermost parts of the mantle are called the lithosphere. Aesthenosphere does not form a part of the lithosphere.
Hence, the correct option is (D).

39. In dry climates, because of high temperature, evaporation exceeds precipitation and hence groundwater is brought up to the surface by capillary action and in the process, the water evaporates leaving behind salts in the soil. Such salts form into a crust on the soil known as hardpans. Salinization leads to intense water logging which means a decrease in the porosity of soil and hence the water-holding capacity. And in the long term, makes the soil impermeable. An estuary is a body of water, partially enclosed by land, where saltwater from the ocean and freshwater from the land can mix. Estuaries can be found in coastal areas of the ocean worldwide.
Hence, the correct option is (A).

40. Equatorial type of climate is associated with all the given features given below:

- The most outstanding feature of the equatorial climate is its great uniformity of temperature throughout the year.
- There is no winter.
- Cloudiness and heavy precipitation help to moderate the daily temperature, so that even at the equator itself, the climate is not unbearable. In addition, regular land and sea breezes assist in maintaining a truly equable climate.
- The diurnal range of temperature is small, and so is the annual range. High temperature and abundant rainfall in the equatorial regions support a luxuriant type of vegetation i.e. the Tropical Rain Forests.
- The equatorial vegetation comprises a multitude of evergreen trees that yield tropical hardwood, e.g. mahogany, ebony, etc. It supports a luxuriant type of vegetation – the tropical rain forest. Amazon's tropical rainforest is known as Selvas. Trees of single species are very scarce in such vegetation. There are smaller palm trees, climbing plants like the lianas or rattan which may be hundreds of feet long, and epiphytic and parasitic plants that live on other plants. Under the trees grow a wide variety of ferns, orchids, and lalang. The tallest trees attain a height of over 150 feet.

Hence, the correct option is (C).

41. The solar output received at the top of the atmosphere varies slightly in a year due to the variations in the distance between the earth and the sun. During its revolution around the sun, the earth is farthest from the sun (152 million km) on 4th July. This position of the earth is called aphelion. On 3rd January, the earth is the nearest to the sun (147 million km). This position is called the perihelion. Therefore, the annual insolation received by the earth on 3rd January is slightly more than the amount received on 4th July. However, the effect of this variation in the solar output is masked by other factors like the distribution of land and sea and the atmospheric circulation.

The insolation received at the surface varies from about 320 Watt/m² in the tropics to about 70 Watt/m² in the poles. Maximum insolation is received over the subtropical deserts, where the cloudiness is the least. The Equator receives comparatively less insolation than the tropics.

Generally, at the same latitude, the insolation is moreover the continent than over the oceans. In winter, the middle and higher latitudes receive less radiation than in summer.
Hence, the correct option is (D).

42. In the southern hemisphere where there is a large expanse of ocean, 40 degrees S to 60 degrees S, Westerlies blow with much greater force and regularity throughout the year. They bring much precipitation to the western coasts of continents. The weather is damp and stormy. It is thus usual for seafarers to refer to the Westerlies as the Roaring Forties, Furious Fifties, and Shrieking Sixties, according to the varying degree of storminess in the latitudes which they blow.
Hence, the correct option is (D).

43. The following countries share their borders with the Mediterranean Sea -

Spain, France, Monaco, Italy, Malta, Slovenia, Croatia, Bosnia and Herzegovina, Montenegro, Albania, Greece, Turkey, Cyprus, Syria, Lebanon, Israel, Egypt, Libya, Tunisia, Algeria and Morocco.
Hence, the correct option is (D).

44. Deciduous Forests are the most widespread forests in India. They are also called the monsoon forests. They spread over regions that receive rainfall between 70-200 cm. On the basis of the availability of water, these forests are further divided into moist and dry deciduous.

These forests are found in the northeastern states along the foothills of the Himalayas, eastern slopes of the Western Ghats and Orissa. Teak, sal, shisham, hurra, mahua, amla, semul, kusum, and sandalwood etc. are the main species of these forests.

Dry deciduous forest covers vast areas of the country, where rainfall ranges between 70 -100 cm. On the wetter margins, it has a transition to the moist deciduous, while on the drier margins to thorn forests. These forests are found in rainier areas of the Peninsula and the plains of Uttar Pradesh and Bihar. As the dry season begins, the trees shed their leaves completely and the forest appears like a vast grassland with naked trees all around. Tendu, palas, amaltas, bel, khair, axlewood, etc. are the common trees of these forests.
Hence, the correct option is (B).

45. The ocean floors can be divided into four major divisions: (i) the Continental Shelf; (ii) the Continental Slope; (iii) the Deep Sea Plain; (iv) the Oceanic Deeps. Besides, these divisions there are also major and minor relief features in the ocean floors like ridges, hills, sea mounts, guyots, trenches, canyons, etc.

Continental Shelf: The continental shelf is the extended margin of each continent occupied by relatively shallow seas and gulfs. It is the shallowest part of the ocean showing an average gradient of 1° or even less.

Continental Slope: The continental slope connects the continental shelf and the ocean basins. It begins where the bottom of the continental shelf sharply drops off into a steep slope.

Continental Rise: The continental rise is found between the continental slope and the abyssal plain. It represents the final stage in the boundary between continents and the deepest part of the ocean. At the bottom of the continental slope, one will find the continental rise, an underwater hill composed of tons of accumulated sediments.

Abyssal Plain: The abyssal plain is an underwater plain on the deep ocean floor, usually found at depths between 3,000 metres and 6,000 metres. It lies between the foot of a continental rise and a mid-ocean ridge.
Hence, the correct option is (B).

46. Variability of rainfall brings droughts or floods every year in some parts of the country.

Sudden monsoon burst creates the problem of soil erosion over large areas in India. The summer rainfall comes in a heavy downpour leading to considerable runoff and soil erosion.

The beginning of the rains sometimes is considerably delayed over the whole or a part of the country. The rains sometimes end considerably earlier than usual, causing great damage to standing crops and making the sowing of winter crops difficult.
Hence, the correct option is (D).

47. Guyot is a flat-topped seamount. They show evidence of gradual subsidence through stages to become flat-topped submerged mountains.

Mid Oceanic Ridges is a mid-ocean ridge (MOR) is a seafloor mountain system formed by plate tectonics. It typically has a depth of around 2,600 meters and rises about two kilometers above the deepest portion of an ocean basin. This feature is where seafloor spreading takes place along a divergent plate boundary. The rate of seafloor spreading determines the morphology of the crest of the mid-ocean ridge and its width in an ocean basin.

Trenches are the deepest parts of the oceans. The trenches are relatively steep-sided, narrow basins. They are some 3-5 km deeper than the surrounding ocean floor. They occur at the bases of continental slopes and along island arcs and are associated with active volcanoes and strong earthquakes.
Hence, the correct option is (D).

48. The Eastern Ghats comprising the discontinuous and low hills are highly eroded by the rivers such as the Mahanadi, the Godavari, the Krishna, the Kaveri, etc. Some of the important ranges include the Javadi hills, the Palconda range, the Nallamala hills, the Mahendragiri hills, etc. The Eastern and the Western Ghats meet each other at the Nilgiri hills.

The Western Ghats are comparatively higher in elevation and more continuous than the Eastern Ghats. Their average elevation is about 1,500 m with the height increasing from north to south. 'Anaimudi' (2,695 m), the highest peak of the Peninsular plateau is located on the Anaimalai Hills of the Western Ghats followed by Dodabetta (2,637 m) on the Nilgiri hills. Most of the Peninsular rivers have their origin in the Western Ghats.

Deccan Plateau is bordered by the Western Ghats in the west, the Eastern Ghats in the east, and the Satpura, Maikal range, and Mahadeo hills in the north. The Western Ghats are locally known by different names such as Sahyadri in Maharashtra, Nilgiri hills in Karnataka and Tamil Nadu, and Anaimalai hills and Cardamom hills in Kerala.
Hence, the correct option is (D).

49. The Jhelum river rises from a deep spring at Vernag, in western Jammu and Kashmir state. Srinagar, capital city of the state of Jammu and Kashmir is located on the banks of Jhelum river.

Jhelum in the valley of Kashmir is still in its youth stage and yet forms meander– a typical feature associated with the mature stage in the evolution of fluvial landform. The river meanders northwestward from the northern slope of the Pir Panjal Range through the Vale of Kashmir to Wular Lake at Srinagar, which controls its flow. It meanders due to the local base level of sediments provided by a primeval lake that existed millions of years ago in Kashmir Valley.
Hence, the correct option is (C).

50. The Tropic of Cancer passes through eight states in India: Gujarat (Jasdan), Rajasthan (Kalinjarh), Madhya Pradesh (Shajapur), Chhattisgarh (Sonhat), Jharkhand (Lohardaga), West

Bengal (Krishnanagar), Tripura (Udaipur) and Mizoram (Champhai) in that order.

Mahi River is the only river in India that cuts the Tropic of Cancer twice, first in Madhya Pradesh from where it flows towards Rajasthan and enters Gujarat where it cuts for the second time. Udaipur in Tripura is the city nearest to the Tropic of Cancer.
Hence, the correct option is (B).

51. Some Famous Local Storms of Hot Weather Season in India are:

Mango Shower: Towards the end of summer, there are pre-monsoon showers which are a common phenomenon in Kerala and coastal areas of Karnataka. Locally, they are known as mango showers since they help in the early ripening of mangoes.

Blossom Shower: With this shower, coffee flowers blossom in Kerala and nearby areas.

Nor Westers: These are dreaded evening thunderstorms in Bengal and Assam. Their notorious nature can be understood from the local nomenclature of 'Kalbaisakhi', a calamity of the month of Baisakh. These showers are useful for tea, jute, and rice cultivation. In Assam, these storms are known as "Bardoli Chheerha".

Loo: Hot, dry and oppressing winds blowing in the Northern plains from Punjab to Bihar with higher intensity between Delhi and Patna. Mustard is a Rabi crop, therefore storms of Hot Weather Season do not assist in its growth.
Hence, the correct option is (C).

52. The continents that the Equator passes through include Australia and Oceania, South America, Africa, and Asia. This imaginary line that circles the world traverses 13 countries:

- Kiribati in Australia and Oceania
- Ecuador, Colombia, and Brazil in South America
- Sao Tome and Principe, Gabon, Democratic Republic of Congo, Congo, Kenya, Uganda, and Somalia in Africa
- Maldives and Indonesia in Asia.

The Limpopo River rises in South Africa and flows generally eastwards through Mozambique to the Indian Ocean. Its length is 1750 km. It passes through the Tropic of Capricorn twice.
Hence, the correct option is (C).

53. The Indian Oceans winter monsoon (Northeast Monsoon), which lasts from October to April, is less well known than its rainy summer equivalent. The dry winter monsoon blows from the northeast. These winds start in the air above Mongolia and northwestern China.

Winter monsoons do not cause rainfall as they move from land to the sea. It is because they have little humidity; and due to anticyclonic circulation on land, the possibility of rainfall from them reduces. So, most parts of India do not have rainfall in the winter season.

On the other hand, the low temperature generally assists in the condensation of water vapors in the atmosphere. But in the case of low humidity, water vapors are inadequate to get precipitated in the form of rainfall. The Winter monsoon causes heavy rainfall in Tamil Nadu. This is because the winds pass over the Bay of Bengal, picking up moisture in the process.
Hence, the correct option is (C).

54. All the statements given in the question are true about the Brahmaputra river. The Brahmaputra River originates from the Mansarovar lake in Tibet. The origin of this river is situated at an altitude of 5,150 above sea level. This river enters India from the west of Sadiya town in Arunachal Pradesh. The Brahmaputra river is known as Tsangpo in Tibet and is called Dihang after entering India from Arunachal Pradesh. In Assam, it is known as the Brahmaputra and in Bangladesh, it is called Jamuna. After the confluence of the Ganges and the Brahmaputra, the combined stream of both is called Meghna. The total length of the Brahmaputra river is 2,900 km and in India, it is 916 km long. Majuli Island, the world's largest river island in the state of Assam, is situated on this river.

Hence, the correct option is (D).

55. Anticyclones are the opposite of cyclones, with high pressure in the centre and the isobars far apart. The pressure gradient is gentle and winds are light.

Anti-cyclones normally herald fine weather. Skies are clear. The air is calm and temperatures are high in summer but cold in winter. In winter intense cooling of the lower atmosphere may result in thick fogs. Anti-cyclonic conditions may last for days or weeks and then fade out quietly.

Winds in anticyclone' blow outwards and are also subject to deflection, but they blow clockwise in the northern hemisphere and anticlockwise in the southern hemisphere.
Hence, the correct option is (C).

56. Strait of Hormuz lies between Iran, Oman and UAE and connects Persian Gulf with Gulf of Oman and Arabian sea. It provides only sea passage from persian gulf to open ocean (Arabian Sea).

Bab-el Mandeb is between Yemen on the Arabian Peninsula and Djibouti and Eritrea on the Horn of Africa. It connects Red sea to Gulf of Aden and Indian Ocean.

Bosphorous Strait is Between Asian Turkey and European Turkey. It connects Black sea to Sea of tched

Magellan Strait is in southern Chile separating mainland South America to the north and Tierra delFuego to the south and is a natural passage between Atlantic and Pacific oceans.
Hence, the correct option is (A).

57. Tropic of Cancer passes through the central part of India in the east-west direction. Thus, the northern part of India lies in the sub-tropical and temperate zone and the part lying south of the Tropic of Cancer falls in the tropical zone.

The tropical zone being nearer to the equator experiences high temperatures throughout the year with small daily and annual range.

Tropic of Cancer lies at 23°27' N of the terrestrial Equator. It is the circle marking the latitude 23.5 degrees north, where the sun is directly overhead at noon on June 21, the beginning of summer in the northern hemisphere. Beyond the Tropic of Cancer, Northern India does not observe the overhead Sun on the

summer solstice of the northern hemisphere.
Hence, the correct option is (A).

58. Jaipur is the capital and the largest city of the Indian state of Rajasthan. It is situated at 75.8°E longitudes.

Bhopal is the capital city of the Indian state of Madhya Pradesh. It is situated at 77°25′E longitudes.

Lucknow is the capital city of the Indian state of Uttar Pradesh. It is situated at 80°57′E longitudes.

Raipur is the capital city of the Indian state of Chhattisgarh. It is situated at 81.63°E longitudes.
Hence, the correct option is (D).

59. P-waves move faster and are the first to arrive at the surface. These are also called 'primary waves'. The P-waves are similar to sound waves. They travel through gaseous, liquid and solid materials. S-waves arrive at the surface with some time lag. These are called secondary waves. An important fact about S-waves is that they can travel only through solid materials.

Different types of earthquake waves travel in different manners. As they move or propagate, they cause vibration in the body of the rocks through which they pass. P-waves vibrate parallel to the direction of the wave. This exerts pressure on the material in the direction of the propagation. As a result, it creates density differences in the material leading to stretching and squeezing of the material. The direction of vibrations of S-waves is perpendicular to the wave direction in the vertical plane. Hence, they create troughs and crests in the material through which they pass.
Hence, the correct option is (D).

60. In the course of a year, the earth's revolution around the Sun with its axis inclined at 66.5 degrees to the plane of the ecliptic changes the apparent altitude of the midday Sun. The sun is vertically overhead at the equator only on two days each year. These are usually 21st March and 21st September. These two days are termed equinoxes.

After the March equinox, the Sun appears to move north and is vertically overhead at the Tropic of Cancer on about 21st June. This is known as the June or Summer solstice when the northern hemisphere will have its longest day and shortest night. By about 22 December, the Sun will be overhead at the Tropic of Capricorn. This is the Winter solstice when the southern hemisphere will have its longest day and shortest night.

The tropics mark the limits of the overhead Sun, for, beyond these, the Sun is never overhead at any time of the year.
Hence, the correct option is (C).

61. It was Alfred Wegener, a German meteorologist who put forth a comprehensive argument in the form of the Continental Drift theory in 1912. It was regarding the distribution of the oceans and the continents. Arthur Holmes primary contribution was his proposed theory that convection occurred within the Earth's mantle, which explained the push and pulls of continent plates together and apart. He also assisted scientists in oceanographic research in the 1950s, which publicized the phenomenon known as seafloor spreading.

According to Wegener, all the continents formed a single continental mass and mega ocean surrounding the same. The supercontinent was named "Pangaea", which meant all earth. The mega-ocean was called "Panthalassa", meaning all water. He argued that, around 200 million years ago, the supercontinent, Pangaea, began to split. Pangaea first broke into two large continental masses as Laurasia and Gondwanaland forming the northern and southern components respectively. Subsequently, Laurasia and Gondwanaland continued to break into various smaller continents that exist today.

Continental Drift theory suggested that the movement responsible for the drifting of the continents was caused by pole-fleeing force and tidal force. The polar-fleeing force relates to the rotation of the earth. The second force was the tidal force which is due to the attraction of the moon and the sun that develops tides in oceanic waters. However, most scholars considered these forces to be totally inadequate.
Hence, the correct option is (B).

62. A long winter night with clear skies and still air is an ideal situation for inversion. The heat of the day is radiated off during the night, and by early morning hours, the earth is cooler than the air above. Over polar areas, a temperature inversion is normal throughout the year.

Surface inversion promotes stability in the lower layers of the atmosphere. Smoke and dust particles get collected beneath the inversion layer and spread horizontally to fill the lower strata of the atmosphere. Dense fogs in the mornings are common occurrences, especially during the winter season. This inversion commonly lasts for a few hours until the sun comes up and beings to warm the earth.

The inversion takes place in hills and mountains due to air drainage. Cold air at the hills and mountains, produced during the night, flows under the influence of gravity. Being heavy and dense, the cold air acts almost like water and moves down the slope to pile up deeply in pockets and valley bottoms with warm air above. This is called air drainage. It protects plants from frost damages.
Hence, the correct option is (B).

63. Jelap La is on Tibet-Bhutan border.

Bomdi La is in Arunachal Pradesh.

Bum La is in india-Bhutan border.
Hence, the correct option is (C).

64. The actual amount of water vapour present in the air, which is expressed in grams per cubic metre, is called absolute humidity. But more important from the point of view of weather studies is the relative humidity. This is the ratio between the actual amount of water vapour and the total amount the air can hold at a given temperature, expressed as a percentage.

Warm air can hold more water vapour than cold air, so if it contains only half the amount it could carry, the relative humidity is 50 per cent. In the equatorial regions, over 80 per cent is common in the morning, 'which means the air contains four-fifths as much water vapour as it can carry. When the relative humidity reaches 100 per cent, the air is completely saturated. The air temperature is said to be at dew-point. Further cooling will

condense the water vapour into clouds or rain. It is thus clear that when relative humidity is high the air is moist, as in the equatorial regions; when it is low, the air is dry as in the deserts. For clouds to form and rain to start, the air does have to reach 100% relative humidity, but only where the clouds are forming or where the rain is coming from.
Hence, the correct option is (B).

65. Eravikulam National Park is located along the Western Ghats in the Idukki district of Kerala in India. It is the first national park in Kerala. Eravikulam National Park is a UNESCO World Heritage Site

The main body of the park consists of a high rolling hill plateau with a base elevation of about 2,000 m. The terrain consists of high-altitude grasslands interspersed with sholas. Anamudi, (2,695 meters), the highest peak in India south of the Himalayas is inside this park. Many perennial streams criss-cross the park. They merge to form tributaries of the Periyar river in the west and of the Cauvery River in the east.
Hence, the correct option is (C).

66. Features of Warm Temperate Eastern Margin Climate (China Type):

- Influenced by the on-shore Trade Winds all the year-round, without any monsoon variations.

- Fairly uniform distribution of rainfall throughout the year. There is rain every month, except in the interior of central China, where there is a distinct dry season. Rain comes either from convectional sources or as orographic rain in summer, or from depressions in prolonged showers in winter.

- It is sometimes referred to as the Gulf type or Natal type of climate

Hence, the correct option is (B).

67. Altitude is one of the factors related to location and relief which determines the climate of a region. Altitude affects various atmospheric parameters in the following manner:

- Temperature decreases with height. The temperature in the troposphere usually decreases with height at the average lapse rate of 6.5 °C per kilometer.

- The density of air decreases with height. There are two reasons- (1) At higher altitudes, there is less air pushing down from above, and (2) Gravity is weaker farther from Earth's center. So at higher altitudes, air molecules can spread out more, and air density decreases

Due to thin air i.e., lower density, places in the mountains are cooler than places on the plains. For example, Agra and Darjiling are located on the same latitude, but the temperature of January in Agra is 16°C whereas it is only 4°C in Darjiling.

Pressure decreases with increasing altitude. The pressure at any level in the atmosphere may be interpreted as the total weight of the air above a unit area at any elevation. At higher elevations, there are fewer air molecules above a given surface than a similar surface at lower levels.
Hence, the correct option is (D).

68. Cirques are the most common landforms in glaciated mountains. The cirques quite often are found at the heads of glacial valleys. The accumulated ice cuts these cirques while moving down the mountain tops. They are deep, long, and wide troughs or basins with very steep concave to vertically dropping high walls at its head as well as sides.

Horns form through headward erosion of the cirque walls. If three or more radiating glaciers cut headward until their cirques meet, high, sharp-pointed, and steep-sided peaks called horns form.

When glaciers melt in summer, the water flows on the surface of the ice or seeps down along the margins or even moves through holes in the ice. These waters accumulate beneath the glacier and flow like streams in a channel beneath the ice. Such streams flow over the ground (not in a valley cut in the ground) with ice forming its banks. Very coarse materials like boulders and blocks along with some minor fractions of rock debris carried into this stream settle in the valley of ice beneath the glacier and after the ice, melts can be found as a sinuous ridge called esker.
Hence, the correct option is (A).

69. Orogeny is a mountain-building process whereas epeirogeny is a continental building process. In the process of orogeny, the crust is severely deformed into folds. Due to epeirogeny, there may be simple deformation.

Orogeny and Epeirogeny both are caused by endogenic forces. Thus, the forces required for them emanate from within the earth. It is mostly generated by radioactivity, rotational and tidal friction, and primordial heat from the origin of the earth.
Hence, the correct option is (C).

70. The continental shelf is a gently sloping and relatively flat extension of a continent that is covered by the oceans. Seaward, the shelf ends abruptly at the shelf break, the boundary that separates the shelf from the continental slope. Continental shelves contain valuable resources, such as oil and gas and minerals. Oil and gas are formed from organic material that accumulates on the continental shelf. Over time the material is buried and transformed into oil and gas by heat and pressure.

A placer deposit is an accumulation of valuable minerals formed by gravity separation from a specific source rock during sedimentary processes. Minerals come from rocks on land and are carried to the ocean by rivers. The minerals are deposited in river channels and beaches. Examples of important minerals on the shelf are diamonds, chromite (chromium ore), ilmenite (titanium ore), magnetite (iron ore), platinum, and gold. Continental shelves are home to the largest concentration of bottom-dwelling marine life, and they are the sites of major fishing grounds.
Hence, the correct option is (D).

71. Classification of Natural Disasters:

- Atmospheric
- Blizzards
- Thunderstorms
- Lightning
- Tornadoes
- Tropical Cyclone

- Drought
- Hailstorm
- Frost, Heat Wave or Loo. Cold Waves, etc.

Terrestrial:

- Earthquakes
- Volcanic Eruptions
- Landslides
- Avalanches
- Subsidence
- Soil Erosion

Aquatic:

- Floods
- Tidal Waves
- Ocean Currents
- Storm Surge
- Tsunami

Hence, the correct option is (C).

72. The Ganges River, also called Ganga, is a river located in northern India that flows toward the border with Bangladesh. It is the longest river in India and flows for around 1,569 miles (2,525km) from the Himalayan Mountains to the Bay of Bengal.

The Ganges passes through the states of Uttarakhand, Uttar Pradesh, Bihar, Jharkhand, and West Bengal. The Ganga enters the plains at Haridwar. From here, it flows first to the south, then to the southeast and east before splitting into two distributaries, namely the Bhagirathi and the Hugli. The river has a length of 2,525 km. It is shared by Uttaranchal (110 km) and Uttar Pradesh (1,450 km), Bihar (445 km), and West Bengal (520 km), and Sahibganj town of Jharkhand is located on the bank of the River Ganges. The Ganga basin covers about 8.6 lakh sq. km area in India alone.
Hence, the correct option is (B).

73. The speed of the wave in the ocean depends upon the depth of water. Water waves travel slower in shallower water. The deeper the water the faster the waves can travel, in fact in the ocean waves speeds can sometimes approach hundreds of miles per hour. As a result of this, the impact of the tsunami is less over the ocean and more near the coast where they cause large-scale devastations. Therefore, a ship at sea is not much affected by the tsunami and it is difficult to detect a tsunami in the deeper parts of the sea.

It is so because over deep water the tsunami has very long wave-length and limited wave height. Thus, a tsunami wave raises the ship only a meter or two and each rise and fall takes several minutes.

As opposed to this, when a tsunami enters shallow water, its wavelength gets reduced and the period remains unchanged, which increases the wave height. Sometimes, this height can be up to 15m or more, which causes large-scale destructions along the shores. Thus, these are also called Shallow Water Waves.
Hence, the correct option is (D).

74. Frequent inundation of agricultural land and human settlement have serious consequences on the national economy and society. Floods do not only destroy valuable crops every year but also damage physical infrastructures such as roads, rails, bridges, and human settlements. Millions of people are rendered homeless and are also washed down along with their cattle in the floods.

Spread of diseases like cholera, gastroenteritis, hepatitis, and other water-borne diseases spread in the flood-affected areas.

However, floods also make a few positive contributions. Every year floods to deposit fertile silt over agricultural fields which is good for the crops. Majuli (Assam), the largest riverine island in the world, is the best example of good paddy crops after the annual floods in the Brahmaputra.
Hence, the correct option is (D).

75. Temperate grasslands of the mid-latitudes produce the greatest quantity of wheat per capita amongst the world's wheat-growing nations. The temperate grasslands are ideal for extensive wheat cultivation. They are, naturally the greatest wheat exporters.

Three-quarters of the world's wheat is winter wheat, i.e. wheat sown in winter or late autumn, and is then harvested in the summer. The cool, moist spring stimulates early growth, and the light showers in the ripening period help to swell the grains to ensure a good yield. The warm, sunny summer is not only advantageous for harvesting but also enables the straw to be dried for farm use. It is a hard wheat with a low moisture content, being ripened in the hot, sunny, continental summer. It is best for bread-making and is extensively traded. Spring wheat is grown in regions where winter temperature is too cold for wheat seedlings to survive. The yield of spring wheat is hard wheat which is suitable for making cakes.
Hence, the correct option is (C).

76. The human population increased more than ten times in the past 500 hundred years. In the twentieth century itself, the population has increased four times.

The highest rate of population growth during the last decade has been observed in Africa and not Asia.

Population growth (annual %) in India was reported at 1.1271% in 2017, according to the World Bank collection of development indicators. As per census 2011 the decadal rate of growth of India's population is 17.70%.
Hence, the correct option is (C).

77. Kandla - It is situated at the head of Gulf of Kuchchh has been developed as a major port to cater to the needs of western and northwestern parts of the country and also to reduce the pressure at Mumbai port. The port is specially designed to receive large quantities of petroleum and petroleum products and fertiliser. The offshore terminal at Vadinar has been developed to reduce the pressure at Kandla port.

Paradip - It is situated in the Mahanadi delta, about 100 km from Cuttack. It has the deepest harbour especially suited to handle very large vessels. It has been developed mainly to handle large-scale export of iron ore. Odisha, Chhattisgarh and Jharkhand are the parts of its hinterland.

Vishakhapatnam - situated in Andhra Pradesh is a land-locked harbour, connected to the sea by a channel cut through solid rock and sand. An outer harbour has been developed for handling iron-ore, petroleum and general cargo. Andhra Pradesh and Telangana are the main hinterlands for this port.

Marmagao - It is situated at the entrance of the Zuari estuary, is a natural harbour in Goa. It gained significance after its remodelling in 1961 to handle iron-ore exports to Japan. The construction of the Konkan railway has considerably extended the hinterland of this port. Karnataka, Goa, Southern Maharashtra constitute its hinterland.
Hence, the correct option is (D).

78. Indira Sagar dam built on the Narmada river. It is a concrete gravity dam, located in the Khandwa district of Madhya Pradesh. Indira Sagar project was the key project on Narmada river providing an excellent storage site of water. Indira Sagar Dam has the biggest reservoir in India.

Krishnarajasagar Dam built across the Kaveri River near Mysore in Karnataka. It is one of the principals and largest dams built on the river Kaveri in Karnataka in, South India.

Mettur Dam built across the Kaveri River at Salem district in Tamil Nadu. It is one the largest and one of the oldest dams built in India. Mettur Dam has the biggest and the most power generating capacity dam in Tamil Nadu.
Hence, the correct option is (C).

79. Oil drilling falls into one of two main categories: offshore and onshore. The location of the drilling is the most obvious difference, but the two types vary in other areas, including cost, profits, timelines for drilling, and processes. India has both on-shore as well off-shore reserves of Natural Gas. One of the off-shore reserves is near Mumbai High in the Arabia Sea.

The majority of the Natural Gas Reserves are concentrated in Eastern and North-Eastern India.
Hence, the correct option is (A).

80. The proportion of the literate population of a country is an indicator of its socio-economic development as it reveals the standard of living, social status of females, availability of educational facilities, and policies of the government.

The age-sex-occupational structure, density of population, and level of development vary between rural and urban areas.

The proportion of the working population engaged in these four sectors is a good indicator of the levels of economic development of a nation. This is because only a developed economy with industries and infrastructure can accommodate more workers in the secondary, tertiary, and quaternary sectors. If the economy is still in the primitive stages, then the proportion of people engaged in primary activities world be high as it involves the extraction of natural resources.
Hence, the correct option is (D).

81. Population aging is the process by which the share of the older population becomes proportionally larger. This is a new phenomenon of the twentieth century. In most of the developed countries of the world, the population in higher age groups has increased due to increased life expectancy. With a reduction in birth rates, the proportion of children in the population has declined.
Hence, the correct option is (D).

82. If a person travels from Srinagar (Jammu & Kashmir) to Kolkata (West Bengal), then the minimum number of states through which he can pass via road is Jammu & Kashmir - Himachal Pradesh - Uttar Pradesh - Jharkhand - West Bengal.
Hence, the correct option is (A).

83. Rainwater harvesting is a method to capture and store rainwater for various uses. It is also used to recharge groundwater aquifers. It is a low-cost and eco-friendly technique for preserving every drop of water by guiding the rainwater to bore well, pits, and wells. Rainwater harvesting has several benefits like:

- Increases water availability,
- Checks the declining groundwater table,
- Improves the quality of groundwater through dilution of contaminants like fluoride and nitrates,
- Prevents soil erosion and flooding and
- Arrests saltwater intrusion in coastal areas if used to recharge aquifers.

Rainwater harvesting has been practiced through various methods by different communities in the country for a long time. There is a wide scope to use rainwater harvesting techniques to conserve precious water resources. It can be done by harvesting rainwater on rooftops and open spaces.
Hence, the correct option is (D).

84. Famous Copper extraction mines in India are Khetri, Alwar, Bhilwara, and Udaipur in Rajasthan, Balaghat in Madhya Pradesh, Hazaribagh, and Singhbhum in Jharkhand.

Famous Bauxite mines in India are Katni, Amarkantak in Madhya Pradesh, Bilaspur and Maikala Hills in Chhattisgarh, Koraput in Odisha.
Hence, the correct option is (C).

85. According to the United Nation's World Urbanisation Prospects 2018, Tokyo is the world's largest city with an agglomeration of 37 million inhabitants, followed by New Delhi with 29 million, Shanghai with 26 million, and Mexico City and Sao Paulo, each with around 22 million inhabitants. Today, Cairo, Mumbai, Beijing and Dhaka all have close to 20 million inhabitants.
Hence, the correct option is (A).

86. Metallic minerals are divided into ferrous and non-ferrous metallic minerals. Ferrous minerals refer to iron. Thus, all those minerals which have iron content are ferrous such as iron ore itself. For e.g iron, manganese etc.

Those metallic minerals which do not have iron content are referred to as non-ferrous such as copper, bauxite, aluminum, brass, lead etc.
Hence, the correct option is (A).

87. The first population Census in India was conducted in 1872 but its first synchronous decennial Census was conducted only in 1881. Since then, censuses have been undertaken uninterruptedly once every ten years.

The census year 1921 registered a negative growth rate of -0.31 percent which happened only once throughout the demographic history of India. It is because of this decline that the year 1921 is called the 'demographic divide' in the demographic history of India.
Hence, the correct option is (D).

88. In southern states and West Bengal, the climatic conditions allow the cultivation of two or three crops of Rice in an agricultural year. In West Bengal farmers grow three crops of rice called "aus", "aman" and "boro". But in the Himalayas and northwestern parts of the country, it is grown as a Kharif crop during the Southwest Monsoon season.
Hence, the correct option is (D).

89. A geographer, Griffith Taylor introduced another concept which reflects a middle path (Madhyam Marg) between the two ideas of environmental determinism and possibilism. He termed it as Neodeterminism or stop and go determinism. The concept shows that neither is there a situation of absolute necessity (environmental determinism) nor is there a condition of absolute freedom (possibilism). It means that human beings can conquer nature by obeying it. They have to respond to the red signals and can proceed in their pursuits of development when nature permits the modifications. It means that possibilities can be created within the limits which do not damage the environment and there is no free run without accidents.
Hence, the correct option is (C).

90. Almost all sectors of the Indian industry depend heavily on the iron and steel industry for their basic infrastructure. The other raw materials besides iron ore and coking coal, essential for the iron and steel industry are limestone, dolomite, manganese, and fire clay.

Coking coal is a vital ingredient in the steel-making process as iron occurs only as iron oxides in the earth's crust. Hence, the ores must be converted, or 'reduced', using carbon. The primary source of this carbon is coking coal.

Limestone is used as a slag former for removing impurities in the extraction of iron ore. Dolomite is used as a slag former, slag modifier, and as a refractory material.

Manganese removes oxygen and sulfur when iron ore (an iron and oxygen compound) is converted into iron. It also is an essential alloy that helps convert iron into steel. Fire clay is used in the iron and steel industry as it can withstand high temperatures and used for making refractories.
Hence, the correct option is (D).

91. New seed varieties of wheat (Mexico) and rice (Philippines) known as high-yielding varieties (HYVs) were available for cultivation by the mid-1960s. India took advantage of this and introduced a packaging technology comprising HYVs, along with chemical fertilizers in irrigated areas of Punjab, Haryana, Western Uttar Pradesh, Andhra Pradesh, and Gujarat.

An assured supply of soil moisture through irrigation was a basic prerequisite for the success of this new agricultural technology. This strategy of agricultural development paid dividends instantly and increased foodgrains production at a very fast rate. This spurt of agricultural growth came to be known as Green Revolution.

This also gave a fillip to the development of a large number of agro-inputs, agro-processing industries, and small-scale industries. This strategy of agricultural development made the country self-reliant in foodgrain production.

The green revolution was initially confined to irrigated areas only. This led to regional disparities in agricultural development in the country until the seventies, after which the technology spread to the Eastern and Central parts of the country.
Hence, the correct option is (D).

92. The Rhine Waterways is located on the continent of Europe. The Rhine flows through Germany and the Netherlands. It is navigable for 700 km from Rotterdam, at its mouth in the Netherlands to Basel in Switzerland.

The Great Lakes – St. Lawrence Seaway is located on the continent of North America. The Great Lakes of North America Superior, Huron Erie, and Ontario are connected by Soo Canal and Welland Canal to form an inland waterway.

The Volga Waterway is located on the continent of Europe. Russia has a large number of developed waterways, of which the Volga is one of the most important.
Hence, the correct option is (B).

93. The age-sex pyramid of Nigeria is a triangular-shaped pyramid with a wide base and is typical of less developed countries. These have larger populations in lower age groups due to high birth rates. If you construct the pyramids for Bangladesh and Mexico, it would look the same.

Australia's age-sex pyramid is bell-shaped and tapered towards the top. This shows birth and death rates are almost equal leading to a near-constant population.

The Japan pyramid has a narrow base and a tapered top showing low birth and death rates. The population growth in developed countries is usually zero or negative. It is not an inverted pyramid.
Hence, the correct option is (A).

94. Plantation Agriculture is a form of commercial farming where crops are grown for profit. The characteristic features of this type of farming are:

- Large estates or plantations
- Large capital investment
- Managerial and technical support
- Scientific methods of cultivation
- Single crop specialization instead of multi-crop specialization
- Cheap labor instead of highly paid workers
- A good system of transportation which links the estates to the factories and markets for the export of the products

Hence, the correct option is (B).

95. In his 1798 work, An Essay on the Principle of Population, Malthus examined the relationship between population growth and resources. From this, he developed the Malthusian theory of population growth in which he wrote that population growth occurs exponentially, so it increases according to birth rate. On

the other hand, food production increases arithmetically (linear), so it only increases at given points in time. Malthus wrote that left unchecked, populations can outgrow their resources.
Hence, the correct option is (A).

96. Sherms is a place dug hollow beneath a thorn tree, surrounded by bushes. Bushmen tribes travel in small family groups and live together in Sherms.

Wurlies are simple shelters made of branches and tufts and grass. Bindibu or Aborigine tribes also travel in family groups and live in Wurlies.
Hence, the correct option is (D).

97. India is the second-largest producer of Sugarcane in the world. The largest producer of Sugarcane in the world is Brazil. The top five Sugarcane producing countries are Brazil, India, China, Thailand and Pakistan.

Uttar Pradesh produces about 40 percent of the Sugarcane of the country. Maharashtra, Karnataka, Tamil-Nadu, and Andhra Pradesh are other leading producers of this crop. The yield of Sugarcane is higher in Southern India as compared to Northern India because of the favorable climate which is free from the effects of summer loo and winter frost. The black soil in the south is also ideal for growing crops like cotton and sugarcane.
Hence, the correct option is (D).

98. The growth rate of the population in India over the last century has been caused by the annual birth rate and death rate and rate of migration and thereby show different trends. There are four distinct phases of growth identified within this period-

Phase I: The period from 1901-1921 is referred to as a period of the stagnant or stationary phase of growth of India's population, since in this period growth rate was very low, even recording a negative growth rate during 1911-1921. Poor health and medical services, inefficient distribution systems of food and other basic necessities were largely responsible for high birth and death rates in this period.

Phase II: The decades 1921-1951 are referred to as the period of steady population growth. An overall improvement in health and sanitation throughout the country brought down the mortality rate.

Phase III: The decades 1951-1981 are referred to as the period of population explosion in India, which was caused by a rapid fall in the mortality rate but a high fertility rate of population in the country. International migration bringing in Tibetans, Bangladeshis, Nepalis, and people from Pakistan contributed to the high growth rate.

Phase IV: In the post-1981 till present, the growth rate of the country's population though remained high, has started slowing down gradually.
Hence, the correct option is (A).

99. During the colonial period (British period) millions of the indentured laborers were sent to Mauritius, Caribbean islands (Trinidad, Tobago and Guyana), Fiji and South Africa by British from Uttar Pradesh and Bihar; to Reunion Island, Guadeloupe, Martinique and Surinam by French and Dutch and by Portuguese from Goa, Daman and Diu to Angola, Mozambique to work as plantation workers.

All such migrations were covered under the time-bound contract known as Girmit Act (Indian Emigration Act). All such indentured laborers are called Girmitiyas.
Hence, the correct option is (A).

100. Red Collar - Primary Activities

Gold Collar - Quinary

White-Collar - Professionals in the High Technology industry

Blue Collar - Workers in industries
Hence, the correct option is (B).

101. Double village settlements extend on both sides of a river where there is a bridge or a ferry.

T-shaped settlements develop at trijunctions of the roads.

In the linear patterns, settlements houses are located along a road, railway line, river, canal edge of avalley.

Cruciform settlements develop on the crossroads and houses extend in four directions.
Hence, the correct option is (B).

102. Industries can be classified based upon various factors such as ownership, inputs, outputs, etc. Basic industries whose products are used to produce other goods.

- Iron and steel industry, copper refining industry is one of the basic industries because steel & copper produced by this industry is used in many other industries as a raw material.

- Some basic industries produce machines that are used to produce other goods.

Hence, the correct option is (C).

103. This canal connects the Atlantic Ocean in the east to the Pacific Ocean in the west. It has been constructed across the Panama Isthmus between Panama City and Colon by the U.S. government which purchased 8 km of an area on either side and named it the Canal Zone.

It shortens the distance between New York (West Coast of USA) and San Francisco (East Coast of USA) by 13,000 km by sea. Likewise, the distance between Western Europe and the West-coast of the U.S.A., and Northeastern and Central U.S.A. and East and South-east Asia is shortened.
Hence, the correct option is (D).

104. The concept of human development was introduced by Dr. Mahbub-ul-Haq. Dr. Haq has described human development as a development that enlarges people"s choices and improves their lives.

People are central to all development under this concept. These choices are not fixed but keep on changing. The basic goal of development is to create conditions where people can live meaningful lives. A meaningful life is not just a long one. It must be a life with some purpose. This means that people must be healthy, be able to develop their talents, participate in society and be free to achieve their goals.
Hence, the correct option is (C).

105. The Bushmen of the Kalahari and the Bindibu of Australia remains so primitive in their mode of living that they barely survive.

The Bushmen roam the Kalahari Desert with their bows and poisoned arrows, spears, traps, and snares. They are not only skillful and strong but have great endurance. In order to capture their prey, they have to be very patient and if necessary run many miles to track down the wounded animals. In this way, they hunt antelope and other smaller animals. The women and children collect insects, rodents and lizards, and gather honey, roots, grass, and grubs. Bushmen either wear a loincloth or go virtually naked.

Hence, the correct option is (A).

106. The eco-development through afforestation, shelterbelt plantation (planting of trees or shrubs in rows in a manner so as to provide protection from wind and prevent soil erosion), and pasture development is necessary for promoting Sustainable Development.

Warabandi System (equal distribution of canal water in the command area of the outlet) can be effectively implemented to reduce the conveyance loss of water and thus promote Sustainable Development.

In general, the cropping pattern shall not include water-intensive crops. It shall be adhered to and the people shall be encouraged to grow plantation crops such as citrus fruits. Intensive agriculture is a kind of agriculture where a lot of capital and labor are used to increase the yield that can be obtained per area of land. It involves large amounts of pesticides for crops, and of medication for animal stocks is common. Intensive agriculture leads to problems of soil and water degradation and compromising sustainable development.

Hence, the correct option is (A).

107. Semi-clustered or fragmented settlements may result from a tendency of clustering in a restricted area of dispersed settlement. More often such a pattern may also result from segregation or fragmentation of a large compact village.

In this case, one or more sections of the village society choose or are forced to live a little away from the main cluster or village. In such cases, generally, the land-owning and dominant community occupies the central part of the main village, whereas people of lower strata of society and menial workers settle on the outer flanks of the village. Such settlements are widespread in the Gujarat plain and some parts of Rajasthan.

Hence, the correct option is (D).

108. The working-age population is defined as those aged 15 to 59.

The basic indicator for employment is the proportion of the working-age population aged 15-59 who are employed (In some cases it may also be considered 15-64 years of age, therefore the important point to remember is that the working-age population begins from 15 years of age and not 18 years). The working population (i.e. women and men of the age group – 15 to 59) take part in various occupations ranging from agriculture, forestry, fishing, manufacturing construction, commercial transport, services, communication, and other unclassified services.

Hence, the correct option is (D).

109. There are only two ways to satisfy the increasing food and other agricultural demands of the country's rising population: either expanding the net area under cultivation or intensifying cropping over the existing area.

The net sown area of the country has risen by about 20 percent since independence and has reached a point where it is not possible to make any appreciable increase.

Thus raising the cropping intensity is the only viable option left. Cropping intensity refers to the raising of a number of crops from the same field during one agriculture year. It can be expressed as cropping intensity = (Gross cropped area / Net sown area) x 100

It increases the total output per unit area of land from all crops grown over one agricultural year by increasing land-use intensity. The advantage is that along with increased output from limited land, it also increases the demand for labor significantly. For a land-scarce but labor-abundant country like India, a high cropping intensity is desirable not only for fuller utilization of the land resource but also for reducing unemployment in the rural economy.

Hence, the correct option is (B).

110. Industries can be classified based upon size ranging from cottage industry to large scale industry. Small scale manufacturing is distinguished from household industries by its production techniques and place of manufacture (a workshop outside the home/cottage of the producer). This type of manufacturing uses:

- Local raw material
- Simple power-driven machines
- Semi-skilled labor

Hence, the correct option is (D).

111. The Mediterranean lands are also known as the world"s orchard lands. A wide range of citrus fruits such as oranges, lemons, limes, citrons, and grapefruit are grown. The fruit trees have long roots to draw water from considerable depths during the long summer drought.

Viticulture is by tradition a Mediterranean occupation and the regions bordering the Mediterranean Sea account for three-quarters of the world's production of wine. In Spain, Portugal, France, and Italy, wine is the national drink. Although grapes may be grown in many parts of the temperate lands, commercial viticulture is almost entirely confined to the Mediterranean regions.

The mountain pastures, with their cooler climate, support a few sheep, goats and sometimes cattle. Transhumance defined as the action or practice of moving livestock from one grazing ground to another in a seasonal cycle, typically to lowlands in winter and highlands in summer is widely practiced along the Mediterranean region.

Hence, the correct option is (C).

112. Permanent pasture is the land used to grow grasses or other herbaceous forage naturally (self-seeded) or through cultivation (sown) and that is not included in the crop rotation of the holding for five years or longer. Most of this type of land is owned by the village 'Panchayat' or the Government. Only a small proportion of this land is privately owned. The land owned by the village panchayat comes under 'Common Property Resources'.

Current Fallow is the land that is left without cultivation for one or less than one agricultural year. Following is a cultural practice adopted for giving the land rest. The land recoups lost fertility through natural processes.

Culturable Waste-Land which is left fallow (uncultivated) for more than five years is included in this category. It can be brought under cultivation after improving through reclamation practices. Hence, the correct option is (A).

113. Entrepot Ports are collection centres where the goods are brought from different countries for export. Singapore is an entrepot for Asia, Rotterdam for Europe, and Copenhagen for the Baltic region.
Hence, the correct option is (B).

114. Hamleted Settlements- Sometimes settlement is fragmented into several units physically separated from each other bearing a common name. These units are locally called Panna, para, Palli, nagla, Dhani, etc. in various parts of the country. This segmentation of a large village is often motivated by social and ethnic factors. Such villages are more frequently found in the middle and lower Ganga plain, Chhattisgarh, and lower valleys of the Himalayas.
Hence, the correct option is (C).

115. Punjab - Sirhind Canal, Bhakra Canal

Uttar Pradesh - Sharda Canal, Upper and Lower Ganga Canal

Karnataka - Vishweshwarya Canal and Malprabha project canal
Hence, the correct option is (B).

116. Surface Mining is also known as open cast mining or quarrying. Sedimentary or bedded ores lying close to the surface are called open cast mines. It is the easiest and the cheapest way of mining minerals that occur close to the surface.

The underground Mining or shaft method is inherently risky due to the possibility of poisonous gases, fires, floods, and cavings that can lead to fatal accidents. In this kind of mining, vertical or inclined shafts and horizontal tunnels are made and connected with underground galleries.
Hence, the correct option is (A).

117. The Ruhr Coal field in Germany has been one of the major industrial regions of Europe for a long time. Coal and iron and steel formed the basis of the economy and are responsible for 80 percent of Germany's total steel production. However, due to changes in the industrial structure and decline in demand for coal, the future prosperity of the Ruhr is based more on the new industries like the car assembly plant, new chemical plants, universities.
Hence, the correct option is (C).

118. The Kharif crops are associated with the monsoon season. They are sown in the months of June and July and are harvested in autumn months i.e., in September and October. Important Kharif crops are rice, jowar, maize, cotton, tur, ragi, bajra,

sugarcane, and jute.
Hence, the correct option is (B).

119. The Diamond Quadrilateral of Indian railways aims to connect metropolitan cities and growth centers of the country (Delhi, Mumbai, Chennai & Kolkata) through high-speed rail connectivity. Diamond Quadrilateral project of Indian railways is similar to the Golden Quadrilateral project for the development of highways.
Hence, the correct option is (B).

120. The Bhilai Steel Plant was established with Russian collaboration in the Durg District of Chhattisgarh and started production in 1959. The iron ore comes from the Dalli-Rajhara mine, coal comes from Korba and Kargali coal fields. The water comes from the Tanduladam and the power from the Korba Thermal Power Station. This plant also lies on the Kolkata-Mumbai railway route. The bulk of the steel produced goes to the Hindustan Shipyard at Vishakhapatnam.
Hence, the correct option is (B).

121. Command area is the total area which can be economically irrigated from the irrigation system (canal system) without considering the limitation on the quantity of available water.
Hence, the correct option is (A).

122. Employment in the service sector has increased steadily in the developed countries during the twentieth century despite low population and significant job losses in manufacturing. In general, the increase in services employment throughout the world is attached to various reasons:

- Rising per capita income in the developed countries has generated proportionately larger increases in the demand for many kinds of services especially healthcare, entertainment, and transport.

- Due to the changing demographic composition of the population in highly industrialized countries, the demand for medical care services is more from the elderly population in Europe, North America, and Japan.

- With the increasing demand for literacy, mathematical, and computer skills at workplaces, there is a rise in demand for educational services at all levels.

Hence, the correct option is (D).

123. Transhumance pastoralists follow a cyclical pattern of migrations that usually take them to cool highland valleys in the summer and warmer lowland valleys in the winter. Thermally contrasting means a significant difference in the prevailing temperature conditions between two places.
Hence, the correct option is (A).

124. Conurbation applies to a large area of urban development that resulted from the merging of originally separate towns or cities. Greater London, Manchester, Chicago and Tokyo are examples.
Hence, the correct option is (B).

125. Coffee is a tropical plantation crop. Its seeds are roasted, ground, and are used for preparing a beverage. There are three varieties of coffee i.e., arabica, robusta, and Liberica. India mostly grows superior quality coffee, arabica, which is in great demand

in the International market. India produces only about 4.3 percent of coffee in the world and ranks seventh after Brazil, Vietnam, Colombia, Indonesia, Ethiopia, and Honduras.

Hence, the correct option is (D).

Q.1 Bishrampur is famous for which of the following mines?

A. Iron ore   **B.** Coal

C. Manganese   **D.** Copper ore

Q.2 The coastline of Tamil Nadu is called-

A. Sirkar coast   **B.** Konkan Coast

C. Malabar Coast   **D.** Coromandel Coast

Q.3 The Chaurabadi Glacier is located at-

A. South of Kedarnath temple

B. West of Kedarnath temple

C. North of Kedarnath temple

D. East of Kedarnath Temple

Q.4 Melting speed of Himalayan glaciers-

A. Is the lowest.

B. Is the most.

C. Similar to glaciers in other parts of the world.

D. Information about melting of Himalayan glaciers is not available.

Q.5 Which of the following glaciers is located in the Kumaon region of Uttarakhand?

A. Hispar   **B.** Jemu   **C.** Milan   **D.** Rupal

Q.6 The northern part of the western coastal plain of India, by whatever name it is known, is-

A. Karnataka coast   **B.** Malabar Coast

C. Konkan Coast   **D.** Coromandel Coast

Q.7 Which of the following is not correctly matched?

(Rates)	(located in the state)
(a) Jelep La	Sikkim
(b) Mana and Niti	Uttarakhand
(c) Shipki La	Jammu and Kashmir
(d) Bomdi La	Arunadhal Pradesh

A. (a)   **B.** (b)   **C.** (c)   **D.** (d)

Q.8 Which of the following passes is located in Uttarakhand?

A. Jelep La   **B.** Lipulekh

C. Nathu La   **D.** Shipki La

Q.9 The 'Mana Pass' is located-

A. Uttar Pradesh   **B.** Uttarakhand

C. Jammu-Kashmir   **D.** Himachal Pradesh

Q.10 What is King-Wing, Neeti-Mana?

A. Pass   **B.** Rivers

C. Mountains   **D.** Religious place

Q.11 Which one of the following peaks is not a location in India-

(a) Gurla Mandhata

(b) Namcha Barwa

(c) Kamet

(d) Nanga Parbat

A. (a) and (c)   **B.** (a) and (b)

C. (c) and (d)   **D.** (d) and (b)

Q.12 In which span is the "Gaurlata" peak located?

A. Samaripat   **B.** Manpat

C. Jashpurpat   **D.** Jarangpat

Q.13 Which of the following pairs is not correctly matched?

(Mountain pass)	(State)
(a) Shipki La	Himachal Pradesh
(b) Bomdi La	Arunachal Pradesh
(c) Nathu La	Meghalaya
(d) Zoji La	Jammu and Kashmir

A. (a)   **B.** (b)   **C.** (c)   **D.** (d)

Q.14 Which of the following passes is the way to Leh?

A. Zoji La   **B.** Shipki La

C. Chumbi Valley   **D.** Banihal

Q.15 Consider the following statements regarding the Western Ghats.

1. It is a fault mountain.

2. Its eastern slope is a blue plateau, respectively.

3. Its northern section is covered with lava (basalt).

Which of the following statements are correct?

A. 1 and 2   **B.** 2 and 3

C. 1 and 3   **D.** 1, 2 and 3

Q.16 Consider the following relief images-

1. Mahadev mountain range

2. Maikal mountain range

3. Chhotanagpur Plateau

4. Khasi Hills

Change the correct sequence of the above reliefs from west to east.

A. 1, 2, 3, 4   **B.** 4, 3, 2, 1   **C.** 2, 3, 4, 1   **D.** 1, 3, 2, 4

Q.17 On which of the following hills does the Eastern Ghats meet the Western Ghats?

A. Palani hills   **B.** Anamudi hills

C. Nilgiri hills   **D.** Shevaroy hills

Q.18 Which of the following is the oldest mountain range?

A. Himalaya   **B.** Aravali

C. Vindhya   **D.** Satpura

Q.19 Which of the following states of India has the longest coastline?

A. Maharashtra   **B.** Andhra Pradesh

C. Kerala   **D.** Gujarat

Q.20 How many states in India are along the coast line?

A. 7 **B.** 8 **C.** 9 **D.** 10

Q.21 In ancient Indian historical geography, the name 'Ratnakar' was indicative?

A. Arabian Sea
B. Bay of Bengal
C. Indian Ocean
D. The confluence of the Ganges, Yamuna and the legendary river Saraswati in Prayag

Q.22 Most coastal erosion occurs-

[Uttarakhand Public Service Commission (UKPSC), 2016]

A. By waves
B. Tide-reflux
C. From streams
D. From tsunami waves

Q.23 Consider the following West Coast cities of India-

1. Janjira
2. Kannur
3. Nagercoil
4. Sindhudurg

The correct sequence of these cities from north to south will be-

A. 1, 2, 3, 4 **B.** 2, 1, 3, 4 **C.** 1, 2, 4, 3 **D.** 1, 4, 2, 3

Q.24 List-I to List-I. Match with and select the correct answer from the codes given below the lists-

List-I (Sagar Pullin)	List-II (State)
a. Digha	1. Tamil Nadu
b. Gopalpur	2. West Bengal
c. Kalangut	3. Odisha
d. Marina	4. Goa

A. 1, 2, 4, 3 **B.** 2, 3, 4, 1 **C.** 2, 1, 3, 4 **D.** 4, 3, 2, 1

Q.25 Which among the following about the Forest Report is/are correct?

1. ISFR is published by Forest Survey of India (FSI) biennially
2. ISFR 2019 is the 16th report in the pattern
3. Apart from forest and tree survey it also measures carbon stock and forest fires related data
4. ISFR 2019 has created the National forest inventory on produce from forests for the first time

Choose the correct option from the codes given below:

A. 1 & 2 **B.** 1, 2 & 4
C. 2, 3 & 4 **D.** 1, 2, 3 & 4

Q.26 Which of the following is the largest glacier?

A. Kanchenjunga **B.** Kedarnath
C. Gangotri **D.** Rundun

Q.27 Two statements are given below, one statement (A) and the other reason (R).

Statement (A)
The most dense seismic zone in India is located in the Himalayan region.

Reason (R)
The Himalayas have several longitudinal transverse zones.

A. Statement (A) and Reason (R) are both correct and Reason (R) is the correct explanation of statement (A)
B. Statements (A) and Reason (R) are both true but Reason (R) is not the correct explanation of statement (A)
C. Statement (A) is correct, but Reason (R) is false
D. Statement (A) is false, but Reason (R) is true

Q.28 Which is the highest quantity of salt found in ocean water?

A. Sodium chloride
B. Magnesium chloride
C. Calcium sulphate
D. Potassium sulphate

Q.29 With reference to the Bio-Technology Industry Research Assistance Council (BIRAC) consider the following statements:

1. It is a non-profit public sector enterprise.
2. It was established by the Department of Biotechnology (DBT), Government of India.

Which of the above statements is correct?

A. Only 1 **B.** Only 2
C. Both 1 and 2 **D.** Neither 1 nor 2

Q.30 The last part of which direction of India's land is called Indira Call?

A. East **B.** West **C.** North **D.** South

Q.31 Nagaland, Manipur, Mizoram and which state is going to touch the border of India and China?

A. Kerala **B.** Punjab
C. Bihar **D.** Arunachal Pradesh

Q.32 In which of the following hemispheres the Humboldt stream flows?

A. Eastern hemisphere
B. Western hemisphere
C. Northern hemisphere
D. Southern hemisphere

Q.33 Which of the following is called the "Warm Blanket of Europe"?

A. Gulfstream Stream **B.** Humboldt Stream
C. Currail stream **D.** None of these

Q.34 What percentage of the entire area of India is found on the plain?

A. 20 percent **B.** 40 percent
C. 44 percent **D.** 48 percent

Q.35 In which of the following countries is the Great Slave Lake located?

A. Japan **B.** India **C.** Africa **D.** Canada

Q.36 Which of the following is the smallest island in Japan?

A. Kyushu **B.** Shikoku
C. Tanegashima **D.** Yonaguni

Q.37 By what factor of erosion is the genesis of jugen?

A. By water **B.** By the wind
C. Both **D.** None of these

Q.38 The liquified cells below the surface of which of the following planets are called magma?

A. Earth **B.** Saturn **C.** Venus **D.** Arun

Q.39 Which of these volcanoes did not originate since historical times?

A. Dead volcano **B.** Gulfstream Volcano
C. Vesuviya Volcano **D.** None of these

Q.40 In which oceans does Mozambique flow?

A. Atlantic Ocean **B.** Pacific Ocean
C. Indian Ocean **D.** None of these

Q.41 Which of the following threats can be posed to the biodiversity of a geographical area?

1. Global heating

2. Fragmentation of the housing

3. Invasion of alien species

Select the correct answer using the code given below:

A. 1, 2 and 3
B. 2 and 3 only
C. 1 and 2 only
D. None of the appropriate

Q.42 With reference to acidic lava consider the following statements:

1. Acidic slag is highly viscous and has a high melting point.

2. It has a high percentage of silica content, low density and light color.

3. Acidic lava flows at a slow rate and rarely spreads far before freezing.

Which of the statements given above is / are correct?

A. 1 and 2 only **B.** 1 and 3 only
C. 2 and 3 only **D.** 1, 2 and 3

Q.43 With reference to the stages of development of the present atmosphere, consider the following statements:

1. The first envelope is marked as the collapse of the fundamental atmosphere.

2. In the second phase, the warm interior of the Earth contributed to the development of the atmosphere.

3. In the third phase, the structure of the atmosphere was modified by the living world through the process of light synthesis.

Which of the above statements is correct?

A. 1 and 2 only **B.** 1 and 3 only
C. 2 and 3 only **D.** 1, 2 and 3

Q.44 With reference to the ecosystem consider the following statements:

1. With the increase in the length of the food chain, the stability of the ecological system also increases.

2. With the increase in the number of chains in the food network, the stability of the ecosystem also increases.

Which of the above statements is correct?

A. Only 1 **B.** Only 2
C. Both 1 and 2 **D.** Neither 1 nor 2

Q.45 Who is called the father of geography?

A. Eratosthenes **B.** Herodotus
C. Hipparkus **D.** None of these

Q.46 In which of these states are the Satpura hills?

A. Delhi **B.** Rajasthan
C. Madhya Pradesh **D.** Uttar Pradesh

Q.47 The crater and caldera topography are related to which of the following?

A. Meteor **B.** Volcanic action
C. Wind action **D.** Glacial verb

Q.48 On which of the following dates the rays of the sun fall directly on the equatorial line-

A. 23 September
B. March 21
C. 21 March and 23 September
D. 20 June

Q.49 The leading producer of copper in the world is-

A. Australia **B.** China **C.** India **D.** Chili

Q.50 Which one of the following cities is closest to the equator?

A. Singapore **B.** Manila
C. Jakarta **D.** None of these

Q.51 Which of the following countries does not pass through the Tropic of Cancer?

A. Zaire **B.** China
C. India **D.** All of these

Q.52 What is the difference between the local time of two places in crossing a longitude?

A. 7 minutes **B.** 0 minutes
C. 4 minutes **D.** 1 minutes

Q.53 What percentage of the terrain is covered by sedimentary rocks?

A. 80% **B.** 75% **C.** 95% **D.** 68%

Q.54 The Sinai Peninsula is located at:

A. Between the Black Sea and the Mediterranean Sea
B. Between the Red Sea and the Arabian Sea
C. Between the Aral Sea and the Caspian Sea
D. Between the Mediterranean Sea and the Red Sea

Q.55 Which is the highest inert gas present in the atmosphere?

A. Krypton **B.** Helium **C.** Argon **D.** Neon

Q.56 Which of the following steel plants is not located in the iron ore zone?

A. Bhadravati **B.** Bhilai
C. Rourkela **D.** Jamshedpur

Q.57 Which line is found on both sides of the calm box?

A. Tropic of Cancer **B.** Equator
C. Tropic of Capricorn **D.** None of these

Q.58 Where is the world's highest volcanic mountain, Cotopaxi, located?

A. India
B. Japan
C. Germany
D. Ecuador

Q.59 What percentage of the world population lives in the plateau areas?

A. 4%
B. 6%
C. 9%
D. 50%

Q.60 On which river is the Hirakud Dam built?

A. Mahanadi
B. Godavari
C. Cauvery
D. Periyar

Q.61 From which surface of the Earth do long radio waves reflect?

A. Ion board
B. Troposphere
C. Plane board
D. All of these

Q.62 In which South American country is the Atacama Desert?

A. Brazil
B. Chile
C. Peru
D. None of these

Q.63 Which island is in dispute between India and Sri Lanka?

A. Delft Island
B. Pamban Island
C. Kachchatheevu
D. None of these

Q.64 The lines in the map where the pressure is even are called-

A. Latitude lines
B. Isobar lines
C. Longitudinal lines
D. Isotopic lines

Q.65 With reference to the global distribution of rainfall, consider the following statements.

1. The latitudes of $35°$ and $40°$ in the north and south of the equator decrease towards the west.

2. However, rainfall occurs between north and south of the equator and between latitudes in the western part of the first continents, which progressively decrease as they move east.

Which of the above statements is correct?

A. Only 1
B. Only 2
C. Both 1 and 2
D. Neither 1 nor 2

Q.66 What type of forests are found near the equator?

A. Deciduous forest
B. Tropical forest
C. Coniferous forest
D. Grassland forest

Q.67 Which one of the following countries is not a major producer of natural gas?

A. South Africa
B. Norway
C. United Kingdom
D. Russia

Q.68 The "Oder-Nees line" is the border between which country?

A. Israel and Palestine
B. Germany and Poland
C. China and Vietnam
D. Mexico and USA

Q.69 Which of the following countries has the world's largest reserves of uranium?

A. Russia
B. Kazakhstan
C. Australia
D. Jordan

Q.70 With reference to the type of mountains, consider the following statements-

1. The earth's crust for the formation of Mount Bhrotshoth involves both compression and tension, while the construction of the mountain mainly involves compression.

2. The Andes is an example of a mountain of fault, while Vosges is an example of a mountain.

Which of the above statement is correct?

A. Only 1
B. Only 2
C. Both 1 and 2
D. Neither 1 nor 2

Q.71 Consider the following statements regarding latitude and longitude:

1. Latitude is measured as the angular distance of a point north or south of the equator on the Earth's surface.

2. Both the latitude and longitude of a place are measured from the center of the Earth.

Which of the statements given above is/are correct?

A. Only 1
B. Only 2
C. Both 1 and 2
D. Neither 1 nor 2

Q.72 Why don't people drown in the Dead Sea?

A. Due to the presence of sea creatures in the sea
B. Lower Dead Sea temperatures provide swimmers greater solidity
C. Excess concentration of salt in the Dead Sea increases the density of water
D. The depth of thermocline (rapid heat change) is located near the surface in the Dead Sea.

Q.73 The National Inland Navigation Institute is situated in which of the following places?

A. Patna
B. Balasore
C. Bangalore
D. Dehradun

Q.74 Consider the following statements regarding earthquakes:

1. All natural earthquakes occur in the lithosphere.

2. The point where the energy comes out is called the epicenter.

Which of the above statements is correct?

A. Only 1
B. Only 2
C. Both 1 and 2
D. Neither 1 nor 2

Q.75 Which of the following areas can best be described through a "bush-weld" landscape?

A. Steppe grasslands
B. Mediterranean region
C. Savanna grasslands
D. Hot desert

Q.76 Referred to in Indian geology, the Malda fault separates:

A. From Satpura mountain range to Vindhya mountain range
B. From the Aravalli mountain range to the Delhi mountain range
C. From Western Ghats to Eastern Ghats
D. From the peninsular plateau to the Meghalaya plateau

Q.77 With reference to the multi-tropical cyclones in the Northern Hemisphere, consider the following statements:

They are manufactured along with the vatras.

They can develop both on site and on water.

They move from east to west.

Which of the above statements is correct?

A. 1 and 2 only
B. Only 1
C. 2 and 3 only
D. 1, 2 and 3

Q.78 Which of the following statements is/are correct with reference to Western disturbances?

These are light cyclonic avalanches originating over the East Sea.

A sudden drop in normal night temperatures indicates their arrival in India.

They are highly beneficial for rabi crops in northern India.

Select the correct answer using the codes given below.

A. 1 and 2 only
B. Only 2
C. 1 and 3 only
D. 1, 2 and 4

Q.79 In the context of Indian geography, Kareva is-

A. Deposition of glacial clay and other substances in the Kashmir Himalayas as a thick layer on the snow
B. Alluvial plume formed by tributaries of Indus in the northwestern region of India
C. Narrow strip of wet and dense forests with low-level runoff in the foothills of the Himalayas
D. Existing deserts in the Thar Desert

Q.80 At which of the following limits of Plato does a new crust be constructed?

1. Convergence limit
2. Divergent boundary
3. Conversion range

Select the correct answer using the codes given below.

A. 1 and 2 onl
B. Only 2
C. 1 and 3 only
D. 1, 2 and 3

Q.81 Rattan and liana are some types of flora, which climate is found in which of the following?

A. In warm desert region
B. In temperate grassland
C. In the arctic region
D. In equatorial region

Q.82 The houses with two huts placed at the right angle and a rectangular courtyard enclosed by the fence are the common features of settlements of which of the following places of India?

A. Northern plains
B. Himalayan regions
C. Peninsular regions
D. Coastal regions

Q.83 Recently, the color of Lonar Lake in Maharashtra changed to pink. In this context, which of the following reasons can cause a change in color?

A. Toxins emitted by a species of crabs
B. Increase in pollution level due to industrial effluents flowing by rivers
C. Chemical reactions caused by meteorite dust falling into the lake
D. Algae behavior change

Q.84 With reference to the Lakshadweep archipelago, which of the following statements is correct?

A. The entire island group is made up of coral deposits
B. Norcondam is a small volcanic island in the Lakshadweep group
C. The highest peak of the Lakshadweep archipelago is Saddle Peak
D. Eleven degree channel separates Lakshadweep from Maldives

Q.85 Singfan Wildlife Sanctuary was declared Elephant Reserve. It is located in the state.

A. Karnataka
B. Kerala
C. Jharkhand
D. Nagaland

Q.86 Which of the following options is characteristic of Stenothermal or Tanupati organisms?

A. These organisms can live only in places with extremely low temperatures
B. These organisms can tolerate only a very limited range of temperature
C. These organisms migrate to hibernation during winter
D. These organisms can tolerate a wide range of temperatures and grow

Q.87 Generally, standards in 'Organic Farming' are designed to encourage the use of which of the following?

A. Natural substances
B. Genetically modified substances
C. Artificial substances
D. Manmade substances

Q.88 Consider the following statements regarding the solstice:

1. During the Yisma solstice in the Northern Hemisphere, the rays of the Sun fall directly on the Tropic of Cancer.
2. The length of day and night are equal during the winter solstice.

Which of the statements given above is/are correct?

A. Only 1
B. Only 2
C. Both 1 and 2
D. Neither 1 nor 2

Q.89 Chakal, a part of bubble gum, is made from which of the following milky juice?

A. Of banana
B. Of rubber
C. Of japota
D. None of these

Q.90 The process of increasing the load of debris and slowing downward as a result of the saturation of debris and weathering strength due to rainfall in the upper part of a slope or valley is called-

A. Landslide
B. Avalanche
C. Slides
D. Indulgence

Q.91 Which of the following factors affects the erosion and transport of rocks?

1. Air
2. flowing water
3. Harmony
Select the correct answer using the code given below.

A. 1 and 2 only
B. Only 3
C. 1 and 3 only
D. 1, 2 and 3

Q.92 Which of the following activities are considered primary activities?

1. Fishing
2. Mining and Excavation
3. Iron and Steel Industries
Select the correct answer using the code given below.

A. 1 and 2 only
B. 2 and 3 only
C. Only 1
D. 1, 2 and 3

Q.93 Which of the following are characteristics of hot, humid equatorial climate?

A. Winter only
B. Rain throughout the year
C. Dry and humid weather
D. Dry weather

Q.94 Which of the following is/are the major source area of air signs?

1. Warm Tropical and Subtropical Oceans
2. Subtropical Warm Desert
3. Relatively cold high latitudinal oceans
Which of the statements given above is/are correct?

A. 1 and 2 only
B. 1 and 3 only
C. 2 and 3 only
D. 1, 2 and 3

Q.95 Which of the following Indian states share a border with China?

1. Assam
2. Punjab
3. Sikkim
4. Arunachal Pradesh
Select the correct answer using the code given below:

A. 1 and 2 only
B. 3 and 4 only
C. 1, 3 and 4 only
D. Only 4

Q.96 When the cold air moves towards the warm air, its convergence zone is called?

A. Permanent atmosphere
B. Cold atmosphere
C. Warm atmosphere
D. Blocked atmosphere

Q.97 With reference to the Masai tribe, consider the following statements:

1. They live in parts of Brazil and Argentina.
2. They are semi-nomadic and cattle herders.
Which of the above statements is correct?

A. Only 1
B. Only 2
C. Both 1 and 2
D. Neither 1 nor 2

Q.98 Which of the following countries/countries has the status of observer state in SCO?

1. Afghanistan
2. Nepal
3. Mongolia
4. Sri Lanka
Select the correct answer using the code given below:

A. 1 and 2 only
B. 1 and 3 only
C. 2 and 4 only
D. 3 and 4 only

Q.99 Igloo, a type of shelter, is a major feature of which of the following?

A. Bushman's
B. Gurjar's
C. Eskimo's
D. Of aborigines

Q.100 The Sargasso Sea in the Atlantic Ocean is notorious for:

A. For a large amount of floating sea weed and poor marine life
B. High storm surge to hamper shipping
C. For high seismic activity for volcanoes and earthquakes
D. Neither of the above

Q.101 With reference to the Panama Canal consider the following statements:

1. It connects the Atlantic Ocean to the Pacific Ocean.
2. It reduces the distance between New York and San Francisco by sea by 130 km.
Which one of the above statements?

A. Only 1
B. Only 2
C. Both 1 and 2
D. Neither 1 nor 2

Q.102 When a village is developed around a lake and tank, which of the following patterns of rural design can be found?

A. Circular pattern
B. Rectangular pattern
C. Star pattern
D. Y shaped pattern

Q.103 With reference to the hot spot volcano, consider the following statements:

1. Hot spot volcanoes originate at the boundaries of the Earth's tectonic plates.
2. The volcano above the hot spot does not always erupt.
Which of the above statements are correct?

A. Only 1
B. Only 2
C. Both 1 and 2
D. Neither 1 nor 2

Q.104 In which year, Arunachal Pradesh became a full-fledged state of India?

A. 1985
B. 1986
C. 1987
D. 1988

Q.105 Which of the following regions in India represents lowest altitude?

A. Kuttanad region in Kerala
B. Saurashtra Region in Karnataka
C. Coromandel of Tamil Nadu
D. Malabar region of Kerala

Q.106 The place "Noonmati" in India, is related to which among the following?

A. Salt Industry   **B.** Petroleum Industry

C. Paper Industry   **D.** Textile Industry

Q.107 Sundarbans in India is a fine example of which among the following kind of forests?

A. Dry Forests

B. Deciduous Forests

C. Tidal Forests

D. Wet Deciduous Forests

Q.108 Consider the following statements:

1. In India, monazite and thorium are the principal source of rare earths elements

2. India is self sufficient in Rare Earth elements

Which among the above statements are correct?

A. Only 1 is correct

B. Only 2 is correct

C. Both 1 & 2 are correct

D. Neither 1 nor 2 is correct

Q.109 All trees/ plants of which of the following sets are abundant in Western Himalayas?

A. Chir, Pine, Deodar, Red Sanders

B. Oaks, Deodar, Coffee, Betel nut

C. Pine, Spruce, Silver Fir, Silver Birch

D. Chir, Pine, Coffee, Deodar

Q.110 With reference to cultivation of Cotton in India, which among the following statements are correct?

1. Approximately 65% of India's cotton is produced on rainfed areas

2. Majority of the cotton is produced in central zone comprising Maharashtra, Madhya Pradesh and Gujarat

Choose the correct option from the codes given below:

A. Only 1   **B.** Only 2

C. Both 1 & 2   **D.** Neither 1 nor 2

Q.111 Rajghat River Valley Project is associated to which river?

A. Yamuna   **B.** Chambal   **C.** Betwa   **D.** Son

Q.112 Consider the following pairs of hills with their states:

List-I (Hills)	List-II (States)
1. Khandadhar	Odisha
2. Biligiriranga	Karnataka
3. Lushai	Assam

Which of the above are correctly matched?

A. 1 Only   **B.** 1 & 2 Only

C. 1, 2 & 3   **D.** None

Q.113 Consider the following statements about the Angami tribals of India:

1. The people from this tribe live predominantly in the extreme north east part of India

2. The main festival of this tribe is Moatsu

3. Christianity is the major religion followed among the Angami tribal people

Which among the above are correct statements?

A. Only 1 & 2   **B.** Only 2 & 3

C. Only 1 & 3   **D.** 1, 2 & 3

Q.114 The Pichavaram mangrove forest is one of the India's largest mangrove forests. Pichavaram mangrove is located in which of the following states?

A. Tamil Nadu   **B.** Kerala

C. West Bengal   **D.** Gujarat

Q.115 Bhalia wheat is a long grain of wheat, which has high protein content and is grown without irrigation for centuries. It is grown in which state of India?

A. Punjab   **B.** Gujarat

C. Madhya Pradesh   **D.** Jammu & Kashmir

Q.116 Which of the following climatic conditions leads to the optimum growth of rubber trees in India?

1. Evenly distributed rainfall of around 250 centimeters without any dry season

2. Temperature in the range 21-27 degrees

3. Flat land with well drained soil

4. High Humidity

Select the correct option from codes given below:

A. 1, 2 & 3 Only   **B.** 1, 3 & 4 Only

C. 2, 3 & 4 Only   **D.** 1, 2, 3 & 4

Q.117 Which mountain of the Himalayan range is the highest mountain of India?

A. Everest   **B.** Cardamom

C. Karakoram   **D.** Kanchenjunga

Q.118 Lakshadweep in India's South Western coast comes from the Sanskrit word for which number?

A. 1,000,000   **B.** 100,000

C. 10,000   **D.** 1,000

Q.119 Which of the following has maximum bio-diversity?

A. River   **B.** Desert

C. Tropical Region   **D.** Polar Region

Q.120 Which among the following South Indian states shared its boundary with the maximum number of other states?

A. Tamil Nadu   **B.** Kerala

C. Andhra Pradesh   **D.** Karnataka

Q.121 The evolution of the peninsular region is considered as the resultant of which of the following?

A. Geosyncline Evolution

B. Cenozoic folding

C. Platform Evolution

D. None of the above

Q.122 The region lies between the Chota Nagpur Plateau on the West and the Ganges Delta on the East is known as which of the following?

A. Dooars   **B.** Rahr   **C.** Tarai   **D.** Bhabar

Q.123 Pir Panjal Pass provides the easiest access between which of the following places?

A. Kashmir and Kargil

B. Jammu and the valley of Kashmir

C. Leh and Siachen Glacier

D. None of the above

Q.124 Which one of the following regions of India has the characteristic features of Deserts, fertile plains and moderately forested mountains?

A. South-Western border along Arabian Sea

B. North-Western India

C. North-Eastern Frontier

D. Coromandel Coast

Q.125 The dependency of fuelwood on the forest is highest in which of the following states of India?

A. Madhya Pradesh

B. Karnataka

C. Maharashtra

D. Gujarat

// Smart Answer Sheet //

Correct	Indicates percentage of students who answered questions correctly.
Skipped	Indicates percentage of students who skipped questions.

Q.	Ans.	Correct / Skipped
1	B	87.42 % / 0.0 %
2	D	46.6 % / 1.83 %
3	C	89.88 % / 0.0 %
4	B	45.59 % / 1.11 %
5	C	81.59 % / 0.0 %
6	C	56.7 % / 1.86 %
7	C	24.52 % / 3.43 %
8	B	56.19 % / 1.81 %
9	B	87.07 % / 0.0 %
10	A	41.85 % / 1.41 %
11	B	29.5 % / 4.57 %
12	A	47.48 % / 1.38 %
13	C	53.74 % / 1.27 %
14	A	41.33 % / 1.96 %
15	D	11.28 % / 4.91 %
16	A	27.27 % / 4.41 %

Q.	Ans.	Correct / Skipped
17	C	52.99 % / 1.24 %
18	B	28.76 % / 3.61 %
19	D	68.24 % / 1.38 %
20	C	77.67 % / 0.0 %
21	C	86.85 % / 0.0 %
22	A	66.3 % / 1.18 %
23	D	14.88 % / 3.1 %
24	B	22.52 % / 4.25 %
25	D	69.69 % / 1.01 %
26	C	69.98 % / 1.07 %
27	A	30.69 % / 3.5 %
28	A	64.03 % / 1.73 %
29	C	65.11 % / 1.96 %
30	C	65.37 % / 1.96 %
31	D	47.33 % / 1.33 %
32	D	11.96 % / 4.76 %

Q.	Ans.	Correct / Skipped
33	A	47.3 % / 1.21 %
34	C	78.84 % / 0.0 %
35	D	69.24 % / 1.02 %
36	B	47.06 % / 1.04 %
37	B	21.85 % / 3.82 %
38	A	77.83 % / 0.0 %
39	A	45.42 % / 1.48 %
40	C	65.98 % / 1.37 %
41	A	32.31 % / 4.79 %
42	D	60.56 % / 1.01 %
43	D	58.83 % / 1.98 %
44	C	52.23 % / 1.41 %
45	A	59.18 % / 1.23 %
46	C	45.18 % / 1.26 %
47	B	63.42 % / 1.34 %
48	C	78.75 % / 0.0 %

Q.	Ans.	Correct / Skipped
49	D	42.8 % / 1.3 %
50	A	63.9 % / 1.93 %
51	A	89.68 % / 0.0 %
52	C	31.08 % / 3.77 %
53	B	63.13 % / 1.3 %
54	D	78.22 % / 0.0 %
55	C	55.51 % / 1.08 %
56	D	57.56 % / 1.16 %
57	B	77.88 % / 0.0 %
58	D	51.31 % / 1.62 %
59	C	66.75 % / 1.81 %
60	A	40.99 % / 1.33 %
61	A	12.62 % / 3.67 %
62	B	53.64 % / 1.37 %
63	C	67.08 % / 1.71 %
64	B	63.01 % / 1.76 %

Q.	Ans.	Correct / Skipped
65	C	14.28 % / 3.55 %
66	B	56.59 % / 1.82 %
67	A	52.13 % / 1.42 %
68	B	21.52 % / 4.2 %
69	C	76.71 % / 0.0 %
70	A	16.44 % / 3.04 %
71	C	32.2 % / 3.96 %
72	C	18.98 % / 4.42 %
73	A	40.63 % / 1.5 %
74	A	28.91 % / 4.74 %
75	C	51.2 % / 1.51 %
76	D	57.03 % / 1.71 %
77	A	21.14 % / 3.52 %
78	C	16.54 % / 4.26 %
79	A	52.57 % / 1.03 %
80	B	63.63 % / 1.37 %

Q.	Ans.	Correct / Skipped	Q.	Ans.	Correct / Skipped	Q.	Ans.	Correct / Skipped	Q.	Ans.	Correct / Skipped	Q.	Ans.	Correct / Skipped
81	D	31.75 % / 4.12 %	90	D	57.7 % / 1.51 %	99	C	50.23 % / 1.03 %	108	A	52.73 % / 1.69 %	117	D	58.65 % / 1.39 %
82	C	44.47 % / 1.77 %	91	D	43.42 % / 1.49 %	100	A	58.01 % / 1.57 %	109	C	60.06 % / 1.49 %	118	B	46.12 % / 1.26 %
83	D	22.22 % / 4.12 %	92	A	53.46 % / 1.18 %	101	A	54.47 % / 1.39 %	110	C	32.06 % / 4.17 %	119	C	56.84 % / 1.25 %
84	A	17.83 % / 4.53 %	93	B	45.44 % / 1.81 %	102	A	41.57 % / 1.51 %	111	C	54.99 % / 1.44 %	120	D	88.69 % / 0.0 %
85	D	89.34 % / 0.0 %	94	D	27.36 % / 3.75 %	103	B	50.27 % / 1.31 %	112	B	78.64 % / 0.0 %	121	C	52.31 % / 1.52 %
86	B	58.35 % / 2.0 %	95	B	87.83 % / 0.0 %	104	C	40.66 % / 1.56 %	113	C	29.95 % / 3.08 %	122	B	57.46 % / 1.3 %
87	A	49.47 % / 1.5 %	96	B	18.49 % / 3.66 %	105	A	56.8 % / 1.31 %	114	A	81.72 % / 0.0 %	123	B	40.3 % / 1.82 %
88	A	19.57 % / 3.55 %	97	B	62.89 % / 1.79 %	106	B	44.35 % / 1.93 %	115	B	44.73 % / 1.65 %	124	B	84.34 % / 0.0 %
89	C	63.56 % / 1.44 %	98	B	62.45 % / 1.88 %	107	C	66.46 % / 1.68 %	116	D	44.66 % / 1.72 %	125	C	57.2 % / 1.3 %

Performance Analysis

Avg. Score (%)	43.06%
Toppers Score (%)	72.94%
Your Score	

//Hints and Solutions//

1. Bishrampur is famous for coal mine. Bisrampur (or Bishrampur) coal mine is a 3 million ton-per-annum (MTPA) coal mine in Chhattisgarh state, India.

Hence, the correct option is (B).

2. The coastline of Tamil Nadu is called the Coromandel Coast. The eastern coastal region is divided into three parts - Utkal Beach, North SirCar or Royal Border Coast and Coromandel Coast. The western coast is divided into the Konkan Coast and the Malabar Coast.

Hence, the correct option is (D).

3. The Chaurabadi Glacier is located to the north of the Kedarnath Temple in the Rudraprayag district of Uttarakhand.

Hence, the correct option is (C).

4. The Himalayan glaciers have the highest melting speed. The Gangotri glacier at the origin of the Ganges River is rapidly melting. As a result, its expansion work has been reduced to almost half as compared to the last 50 years.

Hence, the correct option is (B).

5. The Milan glacier is the main glacier located in the Kumaon region of Uttarakhand. This glacier originates from the Sharda River (Kali Ganga).

Hence, the correct option is (C).

6. The western coastal plain of India is narrow, its northern part is called the Konkan Coast and the southern part is the Malabar Coast, while the eastern coastal plain includes the northern Sircar coast and the Coromandel Coast. The northern Sircar coast extends from the Godavari delta to the northern coastal part, While the Coromandel Coast extends to the Kanyakumari Krishna Delta.

Hence, the correct option is (C).

7. (a) Jelep La Pass connects East Sikkim district with Lhasa (Tibet).

(b) The two passes connecting Tibet in the hills of Garhwal (Uttarakhand) are Niti and Mana (5068 m elevation).

(c) Shipki La Pass (5571 m altitude) connecting Tibet is located in Kinnaur district of Himachal Pradesh.

(d) Bomdi La Pass connects Arunachal Pradesh (Western Kameng District) and Lhasa (Tijat).

It is clear that Shipki La Jammu and Kashmir is not well matched.

Hence, the correct option is (C).

8. The Lipulekh pass is located in the Pithoragarh district of Uttarakhand state, this pass is also used for the Kailash Mansarovar Yatra.

Hence, the correct option is (B).

9. The 'Mana Pass' extends from the Nanda Devi Biosphere Reserve area in the state of Uttarakhand to the eastern end of the Zaskar mountain range.

10. The King-Wing is the Neeti-Mana Passes. Niti Pass is a major pass in the Himalayas connecting the Uttarakhand state of India with Tibet. The Maana or Mana Pass is located between India and Tibet in the Himalayan region, also known as Chiribitiya or Dungri La. In this pass is the Deoria Tal Lake from where Saraswati, a tributary of the Alaknanda, originates.

Hence, the correct option is (A).

11. The Gurla Mandhata mountain peak is not located in India but near the northwest border of Nepal in western Tibet. The same type of Namcha Barwa mountain peak is also located in southeast Tibet (China) near the Arunachal Pradesh border. Thus both the Gurla Mandhata and the Namcha Barwa are not located in India. Kamet Mountains in the Garhwal region of Uttarakhand and Nanga Parbat jams of India. And is located in Kashmir (Pak-occupied territory).

Hence, the correct option is (B).

12. "Gauralata" peak is located on the Chando hill range of Samaripat. It is located in the state of Chhattisgarh. The height of this mountain peak is about 1225 meters.

Hence, the correct option is (A).

13. Shipki La is located in Himachal Pradesh, Bomdi La in Arunachal Pradesh and Nathu La in Sikkim. Zojila was located in Jammu and Kashmir during the Question Hour. From October 31, 2019, Zoji La Nathu La is located in Kargil district of Union Territory of Ladakh. Nathu La is about 55 km from Gangtok, the capital of Sikkim in the Indian territory. Located in the east, which opens into the Chumbi Valley of the Tibetan Plateau in the Chinese region.

Hence, the correct option is (C).

14. Zoji La connects Greenagar to Leh. The Banihal pass connects Jammu to Srinagar, while Shipki La connects Himachal Pradesh to Tibet.

Hence, the correct option is (A).

15. The Western Ghats extend about 1500 km parallel to the Western Sea coast. It is found in the length from the mouth of Tapi in the north to Kumari Antripe in the south. These are the Block Mountains, which have been formed due to the desalination of a section of the site in the Arabian Sea. Its western slope is steep and steep, while the eastern slope is low and sideline or lowered plateau respectively. The Western Ghats up to 16 ° north latitude are mainly composed of basalt rocks and south granite and fine rocks from Goa.

Hence, the correct option is (D).

16. The correct sequence of reliefs given in the question is moving from west to east- Mahadev mountain range, Maikal mountain range, Chhotanagpur mountain range and Khasi hills. The Mahadev and Maikal ranges are located as the eastern extension of the Satpura range. To the east are the Chotanagpur range and the Khasi hills (Meghalaya) in the east.

Hence, the correct option is (A).

17. The Nilgiri hills are located at the meeting point of the Eastern Ghats and Western Ghats of the Indian Peninsula. The Nilgiri hills is also known as the Blue Mountains. Its highest peak is Doddabetta (about 2637 m high).

Hence, the correct option is (C).

18. Aravali range is about 800 km from Palanpur in Gujarat to Delhi via Rajasthan and Haryana. Spreads a length of. It was built in the pre-Cambrian period, which is believed to date from 600 to 570 million years ago. It is the oldest mountain range in India, while one of the oldest mountain ranges in the world. Its highest peak is Guru Shikhar (1722 m).

Hence, the correct option is (B).

19. The total length of India's coastline is 7516 km. A total of nine states and four union territories are located on the coastline of India. The state of Gujarat has the longest coastline in these states.

Hence, the correct option is (D).

20. A total of 9 states of India are along the coast line. In India, the Tropic of Cancer passes through these states. Total 8 states Chhattisgarh West Bengal, Rajasthan, Gujarat, Madhya Pradesh, Mizoram, Tripura, Jharkhand.

Hence, the correct option is (C).

21. Ancient Indian historical evidence relates the Indian Ocean to the Jewel of mine.

Hence, the correct option is (C).

22. In coastal erosion, sea waves, tides, currents, tsunami waves and human activities etc. have a major role. Most of these coastal erosions is caused by waves.

Hence, the correct option is (A).

23. The correct sequence from north to south of the above mentioned cities on the western coast is as follows:

Janjira - In Raigad district of Maharashtra

Sindhudurg - in the Indus Durg district of Maharashtra

Kannur - in Kannur district of Kerala

Nagercoil - in Kanyakumari district of Tamil Nadu state

Hence, the correct option is (D).

24. The reconciliation of the given sea bridges and their respective states is as follows:

List-I (Sagar Pullin)	List-II (State)
a. Digha	1. West Bengal
b. Gopalpur	2. Odisha
c. Kalangut	3. Goa
d. Marina	4. Tamil Nadu

Hence, the correct option is (B).

25. India State of Forest Report (ISFR) is published by Forest Survey of India (FSI) biennially. ISFR 2019 is the 16th report in the pattern. Apart from forest and tree surveys it also measures carbon stock and forest fires related data. ISFR 2019 has created the National forest inventory on produce from forests for the first time.

Hence, the correct option is (D).

26. The lengths of the glaciers given in the above question are as follows:

Gangotri Glacier - 26 km

Rundun Glacier - 19 km

Kanchenjunga Glacier -16 km

Kedarnath glacier - 14 km

Hence, the correct option is (C).

27. The most dense seismic zone in India is located in the Himalayan region. Most of this region falls in Seismic zone IV and V. This region includes the northeastern India, Jammu and the regions of Kashmir, Ladakh, Himachal Pradesh, Uttarakhand, and the Himalayas extend into these areas in India. In the Himalayas, many longitudinal curves and fractures / cracks are found.

Hence, the correct option is (A).

28. The salinity or salinity is the weight of water and the proportion of salts mixed in it. Water is saline due to high salinity in oceans, seas and some lakes, and it is sweet or fresh due to lack of salinity in the water of rivers. The average salinity in oceanic waters is 35% but its volume is found between 30 and 40 in different seas. Sodium chloride (77.8 percent) and magnesium chloride (10.9 percent) have the highest amount of salts found in ocean water. Among other salts, magnesium sulfate (4.7 percent), calcium sulfate (3.6 percent) and potassium sulfate (2.5 percent) are important. There is a significant variation in the amount of salinity in different seas and lakes and in different parts of the ocean for which the factors responsible are rainwater supply, evaporation volume, water supply and expulsion, ocean currents, prevailing wind etc.

Hence, the correct option is (A).

29. The Biotechnology Industry Research Assistance Council (BIRAC) is a non-profit public sector enterprise, established by the Department of Biotechnology (DBT), Government of India. It is an intermediary agency, which aims to promote, nurture and implement research by providing financial, structural, institutional and advisory support to strengthen and empower biotech industries.

Hence, the correct option is (C).

30. The last part of the north of the land of India is called Indira Call.

Indira Call which is a Call or hill pass in Indira Cuttack of Siachen Muztag subcategory of Karakoram ranges. The naming of Indira Call was discovered in 1912 by Bulk Workman.

Hence, the correct option is (C).

31. Nagaland, Manipur, Mizoram and Arunachal Pradesh are going to touch the border of India and China.

Arunachal Pradesh in which the word Arunachal means "Mount of the Rising Sun". Arunachal Pradesh, Nagaland, Manipur, Mizoram touch the border of India and China. This state was granted full statehood on February 20, 1987.

Hence, the correct option is (D).

32. The Humboldt stream flows in the northern hemisphere.

The Humboldt stream, also known as the Piru stream, is an ocean current of cold water flowing into the Pacific Ocean. Which flows from south to north along the west coast of South America, it is called Humboldt stream.

Hence, the correct option is (D).

33. The stream of Gulfstream is called the "Warm blanket of Europe".

The Gulfstream stream is a major ocean water stream flowing into the dark ocean, also known as the "warm blanket of Europe." In this stream, the water becomes blue and hot.

Hence, the correct option is (A).

34. Plain expanse is found in about 44 percent of the area in India.

Hence, the correct option is (C).

35. Great Slave Lake which is the second largest lake in Northern Canada. Its depth is 614 meters.

Hence, the correct option is (D).

36. Shikoku Island is the smallest island in Japan.

Shikoku Island is the smallest island among the four main islands of Japan and is also sparsely populated. It is 225 km long and has a width of 50 to 150 km.

Hence, the correct option is (B).

37. The jugen is produced by the wind of erosion.

The jugen when in the desert areas, rocks with soft formations are laid in a horizontal form on top of hard rocks. The air then cuts off the soft rocks from which the jugen originates.

Hence, the correct option is (B).

38. Magma is a molten form of rock that is formed by solid, half-molten or fully molten rocks and is formed below the surface of the Earth. The exit form of magma is called lava.

Hence, the correct option is (A).

39. Dead volcanoes did not originate since historical times, these are volcanoes that have no possibility of eruption in the future and lakes have been formed due to flooding of their mouths. Kilimanjaro of Africa, Mount Popa of Myanmar, Koh Sultan of Iran and Demband, Chimbarajo of South America.

Hence, the correct option is (A).

40. The Mozambique stream is a warm ocean current flowing in the Indian Ocean, which flows southwards through the Mozambique channel, a branch of the south equatorial stream. This stream is also called Agulhas stream.

Hence, the correct option is (C).

41. All of the above factors pose a threat to biodiversity.

Biodiversity refers to the diversity of plants and organisms located in the world or in a particular habitat, the high level of which is generally considered important and desirable.

Threat to biodiversity:

- Housing fragmentation

- Invasion of alien species

- Pollution

- Global heating

-Climate change

-Deforestation

- Illegal hunting

- Mining

Hence, the correct option is (A).

42. Acidic or mixed slag is highly viscous and has a high melting point. It has a high percentage of silica content, low density and light color.

Acidic lava flows slowly and they rarely spread far before freezing. It forms a cone-like structure, with steep edges.

Acidic lava settles rapidly, thus preventing the flow of new lava, resulting in loud explosions (volcanic bombs).

Hence the correct option is (D).

43. There are a total of three stages of development of the present atmosphere. The first phase is characterized as the collapse of the fundamental atmosphere. In the second phase, the warm interior of the Earth contributed to the development of the atmosphere. Finally, the structure of the atmosphere was modified by the living world through the process of photosynthesis.

Hence, the correct option is (D).

44. Ecosystem refers to the biological community related to the interaction of organisms and their physical environment with the increase in the number of chains in the food network, with the stability of the ecosystem also increasing. And at the same time, with the increase in the length of the food chain, the stability of the ecosystem also increases. This has been proved through various field trials.

अतः विकल्प (C) सही है।

45. Eratosthenes (276 BCE to 195–194 BCE) is called the father of geography. Eratosthenes was a mathematician, geographer, poet, astronomer, and music theorist of Greece. Established geography as a separate study of scripture and used the term GEOGRAPHICA for geography. Therefore, he is also called the father of systematic geography.

Hence, the correct option is (A).

46. The Satpura hills are located in the central part of India. This mountain range extends from Gujarat through Madhya Pradesh and Maharashtra to Chhattisgarh, Satpura and Vindhyachal

mountain ranges divide India into the Gangetic plain and Deccan plateau to the south.

Hence, the correct option is (C).

47. The volcano, or volcanic crater, is a round shaped crater on the ground caused by the eruption of a volcano. Generally the floor of this pit is flat and molten stones, gases and other volcanic materials come out of a hole in it. Many times a cave filled with lava inside the volcano settles down its roof and forms a cavity crater, but it is not a cavity but a volcanic reservoir or "caldera".

Hence, the correct option is (B).

48. The Sun passes through the sky in its occasional move, twice a year, just above the equator on 21 March and 23 September. These days, the rays of the sun at the equator are perpendicular to the surface of the earth.

Hence, the correct option is (C).

49. Chili is the largest producer of copper in the world. After Chili, the United States is the place in which copper is used to make various types of alloys, such as copper and tin mixtures of bronze and copper and zinc are made of brass. Copper is a physical element.

Hence, the correct option is (D).

50. Singapore is closest to the equator (0° latitude). Singapore is located just 137 km from the equator.

Hence, the correct option is (A).

51. The Congo River, also known as the Zaire River, is a major river in Africa. This river, covering a distance of 4,700 kilometers, is the largest in West Central Africa and the longest river in Africa after the Nile River. The Congo River is the second most water-rich river in the world, after the Amazon River in South America.

Hence, the correct option is (A).

52. In crossing a longitude there is a 4 minute difference between the local time of two places.

The Earth rotates 360 degrees on its axis in the day (24 hours = 24 X 60 minutes = 1440 minutes).

So the time taken to cross the 1 degree longitude line $=$
$$\frac{1440}{360} = 4 \text{ minutes}$$

Hence, the correct option is (C).

53. 75% of the surface is covered by sedimentary rocks. The rock formed by sediments as a result of dissolution, separation and breakage of the original rocks by various means of weathering and erosion and their sediments as a result of deposition at some place is called sedimentary rock.

Hence, the correct option is (B).

54. The Sinai Peninsula of Egypt is a disorganized desert region between the Red Sea and the Mediterranean Sea.

Hence, the correct option is (D).

55. The largest amount of inert gas in the atmosphere is an argon. Inert means inert, the maximum amount of Argon Ar is - .934% i.e. about 1%. This is followed by neon and helium.

Hence, the correct option is (C).

56. The Jamshedpur Steel Plant receives iron ore from Noamundi in Sehbhum district of Jharkhand state and Gurumahisani mines in Mayurbhanj district, which is located about 100 km away.

Hence, the correct option is (D).

57. There are low pressure boxes up to 10 ° degrees on both sides of the equator. Winds are peaceful here, so it is called Shanti Patti or Doldrum.

Hence, the correct option is (B).

58. Cotopaxi is one of the highest volcanic mountains in the world. The last originated in it was in 1942 AD.

Located in Ecuador, Cotopaxi is the highest and volcanic mountain in the world. It is currently in active state. Its height is 5911 meters.

Hence, the correct option is (D).

59. Plateau areas are inhabited by 9% of the world's population. Plateau is very important in the second class land forms found on land and they are found on 33% of the total land area.

Hence, the correct option is (C).

60. Hirakud Dam is a dam built on the Mahanadi in Odisha. It is 15 km from Sambalpur. Built on the Mahanadi in 1957, this dam is one of the longest dams in the world. Its total length is 25.8 km. There is a huge reservoir behind this dam.

Hence, the correct option is (A).

61. The highest is in the transmission of radio waves (electromagnetic waves). Gases of the ionosphere are ionized by the sun's ultraviolet rays and by other high-energy rays and granules. The electromagnetic waves are reflected from the E-layer or the Canali heavyside layer, which contains more ions. Some part of the electromagnetic waves from a place moves towards the sky. Such waves are reflected from the ionosphere and reach different places on the Earth. Short waves are transported through the ionosphere for thousands of kilometers.

Hence, the correct option is (A).

62. The Atacama Desert is a dry plateau located in Chile, South America, and extends for a distance of about 1000 km (600 mi) to the Pacific coast of the continent west of the Andes Mountains. According to NASA, National Geographic and many other publications, it is the driest desert in the world.

Hence, the correct option is (B).

63. The island of Kachchatheevu is a deserted island administered by Sri Lanka. Until 1976, the region was disputed between India and Sri Lanka. The island, Neduntivu, lies between Sri Lanka and Rameswaram (India) and has been traditionally used by Tamil fishermen in Sri Lanka and fishermen in Tamil Nadu.

Hence, the correct option is (C).

64. On a map, the line drawn by mixing places with equal air pressure comparable to the lower air pressure of the ocean floor is called isobar line or isobar.

Hence, the correct option is (B).

65. In general, as we move from the equator to the poles, the rainfall continues to decrease. The world's coastal regions receive a greater amount of rainfall than the interior parts of the continents. Being great sources of water, the oceans receive more rainfall than the continents. Between the latitudes of $35°$ and $40°$ in the north and south of the Mediterranean Risa, there is a greater amount of rainfall on the eastern coasts, which is less when moving west. She goes. But, due to the west winds, between the latitudes of $45°$ and $65°$ north and south of the equator, rainfall first occurs in the western part of the continents, which is east. When going towards, it keeps decreasing at least.

Hence, the correct option is (C).

66. Tropical forests are found near the equator. It is an area that is within about 28 degrees to the south or north of the equator, while Australias Africa, South Africa, Central America, Mexico and the Pacific are found on the lamps.

Hence, the correct option is (B).

67. South Africa is not a major producer of natural gas. Natural gas is a mixture of several gases that mainly contain methane and 0–20% of other high hydrocarbon (such as ethane) gases. Natural gas is the major source of fuel. It is found along with other fossil fuels.

Hence, the correct option is (A).

68. The basis of the internal boundary is Germany and Pars. It runs mainly along the Oder and Lusatian Nees rivers and meets the Baltic Sea in the north. The "Oder-Nees Line" marked the border between East Germany and Poland from 1950 to 1990.

Hence, the correct option is (B).

69. Australia has 29 percent of the world's known uranium reserves. It has a quantity of 1.7 million tonnes here.

Hence, the correct option is (C).

70. Mountains make up a large part of the Earth's surface. On the basis of their construction processes, they are mainly classified into four types of mountains: Valla Parbat, Bhrushottha Parvat, Volcano Parvat, Residual Parvat, Vaal Parvat These are created due to the movement of the earth on a large scale when tension arises in the earth's crust.

Mountains make up a large part of the Earth's surface. On the basis of their construction processes, they are mainly classified into four types of mountains: Valla Parbat, Bhrushottha Parvat, Volcano Parvat, Residual Parvat, Vaal Parvat These are created due to the movement of the earth on a large scale when tension arises in the earth's crust.

Hence, the correct option is (A).

71. Both the statements are correct with respect to latitude and longitude. Latitude is considered as the angular distance (on the surface of the Earth) of a point located north or south of the equator. Other latitudes are determined on the basis of the equatorial circle and the equatorial circle is 0 ° latitude. Longitudes are angular distances expressed in degrees to the east or west of the Prime Meridian (Greenwich) on the equator.

Hence, the correct option is (C).

72. The Dead Sea is a landlocked ocean. All the minerals flow from the surrounding rural areas into this ocean, so the rate of water evaporation is high due to the temperature of the sun here. As a result, the salt concentration in the Dead Sea is very high. The salt concentration in water reaches 34%. Due to the extremely high concentration of dissolved mineral salts in water, its density is higher than that of fresh water. Since the weight of our body is lighter (less denser) than the density of this water, our body receives equine buoyancy in the Dead Sea, which makes it easier to swim.

Hence, the correct option is (C).

73. The National Inland Navigation Institute is situated in Patna. The main objective of the institute is to develop human resources for the Inland Water Transport sector.

Hence, the correct option is (A).

74. In simple words, an earthquake means the vibration of the earth. This is a natural phenomenon. The release of energy produces waves, which propagate in all directions to produce earthquakes. Statement 1 is correct: All natural earthquakes occur in the lithosphere. Often the energy is free from the edges of the fault. The deep cracks in the crusts of the earth's crust are debris.

Hence, the correct option is (A).

75. Long grasses and small trees are found in Savanna grasslands. Therefore, it is not correct to describe savanna as a 'tropical meadow', as small trees with abundant grasses are always present here. Therefore, the terms "parkland" and "bush-weld" more aptly describe this landscape.

Hence, the correct option is (C).

76. The northern boundary of the peninsular plot is irregular, starting from Kutch as a disorganized line extending west of the Aravalli mountain range to Delhi and extending to the Rajmahal hills and the Ganges delta parallel to the Yamuna and the Ganges river.

Hence, the correct option is (D).

77. Multitropical cyclones, also known as wave cyclones or mid-latitude cyclones, are a type of cyclonic wind systems that form in the airspace with horizontal temperature variations in the middle or high latitudes.

Hence, the correct option is (A).

78. These cyclones are avadabs (weak temperate cyclones), originating on the eastern equatorial sea and moving eastward and crossing West Asia, Iran, Afghanistan and Pakistan and reach

the northwestern parts of India. These convoys are oriented towards India by the western jet stream.

Hence, the correct option is (C).

79. Kareva is a thick layer deposition of glacial clay and other substances associated with snow. More precisely, kareva sarovari are deposits. According to geographers, Kareva is formed from the Loess brought by the glaciers-rivers-lakes and winds in the Plio-Pleistocene era. The Kashmir Himalayas are also popular for the Kareva structures, Ja Kesar's placeau Kaism Zafran has access to the fields. They lie between the Pir Panjal Range and the Greater Himalayan Range in Northwest India.

Hence, the correct option is (A).

80. When two plates diverge from each other in the opposite direction, then a new layer is formed, such plates are called divergent plates. The place from which the plates move away from each other is called the diffusional place. The best example of divergent boundaries is Mid-Atlantic Cuttack. From here, American plates/plates are diverging from Eurasian and African plates.

Hence, the correct option is (B).

81. High temperatures and abundant precipitation in warm and humid equatorial regions help in the development of a variety of dense vegetation - tropical rain forests. The weather here is humid year after year due to which the nature of the forests developed here is evergreen. The Amazon tropical rain forests are known as Selvas due to their lush green and broad-leaved tree. The vegetation of the region includes evergreen trees which provide tropical hardwood such as mahogany, ebony, rosewood, cabinet wood, etc.

Hence, the correct option is (D).

82. The houses with two huts placed at the right angle and a rectangular courtyard enclosed by the fence are the common features of settlements of Peninsular regions in India. It is found in Kerala, Tamil Nadu, Karnataka, Odisha.

Hence, the correct option is (C).

83. About 500 km from Mumbai Lonar lake located in the distant Buldhana district is a popular tourist center and also attracts scientists from all over the world. Recently, 1.2 km The change in water color of the average diameter lake surprised not only the locals, but also nature enthusiasts and scientists. The pH of the water of this notified National Land Heritage Monument lake is 10.5. Algae are also present in this water body. Salinity and algae may be responsible for this change. There is a lack of oxygen one meter below the surface of the lake water. There is also an example of such lake in Iran, in which the water color turns red due to increasing salinity. Low levels of water can cause salinity to increase and changes in behavior of algae due to atmospheric changes may cause changes in color.

Hence, the correct option is (D).

84. The islands of the Arabian Sea include Lakshadweep and Minicoy. The entire island group is roughly divided by eleven-degree channels (latitude), with Amini Island in the north and Canaanor Island in the south. These islands are spread between 8 ° N-12 ° and 71 ° E -74 ° E longitude. These islands are located at

a distance of 280 km to 480 km off the Kerala coast. The entire island group is made up of coral deposits. The archipelago consists of storm-built bridges, which are found in barren pebbles, shingles, cobbles, and boulders on the eastern seaboard.

Hence, the correct option is (A).

85. Singfan Wildlife Sanctuary has been declared as an Elephant Reserve by the Government of Nagaland making it the 30th reserve for elephants in the country.

Hence, the correct option is (D).

86. Stenothermal or Tanupati organisms are those organisms that have the ability to tolerate only a limited range of temperature. Examples- Penguins, pythons, crocodiles are eurythermal organisms that can tolerate a wide range of temperatures.

Hence, the correct option is (B).

87. Generally, standards in 'Organic Farming' are designed to encourage the use of natural substances. It prohibits the use of synthetic pesticides, antibiotics, synthetic fertilizers, genetically modified organisms and growth hormones.

Hence, the correct option is (A).

88. On 21 June, the Northern Hemisphere tilts towards the Sun. The rays of the Sun fall perpendicular to the Tropic of Cancer. Consequently, more heat is obtained by these regions. Relatively low heat is obtained due to the sun's rays slanting in areas near the poles. Sunlight is experienced for about six months at places north of the Arctic Circle. Since a large part of the Northern Hemisphere receives sunlight, the zeniths north of the equator have a yellow season. On June 21, the length of the day is the highest in the Northern Hemisphere and the length of the night is the minimum.

Hence, the correct option is (A).

89. Chakal is a natural gum, traditionally used in making chewing gum/bubble gum and other products. It is collected from several species of Mesoamerican trees in the genus Manilakara, including M. japota, M. chikal, M. staminodella, and M. bidentate amyl.

Hence, the correct option is (C).

90. The process of increasing the load of debris and slowing downward motion as a result of saturation of debris and weathering material due to rainfall in the upper part of a slope or valley.

When a mixture of rocks, debris, soil and water, etc., moves downwards, it is called mud flow. The speed of this type of landslide depends on the intensity of the slope and the fluidity of the sludge. The fast-flowing crust in a mountain region is called a adebris flow.

Hence, the correct option is (D).

91. Erosion involves the acquisition and transport of rock debris. When massive rocks break into small pieces through weathering and any other process, erosive geomorphic agents such as water,

groundwater, glaciers, air, and waves move it to other locations depending on its mobility.

The friction caused by rocky debris carried by these geomorphic agents also plays an important role in erosion. Erosion leads to collapse of the reliefs.

Hence, the correct option is (D).

92. Primary activities are directly dependent on the environment as they refer to the use of earth's resources such as land, water, vegetation, construction materials and wetlands. As such, it includes hunting, animal husbandry activities, fisheries, forestry, agriculture, and sanitation and quarrying.

Hence, the correct option is (A).

93. The equatorial warm, humid climate is found between 5 ° –10 ° north and south of the Mediterranean racea. The most outstanding feature of the equatorial climate is the uniform temperature throughout the year, which lacks winter. Most of the rainfall is convective rain, which is accompanied by thunderstorms and thunderstorms.

Hence, the correct option is (B).

94. Vayu Raji is classified on the basis of source losses. The total five major source areas are:

(i) warm tropical and subtropical oceans;

(ii) subtropical warm deserts;

(iii) relatively cold high latitudinal oceans;

(iv) Extremely cold snow-covered continents at high latitudes;

(v) Permanently snow-covered continents in the Arctic and Antarctica.

Hence, the correct option is (D).

95. The states of Himachal Pradesh, Uttarakhand, Sikkim and Arunachal Pradesh and Ladakh, a union territory, share a border with China.

Hence, the correct option is (B).

96. When two regions with different physical properties converge, the convergence zone between them is called Vatagra. The process of manufacturing vents is known as ventilation. There are generally four types of Vatagra: (a) Called Vatagra; (B) warm atmosphere; (C) Permanent atmosphere; (D) Entered atmosphere. When the atmosphere is permanent, it is called a permanent atmosphere. When the cold air moves towards the warm air, their convergence zone is called cold ventilation.

Hence, the correct option is (B).

97. There is a Nilot tribal group inhabiting northern, central and southern Kenya and northern Tanzania. They are one of the most popular local tribes internationally due to their habitat near many game gardens of the great lakes of Africa and their unique customs and styles.

Hence, the correct option is (B).

98. The Shanghai Cooperation Organization (SCO) is a permanent intergovernmental organization, which was announced on 15 June 2001 in Shanghai (China) by Kazakhstan, China, Kyrgyzstan, Russia, Tajikistan and Uzbekistan. The former name of this organization was Shanghai Five Mechanism. The eight permanent member countries of SCO include India, Kazakhstan, China, Kyrgyzstan, Pakistan, Russia, Tajikistan and Uzbekistan.

Hence, the correct option is (B).

99. Igloo, also known as Snow House or Snow Hut, is a type of shelter, constructed from snow. Although igloos are often associated with all Inuit and Eskimo peoples, they were traditionally constructed only by people from the Central Arctic of Canada and the Thule region of Greenland.

Hence, the correct option is (C).

100. The Sargasso Sea is a region of the Atlantic Ocean that is surrounded by four streams, forming a bay of the ocean. Unlike all other areas called the sea, it has no land boundary. It is known from other parts of the Atlantic Ocean for its distinctive brown sargassum seaweed and often cool blue waters.

Hence, the correct option is (A).

101. The Panama Canal connects the Atlantic Ocean in the east to the Pacific Ocean in the west.

This reduces the distance between New York and San Francisco by 13,000 km by sea route. Similarly, the distance between the west-coast of Western Europe and America; And reduces the distance between North-East and Central America and East and South-East Asia. The economic importance of this canal is comparatively less than that of Suez Canal. However, it is important for the economies of Latin America.

Hence, the correct option is (A).

102. In a circular pattern, villages develop around lakes, tanks and sometimes the village is planned in such a way that the central part is open and is used to protect animals from wild animals.

Hence, the correct option is (A).

103. A hot spot originates over a region within the eastern mantle from where the heat rises upward through the process of convection. Due to this heat, the rocks on the ground begin to melt, where the upper part of the mantle meets the earth's crust. This molten rock, known as magma, often originates through cracks in the cast to form volcanoes.

Hence, the correct option is (B).

104. Arunachal Pradesh was established as a state in India on February 20, 1987. Arunachal Pradesh was initially a Union Territory which was carved out of Assam.

Hence the correct option is (C).

105. Kuttanad region in Kerala covering Alappuzha and Kottayam Districts represents India's lowest altitudes.

Hence the correct option is (A).

106. Petroleum Industry, located in Assam and known for the first Oil Refinery to be commissioned by the then Indian Oil Company Limited, now known as Indian Oil Corporation Limited.

Hence, the correct option is (B).

107. Tidal forests grows mainly in the deltaic regions of the Ganga, Mahanadi, Godavari and Krishna which are flooded by tides and high sea waves. Mangrove is the representative of this type of vegetation. Sundari is the typical tree of tidal forests. It is found in abundance in the lower Ganga delta of West Bengal. This is the reason why it is popularly known as Sunderban. It is known for its hard and durable timber.

Hence the correct option is (C).

108. China holds the leading position among producers of rare earths followed by Brazil, Malaysia and India. Though China is having only 37% reserves of rare earths, it produces around 97% of world's supply of rare earth. In India, monazite and thorium are the principal source of rare earths elements. Monazite is a prescribed substance as per the notification under the Atomic Energy Act, 1962.

Hence, the correct option is (A).

109. The Western Himalayan region extends from Kashmir to Kumaon. Its temperate zone is rich in forests of Chir, Pine, other conifers and broad- leaved temperate trees. Higher up, forests of Deodar, blue Pine, Spruce and Silver Fir occur.

Hence, the correct option is (C).

110. Approximately 65% of Indian's cotton is produced on rainfed areas and 35% on irrigated lands. Cotton is produced in India in three zones viz., Northern zone comprising the States of Punjab, Haryana and Rajasthan, Central zone comprising the States of Maharashtra, Madhya Pradesh and Gujarat and Southern zone comprising the States of Andhra Pradesh, Karnataka and Tamil Nadu. Besides these nine States, cotton cultivation has gained momentum in the eastern State of Orissa.

Hence, the correct option is (C).

111. Rajghat Dam is an Inter-state Dam project of the Government of Madhya Pradesh and Uttar Pradesh being constructed on Betwa River about 14 km from Historical place Chanderi in Madhya Pradesh.

Hence, the correct option is (C).

112. Lushai hills are mountain range in Mizoram and Tripura states of India. The hills have been in news for various mining activities and environmental concerns.

Hence, the correct option is (B).

113. Angami tribe belongs to the extreme north eastern part of the country, in the state of Nagaland. Tenyidie is the most common language spoken among the Angamis in Nagaland. The total population of the Angamis is around 12 million. Agriculture is the main occupation. They cultivate rice and grains on the hilly terrains. Christianity is the major religion followed among the Angami tribal people. Sekrenyi is the main festival celebrated among the Angamis in Nagaland. The festival falls in the month of February and marks the beginning of the lunar year. This ten day festival is also known as the Phousnyi among the local people.

Hence, the correct option is (C).

114. Pichavaram mangrove forest is located near Chidambaram in Cuddalore district, Tamil Nadu.

Hence, the correct option is (A).

115. Bhalia wheat is a long grain of wheat, which has high protein content and is grown without irrigation for centuries in the Bhal region of Gujarat. Bhalia wheat received GI Tag in 2011.

Hence, the correct option is (B).

116. The climatic conditions for optimum growth of rubber trees are:

- Rainfall of around 250 centimeters, evenly distributed without any marked dry season and with at least 100 rainy days per year
- Temperature range of about 20 to 34 °C, with a monthly mean of 25 to 28 °C
- Atmospheric humidity of around 80%
- Flat land with well drained soil

Hence, the correct option is (D).

117. Everest is the highest peak in the world, but it is located in Nepal, K2, the second highest is located in Pakistan-China border belongs to the Karakoram range of mountains (it is not a peak), while Kanchenjunga is the third highest located in the Indo-Nepal border. Cardamom Hills is not a part of Himalayas, it is located in South India.

Hence, the correct option is (D).

118. The Lakshadweep archipelago gets its name from the Sanskrit words 'laksha' meaning 100,000 and 'dweepa' meaning island, so it literally means "One hundred thousand islands". This archipelago is a Union Territory of India and is inhabited by around 30,000 people and are known for their pristine beaches and coral reefs.

Hence, the correct option is (B).

119. Diversity is higher in the tropics (not just tropical rainforests) primarily because there are fewer ecological obstacles to higher biodiversity. In the tropics, plants and animals have the greatest access to consistent energy, water, and carbon, etc.

Hence, the correct option is (C).

120. The state Karnataka shared its boundary with six other states viz, Kerala, Tamil Nadu, Andhra Pradesh, Telangana, Maharashtra, Goa.

Hence, the correct option is (D).

121. The evolution of the peninsular region is considered as the resultant of Platform Evolution. The five folding zones of the peninsular region are the Dharwar Folding, the Aravalli Folding, the Eastern Ghat Folding, the Satpura Folding, the Delhi Folding.

Hence, the correct option is (C).

122. The region lies between the Chota Nagpur Plateau on the West and the Ganges Delta on the East is known as Rahr plain. Soil erosion is a great problem in this area.

Hence, the correct option is (B).

123. Pir Panjal Pass also known as Peer ki Gali provides the easiest access between Jammu and the valley of Kashmir. It is located at an elevation of 3,490 meters.

Hence, the correct option is (B).

124. The characteristic features of Deserts, fertile plains and moderately forested mountains are found in North-Western India.

Hence, the correct option is (B).

125. The dependency of fuelwood on the forest is highest in the state of Maharashtra. In case of dependency of fodder, small timer and bamboo is highest in the state of Madhya Pradesh.

Hence, the correct option is (C).

Q.1 Tungbhadra multipurpose project is a joint venture of Karnataka and Andhra Pradesh.Tungabhadra is a tributary river of:

A. Krishna **B.** Kaveri

C. Godavari **D.** Sabarmati

Q.2 As per the assessment of tidal energy potential in the country by the Central Electricity Authority, maximum potential for tidal energy in India has been found in:

A. Gulf of Cambay **B.** Gulf of Katch

C. Gulf of Mannar **D.** Bay of Bengal

Q.3 River Brahmaputra passes through which of the following country/countries?

1. Bhutan
2. Myanmar
3. Bangladesh

Select the correct option from the codes given below:

A. 1 and 2 only **B.** 2 and 3 only

C. 3 Only **D.** 1, 2 and 3

Q.4 Match List 1 and List 2 and select the correct answer using the codes given below the list:

List 1 States	List 2 Highest Peak
A. Kerala	1. Dodda Betta
B. Nagaland	2. Nand Devi
C. Uttarakhand	3. Anai Mudi
D. Tamil Nadu	4. Saramati

A. A - 1, B - 3, C - 4, D - 2

B. A - 2, B - 3, C - 4, D - 1

C. A - 3, B - 4, C - 2, D - 1

D. A - 1, B - 2, C - 3, D - 4

Q.5 Which among the following city is called "Zero Mile Centre" because of its location on India's Geographic centre?

A. Bhopal **B.** Jabalpur **C.** Nagpur **D.** Indore

Q.6 Eastern Ghats passes through which of the following states?

A. Odisha **B.** Karnataka

C. Bihar **D.** Punjab

Q.7 Palghat is situated between:

A. The Nilgiris and the Cardamon Hills

B. The Nilgiris and the Annamalai Hills

C. The Annamalai Hills and the Cardamon Hills

D. The Cardamon Hiils and Palini Hills

Q.8 Sink hole is a phenomenon of:

A. Plain **B.** Desert **C.** Tundra **D.** Karst

Q.9 Narmada Valley is an example of:

A. Rift valley **B.** Fault scarp

C. Nappe **D.** Horst

Q.10 Coal mining in Jowai and Cherapunjee, done by family-members in the form of a long narrow tunnel, is known as:

A. Skunk hole mining

B. Rabbit hole mining

C. Earthworm hole mining

D. Rat hole mining

Q.11 Peneplain is related to:

A. Wind **B.** Underground water

C. Glacier **D.** River

Q.12 Mim Kut which takes place in August-September in the wake of harvesting which of the following crops and by which tribe?

A. Maize, Mizos **B.** Rice, Apatani

C. Barley, Gonds **D.** Cashew, Nagas

Q.13 The branch of geography which deals with composition of a particular human population is called:

A. Urban geography **B.** Biogeography

C. Demography **D.** Human geography

Q.14 Which of the following forms of the land is not a result of 'faulting'?

A. Rift Valley **B.** Ramp Valley

C. Horst **D.** Chevron

Q.15 Which Indian National Park is famous for Rhinoceros population?

A. Kaziranga **B.** Jim Corbett

C. Ranthambor **D.** Bannerghatta

Q.16 Which one of the following is the longest mountain range?

A. The Rocky **B.** The Alps

C. The Himalayas **D.** The Andes

Q.17 Match the following:

List-I	List-II
A. Slate	1. Igneous rock
B. Lignite	2. Metamorpric rock
C. Bauxite	3. Non-ferrous mineral
D. Granite	4. Sedimentary rock

A. A-1, B-3, C-3, D-2 **B.** A-2, B-4, C-3, D-1

C. A-2, B-3, C-4, D-1 **D.** A-1, B-4, C-3, D-2

Q.18 Sierra Nevada Mountains are situated in:

A. Alaska **B.** California

C. Texas **D.** Manitoba

Q.19 Africa's highest mountain peak Mt. Kilimanjaro lies in:

A. Kenya **B.** Malawi **C.** Tanzania **D.** Zambia

Q.20 The biggest island of the Indian Ocean is:
A. Maldives
B. Madagascar
C. Lakshadweep
D. Sumatra

Q.21 Which one of the following ocean currents is different from others?
A. North Atlantic Drift
B. Gulf stream
C. Kuroshio
D. Labrador

Q.22 Which one of the following currents has a warming influence on the neighbouring coast?
A. Benguela
B. Agulhas
C. Canaries
D. Oyasio

Q.23 Which one of the following is a warm ocean current?
A. East Australian current
B. West Australian current
C. Benguela current
D. Peru current

Q.24 Canaries Current flows along:
A. Brazilian coast
B. Peruvian coast
C. East African coast
D. West African coast

Q.25 The Agulhas Current flows in:
A. Indian Ocean
B. Pacific Ocean
C. Atlantic Ocean
D. Southern Ocean

Q.26 Which one of the following National Highways passes through Maharashtra, Chhattisgarh, and Orissa?
A. National Highway-4
B. National Highway-5
C. National Highway-6
D. National Highway-7

Q.27 Which of the following statements is not true of Trade Winds?
A. They blow from the Horse Latitudes to the Doldrums
B. They are deflected to the right to become South-East Trades in the southern hemisphere
C. They are constant in strength and direction
D. They sometimes contain intense depressions

Q.28 A level of atmosphere which is composed partly of Electrons and Positive Ions is called:
A. Troposphere
B. Ionosphere
C. Stratosphere
D. Mesosphere

Q.29 Hurricanes __________.
A. Form at the equator
B. Are not as large as tornadoes
C. Develop over warm ocean areas
D. Tend to intensify when they move over land surfaces

Q.30 The tropical cyclones - Hurricanes and Typhoons - develop and mature ______.
A. At the same place
B. Over the land masses only
C. Over the water bodies only
D. Anywhere in the tropical zone

Q.31 Which among the following National Highways of India is the longest?
A. National Highways-1
B. National Highways-2
C. National Highways-3
D. National Highways-4

Q.32 The national highway from Amritsar to Kolkata via Delhi is numbered:
A. 1
B. 2
C. 4
D. 8

Q.33 The climate of India is tropical because of:
A. The location of the Himalayas in its North
B. Major part of India lies within the tropics
C. The overpowering influence of India Ocean
D. The seasonal influence of jet streams

Q.34 What are the two volcanic islands in the Indian territory?
A. Kavaratti and New Moor
B. Bitra and Kavaratti
C. Pamban and Barren
D. Narcondam and Barren

Q.35 Among the following Union Territories of India, which one has the largest size?
A. Lakshadweep
B. Daman and Due
C. Puducherry
D. Chandigarh

Q.36 The Lakshadweep islands are situated in:
A. Indian Ocean
B. Arabian Sea
C. Bay of Bengal
D. None of these

Q.37 Which foreign country is closest to Andaman Islands?
[Territorial Army Officer, 2021]
A. Sri Lanka
B. Myanmar
C. Indonesia
D. Pakistan

Q.38 Which of the following states shares boundaries with the maximum number of other states of India?
A. Madhya Pradesh
B. Uttar Pradesh
C. Assam
D. Bihar

Q.39 The State with the largest area under waste land is:
A. Gujarat
B. Madhya Pradesh
C. Jammu and Kashmir
D. Rajasthan

Q.40 Which state amongst the following has the highest percentage of the Scheduled Caste population of the State's population?
A. Jharkhand
B. Madhya Pradesh
C. Punjab
D. Uttar Pradesh

Q.41 Cape York Peninsula (Australia) is world-famous for which of the following minerals?
A. Gold
B. Bauxite
C. Iron ore
D. Tin

Q.42 Largest industrial gas reserves are found in:
A. Iraq
B. Iran
C. Qatar
D. Russia

Q.43 Which of the following countries is the highest producer of Uranium in Asia?

A. Indonesia
B. India
C. China
D. Kazakhstan

Q.44 Which of the following crops are grown mostly under subsistence forming?

A. Tea and coffee
B. Vegetables and fruits
C. Cotton and Tobacco
D. Millets and Rice

Q.45 Which of the following states does not lie along the border of Pakistan?

A. Rajasthan
B. Himachal Pradesh
C. Gujarat
D. Punjab

Q.46 Ankleshwar, a famous petroleum site, is located in the state of:

A. Gujarat
B. Maharashtra
C. Rajasthan
D. Assam

Q.47 The length of the Konkan Railway is: (Approx)

A. 560 kms
B. 663 kms
C. 757 kms
D. 887 kms

Q.48 What kind of climate is required for cotton textile industry?

A. Cold climate
B. Hot climate
C. Humid climate
D. Subtropical climate

Q.49 Which of the following is not related to the small industries?

A. Paper goods
B. Toys
C. Clay ornaments
D. Furniture

Q.50 Which type of industries developed after the Industrial Revolution?

A. Cottage industries
B. Small industries
C. Large scale industries
D. Chemical industries

Q.51 Which industry is also called axis industry?

A. Cotton textile industry
B. Ferro-steel industry
C. Gems & Jewelery Industry
D. Cement industry

Q.52 Which is the world's largest steel producer?

A. India
B. China
C. Japan
D. United States of America

Q.53 Which of the following is not a source of biogas fuel?

A. Wood
B. Dung Gas
C. Nuclear power
D. Coal

Q.54 An example of forest wealth is:

A. Soil
B. Wood
C. Copper
D. Aluminium

Q.55 Using resources successfully is what is called giving them time to renew?

A. Resource Conservation
B. Sustainable Nutrition Protection
C. Resource Unique
D. Resource Representation

Q.56 Which tributary of Indus river originates from Mansarovar lake?

A. Vyas
B. Jhelum
C. Sutlej
D. Ravi

Q.57 On which river is the Tulbul project located?

A. Indus
B. Ravi
C. Jhelum
D. Vyas

Q.58 In which state in India is the geographical structure called Kayal found?

A. Karnataka
B. Maharashtra
C. Kerala
D. Tamil Nadu

Q.59 Which of the following rivers originates from Amarkantak?

[Soldier GD, 2019]

A. Betwa
B. Mahi
C. Narmada
D. Tapti

Q.60 Who was the first to experience air pressure on the ground?

A. Ak Gan
B. Otto von Guericke
C. Adult Zone
D. George Lane

Q.61 The true statement related to air pressure is:

A. Air pressure is lowest at the equator
B. The pressure on the pole is highest
C. Due to lack of oxygen and air pressure at high altitude, blood starts coming from human nose and ears
D. All of the above

Q.62 The Earth's rotation speed is highest at the equator, due to which the centrifugal force is highest here due to:

A. Air pressure is the lowest
B. Does not pressure
C. Air pressure is high
D. No one

Q.63 Screaming Satha is called:

A. Business winds
B. Polar winds
C. Seasonal winds
D. Westward winds

Q.64 Trade winds of the eastern part as compared to the western part:

A. Less
B. Dry
C. Cold
D. Both (B) and (C)

Q.65 Which of the following mentioned layers is NOT a homosphere?

A. Exosphere
B. Troposphere
C. Ionosphere
D. Mesosphere

Q.66 What kind of rain is accompanied by lightning and thunder of clouds?

A. Mountain rain
B. Cyclonic rain
C. Sustainable rain
D. None of these

Q.67 The rainiest place in the world is-
A. Reunion Island
B. Amazon valley
C. Mawsynram
D. Cherrapunji

Q.68 What does cloud brust mean?
A. Sowing of crop seeds in cloudy weather
B. Manufacture of artificial rain
C. Unseasonably heavy rain with heavy storm
D. The presence of scattered pieces of clouds in the sky

Q.69 Which of the following statements is/are correct on a cyclone?
A. A cyclone is a center of low pressure, that is, a strong storm of hot air around a low atmospheric pressure is called a cyclone.
B. The cyclone is circular in shape, elliptical to 'V' in shape.
C. Cyclones have extreme effects on climate and weather.
D. All of the above are correct.

Q.70 Which of the following statements is/are correct about tropical cyclones?
A. These cyclones develop in areas located between the Tropic of Cancer and the Tropic of Capricorn.
B. Tropical cyclones typically develop during the summer season in the region around the Inter-Tropical Convergence Zone on the warm sea surface.
C. The energy source of tropical cyclones is latent heat of condensation.
D. All of the above are correct.

Q.71 Consider the following statements.
1. The central part of the galaxy is called the bulge.
2. The galaxy has three rotating arms.
3. Concentric wires have excessive concentration of stars.
Which of the above statements are true?
A. 1, 2 and 3
B. 2 and 3 only
C. 1 and 2 only
D. 1 and 3 only

Q.72 Consider the following statements:
1. The stars are formed by the process of nuclear fusion.
2. All the stars are transformed into white dwarfs by the explosion in the blood giants.
Which of the statements given above is/are true?
A. Only 1
B. Only 2
C. Both 1 and 2
D. Neither 1 nor 2

Q.73 Consider the following statements:
1. 1.44 Ms is called Chandrasekhar Seema.
2. A star with a mass less than 1.44 times the mass of the Sun is called a blackhole.
Which of the statements given above is/are true?
A. Only 1
B. Only 2
C. Both 1 and 2
D. Neither 1 nor 2

Q.74 Consider the following statements-
1. Blackhole is a high gravity field.

2. It is not possible to drain any matter or light from the blackhole.

3. The boundary of the blackhole from which no object can escape, is called the event horizon.

4. The event horizon has no effect on a body.
Which of the above statements are true?
A. 1, 2 and 4 only
B. 3 and 4 only
C. 1, 2 and 3 only
D. 1, 2, 3 and 4

Q.75 Consider the following statements-
1. The source of the Sun's energy is the process of nuclear fission.
2. The outermost part of the sun is called the corona.
3. A storm of atoms occasionally emanating from the corona is the Solar Flares.
Which of the above statements are true?
A. 1, 2 and 3
B. Only 2
C. 1 and 2
D. 2 and 3

Q.76 Consider the following statements-
1. Solar stigmas are warmer than the sun's temperature.
2. Solar blur helps in wireless communication system.
Which of the statements given above is/are true?
A. Only 1
B. Only 2
C. Both 1 and 2
D. Neither 1 nor 2

Q.77 Consider the following statements:
1. 50% of the solar system is produced by the Sun.
2. 5% of the solar system is formed by planets.
Which of the statements given above is/are true?
A. Only 1
B. Only 2
C. Both 1 and 2
D. Neither 1 nor 2

Q.78 Consider the following statements-
1. Earth, Mars, Venus, and Mercury are called terrestrial planets.
2. Atmospheres in the planet Mercury are very dense.
3. Venus is called 'sister of Earth'.
Which of the above statements are true?
A. 1 and 2 only
B. 2 and 3 only
C. 1 and 3 only
D. 1, 2, and 3

Q.79 Consider the following statements:
1. Jupiter has the most natural satellites.
2. There are no natural satellites of Mercury and Venus.
Which of the statements given above is/are true?
A. Only 1
B. Only 2
C. Both 1 and 2
D. Neither 1 nor 2

Q.80 Causes of fraternity at different places on the earth during daytime and nighttime?
A. Earth revolves on an elliptical path
B. Tilt of the earth on its axis
C. Earth's rotation on its axis
D. Location specific latitudinal position

Q.81 Consider the following statements.

1. There is a continuous increase in the night time when it goes north in the northern hemisphere in winter.

2. On the 22nd of December, the sun does not rise all day on the Arctic Circle.

Which of the statements given above is/are true?

A. Only 1
B. Only 2
C. 1 and 2
D. Neither 1 nor 2

Q.82 Which of the following statements is/are true?

1. On the equator, the sun shines vertically once a year.

2. When the sun shines perpendicularly on the Tropic of Cancer, it is called Summer Solstice.

3. The condition of even night and day is called solstice.

Give the correct answer based on the following codes:

A. 1 and 2 only
B. Only 2
C. 2 and 3 only
D. 1, 2 and 3

Q.83 Which of the following ocean is 'S' shaped?

A. Atlantic Ocean
B. Pacific Ocean
C. Arctic Ocean
D. Indian Ocean

Q.84 Nagaland was formed in which year?

A. 1947
B. 1956
C. 1963
D. 1973

Q.85 Which forests are always covered with snow?

A. Broadleaved Forests
B. Tundra Forests
C. Mediterranean Forests
D. All of the above

Q.86 Srisailam Dam is constructed on which of the following river?

A. Kaveri
B. Krishna
C. Godavari
D. Musi

Q.87 The longest bridge in India which was inaugurated by Prime Minister of India in 2017 is ___________.

A. Dhola Sadiya
B. Dibang River Bridge
C. Mahatma Gandhi Setu
D. Bandra Worli Bridge

Q.88 Which Mountain is called the Great Escarpment of India?

A. Great Himalayas
B. Satpura Ranges
C. Arawali Ranges
D. Western Ghats

Q.89 Which is the highest mountain peak of Indonesia?

A. Mt. Puncak Jaya
B. Mt. Kosciuszko
C. Mt. Elbrus
D. Mt. Vinson

Q.90 Which country is the largest producer of hydroelectric power?

A. India
B. China
C. USA
D. Australia

Q.91 Who is considered the father of geomorphology?

A. Peshal
B. Davis
C. Pank
D. None of these

Q.92 Who is the scholar defining geography as human ecology?

A. Hetner
B. Jean Brunche
C. Harlan Barrows
D. Eratosthenes

Q.93 Which scholar is responsible for presenting information about the solar system to the world?

A. Copernicus
B. Kepler
C. Galileo
D. Pank

Q.94 What is the celestial body moving around the Sun?

A. Planets
B. Satellite
C. Tail star
D. All these

Q.95 Who said this is a study of ground floor?

A. Varanius
B. Tailor
C. Kant
D. Karl Ritter

Q.96 What is a small celestial body revolving around a planet?

A. Tail star
B. Planets
C. Satellite
D. All these

Q.97 Who propounded the laws of motion of the planets?

A. Kepler
B. Galileo
C. Newton
D. Copernicus

Q.98 Who discovered the solar system?

A. Copernicus
B. Aryabhata
C. Karl Ritter
D. Kepler

Q.99 Who is the father of the solar system?

A. Earth
B. Venus
C. Saturn
D. Sun

Q.100 What is the maximum distance of a planet from the Sun in its orbit?

A. Perigee
B. Aphelion
C. Perihelion
D. Apoji

Q.101 What actions are included on the surface of the Earth in the biosphere?

A. Biological actions
B. Non-biological actions
C. Biological and non-biological actions
D. Resources

Q.102 Which adaptation arises from response to specific stimuli?

A. Hereditary adaptation
B. Acquired adaptation
C. Biological adaptation
D. Abiotic adaptation

Q.103 All organism actions occur:

A. On the surface of the surface
B. In debility board
C. In mental
D. In the core

Q.104 The oxygen and hydrogen requirements of the body are met by:

A. Water
B. The sun
C. Organic components
D. Earth's physical resources

Q.105 After how many kilometers does oxygen and nitrogen gas almost disappear?

A. 50 km   **B.** 20 km   **C.** 140 km   **D.** 150 km

Q.106 The important gas for photosynthesis is:

A. Oxygen   **B.** Carbon dioxide
C. Hydrogen   **D.** Nitrogen

Q.107 Who first used the term biodiversity?

A. Wilson   **B.** Spat
C. Hittington   **D.** Hortsoran

Q.108 The different forms of the same gene in the organisms of any species are called assessments?

A. Genetic diversity   **B.** Ethnic diversity
C. Ecological diversity   **D.** Cultural diversity

Q.109 Forest, desert, meadows, etc., are included in which variety?

A. Genetics diversity   **B.** Ethnic diversity
C. Ecological diversity   **D.** Cultural diversity

Q.110 Approximately what percentage of plant species are found in India?

A. 8%   **B.** 12%   **C.** 2.4%   **D.** 6.5%

Q.111 Which one of the following does not belong to Himalayan rivers?

A. Kaveri   **B.** Brahmaputra
C. Alaknanda   **D.** Gandak

Q.112 The reservoir Govind Ballabh Pant Sagar is located on which river?

A. Betwa   **B.** Ghaghara
C. Kosi   **D.** Rihand

Q.113 Which one of the following rivers flows into the Arabian Sea?

A. Indravati   **B.** Godavari
C. Cauvery   **D.** Narmada

Q.114 Rajarappa is situated on the confluence of which rivers?

A. Damodar — Behera
B. Damodar — Sherbukhi
C. Damodar — Barakar
D. Damodar — Konar

Q.115 Which one of the following is not a tributary of river Alaknanda?

A. Bhilangana   **B.** Pinder
C. Mandakini   **D.** Nandakini

Q.116 Which one of the following is the correct sequence of the given tiger reserves of India from North to South?

A. Dudhwa-Kanha-Indravati-Bandipur
B. Kanha-Bandipur-Dudhwa-Indravati
C. Indravati-Kanha-Dudhwa-Bandipur
D. Dudhwa-Kanha-Bandipur-Indravati

Q.117 Which one of the following national parks are located near Chamoli?

A. Dudhwa National Park
B. Great Himalayan Park
C. Jim Corbett National Park
D. Nanda Devi National Park

Q.118 Which one of the following states has the largest forest area to its total land area?

A. Mizoram
B. Arunachal Pradesh
C. Sikkim
D. Jammu and Kashmir

Q.119 Kanha National Park belongs to which one among the following biogeographical areas in the world?

A. Tropical Sub-humid Forests
B. Tropical Humid Forests
C. Tropical Dry Forests
D. Tropical Moist Forests

Q.120 Among the following states, the literacy rate is highest in:

A. Odisha   **B.** Punjab
C. Maharashtra   **D.** Mizoram

Q.121 The 'Todas' are one of the major tribes found in:

A. Sikkim
B. Assam
C. Nilgiris
D. The Andaman and Nicobar Islands

Q.122 Where are homogenous group "Mangolab" found in India?

A. South-Region
B. Southern-Central Region
C. North-Western Region
D. North-East Region

Q.123 Where are Khasi and Garo tribes mainly found in:

A. Meghalaya   **B.** Nagaland
C. Mizoram   **D.** Manipur

Q.124 India's biggest tribal group is:

A. Bhil   **B.** Gond   **C.** Santhal   **D.** Tharu

Q.125 The tropical rain forests in the Amazon basin is known as:

A. Savanna   **B.** Prairies   **C.** Selvas   **D.** Pampas

// Smart Answer Sheet //

Correct Indicates percentage of students who answered questions correctly.

Skipped Indicates percentage of students who skipped questions.

Q.	Ans.	Correct	Skipped
1	A	40.16 %	1.29 %
2	A	62.25 %	1.1 %
3	C	56.15 %	1.99 %
4	C	31.52 %	4.63 %
5	C	57.89 %	1.84 %
6	A	60.34 %	1.79 %
7	B	68.53 %	1.48 %
8	D	47.72 %	1.88 %
9	A	66.77 %	1.11 %
10	D	59.48 %	1.37 %
11	C	47.12 %	1.12 %
12	A	14.87 %	3.12 %
13	C	65.85 %	1.05 %
14	D	28.49 %	3.94 %
15	A	46.95 %	1.92 %
16	D	43.48 %	1.73 %
17	B	40.39 %	1.96 %
18	B	55.85 %	1.7 %
19	C	53.27 %	1.43 %
20	B	45.48 %	1.97 %
21	D	67.68 %	1.0 %
22	B	40.88 %	1.67 %
23	A	46.81 %	1.27 %
24	D	65.48 %	1.55 %
25	A	47.17 %	1.39 %
26	C	57.21 %	1.85 %
27	B	14.48 %	3.69 %
28	B	65.61 %	1.58 %
29	C	13.99 %	3.17 %
30	D	56.41 %	1.01 %
31	B	45.98 %	1.67 %
32	B	53.27 %	1.25 %
33	A	67.68 %	1.5 %
34	D	58.22 %	1.39 %
35	C	25.61 %	3.56 %
36	B	43.04 %	1.11 %
37	B	40.31 %	1.15 %
38	B	44.45 %	1.22 %
39	D	69.64 %	1.4 %
40	C	63.26 %	1.73 %
41	B	40.14 %	1.92 %
42	D	60.36 %	1.59 %
43	D	55.22 %	1.13 %
44	D	48.85 %	1.85 %
45	B	59.93 %	1.5 %
46	A	65.29 %	1.04 %
47	C	59.0 %	1.58 %
48	C	40.29 %	1.91 %
49	C	62.22 %	1.64 %
50	C	53.05 %	1.42 %
51	B	69.69 %	1.54 %
52	B	67.63 %	1.96 %
53	C	43.68 %	1.43 %
54	B	64.48 %	1.72 %
55	A	54.51 %	1.95 %
56	C	51.48 %	1.23 %
57	C	60.35 %	1.51 %
58	C	63.2 %	1.33 %
59	C	67.86 %	1.55 %
60	B	60.59 %	1.41 %
61	D	31.96 %	4.66 %
62	A	54.0 %	1.86 %
63	D	61.85 %	1.05 %
64	D	41.23 %	1.78 %
65	A	54.69 %	1.41 %
66	C	57.34 %	1.3 %
67	C	67.51 %	1.16 %
68	C	54.37 %	1.99 %
69	D	50.51 %	1.38 %
70	D	47.87 %	1.23 %
71	C	12.48 %	4.0 %
72	A	29.55 %	4.75 %
73	A	59.47 %	1.99 %
74	C	69.95 %	1.21 %
75	B	50.99 %	1.66 %
76	D	40.87 %	1.48 %
77	D	41.52 %	1.42 %
78	C	29.13 %	3.47 %
79	C	62.68 %	1.4 %
80	B	14.21 %	3.65 %

Q.	Ans.	Correct / Skipped
81	C	20.38 % / 3.66 %
82	B	67.08 % / 1.08 %
83	A	40.26 % / 1.21 %
84	C	40.71 % / 1.9 %
85	B	45.09 % / 1.49 %
86	B	69.36 % / 1.06 %
87	A	61.94 % / 1.41 %
88	D	52.59 % / 1.34 %
89	A	57.43 % / 1.73 %

Q.	Ans.	Correct / Skipped
90	B	63.06 % / 1.14 %
91	A	57.85 % / 1.26 %
92	C	16.15 % / 3.85 %
93	A	42.6 % / 1.26 %
94	A	67.73 % / 1.79 %
95	C	54.97 % / 1.6 %
96	C	66.02 % / 1.34 %
97	A	60.98 % / 1.67 %
98	A	17.72 % / 3.46 %

Q.	Ans.	Correct / Skipped
99	D	69.21 % / 1.74 %
100	B	45.99 % / 1.37 %
101	C	60.6 % / 1.11 %
102	B	54.54 % / 1.91 %
103	A	60.69 % / 1.3 %
104	A	51.96 % / 1.25 %
105	C	21.57 % / 3.38 %
106	B	44.67 % / 1.59 %
107	A	45.85 % / 1.52 %

Q.	Ans.	Correct / Skipped
108	A	44.66 % / 1.37 %
109	C	44.49 % / 1.63 %
110	A	12.99 % / 4.89 %
111	A	68.56 % / 1.03 %
112	D	50.72 % / 1.69 %
113	D	54.55 % / 1.65 %
114	A	56.05 % / 1.24 %
115	A	49.06 % / 1.48 %
116	A	10.06 % / 3.71 %

Q.	Ans.	Correct / Skipped
117	D	56.58 % / 1.12 %
118	A	62.62 % / 1.44 %
119	C	46.88 % / 1.64 %
120	D	46.15 % / 1.94 %
121	C	27.51 % / 3.67 %
122	D	42.38 % / 1.83 %
123	A	66.76 % / 1.76 %
124	A	50.64 % / 1.49 %
125	C	60.65 % / 1.11 %

Performance Analysis

Avg. Score (%)	48.0%
Toppers Score (%)	74.82%
Your Score	

//Hints and Solutions//

1. The Tungabhadra Dam is also known as Pampa Sagar is constructed across the Tungabhadra River, a tributary of the Krishna River. The dam is in Hosapete, Vijayanagara district of Karnataka. It is a multipurpose dam serving irrigation, electricity generation, flood control, etc.

Hence, the correct option is (A).

2. The potential capacity of electricity generation through tidal energy system in India is 10,000MW, in which highest potential site is the Gulf of Cambay has approximate 7200 MW and this is followed by the seashore of Kutch & the Ganga delta of Sunderbans.

Hence, the correct option is (A).

3. River Brahmaputra cuts through 3 countries: China, India, and Bangladesh. The river is known by various names in different regions. It is known as Yarlung Tsangpo in Tibet and the Jamuna River in Bangladesh.

Hence, the correct option is (C).

4. Dodda Betta

- It is the highest mountain in the Nilgiri Mountains, Tamil Nadu.
- It is 2,637 metres (8,652 feet) high.
- Doddabetta translates to "Big Mountain".

Nanda Devi

- It is the second-highest mountain in India after Kangchenjunga.
- It is in Uttrakhand.
- It is the 23rd-highest peak in the world.

Anai Mudi

- It is a mountain located in the Indian state of Kerala.
- It is the highest peak in the Western Ghats and South India.
- Anamudi or Anai Mudi means Elephant Peak in Malayalam and Tamil respectively.

Saramati

- It is the highest peak in the state of Nagaland.
- Mount Saramati is a mountain straddling the border of Nagaland and Myanmar.

Hence, the correct option is (C).

5. Nagpur is precisely at the geographical center-point of India and the zero mile marker is located here. The distances of various major cities which are measured from here are carved on the pillar erected at this zero-mile site. Hence, Nagpur is called the zero-mile center.

Hence, the correct option is (C).

6. The Eastern Ghats or Purva Ghat, also known as Mahendra Parvatam in the south, is a discontinuous range of mountains along India's eastern coast.

Starting at West Bengal, Eastern Ghats pass through states like Odisha, Andhra Pradesh, Telangana, and Tamil Nadu to the south passing through some parts of Karnataka.

They are eroded and cut through by the four major rivers of peninsular India, known as the Godavari, Mahanadi, Krishna, and Kaveri.

The highest peak of Eastern Ghats is the Jindhagada peak (1690 meters). It is also known as Arma Konda or Sitamma Konda.

Hence, the correct option is (A).

7. Palghat Gap, a major break in the Western Ghats mountain range, in southwestern India. It is located between the Nilgiri Hills to the north and the Annamalai Hills to the south. It is about 20 miles (32 km) wide and straddles the Kerala-Tamil Nadu border, serving as a major communication route between those two states.

Hence, the correct option is (B).

8. Karst topography is landscape formed from the dissolution of soluble rocks such as limestone, dolomite and gypsum. Sinkhole vary in size from 1 to 600 m both in diameter and depth.

Hence, the correct option is (D).

9. Narmada is one of the rivers in India that flows in a rift valley, flowing west between the Satpura and Vindhya ranges. The other rivers which flow through the rift valley include the Damodar River in Chota Nagpur Plateau and Tapti.

Hence, the correct option is (A).

10. In Jowai and Cherapunjee, coal mining is done by family members by digging a long narrow tunnel, which is referred to as 'Rat hole Mining'. In India, to extract minerals, individual needs the due permission of the government as most of the minerals are nationalized or acquired by the government of the country. In the case of Meghalaya, it is different; coal mines in the tribal areas of North-east India are acquired by the individuals and communities rather than the government. Large deposits of coal, iron ore, limestone, and dolomite, etc are found in Meghalaya.

Hence, the correct option is (D).

11. A peneplain is a low relief plain formed by protracted erosion. The existence of some peneplains, and peneplanations as a process in nature, is not without controversy, due to a lack of contemporary examples and uncertainty in identifying relic examples.

Uplifted peneplains can be preserved as fossil landforms in conditions of extreme aridity or under non-eroding cold-based glacier ice. Erosion of peneplains by glaciers in shield regions is limited.

Hence, the correct option is (C).

12. Mim Kut which takes place in August-September in the wake of harvesting of the maize crop, is celebrated by the Mizo tribe. It is celebrated with great gaiety and merriment expressed through singing, dancing, feasting and drinking of home made rice beer zu. Dedicated to the memory of their dead relatives, the festival is underlined by a spirit of thanksgiving and remembrance of the

years first harvest is placed as an offering on a raised platform built to the memory of the dead.

Hence, the correct option is (A).

13. Demography studies: The processes and trends associated with population like–

- Changes in population size;
- Patterns of births, deaths, and migration; and

The composition and structure of the population, like–

- The relative proportions of men, women and people of different age groups.

Hence, the correct option is (C).

14. Landforms (mountains, hills, ridges, lakes, valleys, etc.) are sometimes formed when the faults have a large vertical displacement. Adjacent raised blocks (horsts) and down-dropped blocks (grabens) can form high escarpments.

A chevron is a wedge-shaped sediment deposit observed on coastlines and continental interiors around the world. The term chevron was originally used independently by Maxwell and Haynes and Hearty and others for large, V-shaped, sub-linear to parabolic landforms in southwestern Egypt and on islands in the eastern, windward Bahamas.

Hence, the correct option is (D).

15. Kaziranga National park is famous for Rhinoceros Population and is located in Assam, India.

Kaziranga National Park is a national park in the Golaghat, Karbi Anglong and Nagaon districts of the state of Assam, India. The sanctuary, which hosts two-thirds of the world's great one-horned rhinoceroses, is a World Heritage Site.

Hence, the correct option is (A).

16. The Andes, in South America, are the world's longest continental range of mountains. About 7,600 kilometres (4,700 miles) in length, they span seven countries and include some of the highest mountains on Earth. Over fifty of the Andes peaks reach over 6,000 metres (20,000 feet) high.

Hence, the correct option is (D).

17. The correct match is:

List-I	List-II
A. Slate	2. Metamorpric rock
B. Lignite	4. Sedimentary rock
C. Bauxite	3. Non-ferrous mineral
D. Granite	1. Igneous rock

Hence, the correct option is (B).

18. The Sierra Nevada is a mountain range in the Western United States, between the Central Valley of California and the Great Basin. The vast majority of the range lies in the state of California, although the Carson Range spur lies primarily in Nevada. The Sierra Nevada is part of the American Cordillera, an almost continuous chain of mountain ranges that forms the western "backbone" of the Americas.

Hence, the correct option is (B).

19. Africa's highest mountain peak mt. Kilimanjaro lies in Tanzania. Kilimanjaro, with its three volcanic cones, Kibo, Mawenzi, and Shim, is a dormant volcanic mountain in Kilimanjaro National Park, Kilimanjaro Region, Tanzania.

Hence, the correct option is (C).

20. The biggest Island of the Indian Ocean is Madagascar. Madagascar, officially the Republic of Madagascar and previously known as the Malagasy Republic, is an island country in the Indian Ocean, off the coast of Southeast Africa.

Hence, the correct option is (B).

21. Labrador is different from other ocean currents. It is cold in nature. The Labrador Current is a cold current in the North Atlantic Ocean which flows from the Arctic Ocean south along the coast of Labrador and passes around Newfoundland, continuing south along the east coast of Nova Scotia.

Hence, the correct option is (D).

22. Agulhas currents has a warming influence on the neighbouring coast. The Agulhas Current is the western boundary current of the southwest Indian Ocean. It flows down the east coast of Africa from 27°S to 40°S. It is narrow, swift, and strong.

Hence, the correct option is (B).

23. East Australian current is a warm ocean current that moves warm water from the tropical Coral Sea. Where it splits from the South Equatorial Current, down the east coast of Australia.

Hence, the correct option is (A).

24. Canaries Current is part of ocean-current system in the North Atlantic Ocean. It branches south from tine North Atlantic Current and flows southwestward along die northwest coast of Africa.

Hence, the correct option is (D).

25. The Agulhas Current is the western boundary current of the southwest Indian Ocean. It flows south along the east coast of Africa from 27°S to 40°S. It is narrow, swift, and strong.

Hence, the correct option is (A).

26. National Highway-6 passes through Maharashtra, Chhattisgarh, and Orissa. National Highway-6 ran through Gujarat, Maharashtra, Chhattisgarh, Odisha, Jharkhand, and West Bengal state in India.

Hence, the correct option is (C).

27. The trade winds of the Southern Hemisphere need to cross the equator in order to reach the ITCZ (Intertropical Convergence Zone). Thus, the trade winds of the Southern Hemisphere cross the equator but are deflected towards the right under the Coriolis Effect.

Hence, the correct option is (B).

28. The layer of atmosphere composed of ionic gaseous molecules helping in propagation of radio waves is Ionosphere. It is the 2nd layer from the top. It ranges from 60 km to 1000 km. It also protects Earth from meteorites.

Hence, the correct option is (B).

29. Only tropical cyclones that form over the Atlantic Ocean or the eastern Pacific Ocean are called "hurricanes." Tropical cyclones are like giant engines that use warm, moist air as fuel. That is why they form only over warm ocean waters near the equator. The warm, moist air over the ocean rises upward from near the surface.

Hence, the correct option is (C).

30. The tropical cyclones - Hurricanes and Typhoons - develop and mature anywhere in the tropical zone. Tropical cyclone, also called typhoon or hurricane, an intense circular storm that originates over warm tropical oceans and is characterized by low atmospheric pressure, high winds, and heavy rain.

Hence, the correct option is (D).

31. National Highway-2 of India is the longest. National Highway-2 is a national highway in India that runs from Dibrugarh in Assam to Tuipang in Mizoram. Its length is about 1,214 km (754 mi).

Hence, the correct option is (B).

32. National Highway from Amritsar to Calcutta via Delhi is called National Highway No. 2. It was called Grand Trunk road and was constructed by Sher Shah.

Hence, the correct option is (B).

33. The climate of India is mainly tropical because of the location of the Himalayas in its North. India is home to an extraordinary variety of climatic regions, ranging from tropical in the south to temperate and alpine in the Himalayan north, where elevated regions receive sustained winter snowfall.

Hence, the correct option is (A).

34. The two volcanic islands in the Indian Territory are Narcondam and Barren Island. Narcondam Island is part of the east volcano island group of the Andaman island group which is located in the northern Andaman sea.

Hence, the correct option is (D).

35. Puducherry has the largest size and has four administrative divisions: four districts, viz. Puducherry, Mahe, Yanam and Karaikal. Puducherry district has the largest area and population.

Hence, the correct option is (C).

36. Lakshadweep, formerly (1956–73) Laccadive, Minicoy, and Amindivi Islands, union territory of India. It is a group of some three dozen islands scattered over some 30,000 square miles (78,000 square km) of the Arabian Sea off the southwestern coast of India.

Hence, the correct option is (B).

37. The Andaman and Nicobar Islands are one of the seven union territories of India. It is a group of islands at the junction of the Bay of Bengal and the Andaman Sea. Myanmar is the nearest mainland to the island.

Hence, the correct option is (B).

38. Uttar Pradesh shares its boundaries with maximum states. Although Uttar Pradesh comes at the fourth place in terms of area, the state shares its borders with as many as 9 states/Union Territories, apart from sharing an International border with Nepal.

Hence, the correct option is (B).

39. Rajasthan is the largest state in the country. According to the barren land also, the area of available barren land in the state is the highest compared to other states.

Hence, the correct option is (D).

40. As per Census-2011, the State of Punjab, has the highest percentage of Scheduled Caste population amongst all the States of the Country. The Scheduled Caste population in Punjab is about 88.60 lac which is 31.94% of the total population of the State.

Hence, the correct option is (C).

41. North of Australia in the Gulf of Carpentaria and to its east is the knife-shaped upward Cape York Peninsula. Here bauxite is extracted from the Waipa mine. China and Australia rank second in the world in the production of bauxite.

Hence, the correct option is (B).

42. Russia has the largest proved natural gas reserves in the world. As of 2019, it had about 38 trillion cubic meters worth of the fossil fuel, four trillion cubic meters more than ten years prior.

Hence, the correct option is (D).

43. Kazakhstan produces the largest share of uranium from mines (42% of world supply from mines in 2019), followed by Canada (13%) and Australia (12%).

Hence, the correct option is (D).

44. Millets and Rice are grown mostly under subsistence farming. Subsistence agriculture is self-sufficiency farming in which the farmers focus on growing enough food to feed themselves and their families.

Hence, the correct option is (D).

45. Four Indian states or Union territories share their boundaries with Pakistan. The states are- Rajasthan, Gujarat and Punjab and Union territory of Jammu and Kashmir. UT of Jammu and Kashmir shares the longest boundary with Pakistan (1222km). The total length of the India-Pakistan border is 3,323 kilometers.

Hence, the correct option is (B).

46. Ankleshwar is a city and a municipality in the Bharuch district of the state of Gujarat, India. The city is located fourteen kilometers from Bharuch. (AIA)-Ankleshwar Industrial Association is the largest organisation in GIDC where over 2000 industries are registered.

Hence, the correct option is (A).

47. The Konkan Railway (abbreviated KR) is a railway operated by the Konkan Railway Corporation, with its headquarters at CBD Belapur in Navi Mumbai, Maharashtra, India. The 756.25 km (approx 757) long railway line connects the states of Maharashtra, Goa, and Karnataka. The first train on the completed track was sent off on 26 January 1998.

Hence, the correct option is (C).

48. Cotton textile industry requires humid climate. Cinema industry requires cloud-free sunlight throughout the year. Due to the appropriate climate, the cotton textile industry in Mumbai and California has grown rapidly.

Hence, the correct option is (C).

49. Machines and driving force are used in small scale industries and they are also employed in small scale labor whereas in cottage industry this is not so. Fabrics, paper goods, toys, ceramics, furniture, dairy products, edible oil extraction industries, basic utensils leather goods etc. are examples of small scale industries.

Hence, the correct option is (C).

50. Development of large scale industries took place after the industrial revolution, in these industries special attention is given to product quality. Specialization in production is an important feature of large-scale industries. Produced goods are exported. Large scale industries were initially set up in Great Britain Western Europe Russia Japan etc.

Hence, the correct option is (C).

51. Iron-steel industry is the cornerstone of modern industrial era, it is a heavy industry and source of raw material for hundreds of people, hence it is called basic industry. Without this, we cannot even imagine industrial development. Hence it is also called axis industry.

Hence, the correct option is (B).

52. China is the world's largest producer of steel, China has enough raw material available for this industry. China's major iron ore producing area is-

1. Manchuria Region
2. North China Region - Near Shanxi Coalfields
3. Yangtze Valley Region

Hence, the correct option is (B).

53. Atomic energy is energy produced by controlled (i.e., non-explosive) nuclear reactions. Currently, commercial plants use nuclear fission for power generation. The heat from the nuclear reactor is used to heat water to produce steam, which is then used to generate electricity.

Hence, the correct option is (C).

54. Building materials are available from the botanical world. Medicines are available from the forests. Bark, wood, fruits, leaves and roots are not only obtained from trees, but also many types of herbs are also obtained from forests. Today only about 16 percent of the country's land is forested.

Hence, the correct option is (B).

55. Conscious use of resources and giving them time for renewal is called Resource Conservation. The need to use resources and balance their conservation for the future is called sustainable development. Everyone can contribute by reducing consumption and recycle and reuse of goods.

Hence, the correct option is (A).

56. The Sutlej River originates from the Mansarovar Lake in Tibet, the river enters the Shipki Pass in Kinnaur district in Himachal Pradesh, India.

The Sutlej River is a Sadanira river flowing in northern India. Its mythological name is Shaturdi. The length of which is the highest among the five rivers flowing in Punjab. It flows from Pakistan. At an altitude of 4,600 meters above sea level in southwestern Tibet, it originates from the Raksha Tal near Mansarovar, where its local name is Langchen Khambab.

Hence, the correct option is (C).

57. The Tulbul project is located on the Jhelum River in Jammu and Kashmir, work on the project started in 1987. But due to non-agreement of this project between India and Pakistan, the work of this project had to be stopped.

Hence, the correct option is (C).

58. Vembanad (Vembanad Kayal or Vembanad Kol) is the longest lake in India, as well as the largest lake in the state of Kerala. With an area of 2033 square kilometers, it is the second-largest Ramsar site in India only after the Sunderbans in West Bengal.

Hence, the correct option is (C).

59. Narmada, also known as Reva, is a river in central India and the fifth longest in the Indian subcontinent. Narmada is a major river flowing in the state of Madhya Pradesh and Gujarat in central India. The Narmada River originated from the Amarkantak peak of Maikal mountain. Its length is usually 1312 km. This river goes towards the west and falls in the Gulf of Khambat.

Hence, the correct option is (C).

60. Air pressure has an effect on air density, temperature, climate volume and gravitational power. Due to all these elements being variable, no direct proportional relationship between altitude and air pressure is found. The first experience of air pressure on the surface was made in 1650 by Otto von Guericke.

Hence, the correct option is (B).

61. On the equator, the rays of the sun are straight throughout the year. Therefore, the temperature is always high and the air pressure is low. The Earth's rotation velocity is highest at the equator. Due to which the centrifugal force is highest here.

In normal conditions there is inverse relation between air pressure and temperature. If the air temperature is high then the pressure is low and if the temperature is low then the pressure is high. This is the reason for greater pressure at the poles and less pressure at the equator.

The balance of pressure inside and outside the body will be disturbed. Apart from this, the people on board the aircraft would also have lack of oxygen. In such a situation, the fingers become numb and there is a slight tingling. Difficulty in breathing, nasal congestion, nosebleeds, ear pain, very severe headache, joint pain and nervousness.

Hence, the correct option is (D).

62. Equatorial Low Pressure Belt: The rays of the sun fall perpendicular to the equator nearly a year. Due to this, the air in the equatorial regions gets heated and rises, which makes the area of low pressure here.

Hence, the correct option is (A).

63. The best development of the westward wind is found between latitudes 40° to 65° south. These akshas here are called thundering chalisa, Prachanda Pachasa and screama satha. All these names are given by the sailors.

Hence, the correct option is (D).

64. Winds that flow continuously throughout the year in both spheres from equatorial low air pressure lanes to regions of southern latitudes, ie subtropical high air pressure lanes, are called trade winds. Since these winds are cold and dry, they do not rain and due to the effect of these winds, the seasonal days remain cool and dry. The northeast monsoon winds pass through the Bay of Bengal to absorb humidity and rain on the Cormandal coast.

Hence, the correct option is (D).

65. Homospheric layers of atmosphere include layers where chemical composition is independent of molecular weight of gases due to mixing by turbulence. Hence the lower layers such as troposphere, ionosphere, and mesosphere are homospheres.

Hence, the correct option is (A).

66. In the equatorial regions, due to excessive sunset during the day, the air expands and rises due to the lightening of the surface. This rising air absorbs humidity from the seas and other reservoirs. It is called Sustainable rain. The rains are accompanied by the glow of lightning and the thunder of the clouds. This type of rainfall mainly occurs in the equatorial regions, where convection currents arise due to the heating of the ground daily till noon and there are dense clouds around 2.3 o'clock. Complete darkness envelops and in a few moments the rain starts.

Hence, the correct option is (C).

67. Mawsynram is a township located in the East Khasi Hills district of the state of Meghalaya, India. It is located about 60.9 km from the state capital, Shillong. It is the most rainy region of India, and possibly also of the world. It receives 11,872 millimeters of rainfall annually and in 1985, 26,000 millimeters of rainfall fell in the Guinness World Records. Meghalaya State Highway 4 passes through here.

Hence, the correct option is (C).

68. Cloudburst is an extreme form of rain. In this event, thunderstorms are sometimes accompanied by thunderstorms. Normally, due to cloudburst, there is torrential rain for only a few minutes, but during this time it rains so much that a flood-like situation arises in the area. Cloud eruption usually occurs at an altitude of 15 km above the Earth. The rainfall due to this is at a rate of about 100 millimeters per hour. More than 2 centimeters of rain falls in a few minutes, causing heavy destruction.

Hence, the correct option is (C).

69. A cyclone is a center of low pressure, that is, a strong storm of hot air around a low atmospheric pressure is called a cyclone. The cyclone is circular in shape, elliptical to 'V' in shape. Cyclones have extreme effects on climate and weather.

Hence, the correct option is (D).

70. Cyclones develop in areas located between the Tropic of Cancer and the Tropic of Capricorn. They typically develop in the summer season in the vicinity of the Inter-Tropical Convergence Zone on the warm sea surface. The energy source of tropical cyclones is latent heat of condensation.

Hence, the correct option is (D).

71. The galaxy is a cluster of vast numbers of stars. Each galaxy contains about 100 million stars. The sky (Milky Way) has about 100,000 million stars. Structurally, the galaxy consists of a central bulge and three rotating arms. Hence statements 1 and 2 are true.

The central part of the Milky Way - the bulge has more stellar deposits than the rotating arms. Hence statement 3 is false.

The Limon is a cluster of giant galaxies and gases 20 light-years wide of the alpha blobs-amoebic structure. Whereas Andromeda is the closest galaxy to our galaxy i.e., Milky Way.

Hence, the correct option is (C).

72. The rotating galaxy affects the cloud of gases present in the universe. In this way, the process of nuclear fusion starts in the central part as a result of mutual gravity. In this sequence, hydrogen is converted into helium. In this state it becomes a star. So, statement 1 is true.

After the formation of star, hydrogen is exhausted in the central part, this part gets compressed and heated but the process of making helium from hydrogen in the outer part continues. After this, its color turns red by slowly cooling, it is called the blood demon. Helium is then converted into carbon and carbon into heavy materials - iron, etc., causing a rapid explosion (supernova explosion) in the stars. After this, relative to the mass of the Sun, it is called white Vamana (fossil star) or neutron star or pulsar. It is important that the white Vamana cools down and turns into Kala Vamana. So, statement 2 is false.

Hence, the correct option is (A).

73. 1.44 Ms is called Chandrasekhar Seema. So, statement 1 is true.

When the mass of stars is less than 1.44 Ms, due to a supernova explosion in blood donation stars, they become white dwarfs. Here 'Ms' refers to the mass of the Sun. These star Vamana stars cool down and become black dwarfs, hence statement 2 is wrong.

It is important to note that in stars with a mass greater than 1.44 ms, the free-moving electrons move out of the nucleus at high velocity and consequently the neutron remains. This state is called neutron star or pulsar. Now the neutron star also shrinks over a long period of time into a liquid mass of high density called blackhole or Krishna hole.

Hence, the correct option is (A).

74. According to general relativity the blackhole is a celestial sphere with high gravity. It is not possible to flee any other material including light from this region. So, statements 1 and 2 are correct.

It is important to note that the boundary of the blackhole from which the transit of an object is not possible is called the event horizon. So, statement 3 is correct. Despite this, the event horizon widely affects the destiny and condition of an object in contact. So, statement 4 is wrong.

In this way Blackhole is an invisible celestial sphere. This concept was formulated by 'John Kheler'.

The rogue blackhole is a cluster of blackholes, while saffron is a luminous celestial body that emits an enormous amount of energy.

Hence, the correct option is (C).

75. The source of the Sun's energy is not nuclear fission but nuclear fusion. So, statement 1 is false. In the process of nuclear fusion, the hydrogen atom in the center of the Sun converts to helium.

The visible part of the Sun is called the Photosphere. While the outer part, which is visible only at the time of solar eclipse, is called corona. So, 2 is true.

Occasional storms of atoms emanating from the Sun, which go beyond the Sun's attraction power into space; It is called Solar Flares. This solar flame originates from the Sun's lighthouse and not from Corona. So, statement 3 is wrong.

This solar flame enters the Earth's atmosphere, after hitting the air and produces colored light. This phenomenon is seen at the North Pole and South Pole which are called Arira Bolialis and Arira Australis respectively.

Hence, the correct option is (B).

76. The temperature of the solar stigma is lower than that of the Sun, about 1500°C. So, statement 1 is false. It is important to note that black spots are visible from the place where the solar flame comes out, this is called solar spots.

Solar stigma emits strong magnetic radiation that disrupts the wireless communication system on Earth, not aid. So, statement 2 is wrong.

It is noteworthy that the process of solar stigma is completed in 11 years, which is called the solar stigma cycle. ISRO has started the construction process of a satellite named Aditya-1 to study the corona and wireless communication system of the Sun.

Hence, the correct option is (D).

77. About 99.85% of the solar system is formed by the Sun, while only 0.135% is formed by the planets. Hence, both the above statements are false.

Hence, the correct option is (D).

78. Among the eight planets of the solar system, Earth, Mars, Mercury and Venus are called internal planets as well as terrestrial planets. So, statement 1 is true. It is important to note that their

earth has a dense and rocky surface, that is why they are called terrestrial planets.

It is noteworthy that Mercury and Venus are also known as Ingraha due to their location between the Sun and the Earth.

Lack of atmosphere is found on the planet Mercury. Due to this, the temperature of the day is very high here, while the nights are icy, consequently life is not possible here. So, it is clear that statement 2 is false.

The planet Venus has been labeled as 'sister of the earth'. Because Venus is very close to Earth in size, mass and density. So, statement 3 is true.

At the same time, Jupiter, Saturn, Uranus and Neptune are called Jovian planets, because they are much larger than the Earth and have gaseous nature similar to Jupiter.

Hence, the correct option is (C).

79. Jupiter is the largest planet in the solar system. It has 67 known natural satellites so far, which is the highest compared to other planets in the Solar System. 'Ganymede' is the largest satellite of Jupiter. Obviously, statement 1 is true. It is noteworthy that Jupiter is called miniature solar system. It has its own radio energy.

There are no natural satellites of Mercury and Venus. They are both inner planets and inner planets tend to have very few or no satellites and rings. So, statement 2 is true.

Hence, the correct option is (C).

80. Due to the inclination of the earth on its own axis, there is fraternity at different places during the day and night time. Had the Earth not tilted on its axis, the duration of day and night would have been equal in all places.

It is important to note that there is a change of seasons due to the orbiter of the Sun. In this way, the combined result of the earth tilting on its axis and orbiting it relative to the Sun is the difference in the time of day and night at different places in different seasons.

Hence, the correct option is (B).

81. The Earth's axis is inclined to its elliptical plane, which results in the difference between day and night time in different seasons.

In the Northern Hemisphere, progressing northward during the winter season (December) progressively increases the time of night. The sun does not come out all day on Arctic Circle (N) in mid-winter season i.e. 22 December. Thus, both the above statements are true.

It is important to note that the number of full nights increases beyond the Arctic Circle. In this way, when we reach the northern pole (90°N), there is a shadow of six months.

It is notable that in summer (June), the opposite is seen in the northern hemisphere.

Hence, the correct option is (C).

82. The sun shines perpendicularly twice a year on the equator. So, statement 1 is false. Generally this situation is on March 21 and September 21, but there are not completely 365 days in a year, so this situation keeps on changing. It is interesting to note that when the sun shines perpendicularly on the equatorial circle, then the duration of day and night is equal everywhere on the earth.

When the sun shines vertically (22 December) on the Tropic of Capricorn, it is called Winter Solstice. In contrast, when the sun shines perpendicularly on the Tropic of Cancer, it is called Summer Solstice. So, statement 2 is true.

It is important to note that when the sun shines perpendicularly on the equator, the duration of day and night is equal everywhere. This condition is called 'even night-day' or 'equinox'. So, statement 3 is false.

Hence, the correct option is (B).

83. The main attraction or main feature of the Atlantic Ocean is the "Middle Atlantic Ridge". Like the ocean, it extends from north to south in the shape of the letter 'S'. It is about 14000 km from Iceland in the north to Bowet Island in the south. It is tall and about 4000 meters high.

Hence, the correct option is (A).

84. On 1st December 1963, Nagaland became the 16th state of India.

Indian President Sarvepalli Radhakrishnan inaugurated the state of Nagaland at Kohima on December 1, 1963.

Ao, Chakhesang, Angami, Dimasa Kachari, Chang, Konyak, Kuki, Lotha, Pochury, Rengma, Sangtam, Sumi, Zeliang, Yimchunger, Phom, and Khiamniungan- are major tribes of Nagaland.

Hence, the correct option is (C).

85. Tundra forests are always covered with snow. Tundra forests are found in the northern and southern hemispheres. Tundra regions are found between the ice-covered poles and the taiga or coniferous forests. There are three regions and associated types of tundra: Arctic tundra, alpine tundra, and Antarctic tundra.

Hence, the correct option is (B).

86. Srisailam Dam is constructed on Krishna River. It has the second largest hydroelectric project in the country. It is located in Kurnool district of Andhra Pradesh near Nallamala Hill.

Hence, the correct option is (B).

87. Dhola Sadiya is the longest bridge in India. It is also referred as Bhupen Hazarika Setu. It is 9.5 kilometres long and built across Lohit river, which is a tributary of Brahamputra. It will connect Assam and eastern Arunachal Pradesh. The construction of the Dhola-Sadiya Bridge began in 2011 by the Ministry of Road Transport along with Navayuga Engineering Company Ltd.

Hence, the correct option is (A).

88. The Western Ghats are called the Great Escarpment of India. They are also known as the Benevolent Mountains. The Western Ghats start from Gujrat and spread in Maharashtra, Karnataka, Goa, Kerala, and Tamil Nadu. Western Ghats are also recognised as the UNESCO World Heritage Site and also a biodiversity Hot Spot. Anaimudi is the highest peak of Western Ghats.

Hence, the correct option is (D).

89. Puncak Jaya is the highest mountain in Indonesia, on the island of New Guinea, it has an elevation of 4808 mt. It is also the highest point between the Himalayas and the Andes. Carstensz Glacier, West Northwall Firn, East Northwall Firn are major glaciers found nearby it. The recent observations of faster melting of glaciers is a major cause of concern. The massive, open cut Grasberg mine is within 4 km of Puncak Jaya.

Hence, the correct option is (A).

90. China produces the most electricity from hydroelectric power approximately 856.4 billion kilowatt hours a year. Brazil and Canada are at second and third positions in production of hydroelectric power in world. Hydroelectricity is electricity made by generators that are pushed by movement of water. When the water is released, the pressure behind the dam forces the water down pipes that lead to a turbine.

Hence, the correct option is (B).

91. Geomorphology is studied in geography, geology, geometry, engineering geology, archeology, and geotechnical engineering, and this broad base of interest generates a wide variety of research styles and interests under the subject. Peshal is considered to be the originator of geomorphology.

The Earth's surface develops in response to a combination of natural and anthropological processes, and responds with a balance between the processes that add and remove materials.

Hence, the correct option is (A).

92. In modern times the term ecology was first used by Ernest Hackel in 1866 and he tried to define it as something like "economics of nature". Harlan Barrows, at the same time, advocated defining human geography as human ecology.

Ecologists who came from biology to ecology often ignored human elements and human ecology, but the history of human ecology has always been a human-centric study.

Hence, the correct option is (C).

93. Poland-born Nicholaus Copernicus (19 February 1473 - 24 May 1543) was a Polish astronomer and mathematician. He gave this revolutionary formula that the Earth is not in the center of space.

Nicholaus was the first European astronomer to consider the Earth outside the center of the universe, applying the Heliocentrism model. Before this, the whole of Europe believed in the concept of Aristotle, in which the earth was the center of the universe and the sun, stars, and other bodies revolved around it.

Hence, the correct option is (A).

94. The celestial bodies revolving around the Sun or any other star are called planets. According to the International Astronomical Union, there are eight planets in our solar system - Mercury, Venus, Earth, Mars, Jupiter, Saturn, Uranus, and Neptoon. Apart from these, there are three dwarf planets - Ceres, Pluto, and Eris. Ancient astronomers differentiated between stars and planets in this way - most of the bodies that shine in the sky

at night always rise from the east, attain a certain speed, and set in the west direction.

Hence, the correct option is (A).

95. Geography is the study of the surface. This statement was said by Kant.

Emanuel Kant (1724–1804) was a German scientist, ethicist, and philosopher. His scientific view is known as the "Kant-Laplace hypothesis" (hypotheosis). According to the above hypothesis, the solar system originated from the Saturn Vapor Nebula. Kant's moral opinion is called the principle of "moral purity" (moral purism), the principle of "duty to duty" or "rigorism" (rigorism). His philosophical view is known as "Critical Philosophy".

Hence, the correct option is (C).

96. Satellite objects orbiting around a planet are called satellites.

In the context of space flight, a satellite is an object that has been put into orbit by human effort. Such objects are sometimes called artificial satellites to distinguish them from natural satellites such as the moon.

Hence, the correct option is (C).

97. Kepler's first rule:

According to this rule, "Each planet moves along the Sun's elliptical path, and the Sun is on one of the ellipses of that ellipse."

Hence, the correct option is (A).

98. In 1543, Nicolaus Copernicus first discovered that the Sun is at the center of the universe, and Nicolaus Copernicus was the first human to develop a solar-centric system from a mathematical predictor. The solar system was discovered by Nicolaus Copernicus.

Hence, the correct option is (A).

99. The Sun is a G-series main-sequence star located in the center of the Solar System around which the Earth and other elements of the Solar System revolve. The Sun is the largest body of our solar system, which comprises 99.76% of the mass of our entire solar system and has a diameter of about 13 lakh 90 thousand kilometers, which is about 109 times more than the Earth.

Hence, the correct option is (D).

100. The maximum distance of the Sun from any planet or other celestial bodies is called Aphelion, and the minimum distance is called Perihelion.

Perihelion and Aphelion are the minimum and maximum distances from the Sun on their orbit of a planet, asteroid, or comet, respectively.

Hence, the correct option is (B).

101. The biosphere is the result of complex interactions between biological and non-biological components found on the Earth's surface. These mutually complex action reactions of these components are studied in ecology. All biological components are sensitive to changes in the environment and most of their

activities are related to finding the appropriate ecological environment and staying away from inappropriate stimulation.

Hence, the correct option is (C).

102. Two types of adaptation are found in organisms.

1. Hereditary adaptation

2. Acquired adaptation

Hereditary adaptation is the adaptation that is derived from birth. Such as the sensory organ while acquired adaptation arises from a response to a particular stimulus. Just as building antibodies to protect against a disease, all organisms have sensitivity to environmental changes as well as the ability to adjust to changes that result in their survival and biospheric balance.

Hence, the correct option is (B).

103. The lithosphere is the solid part of the earth. Approximately 29 points of the entire Earth are as wide as continents and lamps on 2 percent. Its upper surface is made up of unorganized soil beneath which rocks are found, but from the point of view of biosphere, the upper surface of the earth's surface is important because all the organisms get nourishment from soil obtained on the lithosphere.

Hence, the correct option is (A).

104. The ocean is wide at 70.8 percent of the entire Earth. If rivers, ponds, and other aquatic sources are included in it, then about 72% of the area of earth power is covered with water, which is called the hydrosphere. The body's oxygen and hydrogen requirements are met by water.

It is estimated that about 1360 million cubic kilometers of water are available on the Earth's surface, of which 97% i.e., 1320 million cubic kilometers of water is located in the ocean, about 30 million cubic kilometers of water is located in the form of ice. Less than 1% is available as groundwater.

Hence, the correct option is (A).

105. The highest amount of nitrogen in the atmosphere gases is 78% and oxygen is 21%. The remaining 1% includes other gases such as carbon dioxide neon argon ozone etc. that have been obtained from the tests which vary the percentage ratio of atmospheric gases up to 50 km altitude in the mantle.

Heavy and gaseous gases such as carbon dioxide are found only up to an altitude of 20 km. Oxygen and nitrogen gas also almost disappear after an altitude of 140 km. After 150 km altitude, only hydrogen gas is found to be the critical gas.

Hence, the correct option is (C).

106. Oxygen is the most essential gas for the respiration of all organisms, while carbon dioxide is the essential gas for the photosynthetic action of plants. Similarly, nitrogen is an important component in all the organisms that they get from food.

It is clear from appropriate deliberation that all the biological components of the biosphere derive essential elements for life from the 3 divisions. Where life is attained from the atmosphere.

Water is obtained from the same hydrosphere that makes up 75% of the organism's protoplasm.

Hence, the correct option is (B).

107. The number of species of fauna and plants available in a natural state is called biodiversity. The term biodiversity was first used by American insect scientist Wilson in 1986, which was later adopted by other scientists and environmentalists as a concept.

Hence, the correct option is (A).

108. The properties of each organism are determined by genes at the genetic level. Genetic diversity is the estimation of different forms of the same gene in organisms of any species.

Hence, the correct option is (A).

109. The diversity of the natural inhabitants of an area like a forest, desert, meadows, etc. is called ecological conqueror. In ecological diversity, the transfer of energy from one nutrition level to another nutrition level is related to the process of balanced fertilizer water and mineral substances cyclization.

For example, there are different biodiversity in the saline aquatic system of the sea and in the alluvial aquatic system. In saline waters, where large fishes like whale sharks are found, in saline waters such fishes are not found.

Hence, the correct option is (C).

110. About 2.4% of the total land area is located in our country, while 6.5% of the world's fauna species are found in 8% plant species. Therefore, our country is one of the 12 countries with huge biological diversity in the world. So far, after surveying about 70% of the geographical area of the country, 46000 plant species and 81000 fauna species have been classified here.

Hence, the correct option is (A).

111. Indus, Ganga, Brahmaputra, Satluj, Alaknanda, Gandak, Kosi etc, are Himalayan rivers.

The Kaveri (also known as Cauvery, the anglicized name) is an Indian river flowing through the states of Karnataka and Tamil Nadu. The Kaveri river rises at Talakaveri in the Brahmagiri range in the Western Ghats, Kodagu district of the state of Karnataka, at an elevation of 1,341 m above mean sea level and flows for about 800 km before its outfall into the Bay of Bengal.

Hence, the correct option is (A).

112. Rihand Dam also known as Govind Ballabh Pant Sagar, is the largest dam of India by volume. The reservoir of Rihand Dam is called Govind Ballabh Pant Sagar and is India's largest artificial lake. Rihand Dam is a concrete gravity dam located at Pipri in Sonbhadra District in Uttar Pradesh, India.

Hence, the correct option is (D).

113. The Narmada river flows through Madhya Pradesh, Maharashtra, and Gujarat between Vindhya and Satpura hill ranges before falling into the Gulf of Cambay in the Arabian Sea about 10 km north of Bharuch, Gujarat. The total length of the river from the head to its outfall into the Arabian Sea is 1,333 km.

Hence, the correct option is (D).

114. Rajrappa is a waterfall and a pilgrimage centre in the Chitarpur CD block in the Ramgarh subdivision of the Ramgarh district in the Indian state of Jharkhand. It is situated on the confluence of Damodar – Behera rivers.

Hence, the correct option is (A).

115. Bhilangana is not a tributary of Alaknanda. Bhilangna River is a Himalayan river in Uttarakhand, India, which is the major tributary of the Bhagirathi river, the source stream of the Ganges River of India. Bhilangana is a combination of Bhil and Ganga.

Hence, the correct option is (A).

116. The Dudhwa National Park is a national park in the Terai of Uttar Pradesh, India, and covers an area of 490.3 km², with a buffer zone of 190 km². It is part of the Dudhwa Tiger Reserve.

Kanha National Park, also known as Kanha Tiger Reserve, is a vast expanse of grassland and forest in the central Indian state of Madhya Pradesh. Tigers, jackals, and wild pigs can be spotted in Kanha Meadows.

Indravati Tiger Reserves is a Tiger Reserve area in Chhattisgarh. Bandipur National Park, an 874 km² forested reserve in the southern Indian state of Karnataka, is known for its small population of tigers.

Hence, the correct option is (A).

117. The Nanda Devi National Park or Nanda Devi Biosphere Reserve, established in 1982 is a national park situated around the peak of Nanda Devi (7816 m) in the Chamoli district Uttarakhand in northern India. The entire park lies at an elevation of more than 3,500 m (11,500 ft) above mean sea level.

Hence, the correct option is (D).

118. According to the 2011 Forest Survey of India, Mizoram has the third-highest total forest cover with about 1,594,000 hectares and the highest percentage area (90.68%) covered by forests, among the states of India.

Hence, the correct option is (A).

119. Kanha National Park belongs to tropical dry deciduous forest. It is a tiger reserve of India and the largest national park of Madhya Pradesh.

Kanha Tiger Reserve, also known as Kanha–Kisli National Park, is one of the tiger reserves of India and the largest national park of the state of Madhya Pradesh. The present-day Kanha area is divided into two protected areas, Hallon and Banjar, of 250 and 300 km² (97 and 116 sq mi), respectively.

Hence, the correct option is (C).

120. In the given options the literacy of the following states are-

1. Odisha - 72.87%

2. Punjab - 75.84%

3. Maharastra - 82.34%

4. Mizoram - 91.33%

Hence, the correct option is (D).

121. The 'Todas' are one of the major tribes found in Nilgiris. One of the most primitive tribe of the Nilgiris is Todas. Toda people are a Dravidian ethnic group who live in the Nilgiri Mountains of Tamil Nadu.

Hence, the correct option is (C).

122. Mangolabs migrated from China and Mongolia to Sikkim, Arunachal Pradesh and Nagaland, Manipur has a racial division including people of Central and eastern Asia.

Hence, the correct option is (D).

123. Garo and Khasi tribes are mainly found in hilly regions of Meghalaya. The dominance of these tribes is so profound that hills like Garo, Khasi, and Jaintia are named after them.

Hence, the correct option is (A).

124. According to 2011 Census, Bhil is the most populous tribe having a population of about 4,618,068 which is 37% of ST population. It is mainly found in the Malwa region.

Hence, the correct option is (A).

125. The tropical rain forest in the Amazon basin is known as Selvas. The Amazon rainforest, covering much of northwestern Brazil and extending into Colombia, Peru, and other South American countries, is the world's largest tropical rainforest, famed for its biodiversity. It's crisscrossed by thousands of rivers, including the powerful Amazon.

Hence, the correct option is (C).

Q.1 Who among the following first attempted to create a world map on a scale?

A. Homer

B. Anaximander

C. Hipparchus

D. Ptolemy

Q.2 The Dhule and prism used in Ptolemy's map were located:

A. World's farthest north-south place

B. World's furthest east-west place

C. Middle of the world

D. At the equator

Q.3 Which of the following geographers wrote a book called 'Perspective on the Nature of Geography'?

A. Ritter

B. Dudley Stamp

C. Hartshorne

D. Blache

Q.4 Match List-I with List-II and select the correct answer from the codes given below the list:

	List-I		List-II
(A)	Positivist Geography	(1)	Auguste Comte
(B)	Ethical Geography	(2)	William Kirk
(C)	Humanistic Geography	(3)	Yi-Fu-Tuan
(D)	Neolithicism	(4)	Griffith Taylor

A. (A)-(1), (B)-(2), (C)-(3), (D)-(4)

B. (A)-(1), (B)-(3), (C)-(2), (D)-(4)

C. (A)-(1), (B)-(2), (C)-(4), (D)-(3)

D. (A)-(1), (B)-(3), (C)-(4), (D)-(2)

Q.5 Who said 'Chorological Science' of Geography?

A. A. V. Humboldt

B. A. Hettner

C. W. M. Davis

D. F. Ratzel

Q.6 Who said that 'Geography is the science which is related to the art of mapping'?

A. Eratosthenese

B. Hipparchus

C. Hecataeus

D. Ptolemy

Q.7 In what other name is 'Neo-Determinism' known as-

A. Stop Determinism

B. Go Determinism

C. Stop and go determinism

D. All of the above

Q.8 The most important of the changes in geography after World War II was -

A. The emergence of geography as a spatial science

B. Emphasis on the study of human-environment relationships

C. Achieving the central position of human geography

D. The dualism of ordered geography versus territorial geography flourish

Q.9 The Greek scholar who thought that "all history should be examined in geographical perspective and all geography in historical perspective", is-

A. Thales

B. Herodotus

C. Hecataeus

D. Anaximander

Q.10 The concept of 'sequential occupancy' was presented as-

A. Gotman

B. Hager Strong

C. Gaddis

D. Hitlesi

Q.11 Who among the following wrote that "Geography is related to the accurate, systematic logical description and interpretation of the changing nature of the surface"?

A. Karl Ritter

B. Alexander von Humboldt

C. Richthofen

D. Richard Hartshorne

Q.12 Gunnar Myrdal's book 'Asian Drama' is a study-

A. Of the poverty of nations in Asia

B. Of political competition in Asia

C. Of the state of drama in Asia

D. Of economic cooperation in Asia

Q.13 Geography is the mother of all sciences. This statement is related to______

A. From Preston E. James

B. By Richard Hartshorne

C. From E. Huntington

D. From Karl Ritter

Q.14 'Antipode' magazine highlights the problems of which of the following people of the society?

A. Of the urban rich

B. Of politicians

C. Of capitalists

D. Of the poor and deprived

Q.15 "Geography is a field science." Which of the following scholars has given this statement?

A. R. Hartshorn

B. A. Hettner

C. Richthofen

D. A. Wegner

Q.16 Which of the following scholars propounded the theme of positivism?

A. Auguste Comte

B. David harvey

C. R. N. Beck

D. Yi-fu-tuyan

Q.17 Which of the following is the second largest body of the solar family?

A. Sun

B. Jupiter

C. Saturn

D. Uranus

Q.18 How many satellites are used in the Global Positioning System (GPS)?

A. 28

B. 24

C. 26

D. 30

Q.19 What is a 'magnetic storm'?
A. Disturbances in the magnetic fields of celestial bodies
B. Increase in power of magnetic poles
C. Change of north and south poles
D. Storms in the oceans caused by high magnetic currents

Q.20 Which planet does not have a planetoid?
A. Mars   B. Uranus   C. Venus   D. Neptune

Q.21 The word filament is used:
A. In the planetary hypothesis
B. In the tidal hypothesis
C. In the supernova hypothesis
D. In the interstellar dust hypothesis

Q.22 The corpus of the strings of exhausted gas and dust is called:
A. Filament
B. Nebula
C. The planet
D. Bifurcator

Q.23 Where is the longest length of the year?
A. Mercury   B. Jupiter   C. Earth   D. Pluto

Q.24 Which is the nearest planet to the Sun?
A. Venus   B. Mercury   C. Jupiter   D. Mars

Q.25 Identify the factors responsible for climate change on the surface of the Earth.
i. Earth rotation
ii. Revolutions of the earth
iii. Earth tilted on its own axis
iv. Rotation of the sun
A. i and iii
B. ii and iii
C. i and ii
D. i, ii and iv

Q.26 Consider the following statements about the Indian Solar Mission.
1. India is growing rapidly in solar energy.
2. India plans to extend solar power to all parts of the country.
3. South and West India gets more sunlight and solar energy.
Which of the above statements are correct?
A. only 1
B. 1 and 2 only
C. 1 and 3 only
D. 1,2 and 3

Q.27 Match List-I with List-II and select the correct answer using the code given below:

	List-I (Surname)		List-II (Planet)
(A)	Green Planet	(1)	Venus
(B)	Ringed planet	(2)	Mars
(C)	Red Planet	(3)	Urenas
(D)	Morning Sun	(4)	Saturn

A. (A)-(1), (B)-(2), (C)-(3), (D)-(4)
B. (A)-(4), (B)-(3), (C)-(2), (D)-(1)
C. (A)-(3), (B)-(4), (C)-(2), (D)-(1)
D. (A)-(3), (B)-42), (C)-(1), (D)-(2)

Q.28 The interval between two full moon days is approximately:
[UPSESSB PGT Geography, 2019]

A. 26.5 days   B. 27.5 days
C. 28.5 days   D. 29.5 days

Q.29 The theory of heliocentrism was propounded by ___.
A. Copernicus   B. Ptolemy
C. Laplace   D. Chamberlin

Q.30 Which of the following planets has the shortest day?
[UPSESSB PGT Geography, 2019]

A. Earth   B. Mars   C. Mercury   D. Venus

Q.31 What is Hailey, Gayle and Wilson?
A. Meteor   B. Comet   C. Satellite   D. Asteroid

Q.32 In which of the following, in 1543, instead of 'Earth-centered' universe, the concept of a 'Sun-centered' universe was presented?
A. Nicholas Copernicus
B. I. Newton
C. Herodotus
D. Aristotle

Q.33 Which of the following planets is the Brahmi planet?
A. Venus   B. Mars   C. Uranus   D. Earth

Q.34 Which one of the following is more useful for a sailor?
A. Mercator interpolation
B. Nomonic interpolation
C. Universal interpolation
D. Mallweed interpolation

Q.35 On which planet is the huge red spot found?
A. Mars   B. Jupiter   C. Mercury   D. Saturn

Q.36 Under the mantle in the structure of the planet Earth, the core is mainly composed of ___.
A. Aluminum   B. Silicon
C. Chromium   D. Iron

Q.37 The upper part of the mantle above which the earth's crust plumes, is called:
A. Gurumandal (berriesphere)
B. Mososphere
C. Hydrosphere
D. Asthenosphere

Q.38 In which era of Earth's geological history, dinosaurs reached their largest size?
A. Triassic   B. Jurassic
C. Cretaceous   D. Permian

Q.39 Between whom does the Gutenberg disambiguation occur?
A. Crust and cavity
B. Cavity and core
C. Upper core and lower core
D. Upper cavity and lower cavity

Q.40 What sets Gutenberg disambiguation apart?
[UPSESSB PGT Geography, 2019]

A. Upper crust and lower crust
B. Outer innermost and mantle
C. Inner innermost and outer innermost
D. Lower crust and mantle

Q.41 The land-balance hypothesis was interpreted through the coordination of Airy and Pratt's theory.
A. By Heskinen
B. By Holmes
C. By Jolie
D. By Hayford

Q.42 Which one of the following currents is better than the other currents?
A. Brazilian stream
B. Labrador's stream
C. Falkland Stream
D. Canary stream

Q.43 Which of the following is called cold current?
A. Brazil stream
B. Gulf Stream
C. Bengula stream
D. Agulhas stream

Q.44 The speed of ocean current is approximately-
A. 2% of the prevailing wind speed
B. 4% of the prevailing wind speed
C. 6% of the prevailing wind speed
D. 8% of the prevailing wind speed

Q.45 In which ocean does the Bengula streamflow?
A. Pacific Ocean
B. Indian Ocean
C. Atlantic Ocean
D. Arctic Ocean

Q.46 The average depth of the 'equatorial stream' is-
A. 50 m
B. 100 m
C. 150 m
D. 200 m

Q.47 The Gutenberg Discontinuity is found in the following:
A. Upper core and lower core
B. Mantle and core
C. Septum and mantle
D. Upper mantle and lower mantle

Q.48 Excessive folding occurs as a result of-
A. Anteroposterior prolapse
B. Ground
C. Nappy construction
D. Split block

Q.49 Sedimentary rocks are ultimately obtained from ___.
A. Earth movements
B. Marine deposit
C. Weathering of metamorphic rocks
D. Weathering of igneous rocks

Q.50 Which of the following is associated with the "Cretan"?
A. Granite
B. Conglomerate
C. Slate
D. Phyllite

Q.51 Which of the following is evidence in favor of continental displacement?
(a) Jig-Saw fit
(b) Transcurrent fault
(c) Fossils in different areas
(d) Convection in the mantle
A. (a) and (c)
B. (a) and (d)
C. (a) and (b)
D. (a), (c) and (d)

Q.52 Who is related to the quadrilateral theory of the origin of continents and oceans?
A. Lothian green
B. Holmes
C. Wegner
D. Calvin

Q.53 Who among the following first attempted to create a world map on a scale?
A. Lothian green
B. Wegner
C. Lord Calvin
D. Lapworth and love

Q.54 Which of the following ecosystem has been named as 'land of big poachers'?
A. Selva
B. Savannah
C. The prairie
D. Taiga

Q.55 NEERI is concerned with:
A. Energy research
B. Economic research
C. Academic research
D. Environmental research

Q.56 Consider the following statements about the ecosystem and choose the correct answer from the following code:
1. It occupies a fixed area on the ground floor.
2. It is a closed system in which there is a continuous flow of matter and energy.
3. It is powered by different types of energy but solar energy is the most important.
4. It does not have a measuring dimension.
Code:
A. 1 and 2
B. 2 and 3
C. 1 and 3
D. 3 and 4

Q.57 Which of the following does not promote sustainability in ecosystems?
A. The balance between production and consumption of every element in the ecosystem
B. Balance in investment and output of energy
C. The functionality of differential bio-geochemical cycles
D. Demonstrate suitable for human population growth

Q.58 Which of the following is the correct statement?
A. Man is a secondary consumer
B. Chhathundar is a tertiary consumer
C. Grasshopper is a primary consumer
D. Owl is a secondary and fourth consumer

Q.59 Which of the following statements is correct regarding the management of ecological resources -
A. Exploitation of natural resources
B. Rational exploitation and development of natural resources
C. Conservation of all-natural resources
D. Rational exploitation of natural resources and maintenance of the quality of the environment

Q.60 The fundamental element of an ecosystem is-
A. Bio weight
B. Biodiversity

C. Energy flow   **D.** Vegetation density

Q.61 Which of the following is a correct statement?

A. The ecocline represents the biological community, especially the gradient of vegetation change.

B. The EcoCline represents the adult ecology system.

C. The echocline displays a line joining locations of similar ecological resources.

D. Ecocline exhibits ecological climate.

Q.62 By what name is the study of the interrelations of specific organisms and the interconnection with their physical environment?

A. Phenology   **B.** Ecology
C. Biology   **D.** life science

Q.63 The term ecosystem was first used by which scholar in 1935?

A. The berry   **B.** Stodart
C. Tansley   **D.** Davis

Q.64 The transition between two ecosystems is called Kshatra:

A. Biome   **B.** Ecotone
C. Biotope   **D.** None of the above

Q.65 Which of the following geography bench has considered man as a component of the biosphere?

A. Chicago bench   **B.** Berkel bench
C. French bench   **D.** German bench

Q.66 An outbreak becomes a disaster when it adversely affects:

A. To atmospheric transmission
B. Sea creatures
C. To ecology
D. To human habitat

Q.67 The total amount of energy assimilated by the atmospheric primary products is called:

A. Ecological productivity
B. Environmental productivity
C. Gross primary productivity
D. Net primary productivity

Q.68 Which one of the following flora covers the most surface part of the world?

A. Tropical   **B.** Boreal
C. Neo-tropical   **D.** Antarctic

Q.69 In which of the following years was the 'Biodiversity / Biological Diversity Act' passed by the Lok Sabha of India?

A. 2005   **B.** 2001   **C.** 2002   **D.** 2007

Q.70 Which one of the following types of animal diffusion is caused by a long term drought?

A. Forced diffusion
B. Gradual diffusion
C. Biocore diffusion
D. Animocore diffusion

Q.71 Which of the following climate is humid and has more rainy days?

A. Climate similar to western europe
B. Geo-oceanic climate
C. Monsoon climate
D. St Laurence Equal Climate

Q.72 Which of the following is called 'Ecological Terrorist'?

A. Jhuming Agriculture
B. Soil erosion
C. Eucalyptus
D. Chemical fertilizer

Q.73 Where are different types of animals and plants found in maximum numbers?

A. In warm forested forests
B. In warm grasslands
C. In temperate forests
D. In temperate grass

Q.74 What does ecological niches indicate?

A. Interaction between man and environment
B. Functional role of the organism in the ecological system
C. Interdependence of man and plant
D. None of the above

Q.75 Where are hackistothal plants found?

A. Geo-climatic climate
B. Hot desert
C. Equatorial climate
D. Cold desert

Q.76 Which of the following is not a micronutrient of plants?

A. Carbon   **B.** Iron   **C.** Nitrogen   **D.** Oxygen

Q.77 In which era did the Gramyan of plants and animals begin?

A. Palaeolithic period
B. Medieval period
C. New stone period
D. Pre-Paleolithic period

Q.78 The ecological system is functional

A. Through energy flow and circulation of nutrients and minerals
B. Through growing interactions with organisms and their environment
C. Through integration of biological and abiotic components of the environment
D. Through Physico-chemical environment

Q.79 Diet trap is-

A. In a straight link, the person moving is extremely long.
B. Is a mid-sized net with multiple nutritional levels.
C. Is a circular network.
D. There is an intertwined network of food chains.

Q.80 Does the grass area ecosystem contain a biomass pyramid?

A. Upright (base wide)   **B.** Reverse
C. Horizontal   **D.** Parallel

Q.81 Which one of the following is a state of high ecological production?

A. Desert

B. Tropical and Tropical Forest Areas

C. Meadows

D. Arctic snowy region

Q.82 The largest producer of soybeans in the world is-

A. India

B. Brazil

C. United States of America

D. China

Q.83 The largest producer of dates in the world is-

A. Kuwait

B. Egypt

C. Iraq

D. Saudi Arabia

Q.84 In which region of the world cane can be provided to factories almost year round?

A. India

B. Cuba

C. Hawaiian Islands

D. Germany

Q.85 Which of the following rivers is best suited as internal waterways?

A. Danube

B. The Rhine

C. Volga

D. Alb

Q.86 Which of the following is responsible for the radical transformation of the soul and purpose of geography?

A. Postmodernism

B. Humanism

C. Structuralism

D. Quantification

Q.87 Pan America Highway connects-

A. Kordova - Arjul

B. Fire Bank-Saint Untino Oste

C. Prudhe Alaska - Argentina of South America

D. California - Chilly

Q.88 Which place does the Trans Siberian Railway connect?

A. Bludibostak - Saint Pittsburgh

B. Kiev - Moscow

C. Irkstuck - Leningrad

D. Moscow - Amask

Q.89 For what reasons is Japan a leading industrial country in the world?

1. Due to the developed hydropower

2. Due to huge deposits of metallic minerals

3. Due to high level of technological capability

4. Due to island location

A. 1,2,3 and 4

B. 1,2 and 3

C. 1 and 4

D. 2 and 4

Q.90 The main use of maize in the United States is-

A. In human food

B. In animal feed

C. To make starch

D. In preparing alcohol

Q.91 In which island is Japan's 'rice bowl' located?

A. Kyushu

B. Honshu

C. Shikoku

D. Ryuk

Q.92 The final stage in the process of energy resource utilization is:

A. Transportation

B. Storage

C. Disposal of residual material

D. Conversion

Q.93 In which country of the world, petroleum is considered as the 'source of power' and not the economy?

A. United States of america

B. Saudi Arab

C. Iraq

D. Kuwait

Q.94 The major fishery sector 'Grand Bank' is located -

A. In the south atlantic ocean

B. In the southern pacific ocean

C. In the north atlantic ocean

D. In the northern Pacific Ocean

Q.95 Which of the following is famous for producing mineral oil?

A. Karaganda

B. Transvaal

C. Kirkuk

D. Cape York

Q.96 Which of the following is a metallic mineral?

A. Coal

B. Limestone

C. Zinc

D. Gypsum

Q.97 Which of the following elements is not an iron ore?

A. Magnetite

B. Hematite

C. Lignite

D. Siderite

Q.98 Which of the following elements is formed by humans, is not found naturally?

A. Uranium

B. Plutonium

C. Thorium

D. Polonium

Q.99 The representative oil producing country of South-Western Asia is-

A. Iran

B. Kuwait

C. Saudi Arab

D. None of the above

Q.100 Which country has the deepest mine in the world?

A. United States of America

B. India

C. Brazil

D. South Africa

Q.101 Which country is the main producer of asbestos?

A. India

B. USA

C. Brazil

D. China

Q.102 Which one of the following is not a renewable energy?

A. Geothermal energy

B. Hydropower

C. Molecular energy

D. Solar energy

Q.103 Which of the following is not true for non-conventional alternative energy sources?

A. Eco-friendly

B. Light distribution

C. Renewable

D. Everlasting

Q.104 Where is Kirkuk, the most important oil field in the world, located?

A. Iran   **B.** Iraq   **C.** Kuwait   **D.** Russia

Q.105 Rubber, rosewood, palm and mahogany trees are related to which one of the following?

A. From warm tropical monsoon forests
B. Autumn forests
C. From taiga forests
D. From warm evergreen forests

Q.106 In which of the following are the main areas of agricultural cultivation in the world located?

A. In the Mediterranean
B. In dry area
C. In temperate zone
D. In warm region

Q.107 Which countries' farmers are famous for their intensification of agriculture?

A. Brazil and Colombia
B. Myanmar and Thailand
C. China and Japan
D. Malaysia and Indonesia

Q.108 Terraroxa midti is found in:

A. In brazil   **B.** In South Africa
C. In china   **D.** In Ukraine

Q.109 Milpa is known as:

A. For transferrable agriculture
B. For commercial agriculture
C. For sustainable agriculture
D. For food grains cultivation

Q.110 Which of the following is not related to intensive agriculture?

A. Wheat cultivation in china
B. Rice farming in India
C. Wheat Farming in Canada
D. Fruit farming in California

Q.111 The intensive coffee plantation in Brazil is called:

A. Fazenda   **B.** Tresil
C. Corals   **D.** Astonasius

Q.112 In which part of the world is the landscape formed by wind erosion called serir and reggae?

A. Sahara   **B.** Mongolia
C. Thar   **D.** California

Q.113 The drainage system that is not connected to the structure of that area is called ___.

A. Infertile runoff   **B.** Net runoff
C. Pneumatic runoff   **D.** Impounded runoff

Q.114 Levels are the result of negative motions:

A. Regeneration   **B.** Stabilization
C. Dredging   **D.** Saltation

Q.115 Gokhur Lake is known as?

A. Billabong   **B.** Mort Lake
C. Bayu   **D.** All of the above

Q.116 Which of the following is not an extraneous figure?

A. Natural embankment
B. Waterfall
C. Giri Shring
D. Aret

Q.117 The river valleys whose routes are controlled by factors that cannot be determined are called-

A. Subsequent   **B.** Latter
C. Non-recurring   **D.** Newborn

Q.118 Ria is an example of which of the following?

A. Deposited land
B. Submerged highland coastline
C. Embossed highland coastline
D. Irreplaceable topography

Q.119 In dry regions, the sand deposited by the rivers on the mountainous slope slopes is called:

A. Hamada   **B.** Bazada
C. Desertification   **D.** Pediment

Q.120 The delta chem result is:

A. Glacial erosion   **B.** Air deposition
C. River deposits   **D.** Glacial deposits

Q.121 Subsequent runoff usually occurs:

A. Conform to subsequent runoff
B. In contrast to subsequent runoff
C. At the right runoff angle
D. On the diagonal of the follow-up

Q.122 The amount of average solar energy received (calories per square cm per minute) at the top of the Earth's atmosphere, which of the following is true?

A. 1.94   **B.** 2.94   **C.** 1.84   **D.** 2.84

Q.123 Which of the following is correct in increasing order of percentage of atmospheric gases?

A. Helium, ginan, carbon dioxide and argon
B. Ginan, helium, carbon dioxide and argon
C. Helium, carbon dioxide, gynan and argon
D. Ginan, carbon dioxide, helium and argon

Q.124 The reason for the movement (circulation) of air in the troposphere is:

A. Solar wind   **B.** Convection current
C. Gravity   **D.** Air flows

Q.125 Who refracts electromagnetic waves in the following layers of the atmosphere:

A. Troposphere   **B.** Stratosphere
C. Ozone layer   **D.** Ion board

// Smart Answer Sheet //

Correct — Indicates percentage of students who answered questions correctly.

Skipped — Indicates percentage of students who skipped questions.

Q.	Ans.	Correct	Skipped
1	B	65.22 %	0.0 %
2	A	26.09 %	26.08 %
3	C	56.52 %	26.09 %
4	A	60.87 %	26.09 %
5	B	47.83 %	26.08 %
6	D	47.83 %	26.08 %
7	C	60.87 %	26.09 %
8	A	43.48 %	26.09 %
9	B	65.22 %	26.08 %
10	D	43.48 %	26.09 %
11	D	34.78 %	26.09 %
12	A	43.48 %	26.09 %
13	B	30.43 %	26.09 %
14	D	60.87 %	26.09 %
15	B	30.43 %	26.09 %
16	A	60.87 %	26.09 %
17	B	47.83 %	26.08 %
18	B	43.48 %	26.09 %
19	A	39.13 %	26.09 %
20	C	56.52 %	26.09 %
21	B	39.13 %	26.09 %
22	B	52.17 %	26.09 %
23	D	43.48 %	26.09 %
24	B	60.87 %	26.09 %
25	B	52.17 %	26.09 %
26	C	34.78 %	26.09 %
27	C	60.87 %	26.09 %
28	D	43.48 %	26.09 %
29	A	47.83 %	26.08 %
30	A	34.78 %	26.09 %
31	B	47.83 %	26.08 %
32	A	65.22 %	26.08 %
33	C	60.87 %	26.09 %
34	A	56.52 %	26.09 %
35	B	39.13 %	26.09 %
36	D	65.22 %	26.08 %
37	D	60.87 %	26.09 %
38	B	60.87 %	26.09 %
39	B	47.83 %	26.08 %
40	B	47.83 %	26.08 %
41	A	21.74 %	26.09 %
42	A	52.17 %	26.09 %
43	C	56.52 %	26.09 %
44	A	39.13 %	26.09 %
45	C	52.17 %	26.09 %
46	B	26.09 %	26.08 %
47	B	60.87 %	26.09 %
48	C	65.22 %	26.08 %
49	D	43.48 %	26.09 %
50	A	39.13 %	26.09 %
51	A	56.52 %	26.09 %
52	A	52.17 %	26.09 %
53	B	39.13 %	26.09 %
54	B	60.87 %	26.09 %
55	D	56.52 %	26.09 %
56	C	26.09 %	26.08 %
57	D	47.83 %	26.08 %
58	C	60.87 %	26.09 %
59	B	30.43 %	26.09 %
60	C	43.48 %	26.09 %
61	A	26.09 %	26.08 %
62	B	69.57 %	26.08 %
63	C	69.57 %	26.08 %
64	B	69.57 %	26.08 %
65	A	26.09 %	26.08 %
66	D	30.43 %	26.09 %
67	C	30.43 %	26.09 %
68	B	34.78 %	26.09 %
69	C	39.13 %	26.09 %
70	A	43.48 %	26.09 %
71	A	30.43 %	26.09 %
72	C	56.52 %	26.09 %
73	A	52.17 %	26.09 %
74	B	56.52 %	26.09 %
75	D	34.78 %	26.09 %
76	B	21.74 %	26.09 %
77	C	30.43 %	26.09 %
78	A	30.43 %	26.09 %
79	D	47.83 %	26.08 %
80	A	60.87 %	26.09 %

Q.	Ans.	Correct / Skipped
81	B	69.57 % / 26.08 %
82	C	47.83 % / 26.08 %
83	B	52.17 % / 26.09 %
84	C	43.48 % / 26.09 %
85	B	56.52 % / 26.09 %
86	D	39.13 % / 26.09 %
87	C	52.17 % / 26.09 %
88	A	65.22 % / 26.08 %
89	C	30.43 % / 26.09 %

Q.	Ans.	Correct / Skipped
90	B	56.52 % / 26.09 %
91	B	52.17 % / 26.09 %
92	C	60.87 % / 26.09 %
93	A	43.48 % / 26.09 %
94	C	65.22 % / 26.08 %
95	C	52.17 % / 26.09 %
96	C	43.48 % / 26.09 %
97	C	60.87 % / 26.09 %
98	B	39.13 % / 26.09 %

Q.	Ans.	Correct / Skipped
99	C	56.52 % / 26.09 %
100	D	47.83 % / 26.08 %
101	A	39.13 % / 26.09 %
102	C	52.17 % / 26.09 %
103	B	43.48 % / 26.09 %
104	B	47.83 % / 26.08 %
105	D	60.87 % / 26.09 %
106	D	17.39 % / 26.09 %
107	C	52.17 % / 26.09 %

Q.	Ans.	Correct / Skipped
108	A	39.13 % / 26.09 %
109	A	60.87 % / 26.09 %
110	C	39.13 % / 26.09 %
111	A	69.57 % / 26.08 %
112	A	56.52 % / 26.09 %
113	D	43.48 % / 26.09 %
114	A	30.43 % / 26.09 %
115	D	69.57 % / 26.08 %
116	A	56.52 % / 26.09 %

Q.	Ans.	Correct / Skipped
117	C	56.52 % / 26.09 %
118	B	60.87 % / 26.09 %
119	B	39.13 % / 26.09 %
120	D	43.48 % / 26.09 %
121	B	30.43 % / 26.09 %
122	A	47.83 % / 26.08 %
123	B	47.83 % / 26.08 %
124	D	21.74 % / 26.09 %
125	D	65.22 % / 26.08 %

Performance Analysis

Avg. Score (%)	49.65%
Toppers Score (%)	98.35%
Your Score	

//Hints and Solutions//

1.

- Anaximander first attempted to create a world map.
- In his map, Alexander displayed Greece in the middle of the world. The map was circular, surrounded by the ocean surrounding.
- Along with Thales, Anneximander is also considered to be the founder of mathematical geography.

Hence, the correct option is (B).

2. Dhule and dormant space used in Ptolemy's map is the northernmost south place in the world. The major books composed by Ptolemy are-

- Planetary hypothesis
- Almagest
- Geographic Syntax
- Geographia

Hence, the correct option is (A).

3. American geographer Richard Hartshorne developed an idiographic approach to geography. His major books are:

(1) The Nature of Geography (1939)

(2) Perspective on the nature of Geography (1959)

Hence, the correct option is (C).

4.

	List-I		List-II
(A)	Positivist Geography	(1)	Auguste Comte
(B)	Ethical Geography	(2)	William Kirk
(C)	Humanistic Geography	(3)	Yi-Fu-Tuan
(D)	Neolithicism	(4)	Griffith Taylor

Hence, the correct option is (A).

5. Alfred Hettner called geography Chorological Science. Under which the regions are studied. Hettner used the term Landerkunde, which means the surface area of the Earth, in place of Ritter's Ardkunde, the science of chromatography.

Hence, the correct option is (B).

6. Ptolemy said that geography is the science associated with the art of mapping. The major books of Tallami are as follows -

(i) Planetary Hypothesis

(ii) Alnagest

(iii) Geographic Syntaxis

(iv) Analema

Hence, the correct option is (D).

7. Neo-Determinism is known as 'stop and go' Determinism. The proponent of neo-determinism was Griffith Taylor. Griffith Taylor explicitly emphasized that in reality neither nature has complete control over man, nor man is the conqueror of nature. The two have a functional relationship.

Hence, the correct option is (C).

8. The most important of the changes in geography after World War II was the emergence of geography as a spatial science.

Spatial science refers to the organization of data in a geometric space with information about the location of things. Thus, geospatial statistics are statistics that also hold information on the location of things on Earth and in a spatial database they are collected and represented at the primary level through point, line and polygons.

Hence, the correct option is (A).

9. "All history must be examined in geographical perspective and all geography in historical perspective" was the idea of Herodotus, the famous Greek scholar. Herodotus is called the father of history. Herodotus was the first geographer to divide the world plot into three continents Europe Asia and Libya. Herodotus was the first geographer to consider the Caspian Sea as the inner ocean.

Hence, the correct option is (B).

10. Hitlesi introduced the concept of 'sequential occupancy'. Hitlesi divided the world into 13 agricultural regions in the year 1936 AD.

Hence, the correct option is (D).

11. "Geography is concerned with the precise, systematic logical description and interpretation of the changing form of the surface", given by the American geographer Richard Hartshorne. He was educated at the University of Chicago. They were important American geographers of the 20th century. Books written by:

- Nature of geography
- The Perspective on the Nature of Geography
- The Academy Citizen
- Political Geography in the Modern World
- Functional Approach in Political Geography

Hence, the correct option is (D).

12. Gunnar Myrdal's book 'Asian Drama: An Inquiry of Nations in the Poverty' is a study of the poverty of nations in Asia. Myrdal formulated the cumulative resulting theory. According to Myrdal's theory, inequality due to market forces increases rather than decreases because the backward effect is more powerful than the diffusion effect.

Hence, the correct option is (A).

13. "Geography is the mother of all sciences" This statement relates to Richard Hartshorne. Richard Hartshorne was a famous American geographer. He was educated at the University of Chicago. They were important American geographers of the 20th century.

Hence, the correct option is (B).

14. Revolutionary geography was born in 1960. The main reasons for this were the following low incidence in the US in the 1960s. Such as dissatisfaction among students, consequences of Vietnam War, apartheid, exploitation of resources, inequality towards development, etc. Appropriate events resulted in voids against spatial analysis. And the U.S. A. magazine called 'Antipode' was founded in 1969 at Clarke University in Worcester. The first major contribution in these is considered to be 'Prat'.

Hence, the correct option is (D).

15. "Geography is a field science." This statement is by Alfred Hettner. He used a word called 'Landerkunde' which means 'the surface area of the earth in the science of chromatography'.

His major works are:

(i) Visit to Colombian Andes

(ii) Regional Geography of Europe

(iii) Comparative Regional Geography

Hence, the correct option is (B).

16. The attempt to connect science with direct experience is called positivism. Historically, the concept of positivism was introduced after the French Revolution in 1833 by Auguste Comte.

Hence, the correct option is (A).

17. Jupiter is the second largest body of the solar family. The largest body of the solar family is the sun. Jupiter is primarily a gas body whose mass is equal to one-thousandth of the Sun and two and a half times the total mass of the other seven planets in the Solar System. Jupiter is classified as a gaseous planet along with Saturn, Arun and Varuna. It can be seen with naked eyes at night.

Hence, the correct option is (B).

18. The Global Positioning System (GPS) is a satellite-based navigation system used to detect the location of anything, made up of at least 24 satellites. GPS works 24 hours in any season. GPS technology was first used by the United States military in the 1960s.

Hence, the correct option Is (B).

19. Disturbances in the magnetic fields of celestial bodies are called magnetic storms. A geomagnetic storm is a temporary disturbance of the Earth's magnetosphere due to the solar wind shock wave and magnetic field cloud of the magnetic field interacting with the Earth's magnetic field.

Hence, the correct option is (A).

20. There is no planetoid of Venus. Venus is the nearest planet to the Earth. It is the brightest and hottest planet. It is called evening star or morning star. It rotates clockwise unlike other planets. It is called the sister planet of the Earth. This density is similar to the Earth in size and diameter.

Hence, the correct option is (C).

21. The term filament is used under the 'tidal hypothesis'. The tidal hypothesis was formulated by British scholar Sir James Jeans in 1919.

Hence, the correct option is (B).

22. The corpus of star gases and the amount of dust is called nebula (nebula). The nebula is an interstellar cloud located in interstellar space that contains dust, hydrogen gas, helium gas, and other ionized plasma gases. In the old days, "Niharika" used to refer to any elaborate object seen in the astro.

Hence, the correct option is (B).

23. The length of the year is the highest on Pluto. Pluto has one year equivalent to 248 years. While equivalent to 12 years on Jupiter. Equals 365 days on Earth and 88 days on Mercury.

Hence, the correct option is (D).

24. Mercury is the nearest planet to the Sun. All the planets in the solar family revolve the Sun in long circular paths, called orbits. As the distance of the planets from the Sun increases, the time of its rotation also increases. Mercury is closest to the Sun, so it takes 88 days to orbit the Sun. As Mercury is closest to the Sun, it gets the most heat from the Sun. While Jupiter is the largest planet. Venus is the hottest planet. Mars is in the fourth position from the Sun, it is called the red planet.

Hence, the correct option is (B).

25. The rotation of the Earth and the tilt of the Earth on its own axis are the necessary factors for weather changes on the surface of the Earth. The Moon revolves around the Earth in an elliptical path, when the Moon is closest to the Earth, this state is called Perigee. The most distant position of the Moon from the Earth is called apogee.

Hence, the correct option is (B).

26. As a hot tropical country, there is a greater potential for production and utilization of Tire energy in India. Photovoltaic technology converts sunlight directly into electricity. The largest solar plant in India has been set up at Madhopur near Bhuj. The world's largest solar vapor system for cooking has been installed at Mount Abu in Rajasthan.

Hence, the correct option is (C).

27. The correct matched sequence is as follows-

	List-I (Surname)		**List-II (Planet)**
(A)	Green Planet	(3)	Urenas
(B)	Ringed planet	(4)	Saturn
(C)	Red planet	(2)	Mars
(D)	Morning Sun	(1)	Venus

Hence, the correct option is (C).

28. The interval between two full moon days is 29.5 days. The lunar eclipse always occurs on the full moon but not every full moon, because the mutual inclination of $5°$ is found in the earth and the orbital plane of the moon, so the moon is seldom in the bottom of the earth. The state of full moon is also called Vyuti.

Hence, the correct option is (D).

29. The theory of heliocentrism was propounded by Copernicus. Copernicus was a Polish astronomer and mathematician. He gave this revolutionary formula that the Earth is not in the center of space. Copernicus was the first European astronomer to consider the Earth outside the center of the universe, ie the Heliocentrism principle. Before this, the whole Europe believed in the concept of Aristotle, in which the earth was the center of the universe and the sun, stars and other bodies revolved around it.

Hence, the correct option is (A).

30. The above mentioned planets have the shortest day on Earth. The Earth has its own specific shape called a geod. Its shape is also called oblate spheroid. The equatorial diameter of the Earth is 12,757 km with a polar diameter of 12,714 km.

Hence, the correct option is (A).

31. Halley, Gail and Wilson are comets, also known as tail stars. These are objects of celestial dust, snow and glacial gases that live in a cold and dark region away from the Sun. A comet is a solar system that consists of small blocks made of stone, dust, ice, and gas.

Hence, the correct option is (B).

32. Nicholas Copernicus introduced the concept of the Sun-centered universe in place of the Earth-centered universe in the year 1543. Poland-born Nicolas Copernicus (19 February 1473–24 May 1543) was a European astronomer and mathematician. He gave this revolutionary formula that the Earth is not in the center of space. Nicholas was the first European astronomer to consider the Earth outside the center of the universe, and applied the 'heliocentrism model'.

Hence, the correct option is (A).

33. Uranus is the outermost planet. Jupiter, Saturn, Arun (Uranus), Varuna are called external planets. Mercury, Venus, Earth and Mars are called internal planets.

Hence, the correct option is (C).

34. Mercator interpolation is more useful for a sailor. Each straight line drawn on a Mercator projection cuts the latitude lines at a fixed angle. Similarly, any straight line cuts longitudinal lines at a fixed angle. Hence the straight line that joins the two places on the Mercator chart. Mercator interpolation is used in nine operations.

Hence, the correct option is (A).

35. Jupiter is the largest planet in the solar system. A 'huge red spot' is found on this planet, which is a continuous cyclonic storm, while Mars is known as 'Red Planet'.

Hence, the correct option is (B).

36. Under the mantle in the structure of the planet Earth, the core is mainly made of iron. The core is the innermost layer of the Earth and is called the Berisphere. It is mainly made by iron and nickel. Hence it is also called Nife. This layer is found from 2900 km to 6371 km depth.

Hence, the correct option is (D).

37. Earth's crust is found up to a depth of 100 km. The mantle is found on it. And the upper part of the mantle is called the asthenosphere (debilitated), above which the septum floats. An earthquake also originates from this debilitated region. The Gurmandal (Berisphere) is part of the internal structure of the earth found from 2800 km to the center, in which the amount of

nickel and forum are found. The mesosphere is called the middle layer of the atmosphere, while the hydrosphere refers to the atmosphere, under which oceans and oceanic resources are studied.

Hence, the correct option is (D).

38. Dinosaurs reached the largest size in the Jurassic era in Earth's geological history. The first bird archeopteryx from flying reptiles and the kangaroo mammals originated in the Jurassic era. Dinosaurs ended in the Cretaceous era.

Hence, the correct option is (B).

39. The boundary of mantle and core (cavity and core) located at a depth of 2900 km in the inner part of the Earth is called Gutenberg disambiguation, its density suddenly increases from 5.5 to 10.0. Moho disinhibition is found at the boundary of the crust and mantle. Repetite incompatibility is located at a depth (700 km) between the external and internal mantle.

Hence, the correct option is (B).

40. The Gutenberg disambiguation separates the outer innermost and the mantle. Moho's disambiguation separates the crust and mantle. Repeat incompatibility separates the external and internal mantles.

Hence, the correct option is (B).

41. The ground equilibrium hypothesis was interpreted through Heskinen coordinating the theory of Airy and Pratt. The term land balance was first used by the American geologist Dutton in the year 1889. Airy believes that the seals are floating above the boundary, according to them the density of different columns is equal and their depth is different. According to Pratt, the higher the column, the lower its density will be and the lower the column, the higher its density will be.

Hence, the correct option is (A).

42. The Falkland Stream, the Labrador Stream, and the Canary Stream are the colder streams of the Atlantic Ocean, while the Brazilian Stream is the Florida Water Stream, the Ir Miner's Stream, the Gulfstream Stream, and the North Equator Linear Stream, etc. are the warm waters of the Atlantic Ocean.

Hence, the correct option is (A).

43. The Bengula stream is a cold stream that flows northwards along the western coast of southern Africa and merges into the southern equatorial stream. The cold ocean water rises to the surface near the coast of Africa, due to which, this stream becomes colder.

Hence, the correct option is (C).

44. Ocean current is 2% of the prevailing wind speed. Currents are the motion of water flowing in a certain direction in the seas. The following factors affecting ocean currents are salinity, temperature, density, airflow, etc.

Hence, the correct option is (A).

45. The Bengula cold stream flows into the Atlantic Ocean, dividing it into two branches, the Southern Atlantic Ocean, near the Ashe Island of Africa. One branch flows south of Africa and the other branch flows south to north along the west coast. It moves from cold area to hot area, hence the Bengali is called cold stream.

Hence, the correct option is (C).

46. The average depth of the equatorial line segment is 100 m. The origin of this stream lies between the northern equatorial stream and the southern equatorial stream in the Pacific Ocean and the Atlantic Ocean. The direction of the equatorial stream is opposite to the equatorial equator and the equator. The equilateral linear stream is oriented from west to east. It flows due to the gradient.

Hence, the correct option is (B).

47. The Gutenberg discontinuity is found between the lower mantle and the outer core.

Nature of the Earth's internal structure

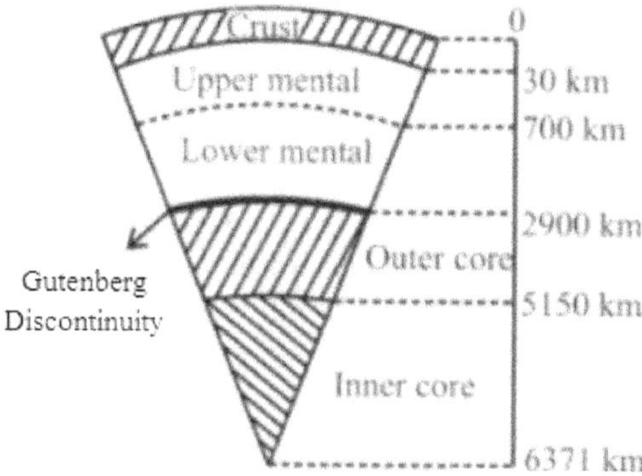

Hence, the correct option is (B).

48. Excessive folding results in the formation of Nappe. Napa or cervix is a sign of intense horizontal movement or compression. In the folded fold, both arms are parallel and horizontal, and on higher compression, one segment of the folded cross climbs to the other. This action is called Utkram. On even more compression, the arm of the fold is twisted so much that it breaks on the axis of the fold and the lower layers come up. In this way, when the horizontal movement and compression continues, the broken arm of the fold goes away from its place and climbs on another type of rock. This is called cervical or nappy.

Hence, the correct option is (C).

49. Sedimentary rocks are ultimately derived from weathering of igneous rocks. Different layers of sediments are found in sedimentary rocks. These rocks contain fossils. 75% of the surface is covered by sedimentary rocks.

Hence, the correct option is (D).

50. The term Cretan was first proposed by Austrian geologist Köber in 1921 as kerogen, referring to stable continents. Cratons are made of ancient crystalline basement rocks. Under which granite and basalt rocks come.

Hence, the correct option is (A).

51. Wegner proposed the continental flow theory in 1912 AD. He gave the following evidence in favor of continental displacement:

In favor of Jig-Saw Fit, Wegner said that geographical homogeneity is found on both the coasts of the Andhra Ocean. That is, both the banks can be mixed with each other. He told that the way pieces of an object can be mixed again. Similarly, the east coast of North America can be linked to the west coast of Europe. Similarly, the eastern coast of South America can be merged with the west coast of Africa.

In the context of fossils in different regions, Wegner said that on both the banks of the Andhramasagar, there is a considerable similarity between the fossils and the remains of vegetation found in the rocks.

Hence, the correct option is (A).

52. The oceans are called continents and first-class reliefs. Many scholars have given different views about their origin. Calvin K. The quadratic hypothesis of Holmes, Wegner, Solus, and Lothian Green is based on contraction. The quadrilateral is composed of four equilateral triangles.

Hence, the correct option is (A).

53. Lothian Green is related to tetrahedron. Wegner's 'Continental Flow Theory'. Lord Kelvin's hypothesis of Nebula Hypothesis, while Lapworth and Love's hypothesis is related to the large-scale folding action on the upper surface of the Earth. In 1909, Love had revised the hypothesis of Lapworth to explain the origin of continents and oceans as the central attracting power of the Earth.

Hence, the correct option is (B).

54. The extension of the savanna biome is found between $10°$ to $20°$ latitudes on either side of the equator. Savannah-type grass biomes are found in Brazil, Africa, North Australia, and New Zealand, etc. in South America. This ecosystem is known as the land of large prey.

Hence, the correct option is (B).

55. NEERI (National Environmental Engineering Research Institute) is concerned with environmental research. Its headquarters is located in Nagpur, Maharashtra state.

Hence, the correct option is (D).

56. The ecosystem is composed of organisms and abiotic components and is relatively stable in homology. This happens in the open system, in which there is a continuous flow of matter and energy. The ecosystem occupies a certain area on the ground floor. The ecosystem has a regional dimension. It also has a measuring dimension.

Hence, the correct option is (C).

57. Every element in the ecosystem is inorganic, the balance in the production and consumption of organic, the balance of energy investment and output, and the smooth functioning of different biochemical cycles enhance stability in the ecosystem. Conditions suitable for human population growth have no relation to ecological status. Rather, where there is a lot of human development or population, the ecosystem is unbalanced. Hence, the correct option is (D).

58. Grasshopper - primary consumer

Moleskin - Secondary Consumer

Owl - Tertiary Consumer

Human - Quartile consumer (omnivores)

Hence, the correct option is (C).

59. Resource management is the rational exploitation and development of natural resources while maintaining the quality of the environment. Resource management is based on the concept of sustainable development.

Hence, the correct option is (B).

60. Energy flow is the fundamental element of an ecosystem. There is a gradual transfer of food items or energy into the food chain. Only about one percent of the solar energy reaching the earth is used in photosynthesis. The process of formation of biological tissues in various organisms is called biosynthesis. In fact the process of biosynthesis represents the conversion of solar energy or light energy into chemical energy.

Hence, the correct option is (C).

61. The slope of flora is called ecocline. With this gradient of vegetation (gradient), the vegetation of different ecosystems changes gradually with changes in environmental conditions.

Hence, the correct option is (A).

62. The term ecology was first used by Ernest Haeckel. Under this, the interaction of all organisms and their physical environment and on the other hand the interaction of different organisms is studied in an ecological system.

Hence, the correct option is (B).

63. The term Ecosystem was first used by A.G. Tansley did it in 1935. According to Tansley, 'ecosystems are a special type of physical systems, composed of organisms and abiotic components. The mechanism created by physical-chemical-biological processes in the time unit is called an ecosystem.

Hence, the correct option is (C).

64. An ecosystem is a basic functional unit that occupies a fixed area of the ground floor, which includes the biological community and the aggregate set of inorganic (physical) components and their mutual interactions within a given time unit and between two ecosystems. The transition zone is called an ecotone.

Hence, the correct option is (B).

65. Special credit for the components of the current biosphere goes to the Chicago bench. The concept of biosphere reserve was implemented in 1974 AD as a part of UNESCO's Standard Biosphere Project 9 which was related to conservation of ecosystems and its present genetic resources. Protected areas of added biosphere reserves and seaside environments where various people are integral components in the system.

Hence, the correct option is (A).

66. An outbreak becomes a disaster when it adversely affects the human habitat. Natural crises are the elements of the situation in the natural environment that have the potential to cause damage to wealth, people or both. They can be very acute or can be permanent aspects of the environment. Natural disasters occur relatively intensely, people have little or no control over them.

Hence, the correct option is (D).

67. The total amount of energy assimilated by atmospheric primary producers is called gross primary productivity. Primary producers are chlorophyll-rich plants, such as moss (algae) grasses and trees. These plants convert carbon dioxide and water into glucose in the presence of sunlight by the action of photosynthesis. Since green plants prepare their own food. They are also called autotrophs.

Hence, the correct option is (C).

68. Temperate angular forest biome - It is also called taga forest biome. This biome is the northernmost biome of the temperate biome. It is found in cold continental or sub-polar climatic regions in North America and Eurasia. The angled tree is the most influential of the flora. This biome is also known as boreal forest.

Hence, the correct option is (B).

69. The Biodiversity Act was passed by the Indian Parliament on 11 December 2002. The National Biodiversity Authority of India was established in the year 2003 with the objective of implementing the provisions of the Biodiversity Act, 2002 and is headquartered in Chennai, Tamil Nadu.

Hence, the correct option is (C).

70. Accelerated and sudden catastrophic events such as prolonged drought, severe floods, forest fire, volcanic eruption etc. that force the animals to migrate elsewhere for their survival are called diffusion of animals.

Hence, the correct option is (A).

71. This climatic zone extends between the latitudes of both spheres $45°$ to $60°$ in the western parts of the continents. The predominant feature of this climate region is the prevailing westerly wind flow from sea to the site, the average amount of rainfall is about 140 cm.

Hence, the correct option is (A).

72. The plant Eucalyptus, once thought to be the origin of ecology, has today been called the circumstantial terrorist. Which is why this plant absorbs about 60 liters of water per day and does not have transpiration.

Hence, the correct option is (C).

73. Rainfall is low and erratic in warm grassland meadows. Its extension is generally found between $5°$ to $20°$ both northern and southern latitudes. The grass that grows in this region is savanna, whose main production area is Africa. Animals and plants are found in large numbers in tropical forests.

Hence, the correct option is (A).

74. Ecological niches indicate the functional role of the organism in the ecological system. Ecology is the science under which the

interrelationships between all organisms and the physical environment and mutual interactions between different organisms are studied.

Hence, the correct option is (B).

75. Hackistothermal plants are found in cold desert. Hackistothermal comes under such plants that can thrive on the continuous frozen surface of the tundra region. Only lichen and moss develop in the lithosol soils here.

Hence, the correct option is (D).

76. Biological and abiotic elements or substances of the biosphere are also called nutritional elements because these substances help in the formation and promotion of the body and tissues of various organisms. Nutritional elements operating in the ecological system are divided into the following classes-

(i) Micronutrients- These elements include oxygen, carbon, hydrogen, nitrogen, phosphorus, potassium calcium etc.

(ii) Microbial elements - iron, copper, manganese etc. come under it. Thus iron is not a micronutrient.

Hence, the correct option is (B).

77. The pastoralism of animals and humans started from the Neolithic period. By this time, the invention of fire, wheels and small tools had been invented. Man had started settling on the banks of rivers and animal husbandry came under his main occupation.

Hence, the correct option is (C).

78. The ecological system is activated through energy flow and circulation of nutrients and minerals. In the ecological system, energy is transferred from one nutrition level to another.

Hence, the correct option is (A).

79. The food network is the ingrained network of food chains. From the point of view of food and energy flow, there is a close relationship between the producing consumer and the decomposer in the food chain. In nature, the food chain is not in a straight line, but all the food chains are interlinked. That is, the organism of one food chain is related to the organism of another food chain. In this way, the interconnection of many food chains is called a food trap.

Hence, the correct option is (D).

80. Pyramids of grassland or crop ecosystems will be formed directly. Through the number of pyramids, the number of primary producers of circumstantial system and producers of different levels is realized. The base of this pyramid always denotes the number of products. The living number pyramid can become both upright and upside down. The pyramid is straightened when the number of producers becomes more factual and the number of consumers becomes progressively less. Conversely, when the number of producers is one and the number of consumers increases, the pyramid will be turned upside down. Like - tree pyramid.

Hence, the correct option is (A).

81. The tropical and temperate forested area is a region of high ecological production. Because these regions are regions with high temperature and high rainfall, due to which high growth of the ecological system is possible.

Hence, the correct option is (B).

82. The United States is the world's largest producer of soybeans. Soybean is extensively cultivated here along with maize cultivation. Soybean is sown in China by North China poor farmers for food grains supply. Though the state of Madhya Pradesh is the first in soybean production in India, most of its production is consumed in India, which is much less than in America. Brazil produces small amounts of soybeans.

Hence, the correct option is (C).

83. Egypt is the largest producer of dates in the world due to the suitability of the Nile River, black soil, and climatic conditions.

Hence, the correct option is (B).

84. 818 quintals of hectare are received in the Hawaiian Islands, here sugarcane is the most important crop, due to which sugarcane is provided to factories throughout the year.

Hence, the correct option is (C).

85. The Rhine River is best suited as an internal waterway. The Rhine River is the world's busiest waterway by which coal is transported the most, as a result it is also known as the Coal River.

Hence, the correct option is (B).

86. Quantification is responsible for the radical transformation of the soul and purpose of geography. After World War II, geographers valued mathematical language more than literary language, especially in developed countries. In this way, more and more mathematical statistics, statistical methods started being used in geography. Called the Quantitative Revolution. The major proponents of the quantitative revolution were Peter Haggett, Richard Sholai and David Harvey.

Hence, the correct option is (D).

87. The Pan America Highway stretches from Prudhe (Alaska) to Argentina in South America. The total length of the Pan America Highway is about 30,000 km.

Hence, the correct option is (C).

88. Following are the major junctions of Trans Siberian Railway - St.Pittsburgh, Moscow, Kazan, Yekaterinburg, Omsk Novosivirsk, Krasnoyvinsk, Irkstak, Ulan Uday Cheetah, Khebrovsk, Bladibostak.

Hence, the correct option is (A).

89. Japan has a developed hydropower technology. Due to which, due to the absence of large deposits of coal and other minerals, it is also developed in a high quality industrial capacity. At the same time, due to the insular position of Japan, it easily imports raw and heavy materials, and manufactures and exports high quality goods from it. Due to the insular location, the climate of Japan is also found to be temperate, which the population there Provides high degree of efficiency.

Hence, the correct option is (C).

90. The United States ranks first in maize production. Santluis is the largest corn market in the world. Here maize is used to feed animals to make them obese. Especially for pigs.

Hence, the correct option is (B).

91. Japan has about 3900 islands, with four large-sized islands - Honshu, Hokado, Kyushu and Shikoku. Honshu Island is the largest island in Japan. On this island, Japan's largest ground, Quanto (rice bowl) is located. And on this island is located the latent volcano Fujiyama. Tokyo, the capital of the country, is located on this island. On this island, 80% population of the country resides.

Hence, the correct option is (B).

92. The final stage in the process of energy resource utilization is disposal of waste material. In today's scientific age, the economic development of any country depends on the industries and businesses that thrive there. Residual materials come out of industries like petroleum industry, sugar mill etc.

Hence, the correct option is (C).

93. Petroleum is considered a source of power in the United States, not an economy. The United States produces 564 million tons of petroleum. The major petroleum producing regions of the United States are the following - Central and East Texas, Oklahoma, Kansas, the northern part of Louisiana, the coastal submerged part of the Gulf, etc.

Hence, the correct option is (A).

94. The Northwest Atlantic region includes the New Zealand region of the United States and the coastal areas of Newfoundland. In this area, George Bank and Grand Bank are the major fisheries sectors of the world. In this area there is a grass called plankton which is the food of the fish.

Hence, the correct option is (C).

95. Kirkuk is famous for producing mineral oil. Mineral oil has its origin in the decomposition of marine organisms and animals which were buried under sediments 10 to 200 million years ago. Among the major mineral oil fields of Iraq are Kirkuk, Mussel, Rumalia, Vasara.

Hence, the correct option is (C).

96. Zinc is a metallic mineral. It is found only in a combined state in nature (usually in the form of sulfides, carbonates and oxides). Its main ores are Zinc Bland and Kalamine. It has an important role in making brass. On the basis of physical and chemical properties, mineral resources have been integrated into two major categories, metallic and non-metallic. The source of the metal is metallic mineral.

Hence, the correct option is (C).

97. The major ores of iron are-

(i) magnetite,

(ii) Hematite,

(iii) Siderite,

(iv) Limonite,

(v) Goethite

Whereas the third option given in the question is the type of lignite coal.

Hence, the correct option is (C).

98. Plutonium is a substance that is obtained by artificial radioactive fission. Whereas in addition all other elements are obtained in the form of ore in nature.

Hence, the correct option is (B).

99. The representative oil producing country of Southwest Asia is Saudi Arabia. It is important to note that the top 5 countries in terms of authentic petroleum reserves are Venezuela, Saudi Arabia, Canada, Iran, Iraq respectively. While South East Asia's most mineral oil producing country is Indonesia.

Hence, the correct option is (C).

100. The deepest mine in the world is the Mponeng gold mine, which is located in the Guteng province of South Africa. Due to the hot stones of Hades, the temperature in the mine is as high as 50 degrees Celsius, so that the miners do not faint due to the heat.

Hence, the correct option is (D).

101. The main producer of asbestos is India. Asbestos is found in many colors (white, pink, green, black) in igneous and metamorphic rocks. It is transparent, flexible and thermally resistant. The main producing states of asbestos in India are Andhra Pradesh, Rajasthan, Jharkhand.

Hence, the correct option is (A).

102. Based on the reuse of energy resources, it has been divided into two categories.

1. Non-renewable energy - ie end-to-end energy sources such as coal, petrol, gas and nuclear-based energy sources, nuclear energy.

2. Renewable energy - ie non-renewable energy sources - such as photoboltaic, solar heat, wind power, hydropower geothermal energy, tidal and ottech energy.

Hence, the correct option is (C).

103. Coal, mineral oil and natural gas are exhausted resources. There is a fear of destruction of our forests and deterioration of ecological balance due to excessive use of wood. Hence, there was a need to find untraceable energy resources that can provide us with energy in the long run. These are called non-conventional energy resources. Biogas, solar energy, wind power, nuclear power, tidal energy, geothermal energy are the prime examples. They are environment friendly, renewable and sustainable.

Hence, the correct option is (B).

104. Oil production in Iraq began in 1627 in place of Baba Gurgur near Kirkuk. The region is located in the northern part of Iraq. At present, Kirkuk is the most important oil producing region of this country. The Jaber oil field is near Basra in the southern part of Iraq. Oil is also found near Gosul in the northern part, Kirkuk is located away from the sea, so the oil of the region is transported by pipeline to the Baniyas of Syria and the Tripoli ports of

Lebanon. Both these ports are located on the eastern coast of the Mediterranean Sea. Iraq's oil is exported to Europe and North America from these ports.

Hence, the correct option is (B).

105. Warm tropical evergreen forests are found in tropical equatorial regions on tropical lowlands and wind-facing ridges. Where there is a lot of rainfall throughout the year and there is no dry season, hard trees like prime rubber, rosewood, palm and mahogany are found in these forests.

Hence, the correct option is (D).

106. Many crops of the world are grown from the commercial point of view of plantations. The distribution of production of miscellaneous crops is also more widespread in this type of (Bagati) agricultural system. But the main areas of agricultural cultivation are in the hot regions.

Hence, the correct option is (D).

107. Intensive agriculture is an agricultural system where food crops are mainly produced for local consumption. Intensive agriculture is done all over South and South East Asia but it is mainly famous in China and Japan, due to limited agriculture in these countries.

Hence, the correct option is (C).

108. Terraroxa soil is most suitable for the production of coffee coffee after lava soil. This soil is found in Brazilian coffee growing areas.

Hence, the correct option is (A).

109. Transfer is an ancient form of agriculture practiced mainly by tribes living in tropical forests. It is known by different names in different regions. Transferable agriculture is known as Milpa in Central America Mexico.

Hence, the correct option is (A).

110. Intensive agriculture is mainly done in areas with high population density. In this type of agriculture, a large amount of capital and labor is used on each of the agricultural land to get maximum production of crops. The main objective of this agriculture is to get more production in less area.

Hence, the correct option is (C).

111. Coffee (Kahwa) is a hot and humid climate and grows from 1500-1800 m below ground in warm tropical regions. Brazil is the world's largest coffee (coffee) -producing country. Here the geographical conditions are favorable for its production. Here Kahwa plants are planted in big gardens which are known by the name of Fazenda.

Hence, the correct option is (A).

112. The landscape created by wind erosion in the Sahara Desert is called Serir and Reg. The Sahara Desert is the warmest in the northern part of Africa and the largest desert in the world. Where the world's highest temperature has been recorded in Al-Algijia located in this desert.

Hence, the correct option is (A).

113. The drainage system which is not connected to the structure of the area is called imputed drainage. All the other drainage systems in question are formed as a result of the surface structure. The pneumatic drainage system is also called plantar drainage pattern. This type of growth is mainly in the flat and flat expansion parts, they are the largest in the granite rock parts. The developed drainage system is developed by a flow network of the principal follow-up sarita and its subsidiary saris developed according to the structure.

Hence, the correct option is (D).

114. The rapid increase in the erosion strength of the aquatic processes (Sarita) is a result of a negative change in the base of the erosion called renewal (regeneration). Due to the innovation, the rivers begin to deepen their valley again by lower erosion. In the state of innovation, the duration of erosion cycle increases. For example, if the aquifer erosion cycle has developed its gradient, slump flow and shallow and wide alluvial valleys. So there will be disruption due to innovation in them and the rivers start deepening their valley by vertical erosion again.

Hence, the correct option is (A).

115. Due to the diversion in the plains, the stream collides at a high speed from the concave bank of the river, due to which the diversion increases. The stream accumulates the severed material of the concave edge at the convex edge. Thus, erosion occurs on continuous concave edge and convection on convex edge. Due to excessive erosion, the path of the river becomes straight and the bended portion is saved. It is called Gokhur Lake. Gokhur Lake is known as Billabong, Mort Lake and Bayu Namo.

Hence, the correct option is (D).

116. The lengthy bounds made by deposition (deposition) of the soil on both sides of the river, which is similar to the low-altitude cuttack, is called the embankment. Since these bonds are made by nature and they are protected during floods, these embankments are also called natural embankments, the rest are all extraneous topographies.

Hence, the correct option is (A).

117. The rivers which do not conform to the territorial gradient and flow in the unfavorable direction and across the physical structure are called invertebrates. Under the erosive drainage system comes the predecessor and preplanned lines.

Hence, the correct option is (C).

118. Ria Nimgan is an example of a highland coastline. The ria edge is formed by partially submerging the site affected by subacrial erosion. In fact, ria is formed when the rivers are submerged. Ria edge is elongated and narrower towards the site. In this way there is a river estuary at the top of the ria and an open ocean at the other end.

Hence, the correct option is (B).

119. In the dry regions, the deposit of sand by the rivers on the mountain slopes is called 'Balu Bazada'. Between the playa and the mountainous façade, there are plains with sloping plains. The lower part of this plain, which meets the playa, is called Bazada. It is formed by the deposition of the Malava. The upper part is called pediment. The bazada is formed by the joining of alluvial wings under the pediment and on the edge of the playa.

Hence, the correct option is (B).

120. The delta chem is the result of glacial deposition. Some debris is deposited as piles or mounds due to melting of snow on the glacial façade. Such mounds are called chem. The sides of the chem are sharp shields. The chem is composed of sand and gravel.

Hence, the correct option is (D).

121. Subsequent runoff usually occurs opposite to subsequent runoff. The first follow-up in any area is the emergence of Sarita. Subsequent rivers follow the territorial gradient, they are called Nati Sarita. Subsequent rivers originate in tributaries in the valleys. Such rivers are referred to as the innovative follow-up Sarita.

Hence, the correct option is (B).

122. The average solar energy gain at the top of the Earth's atmosphere is found to be 1.94 calories per square cm per minute. Every object that has heat radiates, and the warmer the object, the smaller its waves. This is the reason that the energy radiated by the Sun is in the form of small waves. In contrast, radiation from a low-temperature object occurs in small amounts and in the form of long waves. For example, the radiation of energy from the surface of the Earth is in the form of a long wave.

Hence, the correct option is (A).

123. Gas - Percent

Nitrogen - 78.7%

Oxygen - 20.93%

Argon - 0.93%

Hydrogen - 0.005%

Helium - .0005%

Nian - .0015%

Krypton - .001%

Jinan - .0001%

Hence, the correct option is (B).

124. The reason for the movement of air in the troposphere is wind pressure. Air flows from high air to low air. The troposphere is the lowest part of the Earth's atmosphere. In this layer, humidity, water pressure, dust, wind and all the seasonal events occur. It is the densest part of the Earth's air and contains 80% of the mass of the entire atmosphere.

Hence, the correct option is (D).

125. The ionosphere layer in the atmosphere refracts electromagnetic waves. The ionosphere is 80 to 400 km above the median. The ionosphere reflects the radio waves transmitted from the Earth and sends it back to Earth. This helps in radio transmission on Earth.

Hence, the correct option is (D).

// Notes //

// Notes //